IDEAS
that changed the world

FELIPE FERNÁNDEZ-ARMESTO

LONDON, NEW YORK,
MELBOURNE, MUNICH AND DELHI

Project Editor Nigel Ritchie
Editor Cathy Meeus
Editorial Assistant Georgina Garner
Proofreader Lynn Bresler
Indexer Hilary Bird

Senior Art Editor Ina Stradins
DTP Designer Rajen Shah
Picture Researcher Sarah Duncan
Production Controllers Elizabeth Cherry
Melanie Dowland

Managing Art Editor Philip Ormerod
Art Director Bryn Walls
Managing Editor Liz Wheeler
Category Publisher Jonathan Metcalf

Schermuly Design Co.
Creative Director Hugh Schermuly
Designer Sally Geeve

First published in this format in 2004

First published in Great Britain in 2003
by Dorling Kindersley Limited
80 Strand, London WC2R 0RL

A Penguin Company

2 4 6 8 10 9 7 5 3 1

A CIP catalogue record for this
book is available from the British Library

ISBN 1-4053-0593-2

Colour reproduction by GRB, Italy
Printed and bound in Singapore by Star Standard

see our complete catalogue at
www.dk.com

contents

Introduction

The biggest question about history is "How does it happen?" We can see how changeable the human past is when we compare ourselves with other animals. The way they live changes relatively little compared with the convulsions and revolutions typical of our communities.

The structures of even the most complex non-human societies are solid, stable, even stagnant. Baboons, ants, and elephants, as far as we know, have preserved very much the same types of relationships since the first emergence of their species. Between emergence and extinction, nothing much happens. When changes do happen in the "animal world" we think we know why: evolution is the engine, ecology the framework. But for the human world, the rate of change in society, technology, and the arts is giddyingly faster than the pace of evolution.

Contradictory theories of how history happens litter the literature. History is said, for instance, to be subject to laws that govern change, such as class struggle or progress. Or it is a pattern concealed from us only by its complexity, in which all events are linked causes and effects, like vertebrae in a backbone. Or it is determined by some comprehensive mechanism: economics, say, or demographics. Or it has its own momentum – History with a capital "H" – a peculiar force or "World-spirit" (see p.26). Or history is manipulated by providence, for want of a more worldly explanation. Or, perhaps, no explanation is possible – it is all a chaotic system in which things happen randomly.

This book takes a different approach. The pages that follow are about history that happens first in the mind: history driven by ideas. This could be the reason why our human record teems with change. Compared with other species, as far as we know, we have enormously complex facilities for thinking. New thoughts are destabilizing, even dangerous. They generate frustration with the way things are or suggest possibilities about how they might be different. Imagination is surely not a uniquely human property, but it seems likely that human imaginations are uniquely rich. Every event we imagine is a potential new future. I think most historical change has intellectual origins and that ideas are at least as powerful agents for change as material exigencies, economic needs, environmental constraints, and all the other proposed determinants.

To admit that ideas are a source of change begs another question: what is the source of ideas? If it is true that human animals have minds so different from all others, why is that so? Except to appeal to evolution or providence, we have no present way of approaching answers to those questions that are outside the scope of history, even of the kind of meta-history – history contemplating itself – that the most ambitious historians practise and in which readers of this book are invited to join. The effects of ideas are, moreover, sometimes less detectable than those of material forces: some change the world directly by generating palpable consequences; others change it indirectly by affecting the way people perceive it (which then has further consequences in turn).

This book is about ideas that have created both these kinds of change. For each idea, I try to say not only what it is or was, but how it arose and how it registered its influence, so the origins, context, character, and consequences of each idea are crammed into the text. I have tried to make this process of compression seem more like winding springs than squashing stuffing.

The formative power of ideas in general – their strength to affect and even re-shape the world – should emerge from the sheer scope of the book, the sum of its contents, and the way the ideas are grouped. So this is a catalogue-book – a genre intellectuals usually despise – but with an important difference: it has a strong argument. The subject is ideas that have shaped the world as it is now. In consequence, Western ideas predominate in my coverage of periods during which the rise of Western civilization has played a major role in global cultural exchange, spreading ideas around the world. But I have tried to avoid "Westo-centrism" – if there is such a word – by including plenty of ideas that have originated elsewhere.

Uniquely, I believe, for any history of ideas, I have broken with convention to reflect an astonishing but generally unacknowledged fact: most of the ideas that matter today are of ancient origin. Many first arose in people's minds before the invention of writing and can only be excavated archaeologically or re-imagined from rarely surviving works of art. Most histories of ideas start in Ancient Greece, or at best in ancient Mesopotamia and Egypt. This is doubly misleading, first because it privileges the Western tradition to a distorting degree, and secondly because it leaves out the longest era of the story. Those who read this book from cover to cover will find they are well over a quarter of the way through it before they get to the ideas of the Greek sages. Another substantial section is devoted to ideas of the first millennium before Christ. It is humbling for modern people to acknowledge how much of their thinking was anticipated so long ago and how little modernity has added to our basic intellectual equipment.

One important limitation has to be faced: this is a personal selection of ideas. I bear sole responsibility for omissions that annoy readers or inclusions that offend them. Apart from the criteria of major influence and relevance, which were essential to the publishers' original conception of the book, I have tried to keep two further criteria in mind. First, ideas as I understand them are purely mental events. I do not include movements, or inventions, or discoveries, or anything else that happens outside the mind. Secondly, I have tried to focus exclusively on ideas that constitute new ways of envisioning the big picture: of humankind, of the cosmos, or even of other, transcendent worlds. Otherwise, no book would have been possible. If just about everything people do starts as an idea, there will be no end of ideas for inclusion. It would be tempting, for instance, to include great technical innovations on the grounds that most inventions start as ideas, but it is as inventions, not as ideas, that they register their influence.

Felipe Fernández-Armesto

THE MIND OF THE HUNTER

1

30,000–10,000 BC

Excavating the Earliest Ideas

Some of the best ideas were the earliest. Of ideas from the recent past still around today, or those that had the deepest influence – that touched most people, and resonated across most time – were the first to be formulated. Yet most histories of ideas ignore them. Books on this subject usually start the story late in the day, with the invention of writing, at the earliest, or with the great sages of the millennium before Christ. So the ideas of our earliest ancestors are left out.

There are three reasons for this – all of them bad. First, people assume that the only knowable ideas are those that were written down. But most societies, for most of history, have esteemed oral tradition more highly than writing. Their ideas are inscribed in other ways – left in fragments of material culture for archaeologists to unearth, or buried deep in modern minds for psychologists to excavate, or preserved in later ages by traditional societies, where anthropologists are sometimes able to elicit them.

Secondly, a vicious prejudice supposes that there are no ideas worth the name in the mind of the "primitive" or "savage", who is mired in "pre-logical" thought, or retarded by magic, or befogged by myth.

Thirdly, even some enquiries that are unprejudiced by contempt for our remote ancestors tend to be misled by notions of progress. The best thoughts, according to this doctrine, are the latest, so the earlier material can linger in justifiable neglect. In principle, there is no reason why people of the hunter-gatherer era should not have had ideas that anticipate our own. There have been no known changes in human brain capacity since the disappearance of the Neanderthals 30,000 years ago – whose brains, on average, by most computations, were a little bigger than our own – and no evidence of any change in human intelligence over a very much longer period than that. Maybe there was an era – much earlier – when life was "poor, nasty, brutish, and short" and when hominids were scavengers without leisure for reflection. But for hundreds of thousands of years all people, as far as we know, were hunters and foragers. Many of them enjoyed "Stone-Age affluence":

Early flint arrowheads
By learning how to flake flint to give it an edge, early humans could make tools to help them build shelter and prepare food.

abundant game, high levels of nutrition, long days of leisure unequalled in most farming societies, and plenty of time for observing nature and thinking about the observations. The results are visible in the achievements of Palaeolithic art. Like all good jokes, the popular cartoon series *The Flintstones* encloses a kernel of truth. Palaeo-archaeologists date modern humans from about 40,000 years ago. "Cave men" really were like us, with the same kinds of thoughts.

Anthropology can help interpret the material remains. Strictly speaking, there are no primitive peoples: all of us have been on the planet for an equally long time and all our ancestors evolved into something recognizably human an equally long time ago. But some people have more primitive thoughts than others. This does not necessarily mean more simplistic or more unscientific thoughts, just thoughts that occurred earlier. Societies in close touch with their earliest traditions are most likely to preserve their oldest thoughts.

We can therefore check archaeological finds against the evidence of the most traditional societies that survive in today's world, those that still live exclusively by hunting and gathering. The fact that hunter-gatherers today have certain ideas does not mean that people of similar cultures anticipated them tens or hundreds of thousands of years ago. But it raises the possibility and helps make sense of the archaeological evidence.

Material culture, which a lot of digs yield, offers a real clue to what goes on in the mind. You can make informed inferences about a people's religion, morals, politics, or their attitudes towards nature and society, by looking at what they eat, wear, and use to decorate their homes. No other evidence is as good as written evidence, but most of the past happened before writing was invented and it would be an unwarrantable sacrifice to foreclose on so much history. At least in patches, we can clarify pre-literate thinking by careful use of such evidence as we have.

This chapter is about ideas that first occurred as early as the earliest past we can hope to reconstruct or convincingly imagine. Such ideas are hard to recapture, not only because the evidence is unclear, but also because the nature of an idea is so elusive. It is hard to distinguish ideas from instincts. In theory, we can make a pretty clear distinction: ideas arise in the mind, instincts are there "already" – innate or planted, presumably, by evolution.

Some of the notions our species has lived with for longest may have originated in any of these ways. So we have to take great care not to mistake instincts for ideas.

Hard evidence
Material culture, such as these Ancient Egyptian vases, provides clues to how early minds thought.

Standing stones
Carnac in Brittany, France has Europe's largest concentration of standing stones (over 3,000). Dating to over 7,000 years, their layout testifies to a systematic plan of thought.

Eating People

THE IDEA OF CANNIBALISM

Some of the earliest evidence of human thought lies among the detritus of a cannibal feast, eaten nearly half a million years ago. In a cave in Zhoukhoudian, China, the eaters split open the bones to extract the marrow. But there was more to the feast than physical nourishment. These cannibals were intellectuals. They also extracted and presumably ate the brains of their victims.

We have trained ourselves to recoil from cannibalism and to see it as treason against our species: a form of sub-human savagery. The evidence, however, suggests the opposite: cannibalism is typically – you might almost say peculiarly – human and cultural. Human bones snapped and sucked lie under the stones of every civilization. No other mammals practise cannibalism so regularly or on such a large scale as we do: indeed, all others tend to avoid it except in extreme circumstances – which suggests that it did not come "naturally" to our ancestors: they had to think about it.

Evidence about cannibalism assembled by modern anthropology shows that cannibals sometimes eat people for nourishment, to survive famine, or to top up protein-deficient diets. Overwhelmingly, however, most cases have concerned more reflective aims, moral or mental, aesthetic or social: self-transformation, the appropriation of power, or the ritualization of the eater's relationship with the eaten. For the Papuan Orokaiva, it was a way of "capturing spirits" in compensation for lost warriors. The Hua of New Guinea ate their dead to conserve *Nu* – the vital fluids they believe to be non-renewable in nature. The Gimi women of the same highlands consumed their dead menfolk to guarantee the renewal of their fertility, and to encompass masculinity – as in bearing a male child. Such cases have multiple parallels all over the world. Where it is considered normal, cannibalism commonly occurs in war, a symbolic act of dominance over the defeated. Or else human meat is seen as the gods' food and cannibalism a form of divine communion.

So which motive animated the first known cannibals, hundreds of thousands

Hard evidence
A 20,000-year-old human femur bone, with the marrow extracted, provides evidence that early humans practised cannibalism.

Something for the pot
Westerners think cannibalism is something "other" people do. In fact, among humans, it seems to have been practised at some time in every culture.

New Guinea
ceremonial
shield.

"We would not leave a man to rot! We take pity on him! Come to me, so you shall not rot on the ground: let your body dissolve inside me!"

Traditional cry of New Guinean Gimi women on eating their dead menfolk

of years before *Homo sapiens*? It would be idle to speculate; but it is consistent with just about everything we know about the nature of cannibalism to assume that it was not just a survival expedient or an act of hunger or gluttony, but a considered act of ritual, underlain by an idea: an attempt to achieve an effect imagined and immeasurable. If the hominids of Zhoukhoudian were like later cannibals, and devised their cannibal ritual to affect themselves, to enhance their powers, or change their natures, they were launching a bold adventure in thought.

READINGS

F. Lestringant's **Cannibalism** (2000) is the best general history.

P.R. Sanday's **Divine Hunger** (1986) explores the logic of cannibalism from an anthropologist's perspective.

M. Harris's **Cannibals and Kings** (1968) is the classic work of materialist reductionism – wrong but stimulating.

The greatest taboo
Popular interest in Hannibal Lecter, the central character from the 1991 film Silence of the Lambs, *demonstrates the enduring power of the idea of cannibalism – not simply for the satisfaction of hunger, but as a power-taking ritual.*

EATING PEOPLE

Give Me a Sign

THE IDEA OF SYMBOLS

Prehistoric signs
The lozenges on this Palaeolithic bone-fragment from Lorthet, France, provide one of the earliest examples of recorded symbols.

It seems odd that one thing can signify something else. Presumably symbols developed from awareness that some events are cued by others. Language was, probably, the first system of signs people devised: an agreed pattern or code of gestures and utterances with no necessarily obvious resemblance to the things signified.

Controversy about the dating of the first language has been dominated in modern times by strictly irrelevant disputes over the vocal powers – the configuration of jaws and palates – of different hominid species and sub-species: this would affect only the kind of language accessible to them, not the feasibility of language in general. In any case, it is doubtful whether language can be classed as an "idea". Is an articulated feeling a thought? Is it "natural" for us to have it? Or did our ancestors have to think it up from scratch? We may have a "language instinct". Although we have not yet found a real-life Dr Doolittle to master the range, it is clear that some non-human animals have a similar facility. Indeed, some chimpanzees have made better progress in learning English than any human scholars have attained in the effort to learn animal languages.

The earliest evidence of the systematic use of representative symbols occurs, late in human history but absolutely clearly, in Palaeolithic art. Realistic depictions of people made 20,000 to 30,000 years ago show a lexicon of gestures and postures which recur over and over again. Moreover, they often include annotations: what seem to be numbers, signified by dots and notches, and

Signal achievement
Transmitting information through abstract signs, such as semaphore, is not instinctive, but the result of conscious thought.

READINGS

W.V. Quine's **The Roots of Reference** (1973) is a philosopher's exploration of the arbitrary nature of signs.

C. Jung's essay in **Man and his Symbols** (1961) is a classic of psychology, arguing that symbols are products of a collective human "subconscious."

J.T. Bonner's **The Evolution of Culture in Animals** (1980) and S. Walker's **Animal Thought** (1983) are pioneering works on the evolutionary context of gesture and language.

S. Pinker's **The Language Instinct** (1994) is a brilliant introduction to modern scholarship on the subject.

"Angels do not speak. For they understand each other through a sort of instantaneous mental reading, and they know everything they are allowed to know… not by any use of language but by watching the Divine Mind."

Dante Alighieri in *Serendipities* (1998) (summarized by Umberto Eco)

conventional marks which can no longer be interpreted but which are undeniably systematic. Examples include the neat lozenges engraved over a brilliant scene of a reindeer crossing a ford on a bone-fragment found at Lorthet, France, and the widely occurring mark which resembles a "P" and which has been read as a logogram meaning "female" because of a supposed resemblance to the hoop-like form with which Palaeolithic artists described the curves of women's bodies.

The existence of signs raises the question of their reliability. When we signal a state of affairs – the approach of a mammoth, perhaps, or the imminence of fire or ice – we detect part of a world we think is real and represent the reality of it in language (or something like language – gestures, say, or grunts or grimaces). We "name" it: many of the earliest recorded creation-myths make "naming" the first thing the first human did. In most species, at some stages of evolution, the recognition of danger or opportunity seems to be instinctive and unconscious and it can be communicated instinctively: apprehended, for instance, in a sense or a noise or a pang of pain. As soon as it becomes conscious, however, it reflects a concept of truth. It is as pertinent to ask of the first people, "How did they tell truth from falsehood and decide whether their utterances were true?" as it is of the most sophisticated philosophers. When the idea of symbolic representation occurred to them, they had a means of conveying information and making it available for critical examination: it was an advantage over other species and, ultimately, a means of broadening communication and protracting memory.

CONNECTIONS

Symbolic representation takes particular forms, such as: art – see **Picture This** (p.42); writing – see **Take a Letter** (p.78); numbers and numerical codes – see **Seeing Double** (p.46); and language – see **Fast Talking** (p.386)

Body language
Humans have devised a wide vocabulary of gestures (in effect, symbols), whose meaning may change from culture to culture. This facilitates communication, giving humans a unique advantage over other species.

Parting the Mist

THE IDEA THAT OUR SENSES CAN BE DELUDED

Humans have feeble senses. Most of our animal competitors see, hear, and smell more keenly. Reliance on the imaginative gifts in which our species is rich helped us conquer our limitations.

"Truth lies in the depths," said Democritus of Abdera, late in the 5th century BC. He meant that things are not as they seem and that appearance – the evidence on which our senses rely – is often misleading. This is an idea accessible to anyone and there is plenty of evidence that Palaeolithic thinkers knew, or thought they knew, the reality of invisible things: after all, they painted, sculpted, and carved them. Anthropologists are always stumbling in unlikely places on the idea that the world is an illusion. For traditional Maori, for instance, the universe was a mirror,

Fooling the eye
Our senses are easily fooled, as demonstrated by Giulio Romano's masterly use of perspective in his painting Olympus, *from the Palazzo del Te in Mantua, Italy. Recognition of this fact led humans on to a new realm of speculative, imaginative thought.*

reflecting the real but invisible world of the gods. For Dakota priests, before the reception of Christianity on the North American plains, the real sky was invisible: we see merely a blue projection of it. When we behold earth and rock, they maintained, we see only their *tonwampi*, which has been translated as "divine semblance".

An inkling that the senses are delusive may have been one of humankind's first thoughts. One sense contradicts another. The experience of every sense is cumulative, and we can never assume that we have reached the end of semblance. A large block of balsa wood surprises by its lightness. We mistake shapes at a distance. We are attracted by a mirage, repelled by a distorted reflection. There are sweet poisons and bitter medicines.

The idea that our senses are unreliable was a master-idea – a skeleton key to spiritual worlds. It opened up infinite worlds of speculation: domains of thought subsequently colonized by religions and philosophies. Dreams presumably suggested it; hallucinogenics – wild gladiolus bulbs, "sacred mushrooms", and the like – would have confirmed it. The Tikopia of the Solomon Islands call dreams "intercourse with spirits". Among the Lele of the Kasai, diviners are dreamers. More fundamental, perhaps, are the disappointments to which human imaginations are victim: if a man imagines a successful outcome to a hunt for instance, and the expectation is fulfilled, the imagined scene may register in memory as a kind of physical reality, like seeing the shadow of a thing before we see its bulk. Disappointment, however, would alert the hunter to the possibility of purely mental events. This surely is the key to understanding Palaeolithic art, in which events imagined jostle with those observed and recalled.

Distrust of sense-perceptions carries its dangers. It induces people to shift their faith to illusions, which seem more convincing only because they cannot be tested: visions, imaginings, the delusions of madness and ecstasy. These mislead. But they also inspire. They open up possibilities which exceed experience and make progress possible. They launch notions of transcendence, magic, religion. They nourish arts. They make ideas unattainable by experience – such as eternity, infinity, and immortality – conceivable. They empower visionaries and favour charisma over brute force, the spiritually gifted over the physically powerful.

Deceptive nature
Nothing is as it seems, even in the natural world, and appearances often deceive. These leaf insects blend easily into their surroundings, helping to foil potential predators.

CONNECTIONS

Ideas that straddle the threshold of illusion and reality keep recurring in history. See, for example, **Dreamtime** (p.98), **The New Illusion** (p.108), **Impossibilism** (p.132), and **Reality Unveiled** (p.276).

READINGS

C. Lévi-Strauss's **The Savage Mind** (1962) defined the terms of the modern debate.

P. Radin's **Primitive Man as Philosopher** (1957) pioneered unprejudiced study of "primitive" thought.

J.S. Lincoln's **The Dream in Primitive Cultures** (1935) is a valuable guide.

B. Russell's **The Problems of Philosophy** (1939) deals brilliantly with the philosophical problem of evaluating sense-perceptions in its opening chapter.

All Things Invisible

THE IDEA OF A SPIRIT WORLD

All life is sacred
The living environment inspires reverence in many people. Followers of Jainism take a vow of non-violence towards all living creatures – even the smallest bugs, which might be swallowed accidentally.

READINGS

E.B. Tylor's **Primitive Culture** (1871) is the classic study from which all subsequent work departed and (mostly) dissented.

E.A. Nida and W.A. Smalley's **Introducing Animism** (1959) is a masterly survey.

T. Nagel's **Mortal Questions** (1980) is an outstanding philosophical study of spiritual thinking.

Human imagination opened up the possibility that incorporeal beings animate the world or infest perceived things and make them lively. We now think materialism is sophisticated: it is smart science to say that the mind is the same thing as the brain, that thoughts are electro-chemical discharges, that the emotions are neural effects, and that love is, as Diderot said, "an intestinal irritation".

In materialism, there is no room for spirit, or for what observation cannot detect. But is this really modern? It is easy to imagine the earliest of our recognizably hominid ancestors as materialists, for whom everything they knew was physical, thoughts were retinal impressions, and emotions were detectable as bodily urges.

Spirits invaded the human world with the discovery, or delusion, that there are invisible, inaudible, untouchable – because immaterial – realities, inaccessible to the senses but attainable to humans by other means. Metaphorically, we still speak of inanimate things as if they were alive: waves dance, flames leap, winds play, trees whisper, stones witness. In the world's most ancient literature and oral traditions, such usages are surprisingly rare. Instead, some living spirit in the objects is credited literally with lively actions. This is not a crude or "superstitious" assumption. On the contrary, it is an extremely subtle idea: a rational (though not verifiable) inference from the restlessness of the flame or wave or wind, the growth of the tree, the persistence of the stone. Thales, the sage of Miletus who predicted the eclipse of 585 BC and who is widely held to have been the first Greek philosopher, believed that magnets have souls which quickened their mutual attraction and repulsion and that "everything is full of gods".

As well as by observation, the ubiquity of spirits can be suggested by thought. If the cause of some of our qualities – mind, say, or soul or personality – is immaterial, we can never be sure who else has got it:

For ancient peoples, **eclipses** were evidence of incomprehensible realities.

"For the primitive mind, everything is a miracle, or rather nothing is; and therefore everything is credible and there is nothing either impossible or absurd."

Lucien Lévy-Bruhl, *How Natives Think* (1910)

other individuals, people from outside our community, animals, plants, rocks, or, as the Brahmins wonder in E.M. Forster's *A Passage to India*, "oranges, crystals and mud". A living environment inspires poetry and reverence and raises presumptions of immortality. You can douse the flame, break the wave, uproot the tree, shatter the stone, but its spirit lives. Spirit-belief makes many peoples wary of the effects of their interventions in nature: they ask the victim's leave before felling a tree or killing a creature.

By analogy with reports from anthropology, we suppose that early people thought spirits were everywhere and that all matter enclosed them. Science has expelled spirits from what we call "inanimate" – literally, "non-spirited" – matter. But disembodied spirits, or "sprites", most familiar in Western thought as fairies and demons, have proliferated in the meantime, and remain ineradicable from some mind-sets even in scientifically sophisticated societies.

Spectral presence
Early people saw spirits everywhere.
The Northern Lights were viewed as
a powerful spiritual presence by
the Lapps and as messengers
of the gods (Valkyries)
by the Vikings.

CONNECTIONS

The idea of multiple spirits co-exists with that of one all-pervading spirit – see **May the Force…** (p.26) and contrasts with materialism – see **Matter Matters** (p.124). Ideas about relations with spirits are explored in **The Vision Thing** (p.22) and **Return of the Soul** (p.140). Modern "deep ecology" echoes early ideas of a spirit-filled world – see **Silent Springs** (p.384).

Fly Like an Eagle

THE IDEA OF TRANSFORMATION INTO AN ANIMAL OR GOD

Becoming other by the magic of disguise was originally a way of wresting strength from animals and gods. Imagination is what enables us to have ideas: otherwise, we should be unable to think of anything, unless it was already in our experience or implanted in us from outside. The power of self-transformation might be suggested by drugs or dreams; it might merely be an articulation of envy: taking on guises, appropriating power from nature, working magic. Imitation can be part of a strategy of emulation. By donning the disguise of a powerful beast – or of a demon or god, if you believe in such things – you seize its powers.

It is an old idea. Such transformations are among the early subjects of art. One of the earliest known cases is of a human dancer disguised as a bison, who appeared on a cave-wall painted some 20,000 years ago, in the depths of the world's last great Ice Age, at Les Trois Frères cave, Arièges, France. All interpretation has to be tentative when the evidence is so scanty and remote, but the context suggests a hunt. The disguised figure faces its prey head-on in a relationship which evokes a clash of powers. This, in short, seems to be the world's earliest portrait of a shaman, taking on the form of a beast as a means of magical control.

The ubiquity of similar magical practices in traditional societies of the present and recent past means that they are a deeply embedded ingredient of culture. Convincing interpretations of historic rock paintings of South African Bushmen, which resemble those of cave-art, suggest that they record shamanic rain-making rituals. Disguise is not mimicry,

Dragon power
For humans, who are physically weak creatures, the power of other animals inspires awe, envy, and imagination. The dragon in this 14th-century Chinese seal was thought to offer protection from evil spirits.

READINGS

T.D. Price and J.A. Brown's (ed.) **Prehistoric Hunter-Gatherers** (1985) and J.D. Lewis-Williams's **Discovering South African Rock Art** (1990) are indispensable for understanding the shamanism of the cave-painters.

M. Eliade's **Le Chamanisme** (1951) is the now widely repudiated anthropological classic which defined the debate; see J. Dow's **Shamanism** (1990) for a modern survey.

Detail of a **shaman** wearing a bison's head from Les Trois Frères, France.

"We got down and lay on the planking... The rock-vaulting... scraped the tops of the boat's sides... Suddenly, there they were. Pictures. Beasts engraved in the stones... Shamans, too: men wearing beast-masks, uncanny figures and weird."

Herbert Kuhn on the cave art of Tuc d'Audoubert, France

Animal magic
This 8th-century mural from Cacaxtla, Mexico, shows a Mayan female in eagle costume. Self-transformation of this kind suggests a conscious attempt to take on the properties of an animal or god.

of the kind a parrot can perform; nor is it like the self-transformation of the chameleon or the spider-crab, a merely "evolutionary" mechanism to conceal the predator or decoy the prey. Self-consciousness has to precede conscious self-transformation. The notion that virtues are transferable by magic is accessible only to an imagination informed by experience but unrestrained by it.

Self-transformation can go deeper than disguise. The earliest evidence we have of body-sculpting is in the deformed crania of a whole generation of people buried at the deepest stratigraphic layer investigated by archaeologists at Jericho (say, 12,000 years ago). Anthropological evidence suggests that it is often associated with the imitation of other species: scarification resembles a hide or pelt; chiselled teeth acknowledge the superiority of the serrated bite of powerful carnivores; genital mutilation, in parts of Australia, is a tribute to the penis of the kangaroo. Much body-painting and sculpting – most of it, probably, in the modern West – is intended for cosmetic effect, but even this implies an idea which originates in the admiration of nature: the idea of beauty.

CONNECTIONS

The role of the shaman is pursued in **The Vision Thing** (p.22). For more on early ideas about the relationship of humans with non-human species, see **Animal Magic** (p.52). The idea of evolution is taken up in **Tooth and Claw** (p.320).

The Vision Thing

THE IDEA OF COMMUNICATING WITH THE SPIRIT WORLD

In early depictions of animal masks in Ice-Age cave-paintings, we can see the self-transformation of the wearer but not the purpose of the disguise. In cases known from anthropological studies of the recent past, such disguises are normally associated with efforts to communicate with the dead or with the gods: to attain access to "other worlds".

In states of extreme exaltation – ecstasy induced by drugs or dance or drumming – shamans see and hear realms normally inaccessible to the senses and can become the mediums through which the spirits talk to this world. Among the Chukchi hunters of northern Siberia – whose way of life and environment are similar to those of the Ice-Age artists – the vision-event is represented as a journey. The purpose of an animal disguise is to appropriate the fleetness of the creature or, in other traditions, to identify with a totem or a supposed animal "ancestor" (which should not necessarily be understood literally as a progenitor).

This can be an awesome source of authority: the flashpoint of a political revolution which replaces the patriarch or alpha-male, at the top of society, with the seer. Special access to the other world has been an important constituent of political legitimacy in many societies in recent times: the claims of "prophets" to power, or of monarchs to sacrality, or of churches to temporal supremacy have all been based on it. As a way of identifying a ruler, enthronement of the gift of communicating with spirits was clearly an early alternative – perhaps the earliest – to submission to the most physically powerful. Some societies found ways of institutionalizing the practice and perpetuating it in historic times. Cities described in Mesopotamian records of the second millennium BC were abodes of gods, who were the nominal rulers and who communicated their commands – to go to war, to build a temple, to promulgate a new law – by visions confided to their human stewards. The most vivid instance – albeit a rather late one – is depicted in the art and recorded in the epigraphy

Spiritual bloodletting
The ability to communicate with spirits often gave political legitimacy to early rulers. This 8th-century Yaxchilan relief from Mexico shows a Mayan queen achieving ecstasy by drawing a thorn-studded rope through her tongue.

22

CONNECTIONS

For the background to shamanism, see **Fly like an Eagle** (p.20). Other magical routes to human manipulation of the spirit world are followed in **The Golden Key** (p.24) and **Fool's Gold** (p.216).

The **Sybil of Cuma's** predictions were regarded as state secrets in Ancient Rome.

"Suddenly the tone of her rantings changed – her face, her colour, the kemptness of her hair. Her breast billowed. Wildly inside it spun her raving heart. Swell-seeming, sounding weird, somehow inhuman seemed she, as the god's breath blew within her."

Virgil's description of the Sybil of Cuma, from the *Aeneid*

of Mayan monarchs, in what are now Guatemala and neighbouring lands, during the 7th, 8th, and 9th centuries AD. They induced visionary states by bloodletting from their tongues and sexual organs and inhaling narcotic fumes from the drug-steeped, burning bark-paper used to soak up the blood. An ancestral spirit then appeared – usually depicted issuing from the mouth of a vision-serpent – to endorse the monarch's policy: specifically, in most cases, to authorize war with a neighbouring state.

READINGS

L. Schele and M. Miller's **The Blood of Kings** (1986), originally an exhibition catalogue, re-defined under-standing of Mayan royal imagery.

A. Kuper's **The Chosen Primate** (1994) is a brilliant work of anthropology which unfolds the context of early thinking on transcendence.

Spiritual spinners
Communication with the spirit world can be achieved through exaltation induced by chanting and spinning. For followers of the Mevlevi brotherhood (the "whirling dervishes"), it can also be an act of religious worship.

The Golden Key

THE IDEA OF CONTROLLING NATURE THROUGH MAGIC

Early humans knew nature well, so it is not surprising that they tried to control it. Magic was one of the earliest and most enduring ways they devised. There are two distinct thoughts in the idea of magic: first, that change can be effected by causes invisible to experience but accessible to the mind; secondly, that a mind aware of these causes can invoke and apply them. Access to the unseen bestows power over the palpable.

The idea is one of the most powerful the world has known: it recurs in every society and no amount of disappointment can shift it. Most tests find it wanting; no convincing method has ever been proposed for a way of systematizing magic. Yet magicians have inspired fear and hope and attracted deference and reward, despite their failures. Though the evidence is equivocal, scholarship has proposed magic as the origin of religion and science: certainly, all three traditions have been deeply concerned with efforts to extend human control over nature.

It is too much to hope that we can ever be specific about the time or the context in which the idea of magic arose. It is older, no doubt, than the earliest evidence of it, which is found in the archaeological record in traces of the mining of red ochre: the first magician's aid – the earliest substance with what seems to have been a role in ritual. The oldest known ochre mine in the world is at Lion Cave in Swaziland, about 42,000 years old. The vivid, lurid colour was applied in burials, perhaps as a precious offering, perhaps to imitate blood and re-invest the dead with life. The speculation that ochre must also have been wielded perishably – to paint living bodies or as a source of ritual

For my next trick
Those with the apparent power to control the unseen forces of nature have long been revered. Here the British performer "Karachi" demonstrates the Indian rope trick.

CONNECTIONS

For an alternative idea about the origins of magic, see **May the Force...** (p.26). On the exploitation of magic, see **Black Magic** (p.50), and on its modern revival, see **Fool's Gold** (p.216). For further links between magic and scientific thinking or behaviour, see **Parting the Mist** (p.16), **Reading the Stars** (p.44), and **Invisible Powers** (p.228).

Two **alchemists** at work, from a 16th-century woodcut by Ulstadius.

"The earliest scientists were magicians... Magic issues by a thousand fissures from the mystical life... It tends to the concrete, while religion tends to the abstract. Magic was essentially an art of doing things."

Henri Hubert & Marcel Mauss, *Sacrifice* **(1899)**

Fiery transmutation
Perhaps pottery was one of the earliest forms of magic? Early humans discovered that water and clay could be transformed into a water-bearing vessel with the addition of fire.

unction – is hard to resist. Helpful speculations about the prehistory of magic focus on the likelihood of a slow process of mutual nourishment between observation and imagination, deep in the hominid past. Some apparently magical transformations happen by accident and can be imitated by experience: the effect of benign bacteria or mastication, for instance, in making food digestible; or of fire in colouring, caramelizing, and crisping it, or in making clay impermeable; or the conversion of a stick or bone into a tool or weapon. Some transformations, however, require more radical acts of imagination. Weaving is a miracle-working technology, presumably discovered cumulatively in a long history of combining strands of fibre to achieve strength and breadth unattainable by a single strand. Practical measures, extemporized to meet material needs, could act as "cues", stimulating the imagination to make magical inferences.

Houses, for instance, built of mammoth bones – erected by people who hunted mammoths to extinction on the Pleistocene steppes – seem such sublime triumphs of the imagination that it is tempting to assume they must have been temples: reconstructions of mammoth-nature, humanly re-imagined, perhaps to appropriate the mammoth's strength or to magically contrive power over the species. In fact, ordinary, everyday activities went on inside these extraordinary edifices – sleeping, eating, and all the routines of family life.

READINGS

B. Malinowski's **Magic, Science & Religion and other Essays** (1948) remains the best introduction, and is challenged in M. Mauss's **A General Theory of Magic** (1902).

L. Thorndike's **A History of Magic and Experimental Science** (1923) is the unsurpassed classic of the history of magic, while the best modern survey is A.C. Lehmann and J.E. Myers's **Witchcraft, Magic and Religion** (1985).

Mammoth magic
It is impossible to tell when the idea of magic first arose. This 20,000-year-old house built from mammoth bones may have been intended to capture the mammoth's power.

May the Force...

THE IDEA OF A PURPOSEFUL UNIVERSAL FORCE

Manual force field
Some people believe that all living things are surrounded by an invisible force field. Kirlian photography reveals the interaction between the subject's aura and an applied electrical field.

READINGS

R.H. Codrington's **The Melanesians** (1891) introduced the concept of mana to the world, while M. Mauss's **A General Theory of Magic** (1902) generalized it.

See G. Zukaz's **The Dancing Wu Li Masters** (1979) for a discussion of "organic energy".

The question, "What makes objects of perception appear real?" seems sophisticated, but early humans asked it. One possible answer was, "An invisible, universal force." Before there were spirits that are peculiar to the objects they inhabit – so some anthropologists claim – there was "mana", a supernatural force that helps the object to fulfil its purpose.

So when a fishing net is thrown, it is the net's mana that makes the catch; when herbs are prescribed for illness, it is their mana that endows them with healing properties. Mana is a word that science has borrowed from South Pacific languages, but a similar or identical concept is reported from other communities around the world. Known as *arungquiltha* among certain Australian tribes, or *wakan*, *orenda*, and *manitu* in Native America, such a widely dispersed notion is likely to be extremely old.

It is not detectable by archaeology, only in traditions that have lain unrecorded until the fairly recent past. The arguments about it are warped by partisanship, for the controversy over which came first – spirits or mana – is animated by deep ideological divisions. Those who favour the priority of mana want to make animism, or belief in spirits, seem a later, and therefore more "developed", attitude to the world. By implication, this makes animism less "primitive" and part of a more sophisticated and mature realm of human thought and action, a development later than magic and therefore better. There seems, however, no reason why spirit and mana should not have been conceived simultaneously in some cultures, or in conflicting order in others.

A commonly asked – but effectively unanswerable – question about mana is, "Is it manipulable?" Did magic start as an attempt to tease or control it? In some societies, especially among the Maoris and Hawaiians, the authority of chiefs, priests, and nobles is justified on the grounds of their special access or relationship to mana or to some similar

Bronislaw Malinowski (1884–1942) was one of the founders of British anthropology.

"While science is based on the conception of natural forces, magic springs from the idea of a certain mystic, impersonal power... called mana by some Melanesians... a well-nigh universal idea wherever magic flourishes."

Bronislaw Malinowski, *Magic, Science & Religion and other Essays* (1948)

source of power. A deeper question about belief in mana is whether it is valid or not. While most people make a fundamental distinction today between organic and inorganic matter, modern physics identifies all matter as characterized by essentially similar relationships betweeen particles: composed of quantum charges, which are dynamic and formative and so resemble mana in a curious respect. They could reasonably be called a source of "force", though we are reluctant to suppose that they constitute a purposeful force, which, in most versions of the idea, is what mana seems to be. Mana should, in any event, be acknowledged as a sophisticated idea, since it seems to arise from a sophisticated problem: for the peoples who believe in it, it is what makes the perceived world real.

A further question is, "How did the idea of mana contribute to the origins of the idea of a single, universal God?" Some early missionaries who encountered mana-belief in North America and Polynesia identified it with awareness of God and regarded it as a kind of religion. The speculation that God is a sort of outgrowth of mana is a tempting one; really, however, the doctrine of mana seems more closely to resemble some esoteric modern beliefs, such as: the "aura" of alternative health-speak, or the "organic energy" ascribed to all matter by proponents of the oriental-influenced "new physics".

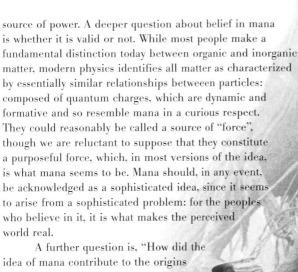

Space mana
In the Star Wars *films, the "Force" (used here by Luke Skywalker to levitate a rock), closely resembles the ancient idea of mana.*

CONNECTIONS

For the idea of multiple spirits, rather than all-pervading mana, see **All Things Invisible** (p.18). On the development of magic, see **The Golden Key** (p.24). For the idea of a unique god, see **No God but God** (p.158). For the background to modern particle physics, see **Warped Universe** (p.346) and **Uncertainty** (p.348).

No Dice

THE IDEA OF AN ORDERLY UNIVERSE

Early humans saw through the apparent chaos of Nature: with a bit of imagination, order was revealed. Animals perceive relationships between events that matter to them: the death of prey and the availability of food, or worsening weather and the need for shelter. The urge to "make sense" of data by juxtaposing, and therefore accumulating them, seems to be a property of the mind, or what people loosely call "instinct". There comes a point, however, when the "sense" we make of knowledge transcends anything in our experience, or when the intellectual pleasure it gives us exceeds material need. At that point, an idea is born.

Once evolution endowed them with sufficient memory, people could observe patchy instances of order in Nature and make mental connections between them: the regularity of the heavenly bodies, the progress of the seasons, the predictability of the life-cycle. But that was only the scaffolding upon which the idea of an orderly Universe was erected. There is a huge gap for the mind to leap, between observations of orderly relationships and the inference that order is universal. Indeed, the claim that order encompasses the whole of Nature is so counter-intuitive and so contrary to experience that it must have originated as an idea. Order is not visible, except in a few fragments; the rest has to be inferred from the clues.

Floral design
Many thinkers have tried to find a pattern that connects humans to nature, in order to understand our place within the universe. The spiral-based arrangement of petals in a dahlia is based on a mathematical pattern found throughout nature, known as the Fibonacci number series.

READINGS

S. Giedon's **The Eternal Presence** (1962) is a stimulating introduction; while E. Neumayer's **Prehistoric Indian Rock Paintings** (1983) displays the evidence from Jaora.

J.E. Pfeiffer's **The Creative Explosion** (1982) is a stimulating attempt to trace the origins of art and religion in Palaeolithic people's search for order in their world.

The idea of order makes the entire cosmos imaginable in a single mind and summons efforts to picture it whole. This fundamental breakthrough in the history of thought obviously happened independently in lots of different cultures, and, in every case, so long ago that we no longer remember when. The first clear evidence is embodied in the earliest cosmic diagrams – artistic or religious or magical depictions of the universe. The oldest I am aware of is in a rock-painting in Jaora in Madhya Pradesh, which, on present calculations, is maybe 8,000 (certainly not more than 10,000) years old. It shows a world divided into seven regions, surrounded by symbols of water and air. Another version decorates a 4,000-year-old Egyptian bowl: the world resembles a pair of pyramids, surrounded by zigzags, between rising and setting suns.

The age of the concept, however, probably greatly exceeds the age of the evidence. For just about all hunter-peoples now known to anthropologists have an overall concept of the cosmos and describe it in their myths. Many of them represent it in rock-painting or body-art: the Caduveo of the Paraguay paint their faces with quarterings that resemble the way they divide up the world. Early descriptions of the world seem echoed in the "dreamtime" of Australian Aborigines, in which the inseparable tissue of all the universe was spun. Dogon goatherds in Mali decorate rocks with diagrammatic representations of a four-quartered world. Kongolese potters make vessels for initiation rites with depictions of the cosmos. Magic and oracular divination seem to pre-suppose an ordered world, bound by predictable, and even manipulable, chains of cause and effect.

Cosmic rock
Like most hunter-peoples, the Dogon of Mali have tried to make sense of the cosmos by representing it in their art. Their myths and rock-paintings display a remarkable knowledge of the solar and Sirius star systems.

CONNECTIONS

Ideas about how to perceive or induce order in the cosmos are also traced in **Around the Clock** (p.30), **Lords of Creation** (p.68). For a more scientific approach, see **Fallen Apple** (p.226), and **Warped Universe** (p.346).

Albert Einstein
(1879–1955),
theoretical physicist.

"You believe in the God who plays dice, and I in complete law and order in a world which objectively exists, and which I, in a wildly speculative way, am trying to capture... "

Albert Einstein, letter to Max Born (1944)

Around the Clock

THE IDEA OF MEASURING TIME

Aztec sun calendar
The idea of time arose from observation of predictable celestial movements. According to Aztec belief, the Sun's movements across the heavens necessitated regular sacrifices.

READINGS

A. Marshack's **The Roots of Civilization** (1972) is a highly controversial but insidiously brilliant study of Palaeolithic calendrical and other notation.

K. Lippincot's (ed.) **The Story of Time** (2000) is the best survey of the whole subject.

J.T. Fraser's **The Voices of Time** (1966) and **Time, Passion and Knowledge** (1990) are fascinating studies of human efforts to devise and improve time-keeping strategies.

Since its first formulation, human beings have used this breakthrough idea as the basis for organizing action and recording experience.

Time is change. No change, no time. Change is observable and you can measure changes roughly against each other, perhaps, without having an idea of time: accelerating, for instance, to elude a pursuer or capture prey, or noticing that different life-forms grow at different rates.

A universal standard of measurement is, however, an idea. It arose, of course, from observation: from awareness that some changes – especially those of the relative positions of celestial bodies – are regular, cyclical, and therefore predictable. The realization that they can be used as a standard against which to measure other such changes transcends observation: it was a perception of commonplace genius that occurred in all human societies so long ago that – ironically – we are unable to estimate a date for it.

It is a fair assumption that it happened in consequence of the congruities between the cycles of the heavens and other natural rhythms – especially those of our own bodies and of the eco-systems to which we belong: the passage of the Sun roughly matches intervals of sleep and wakefulness. The Moon's coincides with the menstrual cycle. Species we eat grow or fatten according to the season. Hence the choice of time-keeping standards. Some human groups keep star-time, usually on the basis of a cycle of Venus, but all, as far as we know, use the solar day and year, and the lunar month. Some, like ours, attempt elaborate reconciliations of the cycles of those two most conspicuous heavenly bodies, while others keep both sets of calculations going in imperfect tandem. It is a safe bet that keeping time by this means is one of the oldest and longest-enduring ideas in the world. It

Monthly **lunar cycles** regulate tides and reproductive ability.

"The sight of day and night, and the months and the revolutions of the years, have created number, and have given us a conception of time."

Plato, *Timaeus* (c. 360 BC)

Neolithic ritual centre
*From 5000 BC onwards,
people started to erect
standing stones to mark the
passage of the Sun. The
great megalithic monument
of Stonehenge on Salisbury
Plain, England, is perfectly
aligned with sunrise on the
summer solstice.*

remained the basis of timekeeping – and therefore of the co-ordination
of all collaborative enterprise – until our own times (when we have
replaced celestial observations with caesium-atomic time-keeping).

But when did it start? The earliest known artefact that looks
as though it might be a calendar was made about 30,000 years ago
in the Dordogne, from a flat bone inscribed with crescents and circles:
the intervals look systematic and have been read as a record of phases
of the Moon. Then there is a yawning gap in the evidence until the 5th
millennium BC onwards, when horizon-marking megaliths appeared,
erected to track the passage of the Sun through the heavens. In the
interim period, many sites have yielded what look like tally-sticks,
or, at least, objects scored with regular incisions, but these are not
securely identifiable as calendars and are as likely to be "doodles"
or games or decorative objects, or ritual aids, or numerical
records of other kinds.

Once timekeeping started, life could never be the
same again. Humans had a unique way of organizing
memory and anticipation, prioritizing tasks, and
co-ordinating collaborative endeavours.

CONNECTIONS

For developments of the
idea of time, see: **Time's
Arrow** (p.112), **Damned
Time** (p.178) – where St
Augustine's idea of time is
discussed – and **Warped
Universe** (p.346). On
change, see **All Change**
(p.110); and for the idea
of progressive change,
see **Getting Better** (p.252),
Tooth and Claw (p.320),
and **Class Struggle**
(p.292).

Wake-up call
*The more precise
measurement of time
facilitated the development
of industrialization. Factory
workers were expected to
work to the clock.*

Mighty and Dreadful

THE IDEA OF DEATH

Burial rites
Ritual burials, such as that of a crippled Neanderthal man from Shanidar, Iraq, provide early evidence of a conscious reverence for life.

READINGS

C. Stringer and C. Gamble's **In Search of the Neanderthals** (1993) is an outstanding introduction, while P. Mellar's **The Neanderthal Legacy** (1996) is a masterly survey of the evidence.

W. Golding's **The Inheritors** (1955) and B. Kurten's **Dance of the Tiger** (1995) vividly re-create the daily life and mental world of that period.

We still find life and death hard to define, but the distinction between them was apparent to people 30,000–40,000 years ago. A Neanderthal family are buried together at La Ferrasie, France: two adults of different sexes are curled into the foetal position characteristic of Neanderthal burials all over what are now Europe and the Near East. Nearby, three children of between three and five years old and a newborn baby lie with flint tools and fragments of animal bones. The remains of an undeveloped foetus, extracted from the womb, is interred with the same dignity as the other family members, albeit without the tools. Other Neanderthal burials have more valuable grave goods: a pair of ibex horns accompanied one youth in death, a sprinkling of ochre was strewn on another. At Shanidar, in what is now Iraq, an old man – who had survived in the care of his community for many years after the loss of the use of an arm, severe disablement to both legs, and blindness in one eye – lies with traces of flowers and medicinal herbs.

All these cases – and many others – of what look like ritual Neanderthal burials have been challenged by sceptical scholars as the results of accident or fraud. But there are too many of them to discount. At the other extreme, credulity has drawn irresponsible inferences from this evidence, crediting Neanderthals with a broad concept of humanity, a belief in the immortality of the soul, a system of social welfare, a gerontocracy, and a political system of philosopher-rule. They may have had such things, but the burials are not evidence of them.

Mere burial is evidence only of material concerns: to deter scavengers, to mask the odour of putrescence. But ritual burial is evidence of an idea, indeed of two ideas – of life and death. We still find it hard to define them and in particular cases – such as impenetrable comas and the misery of the moribund on life-support – to say exactly where the difference between

State funeral
A state funeral – such as the one that followed the assassination of US President J.F. Kennedy in 1963 – provides a ritual focus of mourning.

"… of comfort no man speak: Let's talk of graves, of worms, and epitaphs…"

William Shakespeare, *Richard II* (1597)

Gravestones are an attempt to perpetuate dead identities over bio-degraded remains.

CONNECTIONS

The idea of the afterlife is featured in **Buried Goods** (p.34) and **Conquering Death** (p.92). Ideas concerning the transformations that might accompany or follow death appear in **Judgement Day** (p.94) and **Return of the Soul** (p.140). For afterlife-free ethics, see **Atheist Faith** (p.324).

them lies. But the conceptual distinction we make between them goes back 30,000–40,000 years, when people began to mark it by rites of differentiation of the dead.

These first celebrations of death hallowed life. They constitute the first evidence of a more than merely instinctive valuing of life: a conviction that life is worthy of reverence, which has remained the basis of all human moral action ever since.

Ashes to ashes
Rituals, such as this Hindu cremation in Bali, Indonesia, indicate a clear consciousness of the transition between life and death. Hindus believe that the dead person will be reincarnated.

MIGHTY AND DREADFUL

Buried Goods

THE IDEA OF THE AFTERLIFE

Grave goods yield clues to the origins of one of the most disturbing, yet inspiring ideas humans have ever had: the idea of life after death. Ceremonial burial is not necessarily evidence that people who practise it believe in an afterlife. It might be an act of commemoration or a mark of respect. Goods deposited with the dead may be intended to work their propitiatory magic on the living and to contribute to survival in this world rather than transition to the next. Nevertheless, when grave goods include a complete survival kit – with food, clothes, negotiable valuables, and the tools of one's trade – it is hard to resist the impression that they constitute equipment for a new life.

Such goods became normal in burials all over the inhabited world by

CONNECTIONS

For a materialist take on the afterlife, see **The Family Silver** (p.36) and **The Great Chain** (p.380). Other ideas about the afterlife appear in **Conquering Death** (p.92), **Judgement Day** (p.94), and **Return of the Soul** (p.140).

35,000–40,000 years ago. Gifts of ochre, at least, are found in graves even of people from very modest levels of society, and the incidence of tools and decorative objects constitutes an index of social rank in societies already riven by inequalities. Nor is the survivability of death an idea that is hard to understand. While alive, we all witness constant transformations of our bodies, without losing a sense of the continuity of our identity. If we survive changes as momentous as puberty, the menopause, or traumatic injury without ceasing to be ourselves, why should death, which, after all, is only the most radical of a series of such changes, mark our extinction?

The idea of the afterlife was probably not therefore in itself of great importance: the grave goods of early burials imply that the next life will be a prolongation of this. They affirm the survival of status, rather than of the soul. Indeed, all grave goods seem to have been selected on this sort of assumption until as recently as the first millennium BC, although only in some parts of the world. What mattered were the later (certainly, later-documented) refinements to the afterlife idea, such as the claim that the afterlife would be a place of reward or punishment, or that it would be an opportunity for a new life, perhaps through reincarnation. The way one imagined one's afterlife could then become a moral influence on this world and, in the right hands, a means of moulding society.

Buried status
The idea of the afterlife, as evidenced by the discovery of buried "survival kits", is dramatically shown in the creation of this terracotta army of over 7,000 life-size soldiers. They were intended to provide eternal protection to a 3rd-century-BC Chinese Qin emperor.

READINGS

R. Leakey and R. Lewin's **Origins Reconsidered** (1992) is a lively survey of the evidence of human evolution with special emphasis on early thinking.

C. Renfrew and E. Zubrow's (eds) **The Ancient Mind** (1994) is the best work on very early evidence about cognitive archaeology.

C. Gamble's **The Palaeolithic Societies of Europe** (1999) is ingenious in interpreting all kinds of evidence, and setting that of grave goods in context.

The Family Silver

THE IDEA OF TRANSMITTING STATUS BY HEREDITY

High-ranking remains
The fine ornaments buried with this juvenile skeleton from Sungir, Russia, mark its high social status.

Among the biggest problems for all human societies is how to transmit power, wealth, and rank peacefully. The idea of the hereditary principle supplied one of the earliest answers.

Early human communities did not need an idea of inequality: it came naturally to them. By analogy with other primate societies, individual hominids of exceptional prowess, cleverness, or charisma can fairly be assumed always to have wielded power over their companions. But how could the idea have arisen that acquired status should be transmitted by heredity?

On the face of it, it seems dysfunctional, since parental excellence is no guarantee of a person's merit, and leadership won in competition has the justification of experience to back it. There are no parallels in the animal kingdom. Yet all societies have come to admit the hereditary principle in some measure; most made it, for most of history, the normal means of recruitment to high levels of command.

The plays of the French aristocrat, **Beaumarchais** (1722–99), challenged inherited inequalities.

"Nobility, wealth, rank… What have you done to deserve so many advantages? You have given yourself the trouble of being born, nothing more!"

Pierre-Augustin de Beaumarchais, *The Marriage of Figaro* (1781)

CONNECTIONS

For challenges to inequality, see **A Golden Age** (p.90), **Neverland** (p.250), and **Class Struggle** (p.292). For more on political and social systems that incorporate the hereditary transmission of power, see **Divine Majesty** (p.82), **Noble Education** (p.196), and **Intelligence Test** (p.382). On genetic inheritance, see **The Great Chain** (p.380).

It started early. A representative case is that of a cemetery at Sungir, near Moscow, from around 28,000 BC. At first appearance, the individual of the highest status was an elderly man whose burial goods included a cap sewn with fox's teeth and about 20 ivory bracelets. These could have been the rewards of an active life. Nearby, however, two boys of about eight or ten years old had even more spectacular ornaments. As well as ivory bracelets and pendants, and fox-tooth buttons, they had animal carvings and beautifully wrought weapons, including spears of mammoth ivory, each about two metres (over six feet) long. Almost 5,000 finely worked ivory beads had been drizzled over the head, torso, and limbs of each boy. Here was a society that marked leaders for greatness from boyhood and therefore, perhaps, from birth.

Various explanations have been suggested: as a matter of common observation (for which genetic theory now provides sophisticated explanations), many mental and physical attributes are heritable. This creates a rational bias in favour of the children of self-made leaders. The instinct to nurture children, it is sometimes said, makes parents want to pass their property, including their position, on to their offspring and, therefore, willing to allow others to do so. By deterring competition, the hereditary principle is conducive to the peace of society. Specialization creates disparities of leisure between elites and plebeians, which enables those with specialized roles to train their children to succeed them. Some states still enjoy the advantages of hereditary monarchs and hereditary legislatures, protected from the corruption of popular politics and elevated above conflictive arenas.

THE FAMILY SILVER

Sons and heirs
Throughout history, rulers have striven to pass their property and position down the family line. This formal photograph shows a boy Maharajah from Rajasthan, India, posing with the male members of his family.

READINGS

M.D. Sahlins's **Stone-Age Economics** (1972) is a mould-breaking work in many fields: it explains the basis of economic differentiation in Palaeolithic societies.

Way of the warrior
A specialized warrior class is found in many societies. Around AD 900, Japanese Samurai warriors became a hereditary caste, with a code of honour and the right to bear long swords.

Take, Eat

THE IDEA OF PROSCRIBING CERTAIN FOODS

The common life of early hominids presumably resembled primate bands, bound by kinship, force, and neccessity. What laws turned them into new kinds of societies, regulated by ideas? Though undetectable in the archaeological record, the earliest social regulations are likely, from anthropological evidence, to have been of two kinds: food "taboos" and incest prohibitions. Discrimination in controlling the sex urge, according to some theorists, may have originated as an instinct rather than as an idea, but humans seem less likely to have been naturally fastidious about food, since it is not natural to forego nutrition. Yet all societies proscribe foods, therefore the idea of it must have occurred early in human history.

"Lawful" food
Muslims, like Jews, must make their meat "good-to-eat" by having it ritually slaughtered (drained of blood) and formally blessed. Only then does it become halal ("lawful") or kosher.

Among cases studied by anthropology in an attempt to identify the rationale of dietary rules, that of the Batlokwa, a pastoral people of Botswana, is the most remarkable. They have more forbidden foods than any other community. The aardvark is forbidden to everybody. So is pork. Oranges are banned if grown locally. There are other foods restricted by age and sex, some of which are forbidden in pregnancy. Some prohibitions are seasonal, others enforced only in certain conditions – for instance, when there are sick children in the household. This complexity makes the Batlokwa representative of food taboos worldwide.

Efforts to rationalize food taboos have all failed: in the classic case, the prohibitions encoded in one of the most famous ancient texts, the Hebrew scriptures, defy analysis. The forbidden creatures have nothing in common except that they tend to be anomalous according to some methods of classification. Looked at globally, taboos are too various to yield to overall

READINGS

M. Douglas's **Purity and Danger** (1984) includes the best available interpretative study of food taboos.

M. Harris's **Good to Eat** (1986) is an engaging exposition of the cultural materialist viewpoint.

The Cambridge World History of Food (2000) is a massive compendium of knowledge about foods.

"Animals that have hoofs but not cloven and that are ruminant... those four-footed animals which walk on the flat of their paws... any creature which swarms on the ground... do not defile yourselves with them."

Pork is a proscribed food for both Jews and Muslims, who consider the pig impure.

Leviticus, **11: 3-43**

analysis. The commonest theories do not fit the facts: the claims of economics (that valuable foods tend to become subjects of prohibition) and hygiene (taboos apply when foods are thought to be unhealthy) do not work for most known cases.

Rational and material explanations fail because dietary restrictions are essentially supra-rational and metaphysical. Meanings ascribed to food are, like all meanings, agreed conventions about usage. Food taboos bind those who respect them and brand those who break them. If the rules made sense, outsiders would follow them – but they exist precisely to exclude outsiders and give coherence to the group. Permitted foods feed identity; excluded foods help to define it.

Sacred cows
Hindus do not eat cows because they consider them sacred. As a result, cows are protected by all, and can roam freely, even in the busiest Indian streets.

39

A Family Affair

THE IDEA OF REGULATING INCEST

Dynastic family tree
Marrying outside a family group allows the creation of alliances between different dynasties, as this family tree celebrates.

READINGS

C. Lévi-Strauss's **The Elementary Structures of Kinship** (1949) is the classic study, which, in essence, has withstood innumerable attacks.

R. Fox's **Kinship and Marriage** (1967) is an excellent, dissenting survey.

S. Freud's **Totem and Taboo** (1918) traced incest-prohibition to psychological inhibition, and is one of those ever-admirable books: great, but wrong.

Along with food prohibitions, this idea marks a critical transition from "nature" to "culture". Many non-human animals have gregarious habits and social lives. We usually suppose these are regulated by "instinct" – which you do not have to think about and which falls well short of an idea. Can we find the first clearly non-instinctive rules of social conduct – the origins of the traditions which, in a later stage of their development, we call law?

Evidence of collaborative social projects exists in early remains of hominid material culture; but this does not necessarily imply an idea – merely the development of the survival-instinct evolved by natural selection. So we must turn to anthropology and seek out the most nearly universal feature of culture: this is likely to be the earliest on the grounds that it has had the longest time to become widely practised. The best guess, by these criteria, favours incest-prohibitions. No known human society is without them, though their forms vary astonishingly: some societies permit marriage of siblings, but not of cousins. Some permit only cross-generation cousin-marriage; some treat formal relationships – such as those between in-laws – as if they were blood-relationships.

Because the beginnings of prohibition happened too long ago to be illuminated by evidence, we have to make reasoned guesses about them. It is often supposed that primitive eugenics were responsible: outbreeding reduces the incidence of hereditary defects. This effect may inspire some people with incest-abhorrence, but most people in most societies for most of the time have known little about it and cared less. Incestuous breeding usually produces healthy children. Some societies condone alliances of very near kin – Egyptian pharaohs married their

English **folk dancing.**

"You should make a point of trying everything once, excepting incest and folk-dancing."

Quoted by Sir Arnold Bax in *Farewell to my Youth* (1943)

sisters; Onan's daughters were obliged to "lie with their father"; the Amish in America condone the marriage of cousins and impose prohibitions on marriage to outsiders, even though they may provide better breeding stock.

The most famous and convincing explanation was devised in the 1940s by the French anthropologist Lévi-Strauss, after he watched fellow-countrymen exchanging identical wine in a bistro. Neither party gained from the transaction but it created a relationship between the lunchers. He developed this insight into an argument about incest: women are exchanged to create relationships, binding different families in mutual obligations, and so to make societies of many families cohere and grow. The idea of regulating incest affirmed the idea of society in the minds of people who applied it and enormously expanded the potential of societies that practised it: they got bigger, forged more ties, and so increased in strength. The reason for the universality of the idea is, perhaps, this simple: societies without it are ill-equipped to survive.

Closed community
The idea of sex prohibitions within one's immediate family group affirmed a wider idea of society. However, the Amish of Pennsylvania, USA, discourage marriage with outsiders in order to maintain a narrow, close-knit community.

Parental control
We all have our own marriage taboos. In the film Meet the Parents *(2000), a suspicious father submits his prospective son-in-law to a lie-detector test.*

Picture This

THE IDEA OF ARTISTIC REPRESENTATION

Leaving a mark
In caves from as early as the Palaeolithic era, people painted around their hands and feet with ochre, using one of the earliest artistic techniques: stencilling. This detail comes from the Cave of the Castle in Puente Viesgo, Spain.

Some of the world's best art is the oldest. Nineteenth-century explorers who discovered prehistoric paintings in caves in Spain and France initially could not believe that the works were genuine.

The technology that made them was rudimentary: a palette of three kinds of ochre, applied with wood, bone, and animal hair. Yet even the earliest works appeal instantly to modern sensibilities: the drawing is free and firm, the subjects are shrewdly observed, sensitively captured, products of a mature tradition, drawn by practised, specialized hands. Carvings from the same period exhibit similar accomplishment. Stylized, steatopygous women preponderate: sculptors portrayed their pregnant bellies and powerful hips for many thousands of years over widely spread locations, as far east as Siberia. Realistic images include elegant ivory sculptures in the round: 30,000-year-old, five-centimetre (two-inch) long, arched-necked horses from Vogelherd in southern Germany; and 20,000-year-old female portraits and figures from Brassempouy in France and Vestonice in Moravia. Creatures of the hunt are relief-sculpted on cave-walls or engraved on tools. Other finds from Vestonice include 27,000-year-old fired-clay models of bears, dogs, and women.

These European artworks of the Ice Age survived because they were made in the shelters to which the climate drove the inhabitants, and deep chambers, evidently chosen for their inaccessibility. Other cultures

"Fine art is that in which the hand, the head and the heart of man go together."

John Ruskin, *The Two Paths* **(1871)**

John Ruskin (1819–1900), English art critic.

READINGS

Outstanding surveys include H.G. Bandi's **The Art of the Stone Age** (1961) and A. Sieveking's **The Cave Artists** (1979).

M. Ruspoli's **The Cave Art of Lascaux** (1986) is the best book on the most spectacular cave.

S.J. Mithen's **Thoughtful Foragers** (1990) is a thoughtful, distinctive approach to the problems of interpretation.

of the time also created proficient work: four painted rock slabs at Apollo 11 cave in Namibia are almost as old as any art in Europe. But most prehistoric art has been lost: weathered away on exposed rock-faces, perished with the bodies or hides on which it was daubed, or scattered by wind from the earth in which it was scratched.

A clue to the origins of the idea of representing life in art fades today from a rock-face in Kenniff, Australia, where stencils of human hands and tools were made 20,000 years ago. Traces of similar stencillings are visible on some of the cave-walls that bear paintings in Europe. If stencilling was an early artists' technique, it seems believable that footprints and handprints inspired it. Scholars debate inconclusively the first function of art. It surely told stories and had magical, ritual uses: animal images were scored through or punctured many times over, as if in symbolic sacrifice. A good case has been made out for seeing the cave-paintings as hunters' mnemonics: the shapes of hooves, the spoor, excreta, seasonal habits, and favourite foods of the beasts were important items in the artists' stock of images. Yet the aesthetic effect, which communicates across the ages, transcends any practical function. This was not art for art's sake, but it was surely art: a new kind of power, which, ever since, has been able to galvanize the spirit, capture the imagination, inspire action, represent ideas, and mirror or challenge society.

Imagined hunt
Early cave paintings, like this painted hall of bulls, horses, and stags from Lascaux, France, may have exercised some kind of ritual or magical power on those who looked upon them.

43

Reading the Stars

THE ASTROLOGICAL IDEA

In the absence of books, stars made compelling reading. Stone-Age cave art recorded phases of the Moon and presumably read the rest of the stars, linking their motions to events on Earth.

In some eyes, the stars are pinpricks in the veil of the sky through which light from an otherwise unapproachable heaven is glimpsed. Astrology is close to the threshold between the sublime and the ridiculous. Even the royal astrologers of ancient Babylon were busy with banal and worldly enquiries from their kings: "When Jupiter is in the halo of the moon, the King of Akkad will overcome his enemies. When Regulus is dark, the King will be angry." But they held the stars in genuine awe as the visible face of the sacred world.

It is hard to deny astrology a place among the world's most influential ideas, since so many people have believed in it and continue to do so. But how can astrology survive in our modern, industrialized, "scientific" world? Modern astrologers represent the influence of the stars as part of the web of nature and no different from the interactions of any other parts of the environment. The news from the stars has been stolen from the realms of mystery, and relocated in newspaper-columns and tables of statistics. By a margin slightly greater than average, for instance, sportsmen are born under Mars, actors under Jupiter, and physicians under Saturn. Those who hold planetary influences responsible, explain them by invoking magnetism or electrical fields, or liken them to the effects of the Sun and the Moon on blood albumen and tides. By forfeiting claims to magic, astrology has become more trivial and humdrum than ever and, at the same time, unthreatening and uncrushable. The stars have climbed down from heaven. Instead of being messengers of the gods, astrologers have become mimics of scientific method.

Reading the sky
Stars have always made compelling reading. A planisphere, like this 18th-century example, provides a rough map of the stars above the horizon at any given time, and is used by astrologers to compile horoscopes and star charts.

READINGS

J. Lindsay's **The Origins of Astrology** (1971) is an excellent introduction, while J.D. North's **Stars, Minds and Fate** (1989) has cast much light on the subject.

J. Halliwell's (ed.) **The Diary of Dr. John Dee** (1997) opens a window into the mind of a Renaissance astrologer, who is also the subject of P. Ackroyd's fascinating novel, **The House of Doctor Dee** (1983).

CONNECTIONS

On connections between stargazing and time-keeping, see **Keeping Time** (p.30); for a broader idea about the predictability of the future, see **Deo Volente** (p.96); on astrology as a protean form of science, see **Fool's Gold** (p.216).

In **King Lear** the stars become a metaphor for Lear's tragic downfall.

"It is the stars, the stars above us, govern our conditions…"

William Shakespeare, *King Lear* (1604)

It's in the stars
Astrologers perceive patterns in groups of stars, which are then interpreted. Western astrology associates 12 "constellations" with the characteristics of mythical figures.

Astrology and medicine
Medieval surgery distributed parts of the body among astral spheres of influence. Until the 18th century, the use of the planetary positions in the diagnosis and treatment of illness was commonplace. This medical chart comes from a 15th-century German calendar.

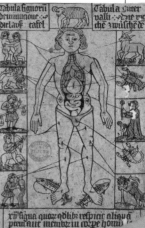

Seeing Double

THE IDEA OF A TWO-FOLD COSMOS

Probably the first idea people had for trying to make sense of the cosmos was to divide it into two. People seek coherence: the feeling that they understand what they sense by matching it with other information. A constant theme of the history of thought is our search for a universal pattern – a meaningful scheme – into which all our information about the universe can be made to fit. As far as we know, the first such scheme people thought of was binarism (traditionally called dualism – but, confusingly, this name has been used for a lot of other ideas as well).

Binarism envisages a two-fold cosmos, satisfyingly symmetrical and therefore orderly, regulated by the balance or flow between two conflicting or complementary principles. Some of the earliest creation myths we know of, including those of the Ancient Egyptians and Sumerians, represent the world as the result of an act of procreation between earth and sky. The idea probably started a long time before it was first documented. Indeed, although anthropologists have found many conflicting descriptions of the cosmos, it does seem that many – perhaps most – peoples inhabit a dual world, envisaged by their remotest ancestors.

This world is seen in uneasy equipoise, or complementarity, between dual forces, such as "male" and "female", "light" and "darkness", or "evil" and "good". A past generation of scholars interpreted the cave-paintings of Ice-Age Europe as evidence of a dualist mental world, in which everything the hunters saw was classified in terms of gender, but the phalli and vulvae they detected in the designs seem equally likely to be weapons and hoofprints, or part of some unknown code of symbols.

Binarism obviously shapes the myths and morals of people who believe in it. Over the last 3,000 years, it has been rejected in more recent systems of thought which have claimed to describe the Universe, but the exceptions include Taoism, which has had a formative influence on China and to the history of thought in many parts of the world. Christianity, while formally rejecting binarism, has absorbed much from it, including the notion, or, at least, the imagery, of a perpetual struggle of angelic powers "of light" against satanic forces "of darkness". For Leibniz, the 17th-century discoverer of binomial theorem, there were only two unquestionable realities: zero and God.

Good and Evil

THE IDEA OF A UNIVERSAL MORALITY

Good and evil are notions of obscure origin – opposites, the difference between which is often hard to establish in practice. Some philosophers, for instance, have defined both as the pursuit of self-interest.

Everybody, at all times, is able to identify practical reasons for action. But there are scruples strong enough to override practical considerations. It is possible that random, or consciously arbitrary, rules distinguishing "right" (which yields good results) from "wrong" (which yields bad ones) may have preceded any attempt at formulating a moral code based on ethical principles. The rules involved in food taboos and incest prohibitions seem to be examples. Yet belief in a universal ethos or a standard of judgement, by which, as a matter of principle, good can be distinguished from evil, is so common among humankind that it is likely to be of very great antiquity. In most societies' origins myths, it is represented as one of humankind's earliest discoveries or revelations. In the Genesis story, it is Man's third step – after acquiring language and society – to distinguish good and evil. And the episode dominates the story disproportionately.

The nearest we can get to trying to date the first emergence of the moral idea is to look in the archaeological record for evidence of apparently disinterested actions. But there are two problems with this method. First, many non-human animals perform disinterested actions without, as far as we know, formulating a moral code (although they can – as in the case of earthquake-rescue dogs – get depressed if their efforts are unsuccessful). Altruism is probably evolutionary – a survival-mechanism which impels us to help each other in the common interest. Secondly, apparently disinterested acts could be explained by calculations unrevealed in the record. The first moral human act known to archaeology is thought to be the Shanidar burial of a crippled, half-blind Neanderthal whose people had nurtured him for years before he died.

Some philosophers argue that the moral idea is a source of weakness: it inhibits humans from maximizing their advantages and their power. More probably it is like all great goals: rarely attained, but conducive to striving, discipline, and self-improvement. It has made societies that take it seriously beloved by their citizens and empowered by loyalty and the spirit of sacrifice. The romantic notion of "poetic justice" – according to which good always proves stronger than evil – is exaggerated, but has some plausibility.

Concentrated evil
If morals are not universal, different cultures can define their own moral communities. Nazis, for instance, excluded Jews and deemed their extermination moral.

CONNECTIONS

Other dualist ideas with a similarly strong moral dimension, are broached in **Wicked World** (p.180). For evil in connection with magic, see **Black Magic** (p.50), On theological responses to the problem of evil, see **Getting Better** (p.252).

READINGS

I. Kant's **The Groundwork of the Metaphysics of Morals** (1798) presents a classic theory of ethics based on rationalism, while A. MacIntyre's **A Short History of Ethics** (1967) surveys the history of moral philosophy.

I. Murdoch's **The Sea, the Sea** (1978) presents a prize-winning fictional treatment of human moral development.

Paradise lost
According to the Bible, humans discovered a moral code after Adam ate fruit from the Tree of Good and Evil, depicted here in Lucas Cranach's The Fall (1537).

Black Magic

THE IDEA OF WITCHCRAFT

Malice aforethought
*In a tradition of malign
attempts to influence nature
magically, the act of
pushing pins into a voodoo
doll is intended to harm the
person the doll represents.*

READINGS

E.E. Evans-Pritchard's
**Witchcraft, Oracles and
Magic among the Azande**
(1929) revolutionized thinking
on the subject.

G. Parrinder's **Witchcraft**
(1959) is a classic from a
psychological point of view;
while J.C. Baroja's **The World
of the Witches** (1964) takes
a more anthropological
approach, with a salutary
emphasis on Europe.

If cause and effect can be invisibly linked and magically manipulated,
harmful magic may be responsible for human ills. Every age has its own
ideas about witchcraft, defining it, for example, as a malign manifestation
of psychic power, or a diabolic pact. But, understood at the most general
level, as the ability of a person to do harm by supernatural means, belief
in it is found in just about all societies – a fact which pushes its probable
origins way back into the past. Many peoples make it central to their
understanding of the world – their explanation of first resort for any
deplorable event. So it is one of the world's most influential ideas.

    The Azande of the Nilotic Sudan are generally treated as a model
case for understanding witchcraft in general, following the pioneering
work on the subject by E.E. Evans-Pritchard. It seems, however, that
their notion of it is quite unusual. They believe that personal misfortune
generally arises from witchcraft, which is not necessarily consciously
applied, and which originates in an inherited physical condition, revealed
in autopsy as a hairy ball in the gut. "Poison oracles" are used to reveal
living witches: poison is forced down a chicken's throat and adjured
to kill or spare the bird according to the truth or falsehood of the
denouncers' accusations. This way of understanding the nature of
witchcraft is different from other common assumptions, such as that
witches are signified by some physical deformity or that evil induces
ugliness in the perpetrator: for the Azande, the
hairy ball is the source of the witchcraft, not
just a sign of it.

    In the world's earliest body of
imaginative literature – that of Mesopotamia
around 2000 BC – witchcraft is frequently
mentioned, especially in incantations intended
to counter its effects: addressed to gods or fire

Witch torture
*During the late
Middle Ages,
witches were
often convicted
with confessions
obtained under
torture.*

*"The purpose both of witches
and wizards... is none other
but that infamous intercourse...
connexion with the Demon."*

L.M. Sinistrari, *Demoniality* (1709)

Korean **demon masks**
are worn in the belief
that they frighten away
real demons .

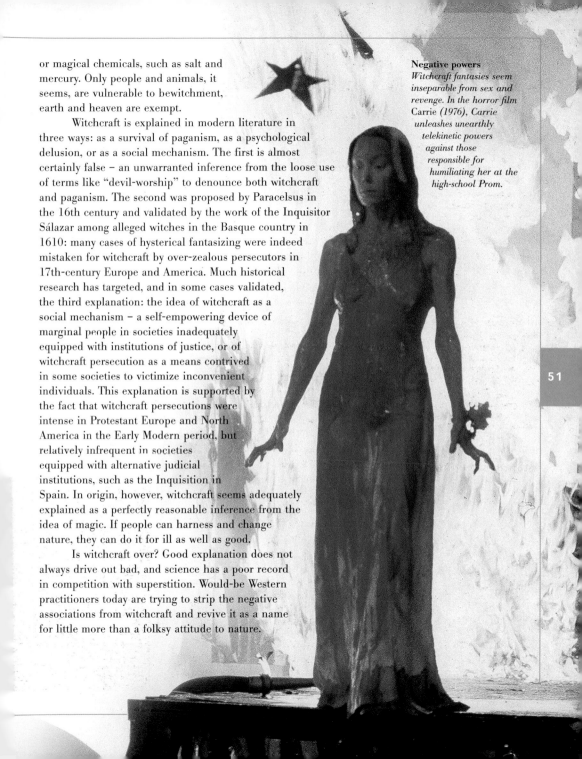

or magical chemicals, such as salt and mercury. Only people and animals, it seems, are vulnerable to bewitchment, earth and heaven are exempt.

Witchcraft is explained in modern literature in three ways: as a survival of paganism, as a psychological delusion, or as a social mechanism. The first is almost certainly false – an unwarranted inference from the loose use of terms like "devil-worship" to denounce both witchcraft and paganism. The second was proposed by Paracelsus in the 16th century and validated by the work of the Inquisitor Sálazar among alleged witches in the Basque country in 1610: many cases of hysterical fantasizing were indeed mistaken for witchcraft by over-zealous persecutors in 17th-century Europe and America. Much historical research has targeted, and in some cases validated, the third explanation: the idea of witchcraft as a social mechanism – a self-empowering device of marginal people in societies inadequately equipped with institutions of justice, or of witchcraft persecution as a means contrived in some societies to victimize inconvenient individuals. This explanation is supported by the fact that witchcraft persecutions were intense in Protestant Europe and North America in the Early Modern period, but relatively infrequent in societies equipped with alternative judicial institutions, such as the Inquisition in Spain. In origin, however, witchcraft seems adequately explained as a perfectly reasonable inference from the idea of magic. If people can harness and change nature, they can do it for ill as well as good.

Is witchcraft over? Good explanation does not always drive out bad, and science has a poor record in competition with superstition. Would-be Western practitioners today are trying to strip the negative associations from witchcraft and revive it as a name for little more than a folksy attitude to nature.

Negative powers
Witchcraft fantasies seem inseparable from sex and revenge. In the horror film Carrie (1976), Carrie unleashes unearthly telekinetic powers against those responsible for humiliating her at the high-school Prom.

51

Animal Magic

THE IDEA OF TOTEMISM

"Totemism" can mean any kind of thinking that closely relates humans and other natural objects. In its most powerful form, the totem becomes a device for re-imagining human social relationships.

Guardian spirits are known in most cultures. They are often associated with individuals (as in the old Jewish, Christian, and Muslim concept of one's personal protective "angel"), but their association with communities may be a clue to the question of how some early human groups formed an idea of the relationships that bound them together.

In totemism, a relationship with a particular animal or, in some cases, plant species, or some other natural object, defines the group and distinguishes it from other groups who form part of the same society. People's relationship with their totem is usually expressed as common ancestry, sometimes as a form of incarnation. This works because it creates obligations that transcend self-interest and constitutes a means of mutual identification. It is a way of keeping track of people of common ancestry in demographically expanding societies. Moreover, although it is strongest and most common as a way of conceptualizing real ties of kinship, it also makes it possible for people who are not tied by real blood-relationships to behave towards one another as if they were: in most societies with totemic practices, one can be ascribed to the totemic "clan" as well as being born into it. It generates common ritual life. Peoples who class themselves according to totemic affiliations usually share rites of veneration of their special animal, and observe peculiar taboos – especially by refraining from eating their totem, or marrying within the group.

It is found in every continent, though it would exceed the evidence to claim that totemism was a universal practice at some early phase of history. Yet it seems to be one of the earliest and most effective ways of forging society, creating and preserving effective bonds between smaller

Defiant bulldog
Nations often choose an animal to embody their identities. During the London blitz of WWII, the British re-adopted the bulldog for its indomitable spirit.

READINGS

C. Lévi-Strauss's **Totemism** (1962) is an ingenious and convincing critique, displacing earlier, but still interesting classics, such as E. Durkheim's **The Elementary Forms of Religious Life** (1912), A. Lang's **The Secret of the Totem** (1905), and S. Freud's **Totem and Taboo** (1918).

groups in expanding societies, and even transforming small families into more numerous bands. Totemic relationships are genuine ideas, often said to have been originally revealed in dreams, which recur to members of the totem group to confirm their status.

How they really start, and what, if anything, the choice of totemic objects means, have been ferociously but inconclusively debated. The common feature of all the theories is that totemism is related to the difference, or "transition", between two very early categories of thought: "nature", represented by the totemic objects, and "culture", understood as the conscious relationships between participants in the group.

Symbol of America
America has chosen the bald eagle (it is found only in North America) as its symbol. Its image adorns many official objects, such as this Presidential Seal.

Tribal identity
A symbolic association with one or more animals is used by many tribes to define their identity. The Native American memorial (or totem) pole commemorates an individual's clan affiliations.

Eat, Drink

THE IDEA OF THE RITUAL SHARING OF FOOD

A peculiar attitude to food – as a socializing influence, a source of magic, and a focus of ritual life – is a characteristic of humankind. But when did the idea that food is more than nourishment arise?

Cooking with fire created a new kind of common life: a routine of fixed mealtimes, a locus of shared activity, which may be presumed to have generated rituals and suggested possibilities. Evidence of ritual slaughter of animals for food goes back to the first known cannibal meal at Zhoukhoudian nearly half a million years ago. The association of food with power may first have occurred to "alpha-male" hominids, who privileged chosen associates when distributing carrion or game millions of years ago.

A further breakthrough, illuminated by a little more evidence, came with the idea of the feast: a ritual sharing of foods, made special by cost or quantity, to mark a special occasion. Some foraging peoples do not have such a practice: the special occasions are large-scale kills by the hunters or the discovery of a carrion-bonanza. So feasting is not as old an idea as those that underlie genuinely universal practices. (It is possible, however, that this is a trick of the evidence: some hunting peoples confine feasts

Feast as metaphor
Real feasts are inclusive. In the parable of Lazarus, a wealthy man ignored a beggar at his door and went to hell.

CONNECTIONS

Other ideas about food occur in: **Eating People** (p.12), **Take, Eat** (p.38), and **All Change** (p.110). On the emergence of chiefly societies, see **The Family Silver** (p.36). On the Christian "love-feast", see **This Is My Body** (p.184).

Thanksgiving turkey
The annual Thanksgiving Day celebrations in North America help to strengthen a common American identity.

*"The art of the chef...
is common to all
civilized nations."*

The **chef's hat** is a sign
of status in the kitchen.

Chevalier Jaucourt, *L'Encyclopédie* (1787)

to remote and secretive locations, far from their usual habitation sites,
such as might not show up in the archaeological record.) Because it
involves a lot of effort and expense, a feast surely needs some
justification: symbolic or magical, at one level; or practical, enhancing the
power, status, or client-network of a feast-giver, creating ties of reciprocity
between feasters, or concentrating labour where feast-givers wanted it, on
another level.

It therefore makes sense to look for the origins of the practice in
periods for which there is other evidence of accumulated food-sources or
of marked social differentiation. Obviously, in early agrarian and pastoral
societies feasting became crucial to social cohesion, as the method by
which surplus production was distributed among the community under
the leadership of chiefs, or, perhaps at a later stage, reserved for elite
gatherings. The earliest clear evidence is at Hallan Cemi Tepesi in
Anatolia, 10,000–11,000 years ago. From recent archaeological work,
however, it looks increasingly as if the practice is much older: originating
in the privileged hunter-societies of the era of Palaeolithic abundance –
the same period that produced surviving cave art, with suggestive
concentrations of remains at sites in northern Spain nearly
twice as old as Hallan Cemi. It has even been suggested
that the tally-sticks that survive from the same region and
period may have been records of expenditure on feasts.

What were such feasts for? To judge from analogies
with modern hunting peoples, the most
likely pretext was alliance-making: if these
had been male-bonding occasions, for
instance, they would probably not have
been close to major dwelling sites. If
they were redistributive feasts, they
would imply a stronger political authority
than we know of in this period from other
sources. From its first emergence, the idea
of the feast had practical consequences:
building and strengthening societies, and
enhancing the power of those who organized
the feasts and controlled the food.

Pork and soda

*Feasting plays a major role
in wedding ceremonies, as
it provides an opportunity
to cement the newly formed
alliance. At Yao wedding
celebrations in Thailand,
guests are invited to feast
on pork and soda at both
the bride's and groom's
houses. Bottled drinks are
served as a mark of status
for the special occasion.*

READINGS

M. Sahlins's **Culture and
Practical Reason** (1976) is
an anthropological classic
that has set the framework
of subsequent debate.

P. Wiessner and W.
Schiefenhovel's **Food and
the Status Quest** (1996)
contrasts culture and
ecology as rival "causes"
of the feast idea.

M. Dietler and B. Hayden's
Feasts (2001) is a superb
collection of essays covering
the field.

EAT, DRINK

Camel convoy
Trade routes (such as the Asian silk route) have often provided the backbone of inter-nation relations. Camels still ply these routes in parts of North Africa.

Evidence of trade
Grave goods often provide evidence of trading contacts. An example is the gold used in this Viking brooch.

Fair Exchange

THE IDEA OF TRADE

Trade presumably arose from gift-exchanges, made in a spirit of reciprocity, even before commerce in goods between different environments became practicable. But what about the idea that trade adds value to goods and can be practised for profit?

It had nothing to do with material needs; nor is it, as economists used to think, the result of a rational system for offloading surplus production. Objects of early commerce seem overwhelmingly to have been traded for ritual purposes. "The outstanding discovery of recent historical and anthropological research," wrote Karl Polanyi, one of the most sophisticated modern critics of capitalism, in 1944, "is that man's economy, as a rule, is submerged in his social relationships. He does not act so as to safeguard his individual interest in the possession of material goods; he acts so as to safeguard his social standing, his social claims, his social assets. He values material goods only in so far as they serve this end." Indeed, anthropologists have revealed many cases of survivals of longstanding practices that not only involve ritual goods but in which the act of trading is itself a rite. The most striking example is the Kula of the islands of the Solomon Sea off eastern New Guinea, in which artefacts made of polished shell were carried laboriously from island to island along routes ordained by custom and repaid at traditionally determined rates and intervals. More or less identical ornaments from identical materials could be manufactured all over the archipelago, but each one was invested with a peculiar character and reckoned at a peculiar value, determined in part by its antiquity. The anthropologist Mary W. Helms points out that in almost every kind of cultural environment, goods from afar carry symbolic associations, crudely proportional to the distance they travel. By interesting coincidence, Hermes, the god of craftsmen, musicians, and athletes, was also responsible for messengers, merchants, and "professional boundary-crossers". This is how goods unremarkable for rarity or usefulness become desirable as objects of trade.

From archaeological evidence or anthropological inference, the earliest goods exchanged between communities seem to have included fire – which, perhaps because of ritual inhibitions, some peoples have never kindled but have preferred to acquire from outside the group – and ochre, the most widespread "must-have" of Palaeolithic ritualists. Large-scale, specialized, systematic trade is probably much older than traditionally supposed. Archaeologists whose predecessors regarded axe-heads of particular patterns or peculiarly knapped flints as evidence of the presence of their producers now recognize that even in the remotest traceable antiquity, such artefacts could have been circulated by means of trade.

READINGS

K. Polanyi's **The Great Transformation** (1944) and **Trade and Economy in the Early Empires** (1957) are the classic works on the subject.

J.W. Leach and E. Leach's (eds) **The Kula** (1983) is the best guide to the Melanesian island system, while J.G.D. Clark's **Symbols of Excellence** (1986) and M.W. Helms's **Ulysses' Sail** (1988) are good on the importance of exotica in the foundation of trade.

Alternative currency
Goods from far away carry a symbolic value relative to the distance travelled. This New Guinean Mount Hagen warrior proudly shows off his shell chest ornament. These desirable objects passed along trading routes that led from the ocean to the mountains.

A 15th-century **French cloth merchant** cuts material to sell to his customers.

"Every man becomes in some measure a merchant."

A. Smith, *Wealth of Nations* (1776)

OUT OF THE MUD 2

10,000–1000 BC

From Settlement to Civilization

After ice, mud. In the last global warming, eco-niches opened for humans to exploit. In environments where water and sunshine were abundant and friable soils could be worked by simple tools, the opportunity to farm emerged. Agriculture probably unfolded in a gradual process of "co-evolution".

Humans shared particular environments with other animals and plants, gradually developing a relationship of mutual dependence. Foragers replanted some crop varieties, selecting as they went. Some new crops developed spontaneously near human camps in waste enriched by rubbish. Some animals became dependent on human care or vulnerable to human herding by virtue of sharing people's favoured habitats. Snails were perhaps the first farmed food-source. Easily gathered and selected, they have been found

Super tuber
The taro root, commonly found in south-east Asia and the Pacific, may have been the world's first farmed plant.

inside prehistoric middens all over the world. These developments happened independently in scattered regions, with various specializations.

Some of the earliest evidence is of taro-planting in New Guinea 9,000 years ago. Farming of wheat and barley in the Middle East, tubers in Peru, and rice in south-east Asia is of comparable antiquity. Cultivation of millet in China, barley in the Indus Valley, and a short-eared grain, known as tef, in Ethiopia, began almost as early. During the periods conventionally known as the New Stone Age and Bronze Age, farming spread or began independently in most Eurasian environments where it was practicable, and in many regions of Africa and the Americas. The consequence was one of the most conspicuous revolutions in world history. Millions of years of evolution were modified as new species arose from what might be called "unnatural selection" – by human agents for human purposes – alongside the "natural selection" which, previously, had been the only means of diversifying creation.

Farming was not an option that suited everybody. Some consequences were malign:

Traditional methods
Agriculture spread even to unforgiving places. This hill farmer in Peru tills the land with an ox-drawn plough in a similar way to his ancient ancestors.

backbreaking work, unhealthy concentrations of people, ecologically perilous increases of population, risks of famine from over-reliance on limited crops, problems of deficient diet, and the incubation of new diseases in new environments. Some human groups preferred to follow retreating ice and fat-rich animals into tundras and uncultivable grasslands, remaining as hunters and foragers, or herding animals.

Where the new ways of life took hold, however, new forms of social and political organization followed. Farming required more than just the right material conditions, it was also the product of an act of imagination – the realization that human hands could re-shape the world, imposing on the land the geometry of cultivated fields and irrigation ditches. The possibilities of great monumental cities arose in minds fed by agriculture. Cultivation generated seasonal food surpluses that had to be warehoused, regulated, and redistributed by strong new states. Kings replaced chiefs. Specialized elites swarmed. Opportunities of patronage multiplied for artists and scholars. Labour, organized on a massive scale, had to be submissive. Armies grew and investment flowed to improve the technology of war: there was an inescapable link between agriculture and tyranny.

One might expect this dynamic epoch to have been productive in ideas.

Bronze-Age dagger
Agriculture and warfare co-existed symbiotically as precious food resources needed to be acquired or defended with improved weaponry.

Civilizing cereal
Millet is a robust type of cereal that thrives in hot and dry climates. It helped to sustain civilizations as far afield as Ethiopia, China, and Mesopotamia.

However, for little-understood reasons, the "great civilizations" of this era were remarkably traditional and static – even stagnant – in their ideas. The best explanation probably lies in their ecological fragility. Most of them occupied a single type of environment and relied on one staple crop. The great exceptions were China and Egypt, which enjoyed unusual environmental diversity and achieved remarkable longevity. Egypt was a granary for millennia, exporting wheat and barley and shovelling large amounts of surplus into grain-fed cattle. From the mid second millennium BC, China encompassed regions both of rice and millet. Even these civilizations, however, were always insecure and needed the order and continuity that tradition provided. Most of the others were less well provided. Civilizations in mutual touch found peace hard to maintain. And there were always enemy "barbarians" on the frontiers – predatory, nomadic peoples envious of sedentary societies' wealth.

For most of the great civilizations, the combination of war and ecological over-exploitation eventually proved fatal. In a period lasting perhaps 200 to 300 years, late in the second millennium BC, cities withered or shrank across a swathe of the Old World, from Greece to central Asia. Egypt tottered and survived. China re-emerged under a new dynasty. Most of the other great civilizations vanished for ever.

Drowning the Deer

THE IDEA OF SACRIFICE

Blood of the bull
*The Muslim holiday
of Kurban-bairam
("Feast of the Sacrifice")
commemorates the prophet
Abraham's willingness to
sacrifice his son Isaac.
In Chechnya, bulls are
sacrificed and children's
faces are painted with
their blood.*

Though the forms, meaning, and purpose of sacrifice vary enormously, almost everywhere people have felt a need to surrender to the gods part of what they wrest from nature.

In 1932 in northern Germany, Alfred Rust was investigating campsites belonging to hunters who had headed north, tracking reindeer with the retreating ice during the last great global warming of about 10,000 years ago. There was none of the great art he hoped for, but in three lakes he found the remains of 30 big, unbutchered reindeer, each of which had been ritually killed, slashed, and sunk, with a big stone implanted between its ribs. Ritual killings are shown in art of the high Ice Age: but these were of rival predators, such as lions and tigers, or preludes to feasts. The lake sacrifices are of another kind, because the food is foregone. This is pure sacrifice: the first evidence of the rise of gods jealous in their hunger and of a religion apparently intended to propitiate them.

Anthropology proposes the most convincing explanation of the origins of this idea. Gifts are a common way of establishing reciprocity and cementing relationships between individuals and human groups: by extension, a gift should also work to bind gods or spirits to the human givers, connecting deities to the profane world and alerting them to its needs and concerns. It is likely that the idea and practice of sacrifice first occurred much earlier than the earliest surviving evidence. There is therefore probably no point in trying to seek a further explanation in the circumstances of the "global warming" that ended the Ice Age. It is suggestive, however, that the first temple we know of – the first space demonstrably dedicated to worship – dates from about the same time. Deep under Jericho, at a level representing settlement in about 11,000 BC,

READINGS

H. Hubert and M. Mauss's **Sacrifice: its Nature and Function** (1899) set the agenda, while M.F.C. Bourdillon and M. Fortes's (eds) **Sacrifice** (1980) gives a modern perspective.

B. Ralph Lewis's **Ritual Sacrifice** (2001) is a useful general history, concentrating on human sacrifice.

I. Clendinnen's **Aztecs: an Interpretation** (1991) offers a fine survey of Aztec mentality.

Mayan **Chac-Mool**
figures provided a
receptacle for offerings
to the gods.

"Sacrifice is a religious act which, by consecrating a victim, modifies the moral status of the person who performs it or the object for which it is offered."

Hubert & Mauss, *Sacrifice: its Nature and Function* (1899)

CONNECTIONS

For a particular example
of sacrifice, see **This Is My
Body** (p.184). Sacrifices
can usefully be compared
with **Buried Goods** (p.34).
On the origins of gift
relationships, see **Fair
Exchange** (p.56).

where a spring once flowed, there
are two stone blocks, pierced to
hold some vanished cult-object, in
a space about 3 by 6 metres (10 by
20 ft), which the worshippers at the
time kept well swept. It is tempting
to draw a connection between a
time of profound environmental
change and the rise of new kinds of
religion, involving the development
of permanent cult-centres and of
new, elaborate rituals of sacrifice.

Despite critics – especially in
ancient Judaism, in modern Islam,
and in the Protestant tradition of
Christianity – who have suspected
sacrifice as a quasi-magical attempt
to manipulate God, it has become
part of most religions during the
last 10 millennia. In the process,
sacrifice has acquired a great range
of meanings: as penance for sin; as
thanksgiving; as homage to divinity;
as a contribution to the well-being
of the Universe; or as a sacralized
gift, considered as an act of worship
or of imitation of God.

Human sacrifice
*Human sacrifice is the most extreme example
of propitiation. The Aztecs believed such rites
(using mainly prisoners) were essential to
feed the "hungry" sun.*

Written on the Wind

THE IDEA OF ORACLES

Readings in the sand
Many societies find clues to the will of the gods or insights into the future in natural phenomena. Here, diviners in Mali inspect a prepared patch of sand for signs of animal disturbance, which can then be interpreted.

The supposed interconnectedness of everything suggests that clues to events in one sphere may be found in another that is apparently quite different. If bird flight, the stars, changes in weather, and individual fortunes are all linked, the links may be traceable. This is the thinking behind the practice of oracular divination.

Intimacy with spirits gives mediums tremendous power. So it is not surprising that most societies have developed alternative means of other-worldly communication, searching for chinks in the wall of illusion, through which shafts of light penetrate from a world that feels closer to truth than our own. Of these methods, the oldest known were oracles, which could be read "in the book of nature".

Tarot cards, which originated in 15th-century Italy, "predict" the future.

> "We know how to say many false things which seem true and to sing truly when we wish."
>
> Hesiod on the Muses, *Theogeny* (c. 9th century BC)

An ominous omen
In the West, comets are traditional omens of political upheavals. Halley's comet (depicted here in the Bayeux Tapestry) was said to have been a portent of King Harold's defeat by William of Normandy at the Battle of Hastings (1066).

The most ancient shrine of the early Greeks was at Dodoma, where they could hear the gods in the babbling of the stream and the whisperings of the wind. The world's earliest surviving literature, from Mesopotamia in the second millennium BC, is full of omens: portents revealed in anomalous weather or rare alignments of celestial bodies. Other oracles commonly identified in writings of the first and second millennia BC, and exemplified in later cases known to history or anthropology, include rarities or "mutations" in the appearance of the sky at night, or of a flight of birds, or of the innards of sacrificed animals (sheep's livers were called "tablets of the gods" in ancient Mesopotamia), or in volcanoes or earthquakes, or apparently spontaneous combustion, or in the behaviour of creatures specially designated for the purpose. The gypsy's tea-leaves are the dregs of a tradition of libations to the gods.

Some early oracles have left records of their pronouncements. In China, for instance, in the silt of the great bend in the Yellow River, hundreds of thousands of such records survive from the second millennium BC on fragments of bone and shell heated to the breaking-point at which they revealed their secrets, like messages scrawled in invisible ink – forecasts made or memories confided by the ancestral spirits could be read from the shape of the cracks. Interpreters or their assistants often scratched these readings alongside, as if in translation. They cover solutions of crimes, disclosures of hidden treasure, and identifications of individuals chosen by the gods for office.

Most of these readings, like the celestial oracles of Mesopotamia, are "official" messages, legitimating state policies. By breaking the shamans' monopoly as spirit-messengers, oracles diversified the sources of power and multiplied political competition. Specialist priests or secular rulers could read them. Political authorities could control fixed shrines and manipulate the messages. The rise of oracles could be considered one of the first great political revolutions, as rulers gradually withdrew patronage from spirit-mediums, usurped their functions, or subjected them to control.

CONNECTIONS

The theme of inter-connectedness also occurs in **May the Force…** (p.26), **No Dice** (p.28), and **All Is One** (p.104). For examples of other attempts at communicating with other worlds, see **The Vision Thing** (p.22) and **Reading the Stars** (p.44).

READINGS

The I Ching or **Book of Changes** (c. 1500 BC) is the world's oldest written oracle, while E.E. Evans-Pritchard's **Witchcraft, Oracles and Magic** (1929) is the classic anthropological case-study.

M. Loewe and C. Blacke's **Oracles and Divination** (1981) covers a wide range of ancient cultures. C. Morgan's **Athletes and Oracles** (1990) is a superb study of oracles in Ancient Greece.

Outside Eden

THE IDEA OF AGRICULTURE

First food
Snails, which are relatively easy to "herd", may have been the first farmed food.

CONNECTIONS

The broader context of this idea is explored in **Lords of Creation** (p.68). Later ideas about the possibilities of human intervention in the process of evolution appear in **Good Breeding** (p.322) and **The Great Chain** (p.380).

About 10,000 or 12,000 years ago, some societies became food-producers: herders and farmers instead of foragers. Debate rages over whether the process started unconsciously or was triggered by an idea. "Some wise old savage," thought Charles Darwin, must have launched our ancestors' first experiments in agriculture, when, "noticing a wild and unusually good variety of native plant… he would transplant it and sow its seeds" – an idea which "hardly implies more forethought than might be expected at an early and rude period of civilization." This makes the idea of producing food by selective cultivation sound rather commonplace. Yet it was extremely powerful: a form of "unnatural selection" – humans' first great revolutionary intervention in evolution.

After millions of years in which hominids relied on scavenging and foraging for their food, it was a radical and surprising innovation. Traditionally, indeed, most historians of agriculture have thought it so extraordinary that it can only have happened once or twice in the history of the world and must have been diffused worldwide from near-unique centres of origin. This view now seems false: there is clear evidence of the independent development of agriculture in at least half a dozen places at different times, during thousands of years of global climatic change which followed the end of the last great glaciation 10,000 to 12,000 years ago.

Conventional explanations cancel each other out: the idea was a response to stress – pressure of rising population and falling game stocks; or it was the result of abundance which gave foragers leisure to think of ways of becoming producers. Alternatively, it was inspired by politics – chiefs who needed spare food-resources for feasts and gifts – or by religion, as people tended, nourished, and transplanted the crops they worshipped. It happened by accident or it happened by design.

"Why farm? Why give up… hunting?… Why work harder for food less nutritious and a supply more capricious? Why invite famine, plague, pestilence and crowded living…?"

In the West, **food** is plentiful and convenient.

Jack Harlan, *Crops and Man* (1992)

The most helpful scenarios are first, of plant-gathering slowly self-transformed into farming, as gatherers re-plant selected specimens or exploit local or temporary climatic conditions to supplement foraging with farming (as the Papago of the Sonora Desert in the North American Southwest do to this day), or hunting transformed into herding, as the hunters' catch is corralled and culled. Secondly, people and the life-forms they eat can be said to "co-evolve", as they grow in mutual dependence: eventually, the first agricultural revolution became complete when species emerged that were incapable of propagation without human help.

Wherever and whenever it happened, farming tended at first to have disastrous consequences: creating new eco-niches in which disease developed; reducing peoples to dependence on a few, fragile staple foods; and encouraging massive farming and irrigation projects, accompanied by despotic regimes. The book of Genesis associated the start of tillage with a time of woe. It made it possible, however, to concentrate populations of a size and density previously unimaginable. All the subsequent developments we associate with what we call civilization depended on the idea of changing what we eat to suit our purposes and to maintain a consistent supply by selective planting and breeding.

READINGS

C. Darwin's **The Variation of Animals and Plants under Domestication** (1868) is the essential starting-point, to be followed by V.G. Childe's **Man Makes Himself** (1936) a ground-breaking though much reviled work.

J.R. Harlan's **Crops and Man** (1992) is an engaging, fiercely argued essay.

D. Rindos's **The Origins of Agriculture** (1984) presents the most cogent theory, while F. Fernández-Armesto's **Food: a History** (2002) gives a concise survey of the literature.

67

Intensive farming
The growth of agriculture on a vast scale (helped by the high-yielding crops of the Green Revolution) has matched the dramatic increase of the world's population, but also contributed to environmental degradation.

Lords of Creation

THE IDEA OF RE-SHAPING NATURE

Chinese rice terraces
Since the earliest days of agriculture, humans have re-shaped Nature to suit their needs. Here, stepped rice terraces transform the landscape.

Man-made skyline
It would be hard to think of a more radical re-shaping of Nature than that represented by the New York skyline. Manhattan's impressive array of skyscrapers has become an icon of urban landscape.

Pre-literate civilizations have left two huge clues to the operation of powerful new ideas: the geometry of their fields and settlements, and the scale of their monumental buildings.

There was never a golden age of ecological innocence. As far as we know, people have always exploited their environment for what they could get out of it. And they have always tended to exceed the rational limits of exploitation: Stone-Age hunters sometimes hunted to extinction the very species on which they depended for food. Neolithic farmers exhausted their soils and dug dust-bowls. Still, the idea of challenging nature – effectively, waging war on other species, re-shaping the earth, re-modelling the environment, re-crafting the eco-system to suit human uses and match human imaginations – was one of the great revolutionary ideas of history. It replaced a method (collaborative) and a model (symbiotic) that had governed human beings' relationships with their environments since the emergence of our species.

Built environments, which smother nature with a geometry of human design, and field-systems, which stamp the land with a regular grid, are the evidence. The earliest remains of this sort date from between 9,000 and 11,000 years ago. In the Jordan valley, Jericho's reputation as "the oldest city in the world" rests on brick dwellings from 10,000 BC, built with walls 60 centimetres (2ft) thick on foundations of stone. The people who lived here ate cultivated strains of wheat and barley. Early

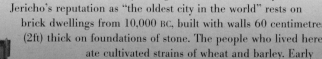

"A social instinct is implanted in all men by Nature and yet he who first founded the city was the greatest of benefactors."

Aristotle, 4th-century BC Greek philosopher.

Aristotle, *Politics* (c. 4th century BC)

CONNECTIONS

For a good example of the role of imagination in the re-fashioning of the environment, see **Outside Eden** (p.66). For ideas of how to control nature, see **The Golden Key** (p.24) and **Fool's Gold** (p.216).

Jericho covered only 4 hectares (10 acres). Çatal Hüyük, built over 7,000 years ago in what is now Turkey, was more than three times larger: a honeycomb of dwellings linked not by streets as we understand them, but by walkways along the flat roofs. The houses were of uniform design: the doorways, hearths, ovens, and even bricks were of standard shapes and sizes. A painted streetscape of a similar city survives on one of the walls.

Citizens of such places may already have thought of the city as the ideal environment to dwell in. That was certainly the prevailing opinion in Mesopotamia by the third millennium BC. The best-known creation myth from the region defines chaos as a time when "a brick had not been made… a city had not been built". By the end of the millennium, 90 per cent of the population of southern Mesopotamia lived in cities. Four thousand years later, the rest of the world is beginning to catch up and we are becoming a city-dwelling species. It has taken that long for us to get close to overcoming the problems of health, security, and viability that arise from massive re-orderings of the natural environment. Some of the consequences are still obscure and we still do not know whether we can avoid the disasters that have overcome every city-building civilization so far.

Ancient metropolis
One of the earliest built environments was the Neolithic city of Çatal Hüyük, Turkey.

READINGS

L. Mumford's **The Culture of Cities** (1938) is an indispensable classic, while P. Hall's **Cities in Civilization** (1999) is a useful collection of case-studies.

For Sumerian cities, see G. Leick's **Mesopotamia: the Invention of the City** (2001). For a modern overview, try F. Fernández-Armesto's **Civilizations** (2000).

The Curse of Work

THE IDEA OF THE WORK-LEISURE DIVIDE

Daily grind
For many, work is a chore to be endured not enjoyed. Here, Charlie Chaplin is a slave to the machine in the satirical film, Modern Times *(1936).*

Blood, sweat, and tears
The invention of the plough in Ancient Mesopotamia and Egypt in about 8000 BC revolutionized farming, while creating a culture of hard work.

A paradox of "developed" societies is that increasing leisure time never liberates us. It makes work a chore and multiplies stress. When did we get into this mess? When did people begin to make the fateful distinction between work and leisure?

In the era of Stone-Age affluence, according to expert reckoning, two or three days' hunting and foraging a week were enough to feed most communities. Work was not, as far as we know, conceptualized as a routine – rather, it was practised as a ritual. Foraging was a collective rite, like the ceremonies and games that preceded and followed it. There was no need or opportunity to separate leisure from work, or to privilege any class or either sex with special access to it.

Agriculture seems to have changed all that by "inventing" work and then compartmentalizing it as an area of life distinct from leisure and pleasure. The legacy of the hunters' approach to life can be observed in many simple agrarian societies, where tilling the soil is also a collective rite, often treated as a form of fun. However, most farming societies in remote antiquity could not afford Palaeolithic levels of relaxation. Soils friable enough to be worked easily with early farming technology were usually either very dry, in which case they needed irrigation, or very wet, in which case canals had to be dug and mounds dredged.

There was a huge increase in the number of hours of dedicated effort required to provide adequate amounts of food. At the same time, work became ever more time-sensitive: sensitive to the rhythms of the seasons, because of the intensive effort demanded during sowing and harvest; and sensitive to the daily tasks of weeding the soil and tending the ditches and dykes. By the period we think of as the Bronze Age, Stone-Age ratios of work and leisure had been reversed through the rise of "hydraulic societies" and "agrarian despotisms" – farming and irrigating civilizations such as those of Ancient Mesopotamia, Egypt, China, and the Indus Valley in India.

Since the work had to be organized, and critically timed, a "leisure class" arose, entrusted with a supervisory role that required no manual labour. Women seem to have been among the biggest losers. In hunting societies, sexual specialization tends to burden men with the most dangerous and physically demanding food-acquiring activities. Agricultural work can be undertaken by women at least as efficiently, on average, as men. In consequence, women, who anyway tended to endure demanding roles in child-rearing and housekeeping, took on more responsibility as providers as farming habits spread.

A further consequence was the emergence of a "work ethic". Contrary to popular belief, it was not a modern invention of Protestantism or industrialization, but a necessary code for all elites to enforce, once work ceased to be enjoyable. Ancient Chinese and Mesopotamian poets rhapsodized about the virtues of unstinting effort in the fields. "Six days shalt thou labour" was the curse of the expulsees from Eden, and to be a "tiller of the soil" was the grim vocation of Cain.

Going nowhere
The pressures of modern life mean that the "work ethic" has come to control our leisure time too, forcing us into timed activity periods such as this "spinning" class.

CONNECTIONS

Other key economic ideas related to work can be found in **Fair Exchange** (p.56), **Human Bondage** (p.150), **Laissez-faire** (p.246), **Workers Unite** (p.248), **Extreme Optimism** (p.290), and **Solid Foundations** (p.370).

READINGS

K. Thomas's (ed.) **The Oxford Book of Work** (2001) is an endlessly entertaining and stimulating anthology.

M. Sahlins's **Stone Age Economics** (1972) defined the notion of Palaeolithic affluence.

J.P. Harlan's **Crops and Man** (1992) is an outstanding survey of the transition to agriculture and its effects on work routines.

The English essayist **Charles Lamb** (1775–1834) is known for his wit and perceptiveness.

"Who first invented Work – and tied the free?"

Charles Lamb, Work (1819)

God Is a Woman

THE MOTHER-GODDESS IDEA

Mistress enthroned
This 7,000-year-old carved, seated female from Çatal Hüyük, Turkey, is a superb example of the many archetypal images of womanhood found among early civilizations.

Claims that the worship of a mother-goddess was the primordial universal religion have often been advanced. Many feminists would like the theory to be true, but is it? Where and when did the idea of the goddess start and how far did it reach?

We do not know the purpose of the little female figures carved by Palaeolithic hunters. Assumptions that they are "idols" representing a "goddess" – perhaps a primeval Earth-Mother who can be posited as the focus of humankind's first and universal religion – are obviously much too rash. Many other functions have been plausibly suggested: talismans, objects connected with birth-rituals, fertility-offerings, even dildos. In early agrarian societies, however, the evidence is overwhelming that female deities often had an honoured place; in many surviving cases, the artworks in which goddesses are represented show remarkably consistent features.

In one of the earliest excavated city-sites, the 7,000-year-old remains of Çatal Hüyük in Turkey, many representations were found of a truly magnificent female, with pregnant belly, pendulous breasts, and broad hips. Naked except for a fillet or diadem, she sits enthroned on a leopard throne, her hands resting on the great cats' heads and their tails curling surrealistically around her shoulders. This image of a "mistress of animals" recurs all over the Near East. One of the earliest stone temples (c. 4000 BC), found at Tarxien in Malta, was dedicated to a similar embodiment of divine motherhood, who lies attended by "sleeping beauties" – smaller female figures scattered around her. Such sites bring rites of female priesthood to mind. A mother-goddess responsible for humankind appears in many Mesopotamian texts of the second millennium BC, being sometimes hailed as "the mother-

READINGS

J.D. Evans's **Prehistoric Antiquities of the Maltese Islands** (1971) published the evidence from Tarxien.

The feminist interpretation is put forward by M. Stone's **When God Was a Woman** (1976), M. Gimbutas's **The Civilization of the Goddess** (1991), and E.W. Gaddon's **The Once and Future Goddess** (1989).

See B.G. Walker's **The Woman's Dictionary of Symbols and Sacred Objects** (1988) for more evidence.

M. Warner's **Alone of All Her Sex** (1976) linked the Christian Mary-cult to the goddess idea.

This 1991 image of actress Demi Moore is a modern celebration of female fecundity.

"… the mother that bore you… knew it all before you… "

R. Kipling, *Mary, Pity Women* (1896)

womb, the creatrix of men". So, even if it is impossible to speak with certainty of a single cult, the evidence of a widespread way of describing and worshipping idealized womanhood is incontrovertible.

Even more impressive, in some ways, is the fact that the way the "goddess" is depicted is essentially identical in cultures with no known connections. The same stylized, big-hipped body (familiar in today's art world to those who know the work of the Colombian painter, Fernando Botero) is found in Native American and Australian Aboriginal art. Goddess-archaeology has stimulated feminism in recent times, yielding two influential theories: first, that the goddess-cult was strangled by men who seized control of religion many thousands of years ago; and secondly, that it was appropriated by Christianity and still survives in the cult of the Virgin Mary.

Cult of the Virgin
The Virgin Mary combines the appeal of the mother-goddess with a role in making real the humanity of God.

Modern goddess
The brothel scenes of contemporary Colombian artist Fernando Botero recycle the broad-hipped amptitude of the ancient mother-goddess shape.

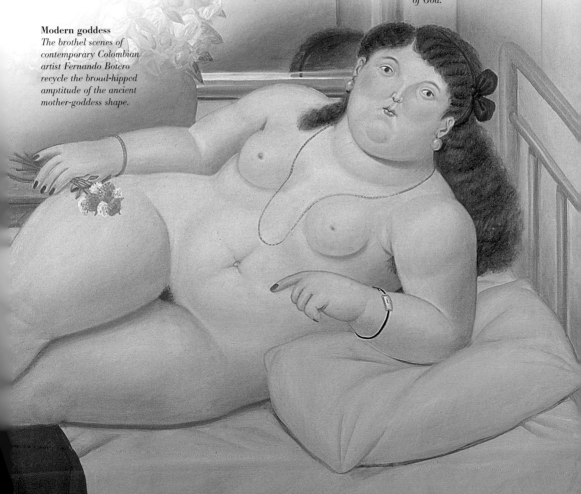

Just Like a Woman

THE IDEA OF SEXISM

Women can do just about everything men can do and almost all of it equally well. They also have a role in reproducing the species, for which most men are strictly superfluous. So why have they had so little power?

On the face of it, women seem more precious than men. A society can dispense with most of its men and still reproduce: that is why men are more commonly risked in war. Women are more easily connected with the sacred forces of nature, because of the obvious correspondences between the cycles of their bodies and the rhythms of the heavens. In what, as far as we know, was the earliest kind of sexual economic specialization – men hunting, women gathering – women's work seems to have been more productive in terms of calorific value per unit of energy expended. The idea we now call sexism – the doctrine that women are inherently inferior – seems so contrary to the evidence as to be irrational, except in particular and peculiar circumstances. When did such circumstances first arise?

The clues seem to be: a shift to patrilineal from matrilineal descent-systems (inheriting status from your father rather than your mother); rapid rises in birth-rates, which tie women to child-rearing; and art depicting women in servile roles, like the pouting, languid bronze dancing girls who figure among the few artworks yielded by excavations of the splendid city-sites of the Indus valley of the second millennium BC. The chronology of female subordination suggests a connection with the rise of agriculture – in farming societies, women appear to bear an unfair share of the burden of work, but the reasons for this have never been satisfactorily explained. The one thing about female subordination on which everybody seems to agree is that men are responsible for it.

But there is scope for doubt: women have frequently been complicit in their own subjection. Sexually differentiated roles suited societies in which children were a major resource, demanding a specialized labour force to breed them and nurture them. The "liberation" of women for what was formerly men's work in industrial and post-industrial society seems, in practice, to have suited men rather well and landed women with even more responsibility than previously. Feminism is still searching for a formula that exempts women from exploitation.

Anything you can do
Men have always been content to open the doors of the workplace to women when it suited them. During WWII, women proved they could do many jobs that had previously been reserved for men.

Double burden
In many societies, women bear the twin responsibilities of farm work and child-rearing.

READINGS

M. Ehrenberg's **Women in Prehistory** (1989) is the best introduction to the archaeological evidence.

B. and R. Allchin's **The Rise of Civilization in India and Pakistan** (1982) is the standard work on the archaeological evidence from the Indus valley.

R. Bridenthal's (ed.) **Becoming Visible** (1994) is a pioneering collection on the re-discovery of the history of women.

Domestic bliss
Since the 1950s, millions of Western women have sought to escape the outdated stereotypes of wife and home-maker.

No Mercy

THE IDEA OF MASSACRE

Exemplary massacre
The fate of 16th-century Dutch rebels was typical of the massacres exchanged by rival sides in Europe's "Wars of Religion". The aim was a kind of ethnocide – the extinction of hated religious traditions.

CONNECTIONS

Other ideas about war or similar types of violent conflict appear in: **All Change** (p.110), **Human Bondage** (p.150), **Nation in Arms** (p.262), **By Other Means** (p.310), and **War Is Good** (p.314).

War in competition for resources is older than humankind. But the idea of waging it to exterminate the enemy was a surprisingly late development. Perfection is a hard idea to access because it is so remote from real experience. Most people's accounts of perfection are pretty humdrum – just more of the same, mere satiety or excess. Most visions of paradise seem cloying. But there were truly radical utopians among early people. They included the first perpetrators of ethnocide and genocide, the first theorists of massacre.

It has often been argued that humans are "naturally" peaceful creatures, who had to be wrenched out of a golden age of universal peace by socially corrupting processes: war, according to the influential anthropologist Margaret Mead, "is an invention, not a biological necessity". Until recently, there was a dearth of evidence with which to combat this theory, because of the relatively scanty archaeological record of inter-communal conflict in Palaeolithic times. Now, however, it seems an indefensible point of view: evidence of the ubiquity of violence has heaped up, in studies of ape warfare, war in surviving forager-societies, psychological aggression, bloodshed, and bone-breaking in Stone-Age archaeology. This bears out Field Marshal Montgomery, who used to refer enquirers who asked about the causes of conflict to Maeterlinck's *The Life of the Ant*.

So aggression is natural, violence comes easily, and war is as old as society. It takes an intellectual, however, to think up a strategy of massacre. It takes little mental effort to wage war to gain or defend resources, to assert authority, to assuage fear, or to pre-empt attack by others: these are observable causes of violence among pack-animals. Massacre

The **atomic bomb** made it possible to kill on a previously unimagined scale.

"Let him who desires peace prepare for war."

Flavius Vegetius, *De Re Militari* (AD 390)

implies a visionary objective: a perfect world, an enemy-free utopia. In some versions of the fate of the Neanderthals, *Homo sapiens sapiens* wiped them out. The evidence is insufficient to support this, but the world's earliest known full-scale battle was fought at Jebel Sahaba about 11,000 years ago, in a context where agriculture was in its infancy. The victims included women and children. Many were savaged by multiple wounds.

The strategy of massacre is found today among peoples who practise rudimentary agriculture. The Maring of New Guinea, for instance, normally try to wipe out the entire population of an enemy village when they raid it. "Advanced" societies seem no different in this respect, except that their technologies of massacre tend to be more efficient. The idea of an enemy-less paradise arose, therefore, at a particular moment of history; but whether we shall ever reach another moment at which we progress beyond it seems doubtful.

The Killing Fields
After a bloody civil war, the Khmer Rouge, who ruled Cambodia from 1975–78, massacred 1.7 million (20 per cent) of their people in a vain attempt to wipe out any opposition to their medieval, utopian vision of "Year Zero".

READINGS

J.A. Vazquez's **Classics of International Relations** (1990) brings together some fundamental texts.

R. Ardrey's **The Territorial Imperative** (1966) and K. Lorenz's **On Aggression** (1963) are the classic works on the biology and sociology of violence.

J. Keegan's **A History of War** (1993) and J. Haas's (ed.) **The Anthropology of War** (1990) set the evidence in broad context.

L.H. Keely's **War Before Civilization** (1996) presents a convincing picture of humankind's violent past.

Plato wrote down the lessons that Socrates confided orally.

" 'I have discovered a sure recipe for memory and wisdom.' 'No, Theuth,' replied Thamus, '... Those who acquire it will cease to exercise their memory and will be forgetful.' "

Plato, *Phaedo* (4th century BC)

Key to the future
The nerve-centre of early 20th-century organizations, the typing pool captured a huge amount of data for many to share. New technology has only accelerated this process.

Take a Letter

THE IDEA OF WRITING

This idea has some claim to be the most powerful in the world – because, ever since its introduction, all other ideas that matter, have been expressed in writing. Writing made communication infinitely elastic and started every subsequent revolution in thought. Its origins, however, were surprisingly humdrum.

Societies that possessed writing could have infinitely long memories. It helped the accumulation and tradition of knowledge – without which human progress would have been stagnant or slow – and conferred new powers of communication and self-expression on its practitioners. It was so important that most people's recorded myths of its origin ascribe it to the gods. Most modern theories suggest that it originated with political or religious hierarchies, who needed secret codes to keep their hold on power and record their magic, their divinations, and their supposed communications with their gods.

Less romantically, the evidence suggests that writing was a mundane invention that originated among merchants between 5,000 and 7,000 years ago. In most civilizations, the earliest known examples are merchants' tags or tallies, which record types, quantities, and prices of goods; or fiscal records. In China, where the earliest known examples were recently discovered, the marks were made on pots; in Mesopotamia, wedge-like symbols were pressed into thin clay slabs; in the Indus valley, they were inscribed on stamps that were used to mark bales of produce. In short, writing started for the purpose of recording trivia – humdrum information that was not worth confining to memory.

Great literature and important historical records were worthy of learning by heart and transmission by word of mouth. The Tuareg of the Sahara, who have their own script, still prefer to leave their best poems unwritten. Most peoples, however, have succumbed to the temptation to use writing for every thought, feeling, or fact that needs to be conserved or communicated. The result of the introduction of writing across society was the first information explosion. The writing revolution is still going on: even in the computer age we have found no better code.

Chinese oracle bone
This early form of writing (c. 1300 BC) comes from an oracle bone inscribed with questions for the gods. The application of a red-hot iron created cracks that were then interpreted as divine responses.

READINGS

G. Sampson's **Writing Systems** (1985) is an ingenious historical account of how writing systems developed worldwide.

F. Coulmas's **Writing Systems of the World** (1989) is an efficient, thoughtful, and comprehensive textbook.

J. Derrida's **Of Grammatology** (1998) is an idiosyncratically challenging text that compels the reader to re-assess the meaning of writing.

> R U COMIN OUT
> L8R 2NITE ?

Txt mssgng
Users of mobile phones have adapted writing for an oral culture, evolving a shorthand "txt" language of their own.

Watching the Flock

THE IDEA OF THE STATE

State control
Citizenship always involves surrender of a degree of one's autonomy to the state. In the early 20th century, American customs officials at Ellis Island subjected new immigrants to a battery of medical and verbal examinations to judge their fitness for entry.

Political scientists commonly make a distinction between "chieftaincy", the structure of political authority typical of foraging cultures, and "the state", which is the political form of herding and farming societies. According to Aristotle, the state evolved as population increased: the first society was the family, then the tribe, then the village, then the state.

The stage before the state was crucial: the village marked the transition to sedentary life, the replacement of hunting and gathering by herding and agriculture. We still rely on this sort of reconstruction of the unknowably distant past. When people formed roving "bands" they were ruled by chieftains. When they settled down, the chiefdoms became

READINGS

K. Butzer and L. Freeman's **Early Hydraulic Civilization in Egypt** (1976) is a brilliant and enduring study of the ecological context of the origins of states.

M. Mann's **The Sources of Social Power** (1986) offers an original perspective on the origins of the state from a historically informed sociologist, while T.K. Earle's (ed.) **Chiefdoms** (1991) is an important collection of essays.

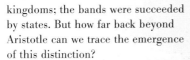

*"L'Etat, c'est moi!
[I am the state]"*

Louis XIV (1638–1715)

The French king **Louis XIV** epitomized the absolutist ruler.

Knowledge is power
England's Domesday Book (1085) provided the new Norman regime with the full record of land ownership and other assets it needed to run an early "state".

kingdoms; the bands were succeeded by states. But how far back beyond Aristotle can we trace the emergence of this distinction?

In Ancient Egypt, the commonest image of the state was a flock, tended by the king in the role of a herdsman. This may represent a real difference between the political ideas of herder-communities and those of the foragers who preceded them. A way of life that involved more competition for space would be bound to strengthen institutions of rulership, as disputes and wars multiplied; increase of war and wealth would be sure to shift patriarchs and elders out of supreme office in favour of elective leaders qualified by prowess or sagacity. It is tempting to identify the rise of a strong executive with the loss of "primitive liberty". Certainly, growing density of population and complexity of society demanded a strengthened state.

Draconian enforcement of obedience was part of Mesopotamian custom – to the vizier in the fields, the father in the household, the king in everything. "The king's word is right," says a representative text, "his word, like a god's, cannot be changed." In Mesopotamian reliefs, the king is commonly the largest figure in any scene that includes him. He receives supplicants and tributaries; he carries bricks to build cities and temples. To form the first brick from the mud was a royal prerogative; bricks from the state kilns were stamped with royal names. The transformation was royally effected magic. Yet this authoritarian autocracy was there to serve the people: to mediate with the gods, to organize the collective effort of tillage and irrigation, to warehouse food against hard times, and to redistribute it for the common good.

Even the most benign state tyrannizes somebody, because the essence of good citizenship is the renunciation to the community of some of those rights which, in a solitary condition, the individual might expect to be able to exercise. However, nobody has yet found any way of regulating the relationships of large numbers of people that is either fairer or more practical.

CONNECTIONS

For further ideas about the state, see **Law Is Order** (p.146), **Rule of the Best** (p.148), **Philosopher-kings** (p.152), **Render unto Caesar** (p.186), **I Am the State** (p.190), **We, the People** (p.260), and **Brother Knows Best** (p.306). ➡

WATCHING THE FLOCK

State boundaries
The Great Wall of China, completed during the Ming Dynasty, demonstrates the state's power to mobilize its subjects' resources and decree arbitrary exclusions from the community.

Divine Majesty

THE IDEA OF THE RULER AS GOD

The claim that the ruler is a god is a handy way of legitimating his power and outlawing any opposition. Anthropologists and ancient historians have collected numerous examples of this phenomenon, of which the earliest documented case is that of pharaonic Egypt.

What did the Egyptians mean when they said their king was a god? He could bear the names and exercise the functions of many gods, so there was no exact identity-overlap with any one of them. A possible aid to understanding is the habit of making images and erecting shrines as places of opportunity for the gods to make themselves manifest. The image "was" the god only when the god inhabited the image. The Pharaoh could provide a similar function.

The idea of the ruler-god had a strong effect on royal power. In the archive of Ancient Egyptian diplomatic correspondence known as the Amarna letters, one can still read the abject language of the Pharaoh's tributaries. "To the king my lord and my Sun-god," wrote a ruler of Shechem in Canaan in the mid 14th century BC, "I am Lab'ayu thy servant and the dirt whereon thou dost tread. At the feet of my king and my Sun-god seven times and seven times I fall." Sehetep-ib-Re, a treasurer around 1800 BC, wrote advice – "a counsel of eternity" – to his children. "The king is Re but he is more. He illumines Egypt more than the Sun, he makes the land greener than the Nile."

A commonsense assumption is that gods came first, kings followed, and kings re-classified themselves as gods to shore up their power. Clearly, however, it did not always happen that way. Maybe the gods were invented by rulers to dull and disarm opposition. That is what Voltaire hinted and Marx believed. There is some evidence that at least in some cases they were right.

READINGS

M. Lichtheim's (ed.) **Ancient Egyptian Literature** (1980) is a wonderful selection from the sources.

J.G. Frazer's **The Golden Bough** (1922) and E. Leach's **Genesis as Myth** (1970) represent the tradition of the anthropological critique of the uniqueness of Christianity, setting in context the Christian traditions of the sacrificed God-king.

CONNECTIONS

For other ideas connected with theocracy, see **The Vision Thing** (p.22) and **Render unto Caesar** (p.186). For ideas of state power, see **Watching the Flock** (p.80), **Legalism** (p.146), **State First** (p.232), and **Brother Knows Best** (p.306).

God and king
Ancient Egyptians placed images of the Pharaoh alongside those of other gods. This vast statue from the Abu Simbel complex depicts Ramses II (c. 1289–24 BC) on a scale calculated to dwarf mere men.

Cartouches showing the names of **pharaohs** inscribed on a tomb.

"Listen to my words. I speak to you. I tell you that I am the son of Re who issued from his own body. I sit upon his throne rejoicing. For he made me king."

Pharaoh tomb inscription (c. 2465–2325 BC)

Universal Rule

THE IDEA OF ONE-WORLD GOVERNMENT

Mongol mayhem
For most of history the establishment of empires has involved armed conquest. The Mongol empire created by Genghis Khan in the 13th century was no exception.

We think of the idea of world government as modern and benevolent. Its first proponents were rulers in antiquity, who intended to achieve it by conquest. Egyptians in pharaonic times, remembered the political union of Upper and Lower Egypt as a remote historical event from which Egypt's greatness flowed. In Mesopotamia, around 2350 BC, Sargon of Akkad is commonly credited with the first empire. From his upland fastnesses, his armies poured downriver and made him "King of Sumer and Akkad". "Mighty mountains with axes of bronze I conquered," he declares in a surviving chronicle-fragment, and dares kings who come after him to do

Temujin, or **Genghis Khan** ("Emperor of all Emperors"), ruled the world's largest empire.

"As the sky is one realm, so must the earth be one empire."

Genghis Khan, cited in *The Secret History of the Mongols* (1240)

Ceremonial weapon
This bronze dagger is from the Shang dynasty (1523–1027 BC), which ruled over numerous city-states in today's Henan province, creating China's first regional super-state.

the same. In China during the second millennium BC, the expansion of the Shang civilization from its heartlands on the Yellow River helped to create a regionally dominant super-state. These practical extensions of rulers' frontiers stimulated boundless political ambitions. Religion and philosophy conspired. A state that touched its limits would fulfil a kind of "manifest destiny" – a reflection of divine order. A tempting analogy between the cosmos and the state prompted rulers to seek a dominion as boundless as the sky's. The idea of political world-unification matched philosophical monism: the idea of the unity of the cosmos.

By the time of the Middle Kingdom, Egyptians thought their state already encompassed all the world that mattered: there were only sub-human savages beyond their borders. In China, imperial rule over "the world" came to be seen as divinely ordained: by the end of the Shang dynasty, the phrase "mandate of heaven" had come into use. On the Eurasian steppes, the far horizons, immense flatlands, and vast skies encouraged similar thinking, though the ambitions of the steppe-dwellers are undocumented until much later. Their projects of conquest repeatedly challenged the empires around the edges of Eurasia in the first millennium BC. Through such expansion they strived to bring into being the empire that later Mongol conquerors called "the realm of Tengri", the god they identified with the sky.

It is probably fair to say that for hundreds, perhaps thousands of years, universalism was the only kind of imperialism there was in Eurasia. It was the programme of every conqueror who re-united China, India, or Europe after every dissolution, as well as of those such as Alexander the Great in the 4th century BC or Attila the Hun in the 5th century AD, who succeeded in establishing empires that exceeded the traditional arenas. Even after the great universalist empires of the West and the Near East – Rome and Persia – collapsed definitively, medieval Christendom and Islam inherited their ambitions. In China, rulers accommodated to the fact that there were "barbarian" realms beyond their reach by asserting theoretical supremacy over them. Even in modern times, when the idea of a politically plural world arose from the bitter experience of the failures of universalism, the idea of world government keeps re-surfacing as part of an ideal vision for the future.

READINGS

A. Pagden's **Peoples and Empires** (2001) is indispensable on the European tradition, as is R. Grousset's **The Empire of the Steppes** (1989) on that of Central Asia.

F. Fernández-Armesto's **Millennium** (1995) focuses on empires from the last thousand years or so.

85

United nations?
The Palace of Nations in Geneva is the European headquarters of the United Nations (founded in 1945), the closest the world has come to an institution of global governance. There are now 188 members.

Family values
The Waltons *was one of America's most popular TV series. Set in Virginia during the 1930s and 40s, it revolves around the sagas of an extended, "ideal" family.*

READINGS

There is no good global study, but M.A. Rauf's **The Islamic View of Women and the Family** (1987), and M. Yalom's **History of the Wife** (2001) together provide a selective comparative overview.

J. Austen's **Pride and Prejudice** (1813) casts a wry eye over early 19th-century attitudes to marriage.

Babylonian King **Hammurabi,** shown in relief on top of the Code of Laws.

Getting Together

THE IDEA OF MARRIAGE

Sexual partnerships can work perfectly well without being formalized; no solemnity guarantees them against breakdown. So where and how did we get the idea of making such alliances the subject of legally binding contracts? Considered from one point of view, marriage is not an idea but an evolutionary mechanism: an information-dependent species like ours needs to devote considerable time to nurturing its young. So we encourage long-term alliances between parents who collaborate in transmitting accumulated knowledge to the next generation. Although the functions of child-rearing are shared in different ways in human societies, the "nuclear family" – the couple specialized in bringing up its own children – has existed since the time of *Homo erectus.*

These alliances are distinguished from other kinds of sexual relationships by the commitment of the contracting individuals and, in most cultures, by the assent of society. The idea of formalizing that assent, and regulating and enforcing the marriage-making distinction, presumably arose in response to practical problems, such as, what happens if sexual partners disagree about the status of their relationship, or their mutual obligations, or if they renounce responsibility for their children? Or, what happens when the relationship ends or changes when a third or subsequent partner is introduced or substituted?

All known societies have rules and institutions for dealing with such cases. The earliest surviving record of such rules – an extremely detailed summary of what were evidently already long-standing traditions – is in the Babylonian code of Hammurabi. Marriage is defined as a relationship solemnized by written contract, dissolvable by either party in cases of infertility, desertion, and what nowadays we should call "irretrievable breakdown". Adultery by either sex is punishable by death. Marriage has been an extraordinarily tenacious institution. The power to control it has been recognized as important in most human societies and has

"If a woman so hates her husband that she says, 'You may not have me,' the city council shall investigate… and if she is not at fault, she may take her dowry and return to her father's house."
Hammurabi's Code of Laws (*c.* 1760 BC)

Eternal vows
Most Hindu marriages are arranged, between "equal-status" families. Gold rings (symbolizing eternity) are exchanged during the ceremony.

been keenly contested – especially, in the modern West, between church and state. But the rationale that underlies the institution is problematical. Except for the religious, who could solemnize their unions according to their beliefs without reference to the secular world, it is hard to see why marriage should be anything other than a private contract. Why should the state privilege some sexual unions over others?

Marriage is maintained in the modern world more, perhaps, by the inertia of tradition than by any abiding usefulness.

CONNECTIONS

Ideas about sex are pursued in **A Family Affair** (p.40) and **Wicked World** (p.180). For the idea of romantic love, see **Love Conquers All** (p.200). For a problem case of modern marriage, see **The Doll's House** (p.288).

For richer, for poorer
Hollywood star Michael Douglas insisted on a pre-nuptial agreement to protect his estate before embarking on his second marriage to Catherine Zeta Jones in 2000.

Written in Stone

THE IDEA OF UNCHANGING LAW CODES

Divine law
Although there were earlier examples of written law, the Ten Commandments were drafted innovatively, as a "covenant" with God. The stone tablets on which they were inscribed symbolized their enduring nature.

The first law codes were probably generalizations from exemplary cases, transformed into precepts – rules which would hold good for whole classes of cases. In Egypt, the law remained in the mouth of the divine Pharaoh and the need for codification was never acute. In Mesopotamia, the king was not a god, which is probably why the earliest known codes come from there. The codes of Ur from the third millennium BC are fragmentary – essentially lists of fines. But the code of King Lipit-Ishtar of Sumer and Akkad, from around 1800 BC, is clearly an attempt at the comprehensive regulation of society. It explains that the laws were divinely inspired and ordained "in accordance with the word of Enlil" (one of their most powerful gods). Their purpose was to make "children support the father and the father children... abolish enmity and rebellion, cast out weeping and lamentation... bring righteousness and truth and give well-being to Sumer and Akkad."

Hammurabi, ruler of Babylon during the first half of the 18th century BC, gets undue credit because his code survives intact, having been carried off as a war trophy to Persia. It is engraved in stone, surmounted

READINGS

M.E.J. Richardson's **Hammurabi's Laws** (2000) is a good study of the text.

H.W.F. Sagg's **The Babylonians** (1995) and J. Oates's **Babylon** (1979) are excellent accounts of the historical background.

CONNECTIONS

For a review of the abuse of the idea, see **Legalism** (p.146). For its origins in prehistory, see **Take, Eat** (p.38), and **A Family Affair** (p.40). For laws relating to marriage, see **Getting Together** (p.86). On anarchism, see **Less Is More** (p.240).

by a relief showing the king receiving the text from the hands of a god. The epilogue makes clear that it was intended to substitute for the physical presence of the ruler. "Let any oppressed man who has a cause come into the presence of the statue of me, the king of justice, and then read carefully my inscribed stone, and give heed to my precious words. May my stone make his case clear to him."

Although the notion of a divine covenant is obviously present in these early law codes, the "Laws of Moses" – the codes of the Hebrews of the first millennium BC – have a novel feature: they are cast as a treaty with God, negotiated by a human legislator. But the law still depends for its legitimacy on divine sanction and was to do so until secular theories of jurisprudence emerged in China and Greece towards the middle of the first millennium BC.

The idea of codified law has co-existed to our own times with rival ideas: that law is a body of tradition, inherited from the ancestors, which codification might reduce and rigidify; and the idea that law is an expression of justice, which can be applied and re-applied independently in every case, by reference to principles. In practice, codification has proved to have insuperable advantages: it helps make judges' decisions seem objective; it can be revised from time to time as circumstances require; it suits democracy, because it transfers power from judges – who, in most societies, constitute a self-electing elite – to legislators, who are supposedly representative of the people.

Gradually, all law has become codified, and where different principles of jurisprudence are in conflict – as in England, where equity and custom still have an entrenched place in judges' decision-making – code-law has tended to gain relative dominance.

Samarian Decalogue
This 2nd-century BC carved stone tablet from Nablos (Ancient Shechem), Samaria, is an early example of written law.

Seat of justice
The Supreme Court of the United States is a symbol of democratic justice, upholding laws drawn up by elected representatives.

St Paul (AD 3–68), denied that law could make people good.

"Where there is no law, there is no transgression."

Letter of Paul to the Romans (*c.* AD 57)

A Golden Age

THE IDEA THAT ALL HUMANKIND IS EQUAL

More equal than others
Occasionally, ideas of equality have inspired violent rebellions. The Bolsheviks, who instigated the overthrow of the Tsarist regime in Russia in 1917, sought to impose a more egalitarian society. Instead, a new hierarchy was substituted for the old one.

The equality of all people is usually thought of as a modern ideal. Although sustained efforts to achieve it have only been made for the last 200 years or so, it crops up in every age. When did it start? It was only possible in a state of inequality; but we know of no time before that. So a doctrine of equality may have been preached for many thousands of years before it was first recorded in a famous Egyptian text – inscribed on wooden coffins from about 2000 BC – from the mouth of Amun-Re. The god says he created "every man like his fellow" and sent the winds "that every man might breathe like his fellow" and floods "that the poor man might have rights in them like the rich", but evil-doing had produced inequalities that were a purely human responsibility.

The **United Nations** flag symbolizes a world unified by peace.

"All men are born free and equal in dignity and rights."

UN Universal Declaration of Human Rights (1948)

New age
The hippy movement of the 1960s promoted ideals of love, peace, and equality. Such notions subverted the more rigid social structures of the post-war world.

This raises a problem: if inequality prevailed everywhere, where did the idea of equality come from? Some thinkers have argued that it was a sort of collective memory from an early phase of the history of society, when inequalities were much slighter than in recorded times. The great historian of China, Joseph Needham, argued that criticism of landlords, common in Chinese songs of the 7th century BC, was inspired by memories of "a stage of early society before… Bronze-Age proto-feudalism and the institution of private property". "You do not sow, you do not reap," as one song reproaches the landlords, "so where do you get the produce of those 300 farms?" The book known as *Chuang Tzu* praised the ancient common life of virtue and natural liberty, when all men and all creatures were one. "This was the state of pure simplicity", corrupted by sages, officials, and artists.

Since no such age existed in reality, it cannot have been remembered. But it can have been imagined. Most cultures have a myth of a "golden age," those "good old days" that can be invoked to denounce the vices of the present. "The times which came after the gods", as Ancient Egyptian proverbial wisdom called them, when "Books of wisdom were their pyramids: is there anyone here like [them]?" Similarly, in Mesopotamia in the second millennium BC, Gilgamesh, king of Uruk, recalled a time when there were no canals, no overseers, no liars, no sickness, and no old age.

Because the idea of equality originated in myth it has generally been treated as a myth: extolled by many, believed by few. Occasionally it has been taken seriously and the results have in almost all cases been violent rebellions of the underprivileged against the prevailing order (whatever that may be, for no lasting order has ever embodied equality). Successful rebellions are revolutions: but although equality has been a common aim of revolutions, especially in modern times, it has never endured as a revolutionary achievement.

READINGS

R. Dworkin's **A Matter of Principle** (1985) treats equality from the perspective of jurisprudence, while R. Nozick's **Anarchy, State and Utopia** (1974) adopts an approach from political philosophy.

The Book of Chuang Tzu (c. 1300 BC) consists of the teachings and stories by Master Chuang, which helped develop Taoism.

CONNECTIONS

The idea of inequality is broached in **The Family Silver** (p.36), **Just Like a Woman** (p.74), **Human Bondage** (p.150), **Inferior by Nature** (p.318), and **The Great Chain** (p.380). For more on equality, see **Neverland** (p.250).

Conquering Death

THE IDEA OF ETERNAL MONUMENTS

CONNECTIONS

Mighty and Dreadful
(p.32) gives the essential
background to this idea.
Other ideas about the
afterlife are explored in:
Buried Goods (p.34),
Judgement Day (p.94),
Damned Time (p.178),
and **Return of the
Soul** (p.140).

Immortal mausoleum
Not so much a tomb as a
physical manifestation of
immortality and "launch
pad" to the afterlife, the
Great Pyramid of Cheops
was built around 2500 BC
for the Fourth Dynasty
pharaohs. Its epic scale and
precision of design reflects
the high importance placed
on planning for death.

Like most monumental builders in remote antiquity, the Egyptians were
inspired by a desire to mirror and reach a transcendent and perfect world.
The Great Pyramid of Cheops is still the largest man-made structure ever
built. Its base forms so nearly perfect a square that the greatest error in
the length of a side is less than 0.0003 centimetres (0.0001in) and its
orientation on a north-south axis varies by less than a tenth of one
degree. It contains about two million stones weighing up to 50 tonnes
each. Shimmering in the desert heat it still makes an impression of
spiritual strength or – on susceptible minds – of magical energy:
a mountain in a desert plain; colossal masonry in an environment
of sand-grains; precision tooling with nothing sharper than
copper. In its day, the whole edifice was faced in smooth,
gleaming limestone and capped with a shining peak,
probably of gold.

We tend to suppose nowadays that great
art is a product of the artist's liberty, but for
most of history the opposite has been true.
In most societies, only the outrageous
power and monstrous egotism of a
tyrant or an oppressive elite have
been able to galvanize the
effort and mobilize the
resources to make
monumental

"O King Unis, thou hast not departed dead. Thou hast departed living."

From a Pyramid text of the 5th & 6th Dynasties (2425–2300 BC)

A modern **funeral urn** is about as far as you can get from the ancient monumental impulse.

achievements possible. To understand why Cheops wanted a monument of such numbing proportions in so original a shape, it is necessary to try to think oneself back into an ancient Egyptian mind-set. A capstone made for a later Pharaoh captures the pyramid's purpose: "May the face of the king be opened so that he may see the Lord of Heaven when he crosses the sky! May he cause the king to shine as a god, lord of eternity… "

Death, to these people, was the most important thing in life: Herodotus reports that they even displayed coffins at dinner parties to remind revellers of eternity. Their tombs survive, not their palaces, because they built solidly for eternity, while they wasted little effort on the flimsy dwelling-places of this transitory life. Pointing heavenward, a pyramid hoisted its occupant towards the realm of the stars and the Sun. No one who has seen the pyramids outlined in the westering light could fail to associate them with the words addressed to the Sun by an immortalized Pharaoh: "I have trodden thy rays as a lamp under my feet!"

READINGS

E.A. Wallis Budge's **The Egyptian Book of the Dead** (1895) is the classic edition of the classic text.

I. Edwards's **The Pyramids of Egypt** (1946) is a model of accessible scholarship.

C. Aldred's **The Egyptians** (1984) is an accessible overview of Egyptian civilization.

93

Judgement Day

THE IDEA OF DIVINE JUSTICE

Heaven and hell
The idea of divine judgement was common in medieval Europe, where elaborate ideas of the afterlife had been developed by the Church. This 15th-century painting shows the Italian poet Dante against a backdrop of heaven and hell.

Ancient ideas about an afterlife generally seem to have assumed that it would be in some ways a prolongation of this life. Early grave goods include the cherished possessions of this world. The next world seems to reproduce the inequalities and lifestyles of this one.

At an uncertain date, however, a new idea of the afterlife emerged: another world, called into existence to redress the imbalances of the one we know. It is particularly well documented in ancient Egyptian sources, where most of the elite seem to have changed their attitude to the

afterlife between the Old and Middle Kingdom periods. Old Kingdom tombs are ante-chambers to a life for which the world is a practical training; those of the Middle Kingdom are places of interrogation for the next life.

The scene – common in wall-paintings from tombs – of the gods weighing the souls of the dead is one of the most familiar images from Ancient Egypt. Typically, the heart, representing the deceased's intent, lies in one scale; a feather, symbolizing truth, lies in the other; while the jackal-headed underworld-god, Anubis, supervises the scales. In accounts of these divine trials, the examined soul abjures a long list of sins, including sacrilege, sexual perversion, and the abuse of power against the weak. Then the good deeds appear: obedience to human laws and divine will, offerings for the gods and the ghosts, and acts of mercy. The reward of the good is a new life in the company of Osiris, ruler of the cosmos. For those who fail the test, the punishment is extinction.

This was an idea with so much practical resonance that it has cropped up independently in most major religions ever since. It is probably one of the ideas the Greeks got from the Egyptians, but in their own myths they traced the teaching back to Orpheus – the legendary character whose sublime music gave him power over nature. For the Jews, it provided a convenient solution to the problem of how an omnipotent and benevolent God could allow injustice in the world: it would all come right in the end. Taoism developed an elaborate image of an afterworld compartmentalized, according to the virtues and vices of the soul, between places of torture and reward. In Buddhism and Hinduism, too, eternity provided an opportunity for present wrongs to be redressed.

Materialists have often claimed that the whole idea of divine justice was thought up by political elites as a means of social control, in which the threat of divine retribution was used to supplement the feeble power of the state. Hope and fear induced social responsibility in people who might otherwise defy authority. If that is how the idea started, it seems to have been an almost total failure.

Some Christian sects practise **self-flagellation** as an act of penance.

"The wicked are more unfortunate if they escape punishment than if they suffer it."

Boethius, *The Consolation of Philosophy* (6th century AD)

Heavenly check-in
In the 1946 film A Matter of Life and Death, *an injured English airman is caught between Heaven and Earth because of a heavenly clerical error.*

CONNECTIONS

For other ideas connected with the idea of eternity, see **Around the Clock** (p.30), **Conquering Death** (p.92), **Time's Arrow** (p.112), **The Great Void** (p.154), and **Damned Time** (p.178).

JUDGEMENT DAY

READINGS

R. Taylor's **Good and Evil** (1970) provides a general introduction, while H. Frankfort's (ed.) **Before Philosophy** (1946) is a richly reflective enquiry into ancient ethics.

W.D. O'Flaherty's **Origins of Evil in Hindu Mythology** (1967) is an interesting case-study.

D. Alighieri's **The Divine Comedy** (1321) offers a brilliant, poetic vision of heaven and hell from the medieval Christian viewpoint.

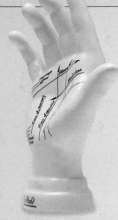

Lifelines
Palmistry, the art of reading a person's future from the lines on their hands, is based on the fatalistic premise that the future is predetermined.

READINGS

Classic works are J.H. Breasted's **Development of Religion and Thought in Ancient Egypt** (1912) and W.M. Watt's **Free Will and Predestination in Early Islam** (1948).

See P. VanInwagen's **An Essay on Free Will** (1983) for a general perspective on various kinds of determinist thinking.

Deo Volente

THE IDEA OF FATE

Common experience suggests that some events are predetermined. Decay, death, the round of the seasons, the recurring rhythms of life and of the heavens are genuinely inescapable.

Three problems arise, which can be assumed to have inspired ideas too early to have been recorded in surviving evidence: first, how are inevitable changes related to one another? Are they all ordained by a single cause? (Most cultures answer, "Yes" and call this cause "fate" or some equivalent name.) Secondly, if so, where does this power of irreversible action come from? Finally, what are its limits? Does it control everything that happens, or are some possibilities open to human endeavour, or left to chance? Can fate be conquered or at least temporarily mastered or induced to suspend its operations?

Broadly speaking, human nature tends to deny fate or circumscribe its supposed power: otherwise, there is little incentive for all the constructive endeavours which seem typical of our species. On the other hand, experience is broadly discouraging. Among the earliest evidence concerning this tension is the Sumerian myth of the god Marduk, who wrested from Fate the tablets on which history was inscribed in advance. This is doubly interesting, as evidence that in early versions, fate is conceived as a power distinct from that of the gods, and is the subject of a cosmic power-struggle. This is also a marked feature of Ancient Greek myths, in which Zeus sometimes seems to control the Fates and at other times to defer to them.

Early Egyptian texts seem buoyant with belief that destiny is manipulable. However, fatalism, the conviction that fate is insuperable, soon sets in. In about the 17th century BC, Egyptian texts become pessimistic about individuals' freedom to impose their own wills on their lives and those around them. "One thing is the word man says, another is what fate does." Or again: "Fate and fortune are carved on man with the stylus of the god." As a Middle Kingdom maxim said, "Cast not thy

Roman emperor
Marcus Aurelius
(AD 121–180) compiled
Stoic sayings.

"Whatever may happen to thee, it was prepared for thee from all eternity; and the implication of causes was from eternity spinning the thread of thy being… It is all part of the great web."

Marcus Aurelius, *Meditations* (2nd century AD)

heart in pursuit of riches, for there is no ignoring fate or fortune. Invest no emotion in worldly achievements, for every man's hour must come."

The idea of fate cannot in itself change the world; but fatalism can – by deterring action. Claims that some cultures are more prone to fatalism than others have often been made in an effort to explain different development rates. It was a strong conviction of what is now called the "Orientalist" school of Western writings on Islam in the late 19th and early 20th centuries that "oriental fatalism" retarded Muslim civilization, but this seems to have been a genuine misunderstanding. The Muslim concept of the "Decree of God" is a philosophical device exempting God, when He so wills, from constraint by the laws of science or logic. It does not deprive people of their ability to exercise free will, which is a divinely commanded gift. No more importance should be attached to proverbial fatalism in Islam than to the old Christian habit of inserting the proverbial phrase "Deo Volente" ("If God wills") into expressions of hope.

Life's lottery
It seems to be a common human evasion to ascribe chance events or random good or ill fortune to predetermined "fate".

CONNECTIONS

Related ideas are taken up in **Around the Clock** (p.30), **Return of the Soul** (p.140), and **Damned Time** (p.178). For materialist forms of determinism, see **Class Struggle** (p.292), **The Great Chain** (p.380), and **Intelligence Test** (p.382).

Dreamtime

THE IDEA THAT THE WORLD IS AN ILLUSION

Ceci n'est pas une pipe.

This is not a pipe
In paintings like this, the Belgian surrealist René Magritte investigated the relationship between representation and reality.

It is one thing to realize that some perceptions are illusory, another to suspect that the whole world of experience is an illusion. Though only late texts survive, the earliest portions of the ancient Vedic text, *Rig-veda*, include hymns transmitted orally for centuries before they were written down: so they contain fragments of thought of the late second millennium BC. They proclaim a spiritual world in which matter is an illusion.

The Upanishads confirm this as one of the oldest and most insistent innovations of Indian thought. The realm of the senses is illusory, or, more exactly, the distinction between illusion and reality is misleading. The world is Brahman's dream; the creation of the world was like a falling-asleep. In consequence, the sense organs can tell us nothing that is true: more than that, speech is illusory, since it relies on lips and tongues and ganglions; thought is illusory, since it happens in – or at least passes through – the body. Most feelings are illusory, because they are registered in our nerves and guts. Only the inarticulacy which later mystics call "the dark night of the soul" is real, and truth can be glimpsed only in purely spiritual visions, or in kinds of feeling, like selfless love and unspecific sadness, which do not have any physical register.

Can this be an idea that "changed the world"? After all, we are in the world, whether illusory or not, and except as an encouragement to inertia the doctrine of all-pervading illusion is not likely to have any practical effect. But it certainly changed the way some people feel about the world. It encouraged mysticism and asceticism; it provided arguments with which some religions could be justified and others attacked. It alienated some thinkers from science and secularism. Few people believe it, but the suspicion that it might be true is never wholly absent.

READINGS

J. Mascaró's **The Upanishads** (1965) is brilliantly translated and accessible, while N.S. Subrahmanian's **Encyclopedia of the Upanishads** (1985) is a good, modern critical survey.

Lewis Carroll's classic works: **Alice in Wonderland** (1865) and **Alice through the Looking Glass** (1871) vividly describe alternative dreamworlds.

Curiouser and curiouser
The distinction between illusion and reality is thoroughly blurred in Lewis Carroll's Alice in Wonderland, *in which the strange adventures of Alice eventually turn out to have been a dream.*

Shiva the "destroyer", one of the chief Hindu deities, performing the cosmic dance.

"The Realization that One is Shiva, the surging holocaust which burns to nothingness the dream-palace of the world, with its infinite, diverse and beautiful chambers."

Abhinavagupta, *The Tantraloka* (c. AD 1000)

THUS SPAKE ZARATHUSTRA

3

1000 BC – 0 AD

The Age of Sages

The second half of the second millennium BC was a bad time for civilization: a protracted "crisis of the Bronze Age". The world's most spectacular empires broke up and progress seemed severed by still-mysterious catastrophes. Centralized economies controlled from palace labyrinths vanished. Trade was disrupted, settlements and monuments abandoned.

In the Indus Valley, the Harappan cities turned to dust. In the late 13th century BC, invaders called the "Sea Peoples" wiped out the Hittite empire in Anatolia and threatened Egypt. When the city of Ugarit in Syria fell, never to be reoccupied, messages begging for seaborne reinforcements were left unfinished. The destruction did not always come by sea. Nubia disappeared from the records. In Turkmenia, on the Iranian plateau, relatively young but flourishing, fortified settlements on the banks of the Oxus, such as Nazmaga and Altin, shrank to the dimensions of villages. At Pylos in southern Greece, the walls of one of many shattered palaces are painted with scenes of combat with animal skin-clad savages.

Stunned by earthquakes, strained by war, the region's last cities were empty by the end of the millennium. In the Aegean, Knossos and Troy survived only in memories. The lavish Cretan city of Akrotiri was buried in volcanic ash under layers of bare pumice; other palaces were rebuilt several times, after repeated crises, before finally succumbing. In Mesopotamia, the ziggurats decayed into ruins. As the millennium

Al fresco
The Bronze-Age Minoan civilization – a predecessor of Classical Greek civilization – flourished in Crete in the second millennium BC. This decorative frieze from Knossos shows an athlete "bull leaping".

drew to a close, Shang China dissolved, though the continuity of civilization hardly seems to have been affected by the political transformation, and competition among warring courts actually multiplied the opportunities for patronage for wise men and literate officials.

Egypt's experience was different. The state survived, but the new millennium was culturally and intellectually arid compared with what had gone before.

In the other affected regions, this "general crisis" was followed by "dark ages" of varying duration. Like most periods of political dissolution and intense warfare, it was a time of technological progress – hotter furnaces, leading to iron weapons and tools – but no traceable innovations in ideas. In Greece and India, the art of writing was forgotten and had to be reinvented from scratch after a lapse of hundreds of years. Recovery happened in new places and among new peoples. In India, civilization gradually re-emerged far from the Indus: in Sri Lanka, where monumental irrigation works and buildings arose, and in the Ganges Valley, where logic, creative literature, mathematics, and speculative science emerged around the middle of the next millennium. Greek civilization crystallized on the edges of the Greek world, in islands and small colonies around the Ionian Sea. Persia's emerging civilization arose in what is now the province of Fars, remote and previously inert.

It seems an inauspicious background to a new age, but it meant a fresh start. In earlier

ages, ideas always arose anonymously. If pegged to a name, it was that of a god. The new ideas of the first millennium BC were the work of schools and sages, who formed four obvious categories: professional intellectuals who sold their services as teachers to candidates for professional or public office; others who sought the patronage of rulers or positions as political advisers; prophets and holy men who emerged from ascetic lives with inspired messages for society; and charismatic leaders with visions to share with and, if possible, impose on their peoples.

This was the millennium of Moses, whom Jewish tradition credits with a crucial role in compiling the teachings and laws at the heart of the Bible, and of Zoroaster, the Persian sage, who founded a religion of fire and light and a philosophy of the struggle of good and evil. It was also the era of Confucius, whose teachings on politics and ethics remain among the most powerful sources of intellectual influence on the modern world. The Greek sages, who are regarded as the founders of Western science and philosophy, overlapped with these figures. It is commonly said that the whole of Western philosophy since the Classical age of Athens has been "footnotes to Plato". These achievements were paralleled in the China of the "Hundred Schools", and in India by the Nyaya school of philosophers.

Between them, these sages came up with ideas so influential on all later ages that scholars call their era the "Axial Age". In the 700 years or so preceding the death of Christ, most of the world's major religious and philosophical traditions began.

Buffalo sage
Lao Tzu's teachings in the 6th-century-BC Tao Te Ching have proved extremely influential in Chinese, and Western, thinking.

Lasting influence
The works of the Greek philosophers, including those of Aristotle – shown here on a 13th-century Turkish manuscript – were re-introduced to Europe during the Renaissance in Arabic translations.

The monotheistic Judaeo-Christian tradition provided the teachings that later became the basis of Islam. About a third of the world's population today belongs to that tradition. The next most widely diffused of the world's religions, Buddhism, was another innovation of the Axial Age. So were the teachings of Mahavira, the founder of Jainism, and the texts that later became the basis of Hinduism. Taoism can be traced to the same period and the works of the sage credited with founding it were written down in the most fruitful period for the generation of sacred texts, soon after the mid-point of the millennium.

It seems astonishing that today, after all the material progress of the past 2,000 years, we should remain so dependent on thought that originated in such a distant period in history and have added so little to it. In the whole of the rest of this book, there are probably no more than a dozen ideas to compare, in their power to change the world, with those of the Axial Age.

philosophy since the Classical age of Athens has been "footnotes to Plato". These achievements were paralleled in the China of the "Hundred Schools", and in India by the Nyaya school of philosophers.

Between them, these sages came up with ideas so influential on all later ages that scholars call their era the "Axial Age". In the 700 years or so preceding the death of Christ, most of the world's major religious and philosophical traditions began. The monotheistic Judaeo-Christian tradition provided the teachings that later became the basis of Islam. About a third of the world's population today belongs to that tradition. The next most widely diffused of the world's religions, Buddhism, was another innovation of the Axial Age. So were the teachings of Mahavira, the founder of Jainism, and the texts that later became the basis of Hinduism. Taoism can be traced to the same period and the works of the sage credited with founding it were written down in the most fruitful period for the generation of sacred texts, soon after the mid-point of the millennium.

It seems astonishing that today, after all the technical and material progress of the last 2,000 years, we should remain so dependent on the thought of such a distant millennium and have added so little to it. In the whole of the rest of this book, there are probably no more than a dozen ideas to compare, in their power to change the world, with those of the Axial Age.

All is One
The idea of monism

Monism is the doctrine that there is really only one thing, in which all the seeming diversity of the cosmos is comprehended. This subtle and stunning idea was a commonplace of the first millennium BC.

Pre-Socratic sages who said the world was one probably meant literally that: nothing is that which is not part of everything else. Anaximander of Miletus in the mid 6th century BC postulated an infinite and ageless reality that must "encompass all worlds". There are, according to this line of thinking, no numbers between one and infinity, which are equal to each other and share each other's boundaries, linking and lapping everything. As a satirist of about 400 BC complained, "They say that whatever exists is one, being at the same time one and all – but they cannot agree what to call it." Wherever ideas were documented, monism appeared. "Identify yourself with non-distinction," said the legendary Taoist, Chuang Tzu. "Love all things equally: the universe is one," was how Hui Ssu put it in the 4th century BC. The Upanishads identified Brahman as the single reality that encompasses all.

The strength and ubiquity of the monist idea during the formative centuries of the history of Eurasian thought are impressive. They raise the suspicion that it must already have been a tradition of great antiquity.

READINGS

D.W. Hamlyn's **Metaphysics** (1984) is a useful introduction to the idea of monism.

E. Deutsch and J.A.B. van Buitenen's **A Source Book of Vedanta** (1971) contains many key texts.

J. Fodor and E. Lepore's **Holism: a Shopper's Guide** (1992) traces the philosophical and practical implications.

Although the Upanishads are difficult to date, the *Kenopanishad* is one of the earliest and enshrines traditions that perhaps go back before the first millennium BC. It tells the story of how the powers of nature rebelled against nature itself; how the lesser gods challenged the supreme god Brahman. But the fire could not burn straw without Brahman. The wind could not blow the straw away without Brahman. This, on its own, might suggest no more than a doctrine of divine omnipotence, similar to that later embraced by Jews, Christians, and Muslims, but in context it seems part of a more general, mystical conviction of the oneness of the Universe – infinite and eternal. It is a "theory of everything", albeit, asserted rather than argued, of a kind not discernible in the thought of earlier civilizations.

Perhaps from a birthplace in India, the monist idea spread and became common in the philosophy of Greece and China during the first millennium BC. It became a prominent theme – possibly the defining doctrine – in Hinduism. Monism is one of those ancient ideas that never stopped being modern, because the oneness of everything and the equation, infinity = one, are profoundly convincing. Practical monism is called "holism" and consists of the belief that since everything is interconnected, no problem can be tackled in isolation. This is a recipe for never getting round to anything, but a weak form of holism has become extremely influential in modern problem-solving. Everything is seen as part of a larger, interconnected system and every difficulty has to be addressed with reference to the systematic whole.

Books of Truth

The idea of infallible holy scriptures

Information overload afflicted the Axial Age. The proliferation of schools, teachings, writings, and mutually contradictory philosophies created the first demand for quick-fix doctrines. Among the consequences, perhaps, was the rise of the all-purpose holy book, which purportedly contained all the truth the faithful needed.

Many of the sages of the Axial Age were indifferent or hostile to written teaching. The Upanishads recollect a time when teaching passed by word of mouth: their very name means something like "the seat close to the master". Christ wrote nothing, except for words he traced in the dirt with his finger. Buddha's teaching, according to his early disciples, was too sacred to commit to writing; only after a couple of centuries – if early traditions can be believed – were they driven to compile a supposedly ungarbled record.

All "divine" revelations have been confided to writing with human help. The claim that any is infallible is therefore deeply unconvincing. All scriptures are selected by tradition, modified by transmission, warped in translation, and misunderstood in reading. Yet the pretence that they

CONNECTIONS

Monism was an alternative to a dualist or "binarist" idea of the cosmos, described in **Seeing Double** (p.46). Modern holistic doctrines about the environment's interconnectedness are examined in **Silent Springs** (p.384).

All important
Powerful in its simplicity, monism makes sense of the complexity of the Universe by suggesting that all things are somehow connected. But without some way of organizing this information, such as the chapters and headings of this book, we risk "information overload".

Books of Truth

THE IDEA OF INFALLIBLE HOLY SCRIPTURES

Information overload afflicted the Axial Age. The proliferation of schools, teachings, writings, and mutually contradictory philosophies created the first demand for quick-fix doctrines. Among the consequences, perhaps, was the rise of the all-purpose holy book, which purportedly contained all the truth the faithful needed.

Many of the sages of the Axial Age were indifferent or hostile to written teaching. The Upanishads recollect a time when teaching passed by word of mouth: their very name means something like "the seat close to the master". Christ wrote nothing, except for words he traced in the dirt with his finger. Buddha's teaching, according to his early disciples, was too sacred to commit to writing; only after a couple of centuries – if early traditions can be believed – were they driven to compile a supposedly ungarbled record.

All "divine" revelations have been confided to writing with human help. The claim that any is infallible is therefore deeply unconvincing. All scriptures are selected by tradition, modified by transmission, warped in translation, and misunderstood in reading. Yet the pretence that they are, or could be, the unalloyed words of gods has been extraordinarily successful. The great Axial-Age texts – the Upanishads, the Buddhist Sutras, the Bible, and the later Quran – have been so successful that they have come to represent a powerful model that other religions try to copy. They have been both a blessing and a blight.

On the one hand, they have fuelled fundamentalist movements and anti-intellectual, literal-minded interpretations of the texts. The Protestants of the Reformation took the Bible so seriously that they thought they could replace the authority of the Church with the authority of scripture. Renegades, terrorists, tyrants, imperialists, and self-proclaimed messiahs have all abused these texts to sanctify their

Divine revelation
Buddha's teachings were initially considered too sacred to write down. Only after a couple of centuries, were his thoughts – like this mid-12th-century Japanese "Sutra of the Mandala of the Eight Great Bodhisattvas" – transcribed. The beauty of the inscription was a tribute to the sacred nature of the text.

The **Ark of the Covenant** housed the Torah – the Jewish holy book.

"He gave him the two tablets of the Testimony, tablets of stone inscribed by the finger of God... The tablets were the work of God and the writing on them was God's writing."

Exodus 31: 18 (c. 1400 BC)

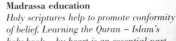

Madrassa education

Holy scriptures help to promote conformity of belief. Learning the Quran – Islam's holy book – by heart is an essential part of the education of these boys at a madrassa *(mosque school) in Pakistan.*

READINGS

H. Coward's **Sacred Word and Sacred Text** (1988) and G. Lanczkowski's **Sacred Writings** (1966) are good comparative studies, while A. Wilson's (ed.) **World Scripture: a Comparative Anthology** (1995) includes extracts from holy texts.

own perverse readings of them. On the other hand, these same Axial-Age scriptures have also offered awe-inspiring guidance. The idea that writing is a suitable medium for sacred messages has now become so commonplace that we do not consider it strange: would-be gurus write their wisdom down and sell it, usually in the form of "how-to" manuals. The books written in the first millennium BC – modified, in the case of the sacred writing of the Jews, by the New Testament and the Quran – have become the basis of the religious beliefs and ritual lives of almost everybody in the modern world, and have deeply influenced the moral ideas even of those who reject religion.

CONNECTIONS

The origins of written texts are explored in **Take a Letter** (p.78). Law codes, which are secular counterparts to sacred scriptures and share some of their functions, are examined in **Written in Stone** (p.88).

The New Illusion

THE IDEA THAT REALITY IS UNKNOWABLE

Shadows on the wall
Plato's suspicion that we experience a world of shadows finds a parallel in these mysterious images created by Balinese shadow puppets.

The idea that the world is illusory goes back many thousands of years. A new idea of illusion, however, can be detected in texts of the Axial Age. We know this idea was new because its proponents argued for it with an intensity that shows they were contending with received wisdom. Chu Tzu dreamed he was a butterfly and wondered, when he was awake, whether he was a butterfly dreaming of being a man. Plato saw shadows on the cave wall and suspected that the perceived world bore a similar relationship to reality.

The invention of geometry showed how the mind can reach realities that the senses obscure or warp: a perfect circle, a line without magnitude. Workers in arithmetic and algebra discovered unreachable numbers – zero and negative numbers, ratios that could never be exactly determined, yet which seemed to underpin the universe: π, for instance ($^{22}\!/_{7}$), the value that determines the size of a circle, or what Greek mathematicians called the "Golden Number" ($^{8}\!/_{5}$), which seemed to represent perfection of proportion. Surds, such as the square root of two, were even more mysterious: they could not be expressed even as a ratio (and were therefore called "irrational").

Science was among the consequences. At the first level of perception, according to the Lü Shih Ch'ung Ch'iu of the 3rd

Platonic solids are believed to represent ideal shapes – having an equal amount of faces at each point.

"Behold people dwelling in a cavern… Like us, they see only their own shadows, or each other's shadows, which the fire throws onto the wall of their cave."

Plato, *The Republic* (c. 4th century BC)

century BC, some metals look soft but can be combined to form hard ones, lacquer feels liquid but can be made dry by the application of another liquid, certain herbs taste poisonous but can be mixed to make medicine. First appearances are deceptive: "You cannot know the properties of a thing merely by knowing those of its components." The aim of this early science was to penetrate the veil and expose underlying truths.

Paradoxically, however, a further consequence was to open a gap between philosophy and science, which has never been rebridged. If the senses are unreliable, according to a tradition that began with Plato, then there is no point in observation or experience: the best laboratory is the mind and the best experiments are thought experiments. The "two cultures" division of our own time, which pits dogmatic science – or "scientism", as its opponents call it – against spiritual and artistic styles of thinking, has old roots.

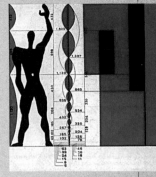

Classical proportions
In 1947, the Swiss modernist architect Le Corbusier updated a harmonic measure relating human size to architectural design, based around the Golden Ratio (3:2).

CONNECTIONS

Earlier ideas about illusion are explored in **Parting the Mist** (p.16). For early scientific ideas arising from the "new" illusion, see pp.128–35. Ideas of the scientific revolution of the 16th and 17th centuries are taken up on pp.216–31.

READINGS

W.H.C. Guthrie's **A History of Greek Philosophy** (1965) and J. Needham's **Science and Civilization in China** (1956) are multi-volume works of dazzling range, which trace the relationship between styles of thinking in the civilizations concerned.

On the artistic grasp and treatment of illusion, see E.H. Gombrich's **Art and Illusion** (1956).

All Change

THE IDEA OF A DYNAMIC UNIVERSE

The violence of nature suggests that cosmic order is fragile and subject to disruption. Hence myths of divine conflict are typical of the ancient stocks of story of all peoples. In the 6th century BC, the sage Heraclitus turned traditional anxiety into a comprehensive description and explanation of how the world worked.

Heraclitus was engaged on what we would now call a theory of everything. Instead of merely accumulating knowledge, he hoped to think his way straight through to "one big thing" – God, Nature, or some universal principle – that encompasses everything else and makes it intelligible. The nearest he got to it was the idea of perpetual conflict.

The way we humans see the world, change is its most obvious feature – an apparently universal law. But it is hard to explain, firstly because there has to be a prior, unchanged state against which to recognize change and, secondly, because if something changes, it is different from what it previously was, so how can we continue to speak of it? "You can never step twice into the same river," was Heraclitus's famous example. His solution was to see the world bound together by tension – like, he said, a bowstring's and a lyre's. Disharmony was the unifying principle.

READINGS

C.H. Kahn's **The Art and Thought of Heraclitus** (1979) is a fine general study of the thinker, while R.G. Geldard's **Remembering Heraclitus** (2000) offers a stimulating interpretation of Heraclitus's key ideas.

R. Dilcher's **Studies in Heraclitus** (1995) is unsystematic, but stimulating, insightful, and abreast of the literature.

Heraclitus (*c.* 540–475 BC) of Ephesus identified change as the only permanent reality.

"God is day and night, summer and winter, war and peace, surfeit and hunger; but he takes various shapes just as fire, when mingled with spices, is named according to the scent of each."

Heraclitus, *Fragment 121* (*c.* 6th century BC)

Conflict soldered the world together, like a raging fire, which fuses rather than consumes. He spun paradoxes into a tight fabric, coining epigrams to show that truth could lie in the depths of apparent contradictions, advocating the power of the human mind to comprehend the cosmos. "What is at variance agrees with itself... War is what is common to all and strife is justice."

He was unpopular in his day and reviled by his successors, but he lit a fire of his own, starting a still-continuing controversy and inspiring thinkers and leaders in every period who have valued competition above collaboration, stress above repose, and struggle above submission. Among the results have been the adventures and miseries that arise from claims that strife is natural and therefore good, conflicts are creative, and wars progressive.

CONNECTIONS

The development of ideas about the value of conflict is traced in **By Other Means** (p.310), **War Is Good** (p.314), and **Axe in the Sticks** (p.364). For the most ancient ethics of conflict we know of, see **No Mercy** (p.76).

Forged in fire
For Heraclitus, fire was the underlying substance of the Universe – a volcanic force – creating everything and making it mutable.

Constructive conflict?
During the 1980s there were many confrontations between South African police and anti-apartheid demonstrators. It could be said that the political change that resulted was an example of the creative value of conflict.

Time's Arrow

THE IDEA OF TIME AS A LINEAR PROGRESSION

The earliest conceptions of time were modelled on the way the heavens revolve: cyclical, unending. But what if time had a beginning and, presumably, an end? Celestial or natural cycles have had a profound and widespread appeal for people seeking standard ways of measuring time. But another method has always been available: instead of relating linear changes to cyclical ones – my (linear) age, say, to the (cyclical) behaviour of the Sun – the timekeeper can compare two or more sequences of linear change. The Nuer of Sudan, for instance, relate major events to the growth-rate of cattle or rites-of-passage ceremonies. Thus famine or war will be dated to "when my calf was so-high" or "when such-and-such a generation was initiated into manhood".

Underlying these different techniques are rival ideas of time: is it endlessly repeated, like a cycle? Or does it have a single, unrepeatable trajectory, like a line? The origins of both ideas are irrecoverably ancient, but the linear concept has gradually gained adherents over the last three thousand years or so, ever since it was adopted by the Jews at the time of the formulation of the Genesis creation-story. Against the beauty of a cycle, which has no beginning and no ending, Genesis proposed that time began with a unique act of creation. Time did not have to be consistently linear in character:

CONNECTIONS

For more ideas about time, see **Around the Clock** (p.30), **Damned Time** (p.178), and **Warped Universe** (p.346). For ideas of progress, see **Getting Better** (p.252), **Class Struggle** (p.292), and **Tooth and Claw** (p.320).

Local time
Traditional societies, like the Nuer of Sudan, often measure time by reference to tangible realities such as the growth of their livestock or important ritual events.

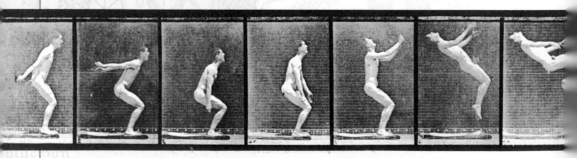

"What is time? If no one asks me, I know; if I try to answer, I know not."

St Augustine, *Confessions* (AD 397)

The Ages of Man
The linearity of human existence makes ageing and death irreversible. This 19th-century Austrian print depicts the chronological development of a human life-span.

it could begin like a loosed arrow or released clockwork and exhibit properties of both, but the Jews adhered to a mainly linear model: particular events might be echoed or repeated, but history as a whole was unique. Building on this idea, St Augustine anticipated most modern thinking about time – realizing that it has no "existence" outside the mind. In compiling historical records, Old Testament writers avoided calculations in years and other astronomical cycles, preferring human generations as units of periodization.

The prestige of Jewish precedents in Christendom and Islam ensured that the modern world inherited the linear model of time. A Christian, indeed, could not entertain a cyclical notion of time without lapsing into heresy. The incarnation occurred once and Christ's sacrifice was sufficient for all time: his second coming will not be a repeat performance, but a final curtain-call at the end of time. This proved an inspiring, as well as a daunting idea, galvanizing people into action in the belief that the world's end might be close at hand, launching millenarian movements, and nourishing the conviction that history is progressive and that all its toils are worthwhile. The leaders of modern movements as diverse as the American and French Revolutions, Marxism, and Nazism were all exhilarated by their sense of participating in the rush of history towards a final goal or climax.

Frame by frame
Humans live and act within a linear framework, as Eadweard Muybridge's famous stop-motion images of people in action showed.

READINGS

S.J. Gould's **Time's Arrow** (1988) is a brilliant study of the concept, while K. Lippincott's (ed.) **The Story of Time** (1999) provides a comprehensive survey of theories of time, and G.J. Whitrow's **Time in History** (1989) looks at different cultures' concepts of time.

M. Amis's **Time's Arrow** (1991) reverses narrative chronology in a brave attempt at dealing with the Holocaust.

Exquisite Reason

THE RATIONALIST IDEA

Thought needs no objects outside itself:
it can make up its own. It is pure. Reason
is therefore chaste rationalism, unravished
by experience.

    "Fire is not hot. Eyes do not see."
The numbing, blinding paradoxes of the
4th-century-BC Chinese philosopher
Hui Shih mean that information acts
directly on the mind, which processes
it before it becomes sensations. This may
be true, but it is such an elusive idea that one
wonders how and when people first thought of it
and how much difference it made to the world.

    The first rationalist we know by name –
who believed that unaided reason is the sole guide
to truth – was the Greek philosopher Parmenides
in the early 5th century BC. He started with
mathematics and geometry, which
Pythagoreans had taught to the previous
generation. If you believe geometrical
figures are real, you believe in the truth of a
world beyond the senses. For a perfect triangle, for
instance, is like God – no one has ever seen one,
though crude man-made approximations are
commonplace. "It is natural," as Bertrand Russell
said, "to go further and to argue that thought is
nobler than sense, and the objects of thought more

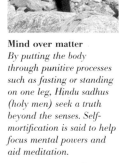

Mind over matter
*By putting the body
through punitive processes
such as fasting or standing
on one leg, Hindu sadhus
(holy men) seek a truth
beyond the senses. Self-
mortification is said to help
focus mental powers and
aid meditation.*

Plato (*c.* 427–347 BC)
examined philosophical
ideas in the form of
dialogues.

*"If a man… will not admit that every
individual thing has its own determinate
Form which is always one and the same…
he will utterly destroy the power of
reasoning."*

Plato, *Parmenides* (4th century BC)

real than sense-perception." The only triangles we know about are those embodied in our thoughts. Parmenides therefore suggested that the same might be true of trees – and everything else.

The consequences are impressive. If, say, a pink rose is real by virtue of being a thought rather than a sensible object, then a blue rose is equally so. The non-existence of anything is an incoherent concept. Few of Parmenides's followers were willing to go that far, but the idea that reason was better than observation or experiment – that it could open secret caverns in the mind, where truths lay buried – contributed all that was best and worst in the subsequent history of thought. Best, because reliance on reason made people question dogma and anatomize lies; worst, because it inhibited science and encouraged self-indulgent speculation. Philosophers have often dangled the tempting hope that reason could be used to re-shape the world, formulate laws, and construct society. In practice, however, it has never had much appeal outside elites and has only rarely ruled entire societies. Chapters on an "Age of Reason" in history books usually turn out to be about something else.

Yet reason has helped to temper or restrain rival approaches to regulating the world such as systems founded on dogma or charisma or emotion or naked power. Alongside science, tradition, and intuition, reason has been part of our essential toolkit for discovering truths.

CONNECTIONS

Logic – reason's counterpart – is examined in **If x then y** (p.122). Reactions against rationalism can be pursued in **Dumbing Up** (p.176), **Impossibilism** (p. 202), **Mu** (p.204), and **Fool's Gold** (p.216).

READINGS

W.H.C. Guthrie's **A History of Greek Philosophy** (1990) is the great multi-volume authority – exhaustive and highly readable.

Plato's **Parmenides** (4th century BC) is the dialogue that defined the debate.

E.R. Dodds's **The Greeks and the Irrational** (1951) was a pioneering exposé of the limits of Greek rationalism.

Voltaire's **Candide** (1759) describes a perfect society run along rational principles.

What's in a name?
The first rationalists thought that objects of thought were more real than the objects themselves. So a blue rose is just as real as a pink one.

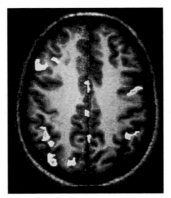

Abstract thought
According to rationalism, thought needs no objects outside itself. This EEG scan shows activity happening all over the brain during an abstract, mathematical problem-solving exercise.

Not a Horse

THE IDEA OF THE EXISTENCE OF UNIVERSAL CONCEPTS

READINGS

F. Fernández-Armesto's **Truth: a History** (1997) sets the broad context of the debate.

R. Collins's **The Sociology of Philosophies** (1998) and J. Goody's **The East in the West** (1996) take different, but equally fascinating, approaches to the comparison of Western and Eastern thought-systems.

Anxiety about illusion focused the thought of the Axial Age on what seemed the most fundamental of problems: "What is real?" For some, knowledge of everything else – in this world and all others – depended on the answer. The teachings collected in the ancient Indian texts, known as the Upanishads, concerning "being" and "Brahman" make this their main focus. "From the unreal", as one of the prayers in the text pleads, "lead me into the real." A practical solution to the problem seemed to lie through the exploration of levels of generalization. If you can be convinced, for instance, of the reality of a particular man, what about "Man" in general?

Moreover, how do you get from specific particularities to vast concepts like "being" and "Brahman"? By the 4th century BC, the Nyaya school of philosophy in India proposed the idea that you can apprehend all instances of a thing, such as Man, within a general statement like "Man is mortal". But is a term like "Man" just a category – a name for the set or class of humans, or is there a sense in which it exists as a universal reality, independent of its instances? Plato and most of his successors in the West believed the latter. Indeed, Plato thought that only universals were real and that specific instances, such as the things themselves, were only "shadowy", imperfect projections of them. So did most of the Chinese and Indian contributors to the debate.

In the 3rd century BC, Kung-sun Lung coined a famous paradox: "A white horse is not a horse." This startling sentence raises a profound philosophical problem: when we apply a general term in a particular instance, do we mean that it refers to something that really exists? We know, as far as

What is a "horse"?
Do the individual attributes of an object separate it from its general category? Does the whiteness of these splendid Camargue horses prevent them from belonging to the general category of all horses?

our senses are reliable, that the white horse exists, along with a lot of other particular creatures we call horses, but what about the horse referred to by the general term – the "horse of a different colour" – who is not grey, chestnut, palomino, or limited by any of the particularities which distinguish one horse from another, but is the horse in general? Kung-sun Lung's paradox suggests that we cannot infer the reality of the general category from the particular instance.

Critics called this "jousting with words", but it has profound implications. If only instances are real, the Universe becomes incomprehensible, except patchily and piecemeal; universal truths and empires are undermined. This idea has inspired radicals in every age since its first emergence and was the philosophy of revolutionaries at critical moments in Western history. In the 16th and 17th centuries it helped Luther challenge the Church, and pitted individualists against old, organic notions of society. In the 20th century, it fed into existentialist and "postmodern" rebellion against the idea of a coherent "system" in which everyone has a place.

Not a chair
The problem of whether universals – like the abstract concept of a "chair" – can really be said to exist, has preoccupied philosophers from time immemorial.

The vastness of the **Universe** suggests realities beyond perception.

"Those who see the absolute and eternal and immutable may be said to have real knowledge and not mere opinion."

Plato, *Phaedo* (4th century BC)

CONNECTIONS

Earlier ideas about the elusive nature of reality and its relationship to the perceived world appear in **Parting the Mist** (p.16) and **Dreamtime** (p.98). Later developments are traced in **Mu** (p.204), and **The Big Idea** (p.274).

Man Is the Measure

THE IDEA THAT TRUTH IS RELATIVE

READINGS

R. Scruton's **Modern Philosophy** (1994) is a toughly argued defence against relativism, while the most sophisticated modern apologia for relativism is R. Rorty's **Objectivity, Realism and Truth** (1991).

R. Akutagawa's **In a Grove** (1922), better known as the film *Rashomon*, tells the story of a rape and murder from the point-of-view of five different witnesses.

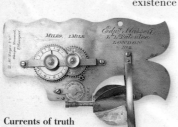

Currents of truth
This 19th-century scientific instrument was dropped overboard to measure the distance a ship travelled. Traditional science relies on the claim that there are objective criteria for assessing truth.

CONNECTIONS

Relativist ideas should be compared with ideas of reality in, for instance, **Not a Horse** (p.116), **Matter Matters** (p.124), **Cogito Ergo Sum** (p.224), **Reality Unveiled** (p.276), **Warped Universe** (p.346), **Common Sense** (p.352), and **Their Own Terms** (p.354).

Truth changes with the perspective of the beholder. Everybody's opinion is as good or as bad as everybody else's. The facts of your history – Black history, gay history, women's history, holocaust history – suit you but are false for me. These sound like modern follies – but are they?

Truth is an abstract idea, but also a practical matter: we want it as a sound basis for our decisions and actions. But when people disagree about it, how do we choose between them? Protagoras became famous in Ancient Greece for waving the question aside, asserting that there is no objective test for what is true. His famous formula read: "Man is the measure of all things, of the existence of the things that are, and the non-existence of things that are not." This sounds obscure, but his colleague Socrates knew exactly what he meant. Truth for one person is different from truth for another. Ask another question instead.

Most thinkers have been unwilling to accept this, on the grounds that it is logical nonsense: as the modern philosopher Roger Scruton said, "The man who says, 'There is no truth' is asking you not to believe him. So don't." Or, in the paradox formulated by the Harvard professor Hilary Putnam, "Relativism just isn't true for me."

Those prepared to set this difficulty aside, however, have been able to embrace some radical conclusions in consequence. Everyone has his own reality, as if each of all possible universes, or as many as there are people to experience them, were separately embodied in different individuals. Why not drop "truth" altogether? Is it not just a rhetorical flourish, an accolade we give to utterances we want to dignify, or a device to oppress anyone who sees things differently? If everyone is the arbiter of his opinions, all views are equally valuable and equally valueless. Rule of the majority, or community consensus, is the only way of regulating society, which is at the mercy of the expression of popular passions. In practice, this is very much how modern democracy works out.

A tree is ideal for a **monkey**, while humans prefer to live on the ground. Relativism suggests both are equally valid.

"Monkeys prefer trees: so what habitat can be said to be absolutely right? Crows delight in mice, fish flee at the sight of women whom men deem lovely. Whose is the right taste absolutely?"

Master Chang (*c.* 290 BC)

Cubist reality
Cubist painters tried to incorporate multiple perspectives within their works, as shown here in Picasso's 1910 portrait of his art-dealer Kahnweiler.

The long and the short of it
Do people with different view-points experience the same reality differently? Or does the reality itself change?

Count on This

THE IDEA THAT NUMBERS ARE REAL

Summing up
Pythagoras deduced that numbers exist independently of the objects they represent. In this example, the sum of five hats from three apples and two penguins is coherent, if absurd.

READINGS

W. Burkert's **Lore and Science in Early Pythagoreanism** (1972) is a stimulating study.

P. Benacerraf and H. Putnam's (eds) **Philosophy of Mathematics** (1983) and J. Bigelow's **The Reality of Numbers** (1988) are clear and committed guides to the philosophical background of mathematical thinking.

Are numbers "real" or conventions for ordering experience?

Counting – to judge from tallies notched on sticks or scratched on cave walls in Palaeolithic times – came easily to early humans. But was it more than just a practical way of organizing experience?

Halfway through the first millennium BC, the question was posed and a striking answer suggested. The Greek philosopher Pythagoras – who accreted mystical stories around him (he communed with the gods, he had a golden thigh bone) – is most famous today for two relatively trivial insights: that musical harmonies can be expressed as arithmetical ratios; and that consistent ratios characterize the lengths of the sides of right-angled triangles. However, his real importance goes much deeper. He was the first thinker, as far as we know, to formulate the idea that numbers are real.

They are obviously ways we have of classifying objects – two flowers, three flies. But Pythagoras thought there was more to it than that – that two and five really exist, quite apart from the objects they enumerate. Numbers are, one might say, not just adjectives but nouns. They would still exist, even if there were nothing to count. Pythagoras went further still, arguing that numbers are the basis on which the cosmos is constructed. "All things are numbers," was his way of putting it. Shapes and structures are determined by numbers – we still speak of "squares" and "cubes" – and numerical proportions underlie all relationships. Geometry, Pythagoras thought, is the architecture of the Universe.

This idea reflected the world that civilization was carving from nature in Pythagoras's day – a geometric grid of cities and fields stamped on the landscape. But it had immense consequences for the future, too. Once it became entrenched in the learned tradition of the Western world, most people believed in – or simply accepted – the reality of numbers. It enabled them to accept that reality can be invisible, untouchable, and yet still accessible to reason. This deduction paved the way for an alliance between science, reason, and religion that has lasted until our own times.

"I sought the truth in measures and numbers," said Confucius, *"but after five years I still had not found it."*

Chuang Tzu (290 BC)

121

Numerical code
Underlying many
post-Pythagorean ideas
is the assumption that
numbers are universal.
Many number codes, such
as the ISBN (International
Standard Book Number)
system of book
classification, remain the
same in all cultures.

If *x* then *y*

THE IDEA OF LOGICAL PROOF

A passion for logic
The international success of Rubik's cube (over 100 million sold), invented by Hungarian professor Erno Rubik, owed much to the complex logical challenge demanded by its design.

READINGS

I. Bochenski's **A History of Formal Logic** (1956) is an excellent introduction.

W.H.C. Guthrie's **Aristotle** (1981) describes brilliantly the author's "encounter" with Aristotle's thought, while J. Lukasievic's **Aristotle's Syllogistic** (1957) is a valuable technical exposition.

C. Habsmeier's **Science and Civilization in China (vol. 7)** (1998), R. Collins's **The Sociology of Philosophies** (1998), and J. Goody's **The East in the West** (1996) help set Greek logic in its global context.

Tweedledum and Tweedledee are Carroll's logic-chopping twins.

This idea first appeared early in the second half of the first millennium BC, when teachers in India, Greece, and China showed an intense interest in formulating rules for the correct use of reason. Practical issues probably underpinned these movements: for pleading in courts, arguing between embassies, persuading enemies, and extolling rulers, it was important to make arguments watertight. There was a vital by-product: rules for differentiating truths from falsehoods.

The most rigorous and systematic exposition was Aristotle's, strapping common sense into intelligible rules. If we think we understand him, it is because he taught us how to think. To this day, even people who have barely heard of him use the techniques he taught, which have seeped into the way we think through the channels of tradition. He was the best-ever analyst of how reason works, inasmuch as it works at all.

According to Aristotle, or to a doctrine he wrote down, all valid arguments can be broken up into more-or-less identical phases, in which a necessary conclusion can be inferred from two premises established by prior demonstration or agreement. If the premises are – in what has become the standard textbook syllogism – "men are mortal" and "Socrates is a man", it follows that Socrates is mortal. There is a flourish of the conjurer's wand about the method. The whole art and science of logic after Aristotle became focused on improving his rules for distinguishing valid arguments from misleading ones (like "Socrates is a mortal; Socrates is a man; therefore all men are mortal"). By the time his followers had finished, arguments seemed unbearably cumbersome, over-analysed into 256 distinct types.

This was a method akin to mathematics: two and two make four, irrespective of whether they are two eggs and two irons, or two mice and two men. The rules of logic yield the same results, whatever the subject matter; indeed, you can suppress the subject matter altogether and replace it with algebraic-style symbols. Clearly the system was imperfect.

"Contrariwise", continued Tweedledee, "if it was so, it might be; and if it weren't so, it would be: but as it isn't, it ain't. That's logic."

Lewis Carroll, *Through the Looking Glass* (1872)

Man versus machine
When chess master Garry Kasparov took on the IBM computer "Deep Blue" in 1986 and 1987, it seemed an ideal way of testing pure logic against the more creative, if erratic, powers of the human brain. Man and machine both won one game each.

There have to be axioms to start from: propositions deemed to be true that cannot be tested within the system. Aristotle saw no conflict between reason and observation or experience, he thought all were means to establishing truth. His legacy, however, made it possible to take sides and people have done so ever since – some mistrusting "science" and doubting the reliability of evidence.

At roughly the same time in India, the Nyaya school of commentators on the ancient texts demonstrated their own confidence in reason and analysed its processes in five-stage breakdowns that resembled syllogisms. Their concept, however, was in one fundamental way different from Aristotle's: they claimed reason was a kind of extraordinary perception, conferred by God; nor were they strictly rationalists, for they believed meaning did not arise in the mind but was conferred on the objects of thought by God, tradition, or consensus.

"Illogical, Captain"
The "mechanical" application of logic – famously championed by the half-Vulcan Mr Spock from the television series, Star Trek – appears alien to some, to others a sign of distinctively human rationality.

Matter Matters

THE MATERIALIST IDEA

Elementary idea
Ancient Indian materialist thought identified the four elements of earth, air, fire, and water. These were later incorporated into the Western astrological system of the zodiac (above, in a 15th-century French diagram).

READINGS

G. Arnaldi's **The Nature of Matter** (1961) remains a good guide to the scientific problems of materialism.

A.T. Embree's **Sources of Indian Tradition** (1988) is useful on the early Indian sources, and on all aspects of Indian thought before about 1800.

D.M. Armstrong's **A Materialist Theory of the Mind** (1968) is an impressive moderate statement of the materialist position.

***Punch**, a British humorous weekly magazine founded in 1841.*

Materialism – the idea that everything is made of "matter" – has no obvious origin: it is merely the common sense of creatures with limited imaginations, such as early hominids and the non-human evolutionary ancestors of humankind, might be presumed to have been.

Early philosophy denied this idea, however, and therefore it could be reasserted, with ever-greater sophistication, by subsequent critics. The first such reassertion we know of, which generated a tradition enduring to this day, occurred in ancient India. At an uncertain date between the 7th and 5th centuries BC, Ajita Kesakambala – a figure whose thought is known from later, outraged denunciations by Buddhist critics – denied the existence of any world beyond the here and now. There is just earth, air, fire, and water, of which everything, including humans, is composed.

Kesakambala argued that, "When the body dies, both fool and wise alike are cut off and perish. They do not survive after death." There followed an interrupted tradition of materialism in Indian thought, which mainstream Buddhist, Jain, and Hindu thinkers deemed heretical but never effectively suppressed. It is not clear how far this tradition overlapped or even influenced the materialism of the Ancient Greeks, represented by the view – associated with Democritus of Abdera in the 5th century BC – that everything is made of material particles called "atoms".

In East and West alike, the doctrine has always appealed to thinkers seeking a short cut to the denial of such metaphysical concepts as God, spirit, soul, heaven, and "mind" distinguished from "brain". In what is perhaps a distinct but related tradition, materialism is the name for a system of values that places quantifiable goods, such as wealth and physical pleasure, above

"What is mind? No matter. What is matter? Never mind."

Punch (1855)

morals or intellectual or aesthetic pleasures, or asserts that the latter are merely misunderstood manifestations of the former. Again, this is anticipated perfectly in the thought ascribed to Ajita Kesakambala, who is said to have claimed that there was no real difference between "good" and "evil" deeds. Confusingly, in a weak sense, materialism has been adopted by some scientists and philosophers as a name for an approach to knowledge that privileges science (even if its evidence is not strictly of a world in which only "matter" exists). In its extreme form, the materialist idea is unconvincing because post-Einsteinian science makes a Universe without strictly immaterial forces – such as energy and anti-matter – hard to reconcile with the evidence. When asked what matter is, materialists often respond with answers as hard to understand as those of out-and-out metaphysicians. Nevertheless, the idea remains influential, especially among proselytizing atheists and philosophical critics of traditional understandings of "consciousness", who attack this concept because it seems to imply a "mind–body dualism". Another important constituency are enthusiasts for "artificial intelligence", who favour a model of mind-as-machine formerly popularized by 18th- and early 19th-century materialists.

Atomic reality
The Greek philosopher Democritus (c. 460–370 BC) created an all-encompassing materialist theory that explained natural events in terms of the arrangement of tiny particles called atoms.

CONNECTIONS

On the gradual erosion of "primitive" materialism, see **Parting the Mist** (p.16), **All Things Invisible** (p.18), and **May the Force…** (p.26). For some later materialist ideas, see **Smashing Atoms** (p.126), **Class Struggle** (p.292), and **Tooth and Claw** (p.320).

The way of all flesh
In its purest form, the materialist idea denies the existence of causes invisible to experience, driving a wedge between the visible body and invisible thoughts and emotions. In this exhibit from Gunther von Hagens' Bodyworlds exhibition of "plastinated" human bodies, the physical structure is revealed in stunning detail.

CONNECTIONS

Related ideas are raised in
Happiness First (p.142),
Invisible Powers (p.228),
and **Warped Universe**
(p.346). For points of
comparison, see **No Dice**
(p.28), **All Is One** (p.104),
Mu (p.204), and
Uncertainty
(p.348).

Smashing Atoms

THE IDEA OF ATOMS

Atomic theory, which says that all matter is made up of minute particles, has guided physics for the last 200 years, but it was first proposed around the beginning of the 4th century BC. In the earliest texts we recognize as "scientific", matter is treated as continuous – infinitely divisible. Democritus generally gets the credit for denying this, and for proposing instead that everything is made up of tiny, discrete particles that make substances different from each other by zooming around in different patterns – like specks of dust in a sunbeam, he said. This is remarkable, because it seems counterintuitive and closely resembles the world depicted by modern science, yet Democritus and his collaborators achieved it by unaided contemplation. Their decisive argument – in their own minds – was that since things move, there must be space between them; but if matter were continuous there would be no space. Not surprisingly, this convinced few opponents and most scientific opinion in the Western world remained hostile to the atomic theory for most of the next 2,500 years.

An important exception, however, was Epicurus, who died in 270 BC. His name has become unfairly associated with the pursuit of physical pleasure – which he certainly recommended, though in a far more disciplined way than the self-indulgent gourmandizing with which "epicureanism" is popularly besmirched. A more important element of his thought was his interpretation of atomic theory: in a world of atoms and voids, there is no room for "spirits"; since atoms are subject to "random swerves" there can be no fate; since atoms are perishable matter and everything is composed of them, there can be no "immortal soul". Gods, if they can be said to exist at all, inhabit an imaginary world from which "we have nothing to hope and nothing to fear". Epicurus's arguments were formidable, and materialists and atheists keep coming back to them.

A world revealed
This false-colour image of sub-atomic particle activity in a bubble chamber provides evidence for atomic-level activity, something that the Ancient Greek philosophers could only speculate about.

READINGS

D.J. Furley's **The Greek Cosmologists** (1987) is the standard work on the Greek origins of atomic theory.

H. Jones's **The Epicurean Tradition** (1992) traces Epicurus's influence in modern times.

M. Chown's **The Magic Furnace** (2000) is a lively popular history of atomic theory.

C. Luthy's (ed.) **Late Medieval and Early Modern Corpuscular Matter Theories** (2001) is a fascinating scholarly collection that fills the gap between ancient and modern atomic theory.

Atoms in a sunbeam
The sight of dust particles swirling in a sunbeam inspired the Greek philosopher Democritus to assert that matter was composed of tiny particles.

Lord Alfred Tennyson (1809–92) was a popular Victorian poet.

*"I saw the flaring atom-streams
And torrents of her myriad universe
Ruining along the illimitable inane."*

Tennyson, *Lucretius* (1868)

Against Supernature

THE IDEA OF SCIENCE

Heavenly colours?
Rainbows have been viewed in varying ways through the different lenses of science and religion: as a refraction of sunlight through droplets of water or as a symbol of God's covenant with Mankind.

READINGS

A. Crombie's **Styles of Scientific Thinking** (1994) is an unwieldy but invaluable source on the Western tradition.

J. Needham's **Science and Civilization in China** (1956) is a truly great multi-volume history of Chinese science.

Of the world's great ghost stories, H. James's **The Turn of the Screw** (1898) most perfectly balances natural and supernatural explanation.

The universality of spirits – an idea the Axial Age inherited from the past and could never quite get rid of – inhibited science because the spirits could be invoked, instead of natural causes, to explain change. The idea of a distinction between what is natural and what is supernatural was, as far as we can tell, an innovation of the Axial Age: previously, the two realms seemed so thoroughly interpenetrated that science seemed essentially sacred, medicine, magical. The earliest clear evidence is Chinese.

In 679 BC, the sage Shen Hsü is said to have taught that ghosts were exhalations of the fears and guilt of those who see them. Confucius deterred followers from thinking "about the dead until you know the living", and defined wisdom as aloof respect for gods and demons. Confucians professed interest in human affairs – politics and practical ethics – and indifference to the rest of nature. As far as they did delve into the subject, it was in an effort to dig out what they regarded as superstition: the imputation of feelings and wills to inanimate substances; the notion that all matter is infused with spirits; and the claim – advanced sometimes by sophisticated thinkers on grounds of cosmic interconnectedness – that the natural world is responsive to human sin or rectitude.

"If one does not know causes, it is as if one knew nothing," says a Confucian text of about 239 BC. "The fact that water leaves the mountains is not due to any dislike on the part of the water but is the effect of height. The wheat has no desire to grow or be gathered into granaries. Therefore the sage does not enquire about goodness or badness but about reasons."

William Wordsworth (1770–1850) was more at ease with nature than with science.

"Science appears but what in truth she is... a prop to our infirmity."

William Wordsworth, *The Prelude* (1805)

This was part of an emphasis on "natural" causes, which displaced magic from the arena of nature in the mainstream thought of all the great civilizations of the Axial Age.

This did not mean that science expelled religion from a role in establishing the relations between people and their environments. In China, the Emperor still performed rites designed to maintain cosmic harmony. In the West, people still prayed for relief from natural disasters and imputed afflictions to their sins.

Science has never been perfectly separated from religion: indeed, each of these approaches to the world has colonized the other's territory. Even today, some scientists are unable to resist religious controversy and advocate atheism as if it were a religion, evolution as if it were Providence, and Darwin as if he were a prophet.

Chinese technology
The Ancient Chinese were perhaps the first to draw a distinction between science and the supernatural. This seismograph alerted the observer to ground vibrations by dropping balls into the mouths of the toads.

CONNECTIONS

On the borderlands between science and magic, see **The Golden Key** (p.24) and **Fool's Gold** (p.216). For later innovations, see **Tooth and Claw** (p.320), **Warped Universe** (p.346), and **Uncertainty** (p.348).

Experimental science
In the 18th century, there was a widespread emphasis on "natural causes" as an explanation for change. This helped to promote scientific investigation, vividly depicted here in Joseph Wright of Derby's painting of "An Experiment on a Bird in the Air Pump".

Nothing Matters

THE IDEA OF A PURPOSELESS WORLD

A consequence of the rise of a scientific point of view was the suspicion that the world is purposeless, or, at least, if God had some purpose in creation, it was inscrutable and beyond useful speculation. In particular, this line of thinking raised an idea that challenged most earlier orthodoxies: if the world was purposeless, it was not made for Man, who was thereby reduced to insignificance.

The idea Aristotle called the "Final Cause" – the purpose of a thing, which explains its nature – becomes incoherent. The world is a random event. In around 200 BC this was

Going nowhere
A hamster running on a treadmill, going nowhere, is a powerful image of futility. But does the lack of a destination make the journey meaningless?

READINGS

J. Thrower's **Western Atheism: a Short History** (1999) is a clear, concise introduction, while J. Maritain's **The Range of Reason** (1952) provides a good critique of atheism.

L. Feuerbach's **Principles of the Philosophy of the Future** (1843) is a classic apologia.

such a dangerous idea that the Chinese Taoist philosopher Lieh Tzu put it into the mouth of a small boy, who challenged a pious host for praising divine bounty that provided good things for his table. "Mosquitoes suck human blood, wolves devour human flesh but we do not therefore assert that Heaven created man for their benefit." Chen Tse, another Chinese thinker, thought "Why?" a pointless question.

The war poet **Wilfred Owen** (1893–1918) was killed a week before the end of WWI.

"Was it for this the clay grew tall?
O what made fatuous sunbeams toil
To break earth's sleep at all?"

Wilfred Owen, "Futility" (1918)

The greatest-ever exponent of a purposeless cosmos was the 1st-century Chinese philosopher, Wang Ch'ung. Humans, he said, live like lice in the folds of a garment. When fleas buzz in your ear, you do not hear them: how could God even hear men, let alone concede their wishes? Some materialist thinkers take pride in asserting that the whole notion of purpose is superstitious and that it is pointless to ask why the world exists or why it is as it is.

In a purposeless Universe, God is a redundant concept. Accusations of atheism in ancient times often seem to imply something less than outright denial of the reality of divinity. Anaxagoras was the first philosopher known to have been prosecuted under the anti-atheism laws of Athens in the mid 5th century BC, but his offence was only to deny the godhead of the Sun ("a hot stone") and the Moon ("made of earth"). Atheism was among the crimes for which Socrates was condemned, but his belief in a god too subtle for popular Athenian taste is well attested. Around the end of the 1st century AD, Sextus Empiricus anticipated Marx's view that religion is the opiate of the masses. As a means of social control, he suggested, "some shrewd man invented fear of the gods". The doctrines of divine omnipotence and omniscience were devised to suppress freedom of conscience. "If they say that God controls everything, they make him the author of evil," he concluded. "We speak of the gods but express no belief and avoid the evil of the dogmatizers."

NOTHING MATTERS

CONNECTIONS

On the ethics of atheism, see **Atheist Faith** (p.324); for the thinking of materialists, see **Matter Matters** (p.124); for an account of the tradition of anti-clerical feeling, see **Cleansing the Temple** (p.254). Random events also occur in **Chaos Theory** (p.350).

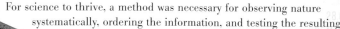

Scientific Method

THE TAOIST IDEA OF KNOWLEDGE

Chinese technology
Chinese science was always stronger on technology than theory. Compasses were used for navigation from the 11th century onwards.

READINGS

N. Sivin's **Medicine, Philosophy and Religion in Ancient China** (1995) is a valuable collection of essays on the links between Tao and science.

J. Needham's **Science and Civilization in China** (1956–) is the fundamental multi-volume work.

F. Capra's **The Tao of Physics** (1975) is a maverick, but influential, work arguing for a Taoist interpretation of modern quantum physics.

For science to thrive, a method was necessary for observing nature systematically, ordering the information, and testing the resulting hypotheses. Habits of observation and experiment probably developed from magical and divinatory practices of early Taoism. The only Taoist word ever used for a temple means "watch-tower" – a platform from which to observe the natural world and launch naturalistic explanations of its phenomena.

Taoism has, in Confucian eyes, a reputation for magical mumbo-jumbo, but Taoists can transcend magic by means of their doctrine that Nature – to the one who would control her – is like any other beast to be tamed or foe to be dominated: she must be known first. Tao has a mystical image in the West, but is rooted in commonplace observations: water, for instance, reflects the world, permeates every other substance, yields, embraces, changes shape at a touch, and yet erodes the hardest rock. Thus it becomes the symbol of an all-shaping, all-encompassing, all-pervading Tao. In the Taoist *yin-yang* image of a circle halved by a serpentine line, the cosmos is depicted as two waves mingling.

Part of the result is that Taoism encourages the rudiments of scientific practice: observation, description, classification, and experiment. The k'ao-cheng tradition, the scientific imperative that arose from some fundamental ethical and religious assumptions, is implicit in some of the earliest Taoist writings. Grand theory is discouraged as an intrusion of reason into the workings of wisdom, which can be attained only through the accumulation of knowledge. Chinese science has always been weak on theory, strong on technology.

It is probably no coincidence that the modern tradition of experimental science in the West began in the 13th century at a time of greatly multiplied contacts across Eurasia, when numerous Chinese ideas and inventions were reaching Europe across the steppelands and the silk routes, via the Muslim world.

Thomas H. Huxley (1825–95) was an enthusiastic defender of scientific attitudes.

"Science is nothing but trained and organized common sense."

Thomas Huxley, *Collected Essays (Vol. 4)* (1894)

Systematic organization
Taoist thinking encouraged thorough observation and classification. The Periodic Table, (devised by Dimitri Mendeleyev in 1869), organized the known elements systematically.

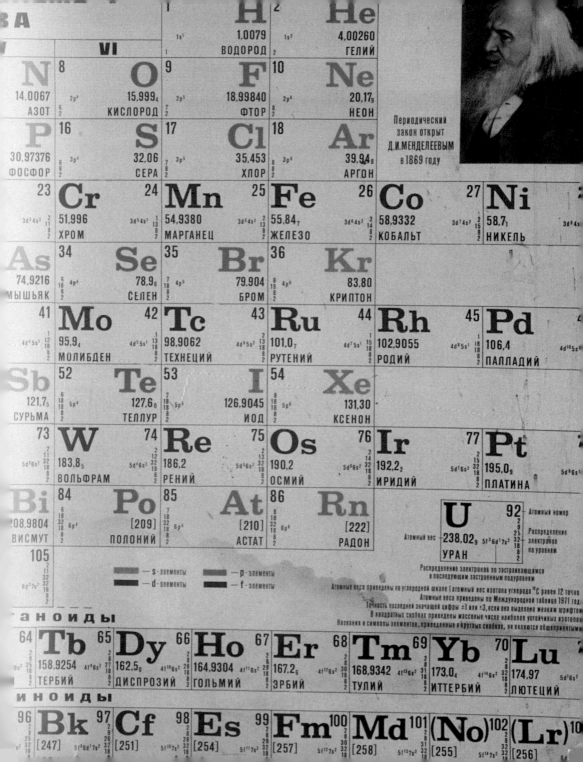

Good Humours

THE IDEA OF MEDICINE AS SCIENCE NOT MAGIC

The four humours
According to the 2nd-century Roman physician Galen, human health was characterized by a balance of the four "humours".

Around the middle of the first millennium BC, the search for a comprehensive theory of the causes of illness prompted a controversy between magic and medicine – or was it just between rival forms of magic? Illness, like any abnormal state, could be the result of possession or infestation by a spirit or a "demon" – to recycle a commonly used word for it. Or some diseases could have material causes, others spiritual, or be a mixture of the two. Or sickness could even be a divine affliction earned by sin. That all illness is physically explicable is a strange idea, which started relatively late in history.

In an incident in China, said to have occurred in 540 BC, an official told his prince to rely on diet, work, and personal morale for bodily health, not the spirits of rivers, mountains, and stars. Officials, however, usually command little prestige as physicians. The controversy that mattered occurred within the ranks of professional healers.

Bedside manner
The physical world may be all there is for modern-day Hippocratic "healers", but there is still some residual "magical" healing in a good bedside manner and a patient's positive attitude.

CONNECTIONS

The context of the origins of science as we now understand it is pursued in **Against Supernature** (p.128) and **The Scientific Method** (p.132). Another case of conflict between scientism and scepticism is pursued in **Impossibilism** (p.202).

"Ars longa, vita brevis"
[The life so short, the craft so long to learn].

Hippocrates, *On Ancient Medicine* (c. 400 BC)

The **caduceus** (a wand with two serpents) has symbolized healing since Classical times.

Bloodletting
Until the 19th century, bloodletting, shown here in this 15th-century manuscript, was a standard medical procedure to re-balance the "humours" and eliminate "poisons".

In late 5th-century BC Greece, a secular school known as the Hippocratic writers made a bid to monopolize the profession, at the expense of rivals who were attached to temples. They had an entirely erroneous theory of how disease works – they thought that health was essentially a state of balance between four "humours" present in human bodies: blood, phlegm, black bile, and yellow bile. Adjust the balance and you alter the patient's state of health. This condemned patients to treatment mainly by diet, emetics, and bloodletting. It was – however – based on observation of the substances expelled from the body in pain or sickness: does it qualify to be called scientific?

A treatise sometimes attributed to Hippocrates advocated a physical explanation for epilepsy, which had previously been assumed to be the result of a form of divine possession. The test was: find a goat exhibiting the same symptoms. "If you cut open the head, you will find that the brain is… full of fluid and foul-smelling; convincing proof that the disease and not the deity is harming the body." The method sounds bizarre but the conclusion is impressive: "I do not believe," the Hippocratic writer went on, "that the 'Sacred Disease' is any more divine or sacred than any other disease, but, on the contrary, has specific characteristics and a definite cause… Personally, I believe that human bodies cannot be polluted by a god."

A similar shift of business into the hands of secular medical specialists occurred in China. Hsün Tzu (305–235 BC) scorned a man who "having got rheumatism from dampness beats a drum and boils a suckling pig as an offering to the spirits". He described the result: "a worn-out drum and a lost pig, but he will not have the happiness of recovering from sickness."

Temple healing survived because it worked. Professional medicine throve alongside it because it sounded convincing. Religious explanations of disease retained adherents when the secular professionals were baffled – which they often were. The history of modern science has, by most accounts, roots in the medicine of the followers of Hippocrates. But their influence is wider and deeper still: they started a presumption that has gained ground ever since – that nothing needs to be explained in divine terms. The physical world is all there is.

READINGS

R. Porter's **The Greatest Benefit to Mankind** (1999) is a vast, readable, and entertainingly irreverent account of the history of medicine.

D. Cantor's (ed.) **Reinventing Hippocrates** (2001) is a stimulating collection of essays.

J. Longrigg's **Greek Medicine** (1998) is a useful source book.

Ethical Beings

THE IDEA THAT HUMAN NATURE IS MORAL

Humans like to claim that they have a unique position in the animal world. But how moral a being is "Man"? It was a key question for the Axial sages and we are still enmeshed in the consequences of their answers. By a large majority, the Axial-Age sages thought human nature was essentially good. Hence the political doctrines of Confucianism, which demanded that the state should liberate subjects to fulfil their potential, and of Greek democracy, which gave citizens a voice in affairs of state even if they were poor or ill-educated.

The evidence, however, was glaringly equivocal: were misdeeds the result of corrupted goodness or inherent evil? "The nature of man is evil – his goodness is only acquired by training," said Hsün Ch'ing, for instance, in the mid 3rd century BC. He believed that the primeval state of humankind was a grim swamp of violence, from which people were painfully raised by progress. "Hence the civilizing influence of teachers and laws, the guidance of rites and justice. Then courtesy appears, cultured behaviour is observed and good government is the consequence." This doctrine has never been displaced: it has resurfaced in the moral pessimism of modern conservative thought, while optimism about human nature has animated liberalism and socialism. Indeed, since the Axial Age, political solutions to the problem of human nature have always been of two contrasting kinds: those that emphasize freedom, in order to release human goodness, and those that emphasize discipline, in order to restrain human wickedness.

So is Man good or bad? The most widely favoured answer was put forward in the Book of Genesis. Man was made good and free, but the abuse of his freedom made him bad. Logically, this was unpersuasive: if Man was good, how could he use freedom for evil? To escape this trap, a diabolical device was added. Goodness was corrupted from outside by "the serpent" (or other "devilish" agents in other traditions). This has left politics with a difficult balancing act to perform, which no system has ever adequately accomplished, between freedom and force.

School democracy
A.S. Neill, founder of the self-governing Summerhill school, believed in the inherent goodness of humans. Pupils at the school are encouraged to exercise their judgement in a weekly General Meeting.

Confucius (551–479 BC) elevated ethics above religion and science.

"Man is born for uprightness. If he lose it and yet live, it is merely luck."

Confucius, *Analects* (c. 440 BC)

Naughty boy
*The Christian doctrine of
"original sin" states that
because of Adam's sin in
eating the apple from the
"tree of knowledge of good
and evil", all humankind is
born sinful. Some people
believe that stern discipline
is needed to control these
inherent failings.*

READINGS

The Marquis de Condorcet's **Sketch for... the Progress of the Human Mind** (1795), written while he was awaiting execution by guillotine, is probably one of the most defiantly optimistic works on the subject ever written, while E.O. Wilson's **On Human Nature** (1978) is one of the most materialist.

A. MacIntyre's **After Virtue** (1981) is a fine introduction.

CONNECTIONS

On the prehistory of ethics, see **Good and Evil** (p.48). Examples of ethical debate generating new ideas are found in **Return of the Soul** (p.140), **Legalism** (p.146), **Human Bondage** (p.150), **Love Above** (p.160), and **Noble Education** (p.196)

Top Ape

THE IDEA OF HUMAN SUPERIORITY

The urge of humans to differentiate themselves from the rest of nature is obviously part of human nature. Yet the idea of the collective superiority of mankind made its first explicit appearance surprisingly late. Early

humans seem to have felt – quite rightly – that they were part of the great animal continuum. They worshipped animals or zoomorphic gods, adopted totemic ancestors, and even – in some cases – buried animals with as much ceremony as humans. Most of their societies had, as far as we know, no concept of mankind, but relegated those outside the group to the category of beasts or sub-men.

The Axial Age differed, developing doctrines of the inferiority of animals and accentuating the unity of mankind.

Two by two
Christian doctrine states that God gave mankind dominion over all the creatures of the Earth. This 16th-century painting of Noah's Ark by Francesco Bassano shows Noah fulfilling his role as the guardian of creation.

In the book of Genesis, God makes "Man in his own image" and gives him dominion over other animals. Early in the second half of the millennium, thinkers in other traditions formulated similar ideas. In the 4th century BC, Aristotle schematized a hierarchy of living souls, in which Man's was adjudged superior to those of plants and animals, because it had "rational" as well as "vegetative" and "sensitive" faculties. The Chinese formula was similar, expressed, for example, by Hsün Tzu early in the next century: "Man has spirits, life, and perception, and in addition the sense of justice; therefore he is the noblest of earthly beings." He could exploit stronger creatures because he was able to act collaboratively.

While some fish still elude our mastery, the **goldfish** has been reduced to a mere ornament.

"… fill the Earth and subdue it. Be masters of the fish of the sea, the birds of heaven, and all the living creatures that move on Earth."

God's command to Mankind, *Genesis* 1: 28 (c. 1400 BC)

There were dissenting traditions. In southern Italy in the late 6th century BC, Pythagoras taught "all things that are born with life in them ought to be treated as kindred". His Indian near-contemporary, Mahavira Vardamana, thought the universality of souls imposed on people an obligation of care of the whole of the rest of creation: because the souls of animals most closely resembled those of people, they had to be treated with special respect. So did human superiority mean human privilege or human responsibility: lordship or stewardship? It was the start of a long, still unresolved debate over the limits of humans' freedom to exploit other creatures for our benefit.

Animal rights?
Belief in human superiority can sometimes lead to indifference or even cruelty to animal species. This Sun Bear is kept caged in cramped conditions in a park in Taiwan, for the entertainment of visitors.

CONNECTIONS

For early ideas about the relationship of humans to other animals, see **Fly like an Eagle** (p.20), **Animal Magic** (p.52), and **Outside Eden** (p.66). For later developments, see **Tooth and Claw** (p.320), and **Silent Springs** (p.384).

READINGS

T. Benton's **Natural Relations** (1993) and R.G. Frey's **Interests and Rights: the Case against Animals** (1980) explain the differences.

M. Midgeley's **Beast and Man** (1980) and P. Singer's **Animal Liberation** (1990) advocate similarities.

F. de Waal's **The Ape and the Sushi Master** (2002) reveals the continuities.

Mandala meditation
Buddhism teaches that the soul is refined through positive thoughts and acts in successive lives. Here, Tibetan Buddhist monks create a mandala (an aid to meditation) out of coloured sand.

READINGS

S.G.F. Brandon's **Man and his Destiny in the Great Religions** (1962) offers a broad synopsis.

J. Head and S.L. Cranston's **Reincarnation** (1977) is a penetrating, dispassionate introduction.

W. O'Flaherty's (ed.) **Karma and Rebirth in Classical Indian Traditions** (1980) is an important collection on the most conspicuous traditions.

Return of the Soul

THE IDEA OF REINCARNATION

This idea has inspired or deluded innumerable individuals and whole societies since its formulation nearly 3,000 years ago. If there is a soul, what happens to it when the body dies? It can become a disembodied spirit, which seems to have been the commonest assumption of the remote past. Or it can go to an afterlife in another world, which was evidently also an early solution to the problem. It can be subject to judgement, as people in agrarian civilizations generally seem to have believed. Or it can migrate at random to a new body – perhaps human, perhaps animal. Or its migrations can be purposeful, perhaps divinely directed: recycled on the wheel of life.

This was the doctrine of the first text in which reincarnation is expressed: the Upanishads, the Indian teachings probably compiled in something like their present form by the 7th century BC. Here, the cycle of reincarnation was represented as fitful but, in the long term, progressive: in the course of a series of lives, the soul could advance towards perfection, when its identity would be submerged in the divine "soul of the world" known as Brahman.

It was echoed in its most developed and influential form in the teachings of Buddha, whose dates are uncertain, but who is usually assigned to the 5th or 6th century BC. Buddhism aimed to liberate the soul from the world, either by individual self-refinement or by the obliteration of the self in altruism. But this was likely to be a long job. In the meantime, the soul could expect to be recycled frequently. The distinctive element in the Buddhist view was that it was ethical: a principle of justice – or at least of retribution – would govern the fate of the soul, which would be assigned a higher or lower body in each successive life according to the virtue of its deeds in its previous incarnation.

The 14th **Dalai Lama** (1935–) is the spiritual leader of Tibetan Buddhism.

"Some people believe I have some kind of magic power. They use words like 'Living Buddha'. These are wrong ideas. I describe myself as a simple Buddhist monk, no more, no less."

The 14th Dalai Lama, Speech at UC–Berkeley (13 June, 1997)

Perfect soul
The Buddhist idea of purposeful reincarnation – governed by a principle of justice – was one solution to the eternal problem of what happens to your soul when your body dies.

Happiness First

THE IDEA OF PRACTICAL ETHICS

CONNECTIONS

This idea can usefully be compared with **Smashing Atoms** (p.126), **Invisible Powers** (p.228), and **Warped Universe** (p.346). For further points of comparison, see **No Dice** (p.28), **All Is One** (p.104), and **Mu** (p.204).

In revolt from unanswerable questions about Nature and reality, philosophers turned first to scepticism, then to practical ethics. One of the great anecdote-inspiring characters of Ancient Greece was Pyrrho of Elis, who was said to have accompanied Alexander to India and to have imitated the indifference of the naked sages. On board ship on the way home, he admired and shared the unpanicky response of a pig to a storm.

He was absent-minded and accident-prone, which made him seem unworldly, but his deepest indifference was to reason. The achievements of the Greek rationalists of the previous 100 years left him cold. Since, he argued, you can find equally good reasons on both sides of any argument, the only wise course is to stop thinking and judge by appearances. More effective was the argument that all reasoning starts from assumptions; so none of it is secure. Mo Ti had developed a similar insight in China around the beginning of the 4th century BC: most problems were matters of doubt. "As for what we now know, is it not mostly derived from past experience?"

One tradition from this line of thought led to scepticism – in its extreme form, the idea that nothing is knowable and that the very notion of knowledge is delusive. Another nourished science or empiricism, since if reason and experience are equally unreliable one may as well prefer experience and the practical advantages it can

The Roman Stoic philosopher **Epictetus** sought a principle to make pain meaningless.

"Show me one who is sick and yet happy, in peril and yet happy, dying and yet happy, in exile or disgrace and yet happy. By the gods, I would see a Stoic!"

Attributed to Epictetus (2nd century AD)

teach. In 2nd century BC China, for instance, the Huai Nan Tzu told of Yi the archer who, on sage advice, sought the medicine of immortality far away in the West, when the weed was growing outside his door. Taoist texts often have amusing dialogues between experienced craftsmen who know their work intimately and interfering rationalists who persuade them to do it differently, with ruinous results. A third strand encouraged thinking about ethics: minds unconcerned about the distinction between truth and falsehood could focus more clearly on good and evil.

Later Greek philosophy emphasized systems that concerned the best practical choices for personal happiness or for the good of society. Stoicism, for instance, which emphasized altruism, moderation, and self-discipline as ingredients of personal happiness, had an enormous effect on Christianity. Further Stoic prescriptions – fatalism and indifference as a remedy for pain – were harder to reconcile with Christianity, but were similar to teachings promulgated at about the same period at the far end of Eurasia, especially by Buddha and his followers.

The "happiness priority" has been sought in so many contrasting ways that it is hard to generalize about its overall effect on the history of the world. Stoicism, however, was certainly its most effective manifestation in the West and has supplied, in effect, the source of the guiding principles of the ethics of most Western elites ever since its emergence.

All-singing stoic
Indifference to reason – as exhibited by Gene Kelly in Singin' in the Rain (1952) – strongly influenced Western moral thinking.

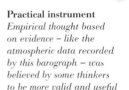

Practical instrument
Empirical thought based on evidence – like the atmospheric data recorded by this barograph – was believed by some thinkers to be more valid and useful than abstract reasoning.

READINGS

A.A. Long's **Hellenistic Philosophy** (1974) is particularly good on Stoicism, while J. Annas and J. Barnes's (ed.) **The Modes of Scepticism** (1985) provides an excellent summary of the main sceptic arguments.

Epictetus's **Discourses** (AD 101) provide an invaluable guide for living, while M. Aurelius's **Meditations** (AD 167) show the Emperor's attempts to live according to Stoic principles.

A Capital Idea

THE IDEA THAT CAPITALISM IS GOOD

Filthy lucre
Throughout history, attitudes to money have fluctuated. This 16th-century Flemish painting of a moneylender is critical of money hoarding.

144

READINGS

K. Marx's **Das Kapital** (1867) remains the great critique of capitalism.

M. Friedman's **Capitalism and Freedom** (1982) mounts an impressive defence.

A. Giddens's **The Third Way** (1998) is the strongest – yet disturbingly vague – voice for a "third way" in economics.

M. Weber's **The Protestant Ethic and the Spirit of Capitalism** (1904) advanced the now discredited claim that capitalism is peculiarly linked with Protestantism.

F. Fernández-Armesto's **Civilizations** (2001) provides a guide to the scattered readings of ancient Jain and Buddhist capitalist texts.

The idea that money-making enterprise is virtuous – or at least compatible with virtue – seems to be unshakeable in the minds of the rich, for whom it is a self-justifying doctrine, and the poor, for whom it is a focus of inspiration. It is well documented in biblical Judaism, which represented worldly success as a sign of divine favour. It is the theme of many early Buddhist stories about the sanctity and nobility of merchants; for example, Jatakas, which perhaps dates from as early as the 3rd century BC.

Yet the idea was challenged by moralists, and many ancient societies evinced hostility towards capitalism by practising state-controlled trade or representing trade as "tribute". The earliest systematic defence of a capitalist way of life was probably drawn up in the 6th century BC by Mahavira, the founding sage of Jainism. Only monastic self-abnegation, in his view, was fully meritorious, but at least he regarded wealth-creation as morally neutral, as long as the rich man relieved the needs of his neighbours and laboured "that many may enjoy what he earns". This anticipates modern capitalist theorists' main moral justification: the wealthy "give employment to the artisan". Their prosperity "trickles down" to enrich the whole of society.

The doctrine has remained contentious. Hindus, for instance, often represent trade as incompatible with high caste. Confucianism regards commerce as an inferior calling. Aristocratic prejudice usually despises it. Christian tradition questions capitalists' fitness for heaven. Poverty is regarded as a qualification for sanctity in many religious traditions. Common experience condemns unregulated enterprise as inherently unjust on the grounds that it rewards the most competitive, the most cut-throat, and the most selfish, and misrepresents greed as good. The consequence, critics say, is a society of exploitation. Socialism proposed an alternative: commerce should become the monopoly of the state. In practice, where this was tried, it simply transferred immorality to the public sphere on a gigantic scale, creating "state capitalism".

Almighty dollar
Many people see money-making not only as a reward for hard work, but as the basis of a modern free society. The American dollar, more than any other currency, symbolizes this view.

The accumulation of **money** is at the root of capitalism.

"Capitalism wisely managed can probably be made more efficient... than any alternative system... but... is... extremely objectionable."

John Maynard Keynes, *The End of Laissez-faire* (1926)

Capitalism has come to mean different things to different people. Karl Marx used it as the name of a historical period – a phase of society in which power is concentrated in the hands of people who dispose of movable wealth, rather than those who own land or make their livings from their labour. Economists treat it as a system regulated by the "invisible hand" of market forces, rather than by the state. The essence of capitalism, however, is always privilege accorded to wealth-creation. Today, capitalism has come to be accepted almost universally as the least-worst basis for an economic system. However, its deficiencies – which take the form of market instability, undemocratic abuses of corporate power, gross social inequalities, and the "fat-cat" behaviour of some capitalists – keep people searching for a "third way", retaining the benefits of capitalism but controlling its excesses.

Princely pose
The fabulously wealthy Jacob Fugger (1459–1525) was part of the great banking family which rose from humble beginnings to found a dynasty of princes.

Legalism

THE IDEA THAT LAW AND ORDER COME FIRST

The only good is the good of the state, and law and order are worth tyranny and injustice: this doctrine was born in a time of great civil disaster and has resurfaced in bad times ever since. The consensus among the Chinese sages was that the ruler should be bound by law: for most, this was a way of restraining tyranny by suborning it to ethics. Confucius even said that ethics should override obedience to the law. The age-old tension between rules and individual rights showed, however, that law could function perfectly well without any consideration for such a moral code.

The Legalists, who formed a school of thought in 4th-century BC China, made a virtue − or pretended virtue − of this deficiency by establishing a basic principle that "goodness" was meaningless. What the law said was irrelevant: all that really mattered was that it should be obeyed. Ethics was a "gnawing worm" that would destroy the state. This was a remarkable new twist in the history of thinking about law: all previous schools had tried to make man-made law more moral by aligning it with "divine" or "natural" law.

The explanation lies in the chaos and terror of the times. The Chinese Legalists were in recoil from generations of disastrous feuding between the "Warring States" − an era in which the empire had

READINGS

A. Waley's **Three Ways of Thought in Ancient China** (1938) is a classic introduction, while S. De Grazia's **Masters of Chinese Political Thought** (1973) prints essential texts in translation.

C. Ping and D. Bloodworth's **The Chinese Machiavelli** (1976) is a lively popular history of Chinese political thought, while B.I. Schwartz's **The World of Thought in Ancient China** (1985) is a more scholarly account.

146

"I am the Law!"
The Chinese Legalist position is updated in the comic-strip story "Judge Dredd". In this dystopic vision of the future, the police and judiciary have merged to form the Judges, of whom Dredd is the most feared.

dissolved into banditry. The ethics-based thinking of the Confucians and Taoists had done nothing to help. The Legalists laughed off the earlier sages' belief in the innate goodness of people. The best penalties were often the most severe: severance at the neck or waist, dismemberment with chariots, boring a hole in the skull, roasting alive, or filleting out a wrongdoer's ribs.

Blind obedience
School discipline is based on unquestioning obedience, and, perhaps also, on the notion that children need to have the "badness" drilled out of them.

The Legalists' ascendancy inflicted so much suffering in China that their doctrines were reviled for centuries. But similar ideas have continued to recur during times of disorder. As well as in the worship of order, Ancient Chinese legalism anticipated modern fascism – for instance, in advocating and glorifying war, recommending economic self-sufficiency for the state, denouncing capitalism, extolling agriculture, and insisting on the need to suppress individualism in the interests of state unity.

CONNECTIONS

Comparable ideas are pursued in **Divine Majesty** (p.82), **Philosopher-kings** (p.152), **State First** (p.232), **Nasty, Brutish, Short** (p.238), **Forced to be Free** (p.256), **Brother Knows Best** (p.306), and **Axe in the Sticks** (p.364).

147

LEGALISM

Thumbscrews were used to extract confessions.

"Benevolence, righteousness, love and generosity are useless, but severe punishments and dire penalties can keep the state in order."

Han Fei (c. early 3rd century BC)

Rule of the Best

THE IDEA OF REPUBLICAN GOVERNMENT

We are not here to serve rulers or support society, although these may be ineluctable duties. The state exists to help individuals fulfil their potential. Chinese and Indian thinkers applied this individualistic doctrine, which gathered strength during the Axial Age, to the state, but they did not go on to question the role of monarchy. The state, after all, was meant to reflect the cosmos; its unity could not be compromised. All that could be expected was that the ruler should consult the people's interests and views, and should face, in case of tyranny, the subject's right of rebellion.

To maximize virtue and prowess in government the obvious step is to multiply the number of people involved in it. So although monarchies preponderated throughout the Axial Age, republican or aristocratic systems, and even democratic ones, had advocates and instances. In Greece, where city-states were practical mechanisms to be tinkered with at need, an enormous variety of political experiments unfolded.

Aristotle made a magisterial survey of them in the 4th century BC. He thought monarchy was obviously the best system in theory, but not in practice, since it was impossible to ensure that the best man would always be the ruler. More practical was aristocratic government, in which administration was shared by a manageable number of superior men, but it tended to generate into the self-interested rule of the wealthy or the perpetuation of power in an hereditary clique. Democracy, in which all

The Great Charter
Republicanism holds that a ruler should consult the people's interests. The Magna Carta – forced on King John of England by his barons in 1215 – ended up enshrining aristocratic tyranny instead.

*"Heaven sees what the people see,
heaven hears what the people hear."*

Mencius, *Meng Tzu* (c. 4th century BC)

Mencius (371-289 BC)
was second only to
Confucius in Chinese
philosophical tradition.

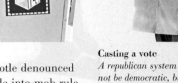
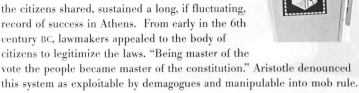

the citizens shared, sustained a long, if fluctuating,
record of success in Athens. From early in the 6th
century BC, lawmakers appealed to the body of
citizens to legitimize the laws. "Being master of the
vote the people became master of the constitution." Aristotle denounced
this system as exploitable by demagogues and manipulable into mob rule.

    The best system was a carefully articulated mixture in which
aristocracy predominated, under the rule of law. Broadly speaking, this
was embodied in the Roman state of the second half of the millennium,
which became, in turn, the model for most republican revivals in Western
history. Even when, at the end of the Axial Age, Rome abandoned
republican government and restored what was in effect a monarchical
system, Romans still spoke of the state as a republic and the emperor as
merely a "magistrate".

    This Classical tradition made republicanism permanently
respectable in Western civilization. The great medieval city-republics of
the Mediterranean modelled themselves on Ancient Rome, as, in the late
18th century, did the USA and revolutionary France. Although most new
states of the 19th century continued to be monarchies, most of
them abandoned that system in the 20th century, when the spread
of the republican ideal became one of the most conspicuous
features of global "Westernization" in politics. By 1952, the King of
Egypt predicted there would soon be only five kings in the world –
and four of those would be found in a pack of playing-cards.

Model government
*The Classical tradition of republican
government provided the model
for future Western governments.
Rule in Ancient Rome was divided
between the magistrates (elected)
and the Senate.*

Casting a vote
*A republican system need
not be democratic, but in
most modern republics,
legitimacy is conferred (or
rigged) through the ballot
box. The first free elections
in South Africa were held
in 1994, after the repeal
of the apartheid laws.*

READINGS

P. Pettit's **Republicanism**
(1997) is a very useful
introduction.

A. Oldfield's **Citizenship
and Community** (1990) and
R. Dagger's **Civic Virtues**
(1997) both take broad looks
at modern republicanism.

CONNECTIONS

On various republican
traditions, see also **The
Social Charter** (p.192),
Heaven's Order (p.240),
Neverland (p.250), **We, the
People** (p.260), **Inalienable
Rights** (p.264), **Extreme
Optimism** (p.290), **Less
Is More** (p.298), and **Just
Say No** (p.308).

RULE OF THE BEST

Human Bondage

THE IDEA OF NATURAL SLAVERY

Most human societies have regarded slavery – or some very similar system of forced labour – as entirely normal and morally unchallengeable. Most have practised it, many have depended on it. But how could they justify it?

In the late 4th century BC, Aristotle produced a long-serviceable answer. Aristotle, however, was aware of the contradiction between enforced servility and the values he espoused – such as the independent worth of every human being and the moral value of happiness. He formulated the world's first justification of slavery: some people are inherently inferior and, for them, the best lot in life is to serve their betters.

For instance, he argued, races inherently inferior to the Greeks could be plundered for slaves; or in wars caused by the resistance of natural inferiors to conquest, captives could be enslaved. In practice, this doctrine was ignored for centuries, because slavery was unquestioned and masters could admit, without prejudice to their own interests, that their slaves were equal to themselves, except in legal status.

But Aristotle's argument became important from the 16th century onwards, when it supplied the basic moral authority for slavery whenever the justice of the institution

Forced labour
Most slaves in Ancient Egypt were prisoners of war, whose servile status, according to Aristotle, reflected their inherent "inferiority".

READINGS

T. Wiedemann's **Greek and Roman Slavery** (1981) covers the ancient context, while A. Pagden's **The Fall of Natural Man** (1982) sets in context the evolution of the doctrine – on which the classic work is L. Hanke's **Aristotle and the American Indians** (1959).

A. Haley's **Roots** (1976) was a bestselling historical biography of the author's (African-American) family, tracing it back to a village in The Gambia, West Africa.

Some white settlers believed that **Native Americans** were not fully human.

"Some men are by nature slaves and others by nature free. And it is just… and fitting that one man should be master and another obey, for the quality of superiority is also inherent in the natural master."

John Mair, justifying enslavement of Native Americans (1513)

was subsequently challenged in the West. It also stimulated racism, and the victimization of people of a particular "race" as slaves, because anyone who was a slave had to be classified as inferior.

In the course of developing the idea, Aristotle also formulated a doctrine of just war. While some societies regarded war as normal, or even as an obligation of nature or the gods, Aristotle regarded war as just, if the victims of aggression were inferior people who ought to be ruled by their aggressors. At least this teaching made war a subject of moral scrutiny, but that would be little consolation to the victims of it.

Instruments of bondage
The institution of slavery required technology – such as these 19th-century leg irons from West Africa – as well as a racial ideology.

Slaves to an idea
Slavery and racism go hand in hand. Those who practised slavery believed that their slaves were naturally inferior.

Philosopher-kings

THE IDEA OF RULE BY AN INTELLECTUAL ELITE

No method of choosing rulers was proof against abuse. In 4th-century BC Athens, Plato thought he could devise a system so perfect that society could rely on a benevolent ruling class. Among philosophers, Plato was surely the best-ever writer and perhaps the greatest-ever philosopher. He was, however, a member of an Athenian brat-pack of rich, well-educated intellectuals, who resented democracy and felt qualified for power.

When he wrote his prescriptions for the ideal state in *The Republic*, they came out harsh, reactionary, and illiberal. The many object-ionable features – censorship, repression, militarism, regimentation, extreme communism and collectivism, eugenics, austerity, rigid class structure, active deception of the people by the state – all had a baneful influence. The key idea, however, is that all political power should be concentrated in a self-electing class of philosopher-rulers called Guardians. Their

In the name of the people
Throughout history, elites – like the highly educated "third estate" shown here on 17 June 1789 vowing to establish a new French constitution – have sought to create the "ideal" state and to rule in the name of the "people".

READINGS

Plato's **The Republic** (380 BC) is the key text, while K. Popper's **The Open Society and its Enemies** (1945) provides the classic critique of Plato's theory.

C.D.C. Reeve's **Philosopher-Kings** (1988) is a historical study of the phenomenon, while M. Schofield's **Saving the City** (1999) studies the idea of philosopher-kings in ancient philosophy.

*"Keep the company of those who seek
the truth, and run away from those
who have found it."*

Václav Havel

Inflammatory texts
*Plato's prescriptions for the
state included censorship,
as a means of social control.
During the 1930s, the
Nazis arranged public book
burnings to demonstrate
state disapproval.*

qualification for office would be intellectual superiority, guaranteed by
a mixture of heredity and education, which would make them selfless in
their private lives and "godlike" in their ability to see what was good for
the citizens. So this repellent system would conform to Plato's declared
"objective in the construction of the state: the greatest happiness of the
whole, and not of any one class". Plato wrote so brilliantly and so persuasively
that this reasoning has continued to appeal to state-builders ever since.
His Guardians are the inspiration and the intellectual ancestors of the
elites, aristocracies, party apparatchiks, and self-appointed "supermen"
whose justification for tyrannizing others
has always been that they know best.

The Great Void

THE IDEA OF NOTHING

CONNECTIONS

Other fundamental ideas about numbers include **Seeing Double** (p.46) and **Count on This** (p.120). For consequences of the idea of nothing see **Power of Thought** (p.156) and **No God but God** (p.158). Also compare with **Mu** (p.204).

154

Middle of nowhere
The idea of nothing is maddeningly elusive. As soon as you try to imagine it, it turns into something.

The idea of nothing may seem uninteresting – but that, in a sense, is what is so interesting about it. It seems strictly unimaginable. Nothing is maddeningly elusive. As soon as you conceive of it, it becomes something. People who have been taught basic numeracy think of it as a familiar concept, because they are used to handling zero. But in mathematical notation, zero does not necessarily imply a concept of nothing: it just means there are no tens or no units or whatever classes of numbers happen to be in question. In any case, notational zero is a surprisingly late innovation in arithmetic, first seen in 7th-century AD inscriptions from Cambodia. Real zero is a joker in arithmetic: indifferent or destructive to the functions in which it appears.

When we begin to appreciate how difficult a concept that of nothing is, we are unsurprised to find that it is a late-comer to the range of ideas. Fittingly, perhaps, its origins are ultimately undetectable. Early in the Axial Age, the Upanishads spoke of a "great void", and Chinese texts of around the middle of the 1st millennium BC refer to a concept

*"Nothing will come of
nothing: speak again!"*

Shakespeare, *King Lear* (1608)

usually translated as "emptiness". But these seem to have
been thought of as spatially located beyond the material
universe, or occupying the interstices between the celestial
spheres; so, really, rather more than nothing. In the
emptiness of the Chinese writings, moreover, "winds" stir, but
perhaps they should be understood metaphorically. All we can say
for certain is that a notion of non-being was known to the sages
of the Upanishads, because they pour scorn on what they see as its
pretended coherence.

Non-existent vacuum
*During the 18th century,
scientists such as Joseph
Priestley disproved the
existence of a void by
separating out the
constituent parts of air.*

Presumably – and it can only be a presumption – the "void"
was postulated by thinkers who supposed that it was necessary to explain
motion (for how could anything move without resistance, except into
nothingness?). But it was rejected in most of the world for two reasons:
firstly, the discovery of air cast empirical doubt on the void; secondly,
there was an apparently invincible logical objection, formulated thus in
5th-century BC Greece by Leucippus: "the void is a non-being; and no
part of what is can be a non-being, for whatever is, strictly speaking,
is absolutely."

Once you have got your head around the concept of nothing,
anything is possible. It becomes possible to eliminate awkward realities
by classifying them as non-being – as Plato did with all matter, or to see
nothingness as the be-all and end-all of existence: the source and
destination of life and the context which makes it meaningful. This
unencouraging conclusion is advocated by some of the modern thinkers
who are called "existentialists". The idea of nothing even makes it
possible to imagine creation from nothing: the key to a tradition of
thought that is crucial to most modern people's religions.

READINGS

R.M. Gale's **Negation and
Non-being** (1976) is a good
philosophical introduction.

J.D. Barrow's **The Book
of Nothing** (2000) is
fascinating, wide-ranging,
and good on the science and
mathematics of zero.

R. Kaplan's **The Nothing
that Is** (1999) is an engaging,
clear, and straightforward
approach to the maths
involved.

Power of Thought

THE IDEA THAT THOUGHT ALONE CREATED THE UNIVERSE

Thought is obviously powerful as a stimulus to action. But how much deeper does its power reach? Thinkers in Ancient Egypt and India saw it as the starting-point of creation – the power that brought everything else into being. An Egyptian text known as the Memphite Theology (allegedly thousands of years old when it was recorded in about 700 BC) depicts Ptah "who gave birth to the gods": chaos personified and endowed with the power of thought. "Indeed all the divine order really came into being through what the heart thought and the tongue commanded."

The power of utterance was already familiar. The initiation of a dynamic process by thought alone – the priority of thought over utterance – was a new idea. There seems to be a parallel in India in the Mundaka, one of the earliest and surely one of the most poetic of the Upanishads, which may go back to before the first millennium BC. The world, says the text, began by emission from Brahman – the one who is real, infinite, and eternal – like sparks from flame or "as a spider extrudes and weaves its thread, as the hairs sprout from a living body, so from that which is imperishable arises all that appears".

So Ptah or Brahman thinks the world into being out of himself. This does not quite amount to the ultimate claim for the power of thought: the theory that the world was created out of nothing. "How could it be so," sneered a text of the Upanishads, "that being was produced from non-being?"

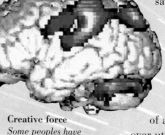

Creative force
Some peoples have conceived thought as the source of creation, specifically – according to ancient Hindu tradition – that of the world. Millions of electro-chemical reactions (illuminated above) help to shape our actions and sense of reality.

John the Evangelist identified Jesus with the Logos – the divine "Word" made human.

"In the beginning was the Word and the Word was with God and the Word was God."

The Gospel according to John 1: 1 (1st century AD)

Let there be... Bang!
The Big Bang theory, which posits an explosive redistribution of matter in space, resembles many early creation myths.

156

Most Classical-age philosophy recoiled from the idea. Plato's creator-god did not create the Universe out of nothing but re-arranged what was already there. The Big Bang theory resembles many early creation myths: matter was already there when the bang happened, dynamically re-distributing it in space.

Very rarely, peoples have thought up creation-myths of a rival kind, according to which the material world was preceded and produced by purely spiritual or emotional or intellectual being. According to the Winnebago people of North America, feelings are the source of creative power: their creator, "Earthmaker", realized that his feelings became things when the tears he shed in his loneliness became the primeval waters. For some Ancient Greek sages it was thought. Indeed, feeling and thought can be defined in terms of each other: feeling is thought unformulated, thought is feeling expressed in communicable ways.

The mysterious notion of a world spawned by an intellectual act was articulated in the age of the Christian gospels by a formula derived from Greek philosophy: "In the beginning was the Logos" (literally, the Thought) – usually translated as "the Word". The Old Testament has the most challenging account of this kind: the world is an extrusion of the power of thought: no more, no less. The idea is obviously problematical, but has gradually convinced most people who have thought about it, while becoming the unthinking assumption of most who have not.

READINGS

H.H. Price's **Thinking and Experience** (1953) is a good introduction to the problem, while G. Ryle's **On Thinking** (1979) famously proposed that thought is just chemical activity in the brain.

See S. Quirke's **Ancient Egyptian Religion** (1973) for the context of Memphite theology, while K. Ward's **Religion and Creation** (1996) takes an arresting, comparative approach.

Thought into matter
The North American Winnebago believe that the primeval waters and the material world were created from the tears of their creator.

No God but God

THE IDEA OF ONE ALL-POWERFUL DEITY

Jain street shrine
*Henotheistic religions,
such as Jainism in India,
represent a stage between
polytheism (multiple gods)
and monotheism (one god).
A single god may be
specially venerated but
not to the exclusion of
all other gods.*

Belief in a unique and omniscient creator is so familiar nowadays, through the popular religions of Judaism, Christianity, and Islam, that we no longer sense how strange it is. Until the first millennium BC, as far as we know, most people who thought about it assumed that the Universe had always existed. People who imagined an invisible world – beyond Nature and controlling it – supposed that it was diverse: crowded with gods, as Nature was crammed with creatures. Various attempts to systematize the world of the gods are documented in major civilizations in the thousand years or so before Christ. Greeks arrayed gods in order. Persians reduced them to two – one good, one evil. In Indian "henotheism", a multiplicity of gods collectively represented divine unity.

The most powerful formulation developed in the sacred writings of the Jews, probably quite early in the first half of the millennium. Yahweh, their tribal Deity, was, or became, their only God. Their writings called Him "jealous" – unwilling to allow divine status to any rival. Fierce enforcement of His sole right to worship was part of a supposed "covenant", in which Yahweh's favour was exchanged for obedience and veneration. Jews were not obliged to impose the Yahweh-cult on others: on the contrary, for most of history they treated it as a treasure too precious to share. Three developments, however, conspired to make the God of the Jews the favourite Deity of the world. First, the Jews' own "sacred" history of sacrifices and sufferings gave a compelling example of faith. Secondly, a Jewish splinter-group, which recognized Jesus Christ as the human face of God, opened its ranks to non-Jews: Christianity built up a vigorous and sometimes aggressive tradition of proselytization, and – thanks in part to a compelling gospel of salvation – became, over a period of nearly 2,000 years, the world's most widely diffused religion. Finally, early in the 7th century AD, the prophet Muhammad, who had studied Judaism and Christianity, incorporated the Jewish understanding of God in the rival religion he founded, which became in its turn – in many of the places where it was propagated – at least as appealing as Christianity. By the end of the second millennium AD, it had attracted almost as many adherents.

On its own, the idea of God's uniqueness might have remained a mere philosophical curiosity. But,

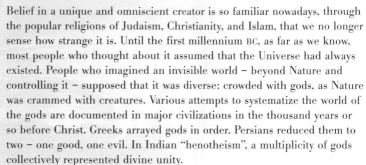

CONNECTIONS

For the possibility that the idea of God grew out of an earlier idea of a universal spirit-force, see **All Things Invisible** (p.18) and **May the Force...** (p.26).

The monotheistic tradition is pursued, with particular reference to Christianity, from **Love Above** (p.160) to **Render unto Caesar** (p.186), while Islam is discussed discretely in **Islam** (p.188).

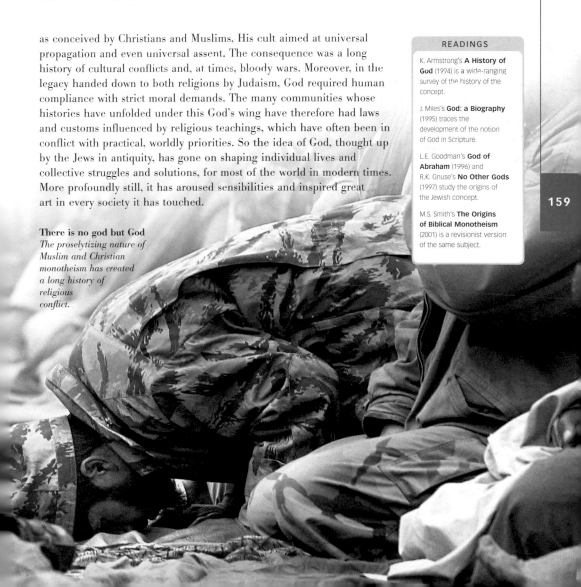

*"I am Yahweh your God... You shall have no other gods to rival me...
You shall not bow down to them or serve them. For I, Yahweh your
God, am a Jealous God, and punish a parent's fault... but I act with
faithful love towards thousands of those who love me and keep my
commandments."*

William Blake's
depiction of **God**
as architect of
creation.

***Exodus** 20: 1–6 (c. 1500 BC)*

as conceived by Christians and Muslims, His cult aimed at universal
propagation and even universal assent. The consequence was a long
history of cultural conflicts and, at times, bloody wars. Moreover, in the
legacy handed down to both religions by Judaism, God required human
compliance with strict moral demands. The many communities whose
histories have unfolded under this God's wing have therefore had laws
and customs influenced by religious teachings, which have often been in
conflict with practical, worldly priorities. So the idea of God, thought up
by the Jews in antiquity, has gone on shaping individual lives and
collective struggles and solutions, for most of the world in modern times.
More profoundly still, it has aroused sensibilities and inspired great
art in every society it has touched.

There is no god but God
*The proselytizing nature of
Muslim and Christian
monotheism has created
a long history of
religious
conflict.*

READINGS

K. Armstrong's **A History of
God** (1994) is a wide-ranging
survey of the history of the
concept.

J. Miles's **God: a Biography**
(1995) traces the
development of the notion
of God in Scripture.

L.E. Goodman's **God of
Abraham** (1996) and
R.K. Gnuse's **No Other Gods**
(1997) study the origins of
the Jewish concept.

M.S. Smith's **The Origins
of Biblical Monotheism**
(2001) is a revisionist version
of the same subject.

Love Above

THE IDEA THAT GOD LOVES PEOPLE

The chosen people
The idea of a loving God followed the Jewish doctrine of creation. Jews were the first to talk of a special loving relationship between God and his "chosen people".

It seems outrageously egocentric to suppose that the cosmos is all about us – a puny species, clinging to a tiny speck. Yet when the doctrine of a God of love emerged, it had intellectual as well as emotional appeal. The idea that God exists is perfectly reasonable. The idea that the Universe is a divine creation is intellectually demanding, but not impossible. Indeed, it is at least as commendable as the alternative view, which is that the Universe has always existed. The further idea, however, that God should take an abiding interest in creation and especially in some particular part of it seems rashly speculative. Most Greek thinkers of the Classical era ignored or repudiated it. Aristotle described a perfect Deity as one who needs nothing else, who has no uncompleted purposes, and who feels neither sensibility nor suffering. After all, God might have created the world capriciously or by mistake.

The claim that God's interest is focused on a particular part of creation – namely humankind – seems suspiciously self-centred. That God's interest should be one of love is stranger still. This most human of emotions that makes us weak, causes us suffering, and inspires us to self-sacrifice, challenges commonplace notions of what it might be to be omnipotent. So where does the idea come from? Who

Loving embrace
Evangelical churches call on worshippers to "feel" God's love, rather than think about it or act it out.

thought of it first? "The peak of the West is merciful if one cries out to her" was an Egyptian adage of the Middle Kingdom period, but this seems to belong to the context of the Egyptian view of divine justice, rather than divine love. "The benevolence of heaven" was a phrase much used in China around the mid-point of the millennium, but this, too, seems a long way short of love. Mo Tzu, a 5th-century-BC Chinese philosopher, anticipated Christianity over 400 years before Christ.

John the Evangelist, said to be the disciple closest to Christ, attended the crucifixion.

"For God so loved the world, that he gave his only begotten Son, that whosoever believeth in him should not perish, but have everlasting life."

The Gospel according to John 3: 16 (1st century AD)

As even Mo Tzu's philosophical adversaries admitted, he "would wear out his whole being for the benefit of humankind". But his vision of humankind bound by love was not theologically inspired; rather, he had a romantic vision of a supposed golden age of "Great Togetherness" in the primitive past.

The starting-point of the thinking which led to the idea of a God of love was raised by the ancient Jewish doctrine of creation. If God created the world, what was in it for him? The Old Testament compilers had no obvious answer, but they did postulate a special relationship between God and his "chosen people". Occasionally, they called this "faithful, everlasting love" and likened it to the feelings of a mother for a child at the breast. More usually, however, they spoke of a "covenant" – a two-sided bargain rather than freely given love. Late in the Axial Age, some Jewish groups reverted to the idea of divine love in an effort to re-define God.

The identification of God with love, which was enthusiastically taken up by Christ and his followers, was emotionally satisfying – a powerful, spiritual, creative emotion, known to everyone from experience. By making God's love universally embracing, rather than favouring a chosen race, Christianity acquired universal appeal. The creation could be shown as an act of love consistent with God's nature. But while a lot of problems were solved, another – why a loving God permits evil and suffering – was raised.

The ultimate sacrifice
Christ's sacrifice on the cross, to "wash away" the sins of humankind, is taken to be the ultimate proof of God's love. Among the numerous works of art it inspired is this painting by Diego Velasquez.

READINGS

M.J. Dodds's **The Unchanging God of Love** (1986) is a study of the doctrine of universal love in the form Aquinas gave it, while C.S. Lewis's **The Four Loves** (1960) sets the idea of divine love in context.

Mo Tzu's **Basic Writings** (c. 4th century BC) is a posthumous compilation.

LOVE ABOVE

CONNECTIONS

In **No God but God** (p.158), the starting-point of the Christian understanding of God is traced and then further covered between pp.166–73. On alternatives to it, see **Islam** (p.188), **Impossibilism** (p. 202), and **Atheist Faith** (p.324).

THINKING RELIGIONS

AD 0–1400

4

The Rise of the Great Faiths

The Axial Age was so fertile in ideas that the following centuries were unsurprisingly fallow. Major new religions – Christianity, the last great innovation of the Axial Age, and Islam – opened up areas for new thinking. Both owed their main principles to Judaism. Christ was, in effect, a freelance rabbi with a marginal following. All his early disciples were Jews, as were the twelve "apostles" to whom his movement was entrusted after his death. He declared that "salvation comes from the Jews", and all his recorded teachings were saturated in references to Jewish scriptures. His followers saw him as the Messiah foretold by Old-Testament prophecy, and made great efforts to ensure that the version of his life defined by tradition conformed to the prophets' predictions. Though Muhammad was not a Jew, a formative part of his life was spent in Palestine among Jewish communities, and his familiarity with Jewish scriptures is apparent on every page of the revelations confided to him by his angelic interlocutor and collected in the Quran.

From Judaism, both religions adopted the idea of the uniqueness of God and that of the creation from nothing. Both, however, modified Jewish ethical teaching as derived from the laws of Moses: Christianity, by replacing law with grace as an agent of salvation; Islam, by substituting laws of its own.

Circling the Ka'ba shrine
Islam (peace through "surrender to God") is a religion of laws. Pilgrimage to Mecca (above) is one of the five pillars of Islam that provide the foundation of Muslim life.

Both faiths found constituencies and arenas of expansion in and around the former Roman Empire. The results for both religions included a long series of debates about how law and religion connected and about how Jewish traditions could be made to square with those of classical learning.

In both cases, the task was made harder by the social contexts from which the new religions sprang. Christianity was "a religion of slaves and women" that appealed to victims of social exclusion and poverty. For the first couple of centuries of the religion's history, high-ranking converts tended to be shamefaced about the derogatory implications of conversion. Christ's human father was an artisan of modest background; his disciples were chosen from low social ranks. The gospel-writers were poorly educated; even the most intellectually able contributors to the New Testament – St Paul and St John – were not easily able to command the respect of the elite. Muhammad came from a prosperous family, but was self-marginalized by his ascetic practices and prophetic vocation, finding acceptance not in the streets of Mecca and Medina but among the desert nomads whose leader he became in exile. In consequence, the rise of the new religions has always seemed inseparable from the story of "the rise of barbarism" or, at least, of the conquest of elites from outside and below.

Meanwhile, the third great global faith – Buddhism – suffered a check. This is one of the great unsolved mysteries of history. In the 3rd century BC, when the Buddhist scriptures were codified, Asoka built an India-wide empire in which Buddhism was, in effect, the state religion. This might have been a springboard for Buddhism, rather as the Roman Empire was for Christianity, or that of Muhammad's successors for Islam. During the great periods of Christian and Muslim expansion, in what we think of as the early Middle Ages, Buddhism demonstrated a similar elasticity, overspilling India, attaining enormous influence in China, becoming the major influence on the spirituality of Japan, and colonizing much of south-east Asia. There were frequent moments when it seemed likely to take over the Chinese court and become the imperial religion in the world's mightiest state. Yet it never quite happened – the Taoist and Confucianist establishments in China kept it at bay.

Buddhism did not capture exclusively the institutional allegiance or elite devotion of any state, except in Burma (Myanmar) and, at a relatively late stage, in Siam (Thailand) and Tibet. Elsewhere Buddhism survived, and continued to make enormous contributions to culture, but the rise of Hinduism largely displaced it from India and competed with it in much of western Indochina. Buddhism did not compete with Islam and Christianity in the global arena until the late 16th century, when a new era of expansion in central Asia began. It was only in the 20th century that Buddhism began to make extensive conversions elsewhere in the world.

Lord of beginnings
In India, the rise of Hinduism – whose gods include the popular Ganesha – displaced Buddhism from its birthplace.

From the Axial Age to modernity, the ideas that produced the world that we now inhabit tended to be overwhelmingly of Christian and Muslim origin; and Christian rather than Muslim, because Christianity demonstrated, in the long run, greater cultural "elasticity", or adaptability. Since Muhammad himself, all advocates of Islam have represented it as a way of life, with strong prescriptions about society, politics, and codes of behaviour. This makes it highly suitable for some societies, unworkable in others. You can map the global reach of Islam and see how its triumphs have been confined to a visible belt of the world – a swathe of fairly consistent environments and social traditions of the Old World, between the temperate zone of the northern hemisphere and the tropics. Outside this zone, it has spread recently, but only by migrations and, in the case of North America, by the rise of a "Black Muslim" movement.

Christianity is a much less prescriptive religion, with a more malleable moral code. Throughout its history, it has been able to penetrate just about every type of society and every habitable environment, undergoing numerous transformations, and experiencing the arrival of many new ideas along the way.

Everlasting flame
The Western monotheistic tradition sprang from Judaism, in which candles – such as this ceremonial menorah – are a reminder of God's eternal presence.

Manjusri on a lion
*Mahayana Buddhism,
represented here by the
sage Manjusri, promoted
ideas of universal love.*

READINGS

I. Singer's **The Nature of
Love** (1989) is a good
introduction to the
philosophical problem
of what love means.

C.S. Lewis's **The Four Loves**
(1971) is a great classic essay
setting out the idea of divine
love in the context of more
worldly notions of love.

Yi-Pao Mei's **Motse: The
Neglected Rival of
Confucius** (1973) offers a
comprehensive and thematic
introduction to Mo Tzu's
thought.

Big Brotherhood

THE IDEA OF UNIVERSAL LOVE

Christ added universal appeal to an ethic of loving one's neighbour, which
emerged from a Jewish tradition, and perhaps borrowed from Chinese and
Indian philosophies.

Wide sympathies have always challenged narrow nationalism. "I am
a citizen of the world," said Diogenes. By the time of Epictetus, however,
around AD 100, the same maxim meant something new. God is the father
of men: all men are brothers. Slaves are the equals of other men – a
poignant doctrine, since Epictetus was a freed slave and walked with a
limp sustained through the cruelty of a former master. While these
sentiments developed in the Greek tradition, they were paralleled – and
perhaps fed – from among the Jews. Already, in the century before the
birth of Christ, the ascetically inclined Jewish sect of the Essenes were
questioning the Jewish self-perception of a race uniquely beloved of God.
Their precepts enjoining love of neighbour and "of all men with a true
heart" flowed into the teachings of Jesus.

An unanswered question is whether these developments in the
West were connected with similar ideas in China and India about
common humanity and the common obligations of care we owe each
other. They may have been independent developments, but by the
time of Christ, the transmission of culture across Eurasia had
been facilitated by travellers on the Silk Road, which is
documented from 138 BC onwards. So Chinese and Indian
ideas were flowing westwards.

Mo Tzu therefore perhaps deserves credit for this
idea. According to his teachings, in early 5th-century BC
China, loving all meant treating all equally: it was therefore
a doctrine of social equality, with a message addressed
particularly to those in positions of power. The teachings
of Buddha – which resemble those of Christianity in being
addressed to individuals – could have represented a sort of

The teachings of **Christ**
give one of the clearest
expressions of the idea
of universal love.

*"There is neither Jew nor Greek, there is neither
bond nor free, there is neither male nor
female: for ye are all one in Christ Jesus."*

Letter of Paul to the Galatians 3: 28, 1st century AD

One happy family
*Several religions promote
universal love, but most
people experience only a hint
of what this might mean at
times of celebration.*

"halfway house" of transmission between China and the Near East. Buddha enjoined love for the sake of the good of the self and Mo Tzu for that of society, but teachers of the Buddhist tradition known as Mahayana developed a distinctive idea in the 2nd century BC: love was meritorious only if it was selfless and unrewarded – a free gift of the enlightened towards all their fellow-humans. This seems very close to Christ's way of understanding it.

Since then, this has been, perhaps, the world's most startling case of an idea honoured in the breach. Almost everybody can see its value. Almost nobody practises it. Yet it has been an enormously influential aspiration. The effort to love universally may be beyond ordinary human competence, but it inspires successful attempts to love selectively and to stretch the limits of one's altruism.

Early influence
The Dead Sea Scrolls were the work of the Jewish Essene sect, whose belief in God's universal love is believed to have influenced Jesus's teachings.

Word Made Flesh

THE IDEA OF DIVINE INCARNATION

Incarnate father
The Reverend Sun Myung Moon believes he is the reincarnation of God, sent to rectify Jesus's failure to marry and become humanity's "True Parent".

CONNECTIONS

Related ways of thinking about the Church are explored on pp.168–73. The comparison with Islam can be pursued in **Islam** (p.188). For later departures, see **Impossibilism** (p.202), **Cleansing the Temple** (p.254), and **God Is Dead** (p.324).

The claim that a particular historic personage was God incarnate is the defining feature of Christianity: but how distinctively Christian is it? After Christ's death, the doctrine that he was God incarnate gained ground. St John's gospel does not just tell the story of a human "Son of God" or even of a man who represented God to perfection, but of the incarnate *Logos* – the thought or reason that existed before time began. Sonhood was a metaphor expressing the enfleshment of incorporeal divinity.

Ideas of a similar kind, however, are older and more widespread. In ancient shamanism, in divine-king myth, in the habit of human or, indeed, animal disguise evinced by so many ancient gods, the idea that a god might take flesh was well known for thousands of years before the time of Christ. Buddha was more than human in the opinion of some of his followers: enlightenment united him with transcendent reality. Anthropologists with a sceptical attitude to Christianity, from Sir James Frazer in the 19th century to Edmund Leach in the late 20th, have found scores of cases of incarnation – often culminating in a sacrifice of the man-god similar to Christ's own – among the religions of the world.

In the 4th century AD, a similar idea surfaced in a Hindu context: Vishnu appeared on Earth in various human lives, undergoing conception, birth, suffering, and death. Islamic (or originally Islamic) sects have sometimes adopted heroes as incarnations of God. For the Druzes of Lebanon, the mad 11th-century Caliph al-Hakim fulfils this destiny. So how new was the Christian idea and how distinctive did it remain?

In all these other cases, as in the many reincarnations of gods and Buddhas with which the history of south, east, and central Asia is strewn, the model was similar: a spirit "entered" a human body – variously before, at, or after birth. The human being was either displaced by the god, or persisted alongside the god. But in the Christian model, the body itself was divinized: Christ's human and divine natures did not remain entirely distinct, but were joined in one "person".

John the Evangelist
related the divinity of Jesus to the Greek idea of Logos.

"The Word was made flesh and dwelt among us and we have seen His glory... full of grace and truth."

The Gospel according to John 1: 14 (1st century AD)

Mortal remains
Christ was at his most human when he was dead, so his purported burial shroud (known as the Turin Shroud), which bears an image venerated as miraculous, is a potent relic of his humanity.

READINGS

G. O'Collins's **Incarnation** (2002) is a straightforward but stimulating account of the doctrine.

B. Hume's **Mystery of the Incarnation** (1999) is a valuable and spiritually sensitive introduction.

S. Davis's (ed.) **The Trinity** (2002) is an outstanding collection of essays setting the doctrine in its theological context.

The tenacity with which Christian theology has always insisted on this formula shows how important it is: that importance, I think, arises from the fact that it really is distinctively Christian.

The idea was copied many times: a constant stream of so-called messiahs claimed the same attributes as Christ or were credited with them by their supporters. But this seems to have been effectively an unrecyclable idea. After Christ, it never again seemed convincing to large numbers of people.

Incarnate lover
The Hindu god Vishnu has many human incarnations. Krishna, depicted here (also known as the "divine lover") is Vishnu's ninth incarnation.

One in Substance

THE CHRISTIAN IDEA OF THE TRINITY

Imperial arbiter
*In AD 325, the Roman
Emperor Constantine
convened the Council of
Nicaea to settle a squabble
within the Church over the
precise nature of Christ's
divinity. In a diplomatic
master-stroke, the key
idea of* homoousion –
*"of one being" – was
established.*

As a religion of universal appeal Christianity has one big disadvantage: a
bafflingly complex theology, involving a single deity that is the union of
three aspects: Father, Son, and Holy Spirit. This complexity excludes those
who do not understand it and divides those who do.

In the early 4th century, a Church Council devised a formula for
overcoming that problem. Most religions present a set of doctrines
– usually ascribed to an authoritative founder – and invite or
defy dissent. Really, however, heresy always comes first:
orthodoxy is refined out of competing opinions. In Christian
history, struggles among the apostles are evident: was the
Church Jewish or universal? Was its doctrine confided to
all the apostles or only some? Did Christians earn
salvation or was it conferred irrespective of
personal virtue? In the long run, some of the
most contentious issues within the early
Christian Church concerned the nature of
God. Traditional formulae seem full of
fudge or compromise: one God in three
Persons, which – as an early creed, still
endorsed by most Christians, says – "are
not three incomprehensibles but one
incomprehensible". That this God should have,
or in some sense be, a Son, and that the Son
should be both fully God and fully human, are
slippery doctrines, defiantly rich in apparent
absurdity. The gospel writers and St Paul had
some notion that Christ was more than just a
man and that he participated, in a profound
and peculiar sense, in the nature of God; but
their utterances on this were ambiguous, vague,
and clouded by affected mystery. It took extremely subtle
thinking to make the doctrine of the human God seem
consistent and reasonable.

The key idea was formulated early in the 4th
century AD at the Council of Nicaea. Most communities
that call themselves Christian still subscribe to its
creed. Its term for the relationship of the Father to

READINGS

W.H. Bright's (ed.) **The
Definitions of the
Catholic Faith** (1874) is
a classic work.

H. Chadwick's **The Early
Church** (1993) is the best
historical survey, while
J. Danoelou's **History of
Early Christian Doctrine**
(1977) gives the theological
background.

"The Divine Word must be one with the God of the Universe and the Holy Spirit must dwell in God, and so it is absolutely necessary that the Divine Triad be gathered and enclosed in unity."

Pope St Dionysius, *Papal Epistle* (AD 267)

the Son was *homoousion*, a Greek word traditionally translated as "consubstantial", and rather inaccurately rendered in modern translations as "of one being" or "of one nature". This kept at bay constructions of Christ's godhead that might weaken the Christian message, including suggestions that his divinity should be understood only in some metaphorical sense or that his "sonship" should be taken literally. Though Christians continued to disagree about how the third party in the Trinity – the Holy Spirit – fitted into the picture, the *homoousion* idea effectively fixed the limits of debate on the issue. The "consubstantiality" of Father and Son had to embrace the Holy Spirit.

Who thought of the idea? The concept of *homoousion* was one of many bandied about among theologians of the period. Its use is attributed to the Roman Emperor Constantine, who presided over the Nicene Council. He was a recent convert to Christianity and theologically illiterate, but he was an expert power-broker and knew a good negotiating formula when he saw one.

As well as in theological debate, the inseparability, or the single nature, of the persons of the Trinity was elaborated in folksy images developed by preachers. The most famous were St Patrick's shamrock – one plant, three leaves; one nature, three persons – and the clay brick that St Spiritus crushed before his congregation and which miraculously dissolved into its constituent earth, water, and fire. These have been the prevalent images on which most Christians have relied for explanations of their intellectually elusive faith.

CONNECTIONS

For the context of Christian theology, see **Big Brotherhood** (p.166), **This Is my Body** (p.184), and **God's Free Love** (p.172). For related but different ideas of God, see **All Is One** (p.104), **No god but God** (p.158), and **Islam** (p.188).

Deposition of Christ
The Church's idea of the Trinity is depicted in this 1798 painting by Antonio Canova: the radiance of the Father, the mortality of the Son, and the luminous transfiguration of the Holy Spirit.

Three in one
St Patrick used the shamrock as a natural analogy for the Trinity – "one plant, three leaves; one nature, three persons".

God's Free Love

THE CHRISTIAN IDEA OF GRACE

The most radical idea St Paul contributed to Christianity proved also to be the most inspiring and the most problematic. St Paul has been praised or blamed for creating or corrupting Christianity. He certainly developed Christ's teaching, perhaps in ways Jesus did not envisage. One of his most dazzling contributions was the idea of grace.

Grace means that God grants favours to people – gifts in this world and salvation in the next – independently of the recipients' deserts. "It is through grace that you have been saved," St Paul wrote to the Ephesians – not, as he constantly averred, through any merit of our own. Indeed, in an extreme form of the doctrine, which Paul seems to have favoured at some times and which the Church has always formally upheld, recipients have no merit: they are children of original sin and any good they do is the effect of God's favour. "No distinction is made," Paul wrote to the Romans. "All are sinned and lack God's glory, and all are justified by the free gift of his grace."

Clearly this is a liberating and appealing idea. No one can be self-damned by sin. No one is irredeemable if God chooses otherwise. The value of the way a life is lived is calibrated not by external compliance with rules and rites, but by the depth of the individual person's response to grace. The idea can, however, be taken too far. St Paul hammered home his claim that God chose the recipients of grace "before the world was made" – an apparently premature decision on God's part, which made the world seem pointless. Some heretics treated it as a licence to do what they liked: in a state of grace, their crimes were no sin but "holy and faultless". Some of Paul's apostolic colleagues

Counting the beads
Catholics use the rosary – a cycle of prayers counted on beads – to concentrate the mind on scenes from the life of Christ and his mother. Recitations of the rosary may be required by the priest as an act of penance for sins confessed.

Grace made it possible for **St Augustine** (AD 354–430) to be both a sinner and a saint.

"A man's free will serves only to lead him into sin, if the way of truth be hidden from him."

St Augustine, *Confessions* (c. AD 400)

READINGS

M. Grant's **St Paul** (2000) is an excellent readable account of the saint, while A.F. Segal's **Paul the Convert** (1990) is good on the Jewish background.

G. Greene's **The Power and the Glory** (1940) is a powerful novel inspired by the problem of grace.

disapproved of this doctrine, which apparently exonerated Christians from doing good. James issued what modern spin-doctors would call a "clarification", insisting that to "love your neighbour as yourself" was an ineluctable rule and that "faith without deeds is useless". A long controversy began between those who saw grace as a collaborative venture, in which the individual has an active role, and those who felt that to acknowledge any initiative on the sinner's part diminished God's omnipotence and love. At the Reformation, the latter group seceded from the Catholic Church, citing St Paul in support of their views, and founded Protestantism.

CONNECTIONS

The idea of grace is related to the idea of God's love discussed in **Love Above** (p.160). On the overlap with ideas about predestination, see **Deo Volente** (p.96) and **Damned Time** (p.178). On human responsibility for goodness, see **Ethical Beings** (p.136).

No one is damned by sin
As long as they repent, even those who have committed serious sins can be saved by God's grace, including those, such as the Mafia characters in the Godfather *film trilogy, who have made a career of crime.*

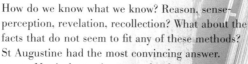

Lightning Flash

THE IDEA OF ILLUMINATION

CONNECTIONS

Communication with transcendent beings is also discussed in **Fly Like an Eagle** (p.20) and **The Vision Thing** (p.22). For more on how knowledge is knowable, see **The New Illusion** (p.108), **Not a Horse** (p.116), and **The Big Idea** (p.274).

How do we know what we know? Reason, sense-perception, revelation, recollection? What about the facts that do not seem to fit any of these methods? St Augustine had the most convincing answer.

Mystical experiences tend to be unimpressive – indeed, uncommunicable – to those who have not had them. That is why the ideas of mystics rarely appear in this book. But St Augustine was no mystic. His idea of what is usually called "illumination" does not involve any extraordinary experience; merely the recognition that only by direct mental apprehension can we attain the knowledge that is beyond reason or the senses – ideas, St Augustine thought, that God puts into our minds. These include mathematical axioms, or the existence of such ideals as beauty or goodness, or perhaps even the existence of God Himself.

The saint described illumination as validation "in that inward house of my thoughts, without help of the mouth or the tongue, without any sound of syllables". This suggests, I think, how he got the idea. His way of putting it suggests a deepening of self-awareness induced by the habit of silent reading – a practice then thought to be rare and mysterious. The saint's personality also helped to shape his thinking. Like many people of genius, he was selectively humble and felt inadequate to understand unaided all the mysteries of life. So what was unintelligible to his own mental powers had to be illuminated by flashes from God.

Plato had a similar theory: that knowledge is innate and we become aware of it through recollection. The purpose of education is to remind us of it.

Transcendent meditation
Many forms of mysticism use meditation to expand self-awareness. Followers of the Indian guru, the Maharishi Mahesh Yogi (shown with The Beatles in 1968) sometimes levitate as well.

Indeed, this seems to have been a primitive Greek idea: the normal Greek word for truth was *aletheia* – literally, "things unforgotten". It is one thing, however, to say that we retrieve knowledge from within ourselves by our own efforts, and quite another to make us reliant on impressions from outside. Without necessarily intending it, St Augustine had produced an intellectual licence for mystics to represent their transports as revelations.

For the history of Christianity, this was a serious matter. As well as reason, experience, scripture, and tradition, there was another way to acquire knowledge – every individual's unique hotline to God. Mysticism had been practised among Christians from the time of the apostles – St Paul twice describes what seem like mystical experiences. But the purpose of the mystics' raptures was always to get a sense of union with God, an emotional self-identification with His loving nature. St Augustine's idea made it possible to get explicit messages, which, potentially, might conflict with the Church. The Church therefore had to police mysticism (and the heresies it might reveal) very carefully. It also meant that Western mysticism became largely a matter of introspective meditation. The alternative of "nature mysticism" – the contemplation of the external world in an effort to arouse a mystical response – never commanded much intellectual respect.

Penetrating moment
Perhaps divine intervention can help us to know the unknowable. Gianlorenzo Bernini's sculpture of The Ecstasy of St Theresa *(1652) portrays one such revelatory moment.*

*Ecclesiastes describes the attempt to "see the **light**", or search for meaning in life.*

"Wisdom exceedeth folly as light excelleth darkness."

Ecclesiastes 2: 13

READINGS

R.H. Nash's **The Light of the Mind** (1969) is a clear and shrewd study of St Augustine's idea of illumination.

D. Knowles's **What is Mysticism?** (1967) is the best short introduction to the subject.

The high life
The quest for communion with God has led to some extreme forms of devotion. St Simeon, depicted here in a 16th-century Russian icon, was a "pillar hermit" said to have spent 36 years alone on top of his column.

LIGHTNING FLASH

Dumbing Up

THE IDEA THAT TOO MUCH LEARNING IS BAD

Picture message
Illiterates learned Christianity in the Middle Ages from pictures. This stained glass detail from Chartres Cathedral shows Christ appearing before Mary Magdalene.

"The folly of God," said Christ, "is wiser than the wisdom of men." The gospels were badly written by the standards of the schools of the day. St Paul was the cleverest apostle, but he wrote appalling Greek.

The elite of the Roman world adopted Christianity in love of its doctrines but in revulsion at the way they were expressed. In the late 4th century AD, St Jerome, a learned, fastidious, and aristocratic bishop, found himself drawn back to the elegance of the pagan classics, and repelled by the "rudeness" of the prophets. In a vision he told Christ he was a Christian. "You lie," said Christ. "You are a follower of Cicero," referring to his love of classical writings. Jerome vowed never to read "good" books again, and when he translated the Bible into Latin – the version that has remained the standard text of the Catholic Church to this day – he deliberately chose a vulgar style, much inferior to the classical Latin he used and recommended in his own letters.

At about the same time, St Augustine found many classical texts distastefully erotic. Two hundred years later, Pope Gregory the Great denounced the use of the classics in teaching, since "there is no room in the same mouth for both Christ and Jupiter". In the 13th century, followers of St Francis, who enjoined a life of poverty, claimed to renounce learning on the grounds that it was a kind of wealth.

A similar trend can be detected in Islam, at least from the 11th century onwards, extolling popular wisdom and mystical insights against classical philosophy. "Rather," wrote al-Ghazali, one of the great Muslim apologists for mysticism, "belief is a light God bestows… sometimes through an explainable conviction from within, sometimes by a dream, sometimes through a pious man… sometimes through one's own state of bliss." In practice, in all these cases, mistrust of learning was a mere

Forrest Gump, the tale of a simple man with a big heart touched a popular nerve.

"I'm not a smart man, but I know what love is."

Forrest Gump, in the film *Forrest Gump* (1994)

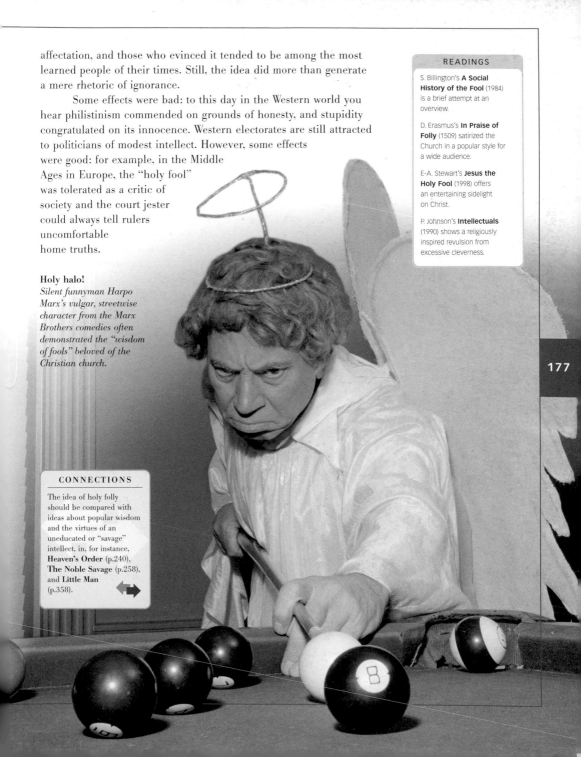

affectation, and those who evinced it tended to be among the most learned people of their times. Still, the idea did more than generate a mere rhetoric of ignorance.

Some effects were bad: to this day in the Western world you hear philistinism commended on grounds of honesty, and stupidity congratulated on its innocence. Western electorates are still attracted to politicians of modest intellect. However, some effects were good: for example, in the Middle Ages in Europe, the "holy fool" was tolerated as a critic of society and the court jester could always tell rulers uncomfortable home truths.

Holy halo!
Silent funnyman Harpo Marx's vulgar, streetwise character from the Marx Brothers comedies often demonstrated the "wisdom of fools" beloved of the Christian church.

CONNECTIONS

The idea of holy folly should be compared with ideas about popular wisdom and the virtues of an uneducated or "savage" intellect, in, for instance, **Heaven's Order** (p.240), **The Noble Savage** (p.258), and **Little Man** (p.358).

READINGS

S. Billington's **A Social History of the Fool** (1984) is a brief attempt at an overview.

D. Erasmus's **In Praise of Folly** (1509) satirized the Church in a popular style for a wide audience.

E-A. Stewart's **Jesus the Holy Fool** (1998) offers an entertaining sidelight on Christ.

P. Johnson's **Intellectuals** (1990) shows a religiously inspired revulsion from excessive cleverness.

Moral maze
According to St Augustine,
God is unconstrained by
human limitations of time
and place, seeing all of our
lives simultaneously. The
choices we make, such as in
this maze, do not undermine
God's omniscience.

READINGS

W. Hasker's **God, Time, and
Knowledge** (1989) is a good
introduction to the Christian
idea of predestination.

J. Farrelly's **Predestination,
Grace, and Free Will** (1964)
and G. Berkouwer's **Divine
Election** (1960) discuss the
theological implications.

Damned Time

THE CHRISTIAN IDEA OF PREDESTINATION

Time was a big problem for Christians until St Augustine, one of the world's clearest-headed thinkers, addressed the question at the end of the 4th century AD. Christ's mission to save humankind came at a particular moment in history – so what about the salvation of everyone up to then?

Worse still, if God was omniscient, how could people obtain that precious "free will" that was supposed to be one of God's great gifts to us? If He knew "from before time began" – as St Paul put it – who was going to end up in heaven, the damned had no real chance of redemption. Where did that leave God's claim to be "just" and "righteous"? St Paul imagined his correspondents asking: "How can He ever blame anyone, since no one can oppose His will?" St Augustine endorsed St Paul's chillingly logical opinion: since everyone is sinful, justice demands damnation for all. It is a measure of God's mercy that He exempts those He has chosen.

It was a powerful solution – but forbidding, unloving, and unappealing to Christians, who prized God for His generosity, not His justice. A better answer arose from another problem Augustine illuminated: the problem

St Paul's letters spread the "good news" of unearned salvation.

"He decided beforehand who were the ones destined... It was those so destined that he called, those that he called, he justified."

Paul's letter to the Romans (c. AD 57)

of time. He wrote a remarkable dialogue with his own mind, in the course of which he discovered that "'tis in thee that I measure my times. It seems to me that time is nothing else but a stretching out in length; but of what I know not and I marvel if it be not of the very mind."

Time is a mental construct, a way we devise of organizing our experience, not part of the real world known to God. God's mind can do rather better than ours, apprehending all of what we think of as time from the outside – simultaneously, if you like. Time can also be like a journey. On the ground, you might feel as if New York precedes Chicago, which in turn precedes Los Angeles. But from a godlike height, it is possible to see them all at once. Shortly after Augustine, Boethius, the philosopher and finance minister of the Ostrogothic kingdom of Italy, proposed this as a solution to the problem of predestination (the question of "fixed fate" – whether souls are to be saved or damned).

Most alternative efforts have separated foreknowledge from predestination. God knows in advance what your free will shall induce you to do. So he can see you today making a free choice tomorrow. "If I foreknew, foreknowledge had no influence on their fault," are words Milton put into God's mouth, concerning the fall of Adam and Eve. This seems just about intelligible. Equally, it seems unnecessary to see human freedom as compromising God's omnipotence. Free will could be a concession He chooses to make but has the power to revoke.

Thanks to the expediency of these arguments, Christian philosophy has always managed to preserve an uneasy balance between free will and predestination in the doctrine of the Church. On the one hand, there is an over-optimistic view of human nature unravaged by original sin; on the other, there is a doom-fraught conviction that most of us are helplessly damned. Even so, those who tend to one or other extreme are always dropping out of communion with other Christians. The Calvinists split with the Catholics and the Armenians with the Calvinists over this issue, and it has generated untold controversy. Islam has developed the idea of *Bada* – in a nutshell, the claim that God can change his mind in favour of a repentant sinner – but the orthodoxy of this has remained a matter of dispute.

Power and the glory
An omniscient God, as imagined here in Henry Stock's painting (1911), has always been difficult to reconcile with "free will".

CONNECTIONS

On divine grace, see **God's Free Love** (p.172). For other ideas about the afterlife, see **Buried Goods** (p.34), **Conquering Death** (p.92), and **Return of the Soul** (p.140). Materialist forms of determinism are discussed in **Intelligence Test** (p.382).

Making a difference
By risking his life to save over 100,000 Jews during World War II, Raoul Wallenberg, a Swedish diplomat, thwarted what appeared to be inevitable.

Wicked World

THE IDEA THAT CREATION IS EVIL

Natural urge
Sex is instinctive, therefore animal. So, for some religions, it is human to resist its urging. According to St Augustine, celibacy is a triumph of free will.

READINGS

J. Bowker's **Beyond Worlds** (1997) is fundamental, while G. Filorano's **Gnosticism** (1990) is a good introduction.

P. Brown's **The Body and Society** (1988) is a brilliant investigation of the early history of Christian celibacy, while P. Aries and A. Bejin's **Western Sexuality** (1985) enjoys a classic status.

Christianity faced a high-minded challenge from thinkers intolerant of the world's imperfections. In the struggle between good and evil, creation seemed to be on the Devil's side. Plato had said the world was a mere shadow of perfection: so, for some of his readers, the world was bad. Many teachers of the Axial Age, including Zoroaster and Lao Tzu, had thought they could detect a perpetual struggle between good and evil: so didn't the world – with all its woes – belong to the evil part? In Christian and Jewish traditions, the world was the realm of the Prince of Darkness. Matter was evil. So, therefore, was the human body. The world, the flesh, and the Devil formed one horrific continuum.

This idea, called gnosis – literally, "knowledge" – by those who held it, was problematic for Christians. Christian gnostics had to deny the Incarnation: God could not have been so tasteless as to be born of woman, take on the foul pollutant of flesh, and allow himself the indignity of the cross. The world cannot have been God's creation: it must have been made by a "demiurge" or rival god. Most Christian thinkers realised that this would make God meaningless and Christianity pointless. But gnosticism left an indelible legacy. Martyr-cults seem indebted to gnostic ennui: the world is darkness; the body a prison of the soul; martyrdom is escape. In real revulsion from the flesh, ascetics have punished their bodies with the lash, starvation-level fasting, and hair shirts. Celibacy, which was strong in the early Church, probably owed a lot to gnostic influence: it re-surfaced in the menu of disciplines recommended by a long series of heresies throughout the Middle Ages. In his youth, St. Augustine had subscribed to one of them, despising reproduction as a means of perpetuating diabolic power.

St Augustine of Hippo (AD 354–430) believed that sexual desire was diabolic temptation.

"Out of the squalid yearnings of my flesh bubbled up the clouds and scum of puberty... so that I could not tell the serenity of love from the swamp of lust."

St Augustine of Hippo, *Confessions* (c. AD 400)

CONNECTIONS

On related ideas of good and evil see **Seeing Double** (p.46), **Good and Evil** (p.48), and **Getting Better** (p.252). For other ideas about the nature of sex, see **A Family Affair** (p.40), **Getting Together** (p.46), and **Love Conquers All** (p.200).

He formulated a new objection to sex on the grounds that it infringes freedom of will. A modern way of putting it might be to say that sex is instinctive, therefore animal, so we make ourselves more human by resisting its temptations. An ancient or medieval way of putting it is to say that you do not choose your sex-urges, so they are an infringement of your freedom of will. God wants you to be free, so sex urges must come from the Devil.

This argument has shaped Christian ambivalence about sex ever since. Still, most religions strongly favour sex. Some religions delight in it, for example, Tantrism or the Taoist tradition of *fang-chung shu*, which seeks immortality through "arts of the inner chamber". Some – including Christianity – selectively license or even sanctify sex, seeing the loving union of man and woman as a metaphor for the mutual love of God and His creatures. Many proscribe infertile sexual practices, such as onanism and homosexuality, or others that are thought to be anti-social or subversive of marriage, such as incest, promiscuity, or sexual infidelity. Moreover, religions that value celibacy or virginity do not necessarily do so out of disapproval of sex, but in esteem of a sacrifice made for God.

Celebration of sex
Hindu and Jain traditions celebrates sexual union, as seen in the erotic carvings that adorn the temples of Khajuraho, India.

Devilish temptation
The fleshly temptations of "red light" districts, would seem to some to be confirmation that the world is the work of the devil.

Centre of the World

THE IDEA OF CHINESE SUPERIORITY

Sinocentric vision
This 18th-century Chinese world map demonstrates China's self-perception of its central position within a global setting.

The Forbidden City
The location, size, and extensive layout of the Forbidden City of Beijing reflected the emperor's status as the Son of Heaven. Designed as an imperial palace for the Ming dynasty, who moved to Beijing in 1421, it took only 16 years to build.

"Middle Kingdom" or "Central Country" is one of the most persistent names the Chinese have given their land. In a sense it is a modest designation, since it implicitly acknowledges a world beyond China, as certain alternative names – "All Under Heaven", "All Within the Four Seas" – do not. But it conveys unmistakable connotations of superiority: a vision of the world in which the barbarian rim is undeserving of the benefits and unrewarding of the bother of Chinese conquest.

Orthodox Confucianism stated that barbarians could be attracted to Chinese rule by example: awareness of China's manifest superiority would induce them to submit without the use of force. To some extent, this improbable formula worked. Chinese culture did attract neighbouring peoples. Koreans and the Japanese largely adopted it; many central and south-east Asian peoples were deeply influenced by it. Conquerors of China from the outside have always been seduced by it.

It is generally said that the name of Central Country was first adopted by the Zhou dynasty, towards the end of the second millennium BC. China constituted all the world that counted, and the rest of humankind were barbarians clinging to the rim. This principle could be compromised from time to time, and barbarian kingdoms ranked in greater or lesser proximity to China's unique perfection. At intervals, powerful barbarian rulers attracted titles of equal resonance or could exact treaties on equal terms from the Chinese. Tribute due to patrons of equal, or even superior, status could often be extorted from a court willing to purchase security, though the Chinese clung to the convenient fiction that such remittances were no more than acts of condescension.

"Who would exhaust China's resources to quarrel with serpents and swine?"

Ou-yang Hsiu, Chinese poet (11th century)

The pig and the snake are two of the 12 signs of the **Chinese horoscope**.

READINGS

S. de Grazia's (ed.) **Masters of Chinese Political Thought** (1973) has some useful texts, while Jung-shen Tao's **Two Sons of Heaven** (1988) is extremely interesting on the consequences of Chinese universalism.

W.I. Cohen's **East Asia at the Centre** (2001) discusses the context of a Sinocentric vision of the world.

J. Harley and D. Woodward's (eds) **Cartography in the Traditional East and Southeast Asian Societies** (Vol 2, Book 2) (1994) gives a fascinating, illustrated insight.

In what we think of as the Middle Ages, the name reflected a world picture, with Mount Chongshan in Henan province at the exact centre of the composition, the true nature of which was much disputed among scholars. In the 12th century, for instance, the prevailing opinion was that, since the world was spherical, its "centre" was a purely metaphorical expression. The world, represented in the most detailed surviving maps of the 12th century, was divided into China and the barbarian countries.

In 1610, Matteo Ricci, the visiting Jesuit who introduced Western science to China, was criticized for failing to place China centrally in his "Great Map of Ten Thousand Countries". This did not mean that Chinese scholars had an illogical world-view, only that the symbolic nature of China's centrality had to be acknowledged in representations of the world. Cartographic conventions do, however, tell us something about the self-perception of those who devise them: like the fixing of the Greenwich meridian, which defines one's place in the world by one's distance from the capital of the British Empire; or Mercator's projection, which exaggerates the importance of northerly countries.

China was psychologically unprepared for the experience of the 19th century, when European superiority, first in war, then in wealth, became apparent. China seemed stunned into backwardness, from which it is only beginning to re-emerge today.

"Foreign devils"
The 1900 Boxer Rebellion was a reaction to the presence of too many "foreign devils" in China. It was quickly quelled by an international relief force that occupied Beijing.

CENTRE OF THE WORLD

This Is My Body

THE IDEA OF THE CHRISTIAN CHURCH

Immersed in faith
For Christ's followers, the sense of being God's "elect" is perpetuated by the rite of baptism – mimicking Jesus's own baptism by John the Baptist in the river Jordan.

At his death, Christ left his disciples with the idea that his presence could be perpetuated in a physical way in the bodies of his followers. Before this time, the traditions of the great teachers of the Axial Age were preserved in two main ways: some sages had followers or initiates who were expert in their own doctrines, while the teachings of the Jewish prophets were entrusted to an entire "chosen people".

Initially, Christ's legacy was perpetuated in both ways: a body of apostles to whom his message was confided, and Jewish congregations who regarded their Master as their traditionally prophesied Messiah. During the first few Christian generations, as the religion embraced large numbers of gentiles, a new model arose: that of the Church, in which Christ's continuing presence in the world was collectively embodied, and which spoke with his authority.

The idea of a tradition of apostleship was maintained among cadres of Christian community leaders, chosen by "apostolic succession" and called "overseers" or "bishops". The sense of a chosen people, meanwhile, was perpetuated by rites of baptism, which guaranteed a place among God's "elect", literally "chosen" for salvation. Moreover, after the Romans destroyed the temple of Jerusalem in AD 70, Christians adopted many of the temple rites.

The idea of the founder's perpetual embodiment was signified by the Eucharist, the common meal of bread and wine that Christians shared in worship – the body and blood of Christ, physically divided and then re-unified by being shared and ingested – and in the language in which Church members were self-represented as the body of Christ. It may have been Christ's idea, since all the early texts – the letters of St Paul, and the gospels, which were probably written soon afterwards –

READINGS

J. Emminghaus's **The Eucharist** (1978) is a good introduction, while R. Duffy's **Real Presence** (1982) sets the Catholic doctrine in the context of its sacraments.

M. Rubin's **Corpus Christi** (1991) is a brilliant study of the Eucharist in late medieval culture.

The **wafer and wine**
represent the body and
blood of Christ.

*"As there is one bread, so we, although there
are many of us, are one single body, for we
all share in the one bread."*

First Letter of Paul to the Corinthians **10: 17 (1st century** AD**)**

CONNECTIONS

Related ways of thinking
about the Church are
explored on pp.168–73. The
comparison with Islam can
be pursued in **Islam** (p.188).
For later departures, see
Impossibilism (p.202),
Infamous Superstition
(p.254), and **Atheist
Faith** (p.324).

ascribe it to him. He was, as he said, "with you always" in the consecrated
bread and, literally, in those who shared it.

The idea worked. The Church, in terms of appeal and durability,
has been the most successful institution in the history of the world. But
it was also a problematic idea. Baptism as a guarantee of preferential
treatment in the eyes of God is hard to reconcile with the idea, equally
Christian – or even more so – of a universally benign deity who desires
salvation for all people. While the Church remained unitedly Christ's
body, it was always divided over the interpretation of his will. Christians
repeatedly challenged the idea, and some "schismatics" rejected it. Many
of the Protestants of the Reformation, for instance, emphasized individual
relationships with scripture and insisted that the real Church consisted
of "the elect known only to God".

In Islam, common identity with fellow Muslims is signified by a
simple device: the believer's affirmation of a one-line profession of faith
and the practice of a few simple rituals. For Christians, with their complex
theology and cumbersome creeds, this was never an option. Which works
better, in terms of ever-widening appeal, remains a moot question. Islam
has experienced phases of astonishing growth, but has never matched the
truly global range of cultures and natural environments in which the idea
of the Christian Church has taken root.

Perpetual embodiment
*Christians of all
denominations assert their
faith through participation
in the the sacrament of the
Eucharist, which originated
in the last supper Christ
shared with his disciples
before the crucifixion.
Leonardo da Vinci's famous
1498 fresco,* The Last
Supper, *is pictured below.*

185

THIS IS MY BODY

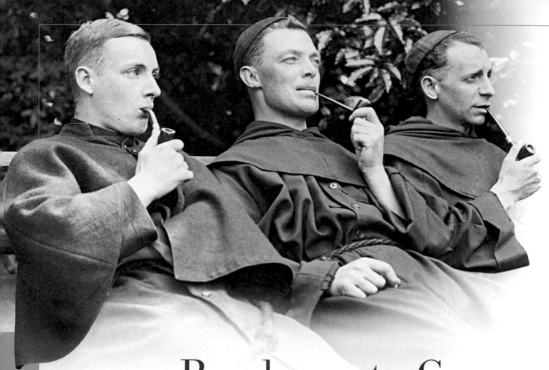

Render unto Caesar

THE IDEA OF THE SEPARATION OF CHURCH AND STATE

A life of contemplation
The Church has never been completely separate from secular life; clerics have always been involved in politics and government. Here, monks take time out to enjoy earthly pleasures.

That which is Caesar's
Christ's words seemed to justify the levying of taxes by Rome and by secular authorities down the ages.

One of Christ's enigmatic jokes started an idea that shaped the subsequent political history of the Western world. Jesus's teachings were honoured in the breach: even his most enthusiastic followers found it hard to practise altruism, meekness, marital fidelity, and "hunger and thirst after righteousness". But one command that resonated through the centuries was, "Render unto Caesar that which is Caesar's, and unto God that which is God's." Rulers interpreted it to mean "Pay your taxes" and "Respect the distinction between the secular and spiritual realms". But is this what Christ meant? He wanted to sanctify real life and make this world conform to the "Kingdom of Heaven". For him, everything was God's, but he wanted his followers to reach this conclusion for themselves. His subtle message was radically misunderstood across chasms of time and culture.

The Church insisted that Christ meant the state had no rights over "things of God", so the clergy should enjoy legal immunity and fiscal privileges. Moreover, some religious people followed Christ's declaration

"Truly he who denies that the temporal sword is in the power of Peter misunderstands the words of the Lord."

Pope Boniface VIII (1235–1303) relished struggles with kings, even when he lost.

Pope Boniface VIII's Bull, *Unam Santam* (1302)

CONNECTIONS

Other ideas that implicate the Church in the world are examined in **Scattered Grains** (p.194), **Noblesse Oblige** (p.198), **Love Conquers All** (p.200), **Holy Terror** (p.208), **Christian Soldiers** (p.210), and **The Third Way** (p.386).

that "my kingdom is not of this world"; ascetics literally withdrew to hermitages and launched Christian monasticism. Yet Church and state always got entangled. Because of their education and objectivity, monks became magistrates and anchorites administrators. Popes came to do emperors' jobs. In the 4th century, Christianity became the state religion of the Roman Empire and the Church became an arm of the state. Government needed the Church: this was where learned, disinterested personnel could be recruited. The Church wanted influence over government: laws that saved souls; treaties that kept peace; crusades that deflected aggression against the infidel.

Some theorists responded with the idea that the Church should rule the world. The 5th-century pope Gelasius argued that when Christ told Peter to "sheathe his sword", it stayed ready for action at the Church's command. In 1302, Pope Boniface VIII delivered the most trenchant utterance yet in this tradition: "Temporal authority should be subject to spiritual [authority]." The position was unsustainable in practice: states simply had bigger battalions than churches. But Christianity remained enmeshed in politics. The pope was a useful arbiter in the power-struggles of states, imposing truces, organizing crusades, and settling disputed frontiers. In modern times, churches continued to interfere in politics, supporting political parties or movements, organizing trades unions, and publicly endorsing or condemning policies according to how well they conform to the gospel or suit the interests of Christians.

The story is not over. "The Pope? How many divisions has he got?" sneered Stalin in response to a suggestion that he should allow Catholicism into the Soviet Union; and Christians proved impotent before the great dictators during World War Two. Yet in the pontificate of John Paul II, the Church re-entered the political arena. Partly, this was the result of this Pope's initiatives in subverting communism, challenging capitalism, and resuming international arbitration. It also was in part a consequence of grass-roots initiatives by religiously committed activists, such as Latin American revolutionaries inspired by "liberation theology" to demand rights for poor peasants and underprivileged indigenous communities. It was also the result of voters in democracies seeking a "third way" in place of discredited communism and insensitive capitalism.

READINGS

J. Maritain's **Man and the State** (1949) is the classic musing of a seminal modern thinker on Church-state relations, while R.W. Southern's **Western Society and the Church in the Middle Ages** (1970) is the best introduction to medieval church history.

Modern fiction on the theme of Church-State relations includes F.W. Rolfe's **Hadrian VII** (1967), and M. West's **In the Shoes of the Fisherman** (1963).

RENDER UNTO CAESAR

Church meets state
Pope John Paul II makes many state visits as part of his role. In 1999, he met President Bill Clinton and Hillary Rodham Clinton.

Call of Islam
Every mosque features one or more minarets from which the call to prayer is made by a muezzin: "Allahu akbar!", "God is greater than everything!" This minaret is part of the Al-Alzhar mosque in Cairo.

Islam

THE IDEA OF RELIGION AS LAW

Christians thought Jewish tradition was too legalistic and tried to cut out the rules from religion. In the 7th century Muhammad re-instated them centre-stage. He constructed a religion that was as rigorously monotheistic as Judaism, as universal as Christianity, as traditional as paganism, and more practical than any of them. For his followers, he was both prophet and ruler. And his teachings were a blueprint for running a state as well as a religion.

Whereas Christ invited individuals to respond to grace, Muhammad, more straightforwardly, called them to obey God's laws. "Islam" literally means submission or resignation. Whereas Moses legislated for a chosen people and Christ for a "kingdom not of this world", Muhammad aimed at a universal code of behaviour covering every aspect of life. The idea was Muhammad's (suggested to him by his angelic source of inspiration). He failed, however, to leave a code that was anything like comprehensive. So schools of jurisprudence set out to fill in the gaps by inferring Muhammad's principles from such laws as he did make in his lifetime, applying them more generally, and, in some cases, adding insights from reason, common sense, or custom. One consequence was that where Jesus had proclaimed a sharp distinction between the

Muhammad
(569-632) left his followers laws governing many aspects of life.

"We gave you a Sharia in religion, so follow it and do not follow the passions of those who do not know."

Quran (c. 7th century AD)

READINGS

M.A. Cook's **The Kuran: A Very Short Introduction** (2000) is the best introduction to the key text, while J.N.D. Anderson's **Islamic Law in the Modern World** (1959) is also useful.

A. Rashid's **Taliban** (2000) presents a case-study of the rule of an Islamic state in Afghanistan.

The reaction to S. Rushdie's **The Satanic Verses** (1988) showed the dangers of treating the central figures of Islam in a work of fiction.

secular and the spiritual, Muslims acknowledged no difference. Islam was both a way of worship and a way of life. The caliph – literally, the "successor" of the Prophet – was both "pope" and "emperor". The corpus of Islamic laws, the Sharia – literally, "the camel's way to water" – was both a religious discipline and a law code for the state. The principles of law were immutable: revealed to the masters of the 8th and 9th centuries, whose interpretations of Muhammad's tradition were regarded as divinely guided. The need to reconcile the opinions of the various schools, however, has always allowed some opportunities for the development of Islamic law.

The practical problems were as great as in Christendom, but different. Within a generation of Muhammad's death, the problem of identifying the caliph rent Islam asunder between rival claimants. The rift never healed and the schisms multiplied. Most Islamic states opted for vesting caliphal or quasi-caliphal authority in the state. Whenever observance of the Sharia has slipped, revolutionary movements have found it convenient to claim that this is a sign of the state's illegitimacy. In modern, secularizing times, this has become an ever more frequent occurrence. The Sharia needs adaptation to an increasingly inter-connected world in which common notions about human rights owe more to Christian and humanist influence than to Islam. The problem of who has the right to re-interpret the Sharia has, however, no agreed solution. States that try to embody Islam in state law are vulnerable to takeover by theocracies. Attempts to modernize leave states vulnerable to accusations of apostasy and expose them to political activism from "Islamist" movements, or even to fundamentalist terrorism.

Illuminated words
This elaborately embellished, 17th-century Quran shows a deep reverence for the word of the Prophet.

I Am the State

THE IDEA OF UNRESTRICTED ROYAL POWER

Modern monarch
Some kings are still enthroned above the constitution, like King Gyanendra of Nepal, who appoints the government, even after constitutional reforms made in the 1990s.

READINGS

J.R. Figgis's **The Divine Right of Kings** (1914) and M. Wilks's **The Problem of Sovereignty in the Middle Ages** (1963) are outstanding studies.

Q. Skinner's **Foundations of Modern Political Thought (Vols 1 & 2)** (1980) is an invaluable guide to all the major themes of late medieval and early modern politics.

In theory, the sovereign power of medieval rulers was limited. First, it was conceived essentially as a matter of jurisdiction – the administration of justice. Legislation, the right to make and unmake laws, which we now think of as the defining feature of sovereignty, was a relatively minor area of activity, in which tradition, custom, divine law, and natural law covered the field and left little scope for innovation.

Secondly, royal power was limited by the notion of a community of Christendom, in which the king of a particular country was not the ultimate authority: the pope had, at least, a parallel supremacy. Notionally, too, the idea persisted that the Roman Empire had never come to an end and that the authority of the emperor over Christendom continued to repose in the person of the pope or the elected head of the German Reich, who was actually called "Roman Emperor". Finally, kings were lords among lords and were obliged to consult their "natural counsellors" – that is, the nobles, who, in some cases, derived their power from royal favour, but in other cases claimed to get it directly from God.

In the late Middle Ages, kings challenged these limitations systematically. Fourteenth-century French and Castilian kings, and a 16th-century English one, called their own kingdoms their "empires" and proposed that they were "emperors in their own realms". The imagery of majesty surrounded them – strategies devised by propagandists. The French king's office was deemed miraculous, endowed by God with "such a virtue that you perform miracles in your own lifetime". The earliest recognizable portrait of a French king – that of John the Good, dating from the mid 14th century – resembles the depiction of a Roman emperor on a medallion and a saint in a nimbus of glory. Richard II of England had himself painted staring in majesty from a field of gold, and receiving the body of Christ from the hands of the Virgin.

The idea never quite took hold in practice. Nevertheless, the period from the 16th to the 18th centuries in Europe is generally characterized by historians as an "age of absolutism".

François I (1515–47), shown on this medal, was an absolute ruler only in theory.

"You have the power to do what you like. But you do not or should not wish to do it."

The Parlement of Paris addressing King François I

Absolutely divine
Monarchs of 17th-century Europe, such as Louis XIV of France, claimed absolute power by divine right.

The Social Charter

THE IDEA OF THE SOCIAL CONTRACT

Popular power
Fifteenth-century theorists argued that the power of monarchs, such as Elizabeth I, owed nothing to God and everything to the "rights" entrusted to her by her subjects.

READINGS

J.H. Burns and T. Izbicki's (eds) **Conciliarism and Papalism** (1997) is an important collection.

J. Ryan's **The Apostolic Conciliarism of Jean Gerson** (1998) is excellent on the development of the tradition in the 15th century.

A. Gerwirth's **Marsilius of Padua** (1960) is the best study of this thinker.

J. Rawls's **A Theory of Justice** (1971) is an impressive attempt to bring social contract theory up to date.

For anyone who values freedom, or thinks collaboration in civil society is natural for our species, the state is a limitation or even an almost inexplicable burden. The problems of explaining and justifying it came together in social contract theory.

"The powers that be are ordained of God," said St Paul, but how did His legitimation get transmitted? Did it descend from heaven upon His anointed, or did it arise via the people by popular election – "the voice of God"? Christ inaugurated a deeply democratic tradition. He came to call tax-collectors and sinners, summoned the rich to poverty, and welcomed the discipleship of fishers and prostitutes. And for Christ, no one was too lowly for God's love. Early in the 14th century, at a time when the papacy was in conflict with kings over power and money, Marsilius of Padua exploited this tradition in propaganda against Rome, arguing that God chose the people; the people chose their delegates, who might be assemblies or monarchs. He even raised the question of whether bishops should be popularly elected.

Potentially, these were highly subversive suggestions. Marsilius's main influence, however, was to encourage nobles to claim a share of power with kings, and bishops with popes. In the 15th century, Jean Gerson, a theorist working on behalf of bishops, went further, developing a theory of the origins of the state that has affected politics in the Western world ever since. The state arose because of sin: outside Eden, there was no limit to iniquity except that which men established by agreement to pool resources and to limit liberty in the interests of peace. The agreement of the citizens is thus the only legitimate foundation of the state. In contrast to the Church, which is God-given, the state is a creation of human free will, made by a historic contract and sustained by the implicit renewal of that contract. In the case of a monarchy, the power of the ruler owes nothing to God, and everything to the covenant by which the people entrust their rights to his keeping.

For **Thomas Hobbes** (1588–1679), absolute monarchy was the most rational system of rule.

"Covenants without the sword are but words and of no power to bind a man."

Thomas Hobbes, *Leviathan* (1651)

The idea of the contractual foundation of the state encouraged representative institutions in many European states to claim equality with kings in making laws and raising taxes. By providing a justification for the state without reference to God, it has been particularly useful in the modern, secular world. In the long run, it has helped to nourish constitutionalism and democracy. There were, however, some critical weaknesses in the idea as Gerson devised it. He made the ruler party to the contract – leaving open the possible objection that the ruler was actually outside it and not bound by its terms. He also made challengeable assumptions about the "clauses" of the contract; apologists for absolutism could argue that the other parties surrendered their rights to the state, rather than merely placing them in trusteeship.

Holy smoke
Popes are ordained by God, but are elected by a conclave of cardinals. A puff of smoke announces the election of a new pope.

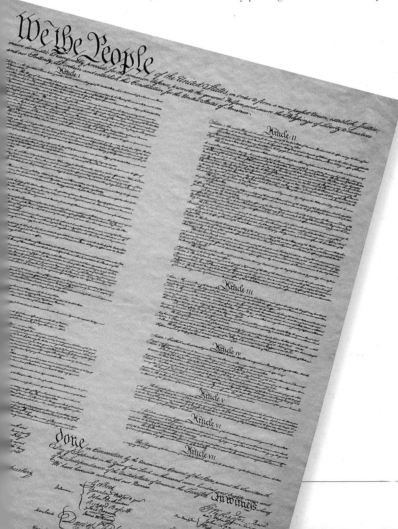

Written constitution
Jean Gerson hailed the agreements of the citizens as the only legitimate foundations of a state. This theory permeates Western politics, most notably in the US constitutional document, the Bill of Rights (1791).

CONNECTIONS

Ideas related to social contract theory are discussed in **Rule of the Many** (p.148), **Heaven's Order** (p.240), **Forced to be Free** (p.256), **We, the People** (p.260), **Nation in Arms** (p.262), and **Inalienable Rights** (p.264).

Scattered Grains

THE IDEA OF JAPANESE SUPERIORITY

An honourable death
Belief in the "divinity" of their nation and a sacred duty to their emperor led "kamikaze" pilots to die for their country.

Sayonara shinkansen
In an image of modern-day "Japaneseness", Mount Fuji, the traditional focal point of Japanese identity, is a backdrop for the Shinkansen, the world's fastest train, an icon of Japan's modernity.

From the first great era of Chinese influence in Japan in AD 700, the Japanese submitted to Chinese cultural superiority, as Western barbarians did to that of Ancient Rome. But they never accepted that this implied political deference.

The Japanese world-picture was twofold. First, in part, it was Buddhist and the traditional world-map was borrowed from Indian cosmography: India was in the middle, with "Mount Meru" – perhaps a stylized representation of the Himalayas – as the focal point of the world. China was one of the outer continents and Japan consisted of "scattered grains at the edge of the field". Yet at the same time, this gave Japan a critical advantage: because Buddhism arrived late, Japan was the home of its most mature phase, where purified doctrines were nourished.

Secondly, there was an indigenous tradition of the Japanese as the offspring of a divine progenitrix. In 1339, Kitabake Chikafusa began the tradition of calling Japan "divine country", and ascribed to it a limited superiority: proximity to China made it superior to all other barbarian lands. Japanese replies to Chinese tribute-demands in the Ming period offered an alternative vision of a politically plural cosmos and a concept of territorial sovereignty: "Heaven and Earth are vast; they are not monopolized

Go-Toba, a 12th-century **Emperor of Japan**, wearing his hair in the traditional style.

"The Sacred Throne was established when the heavens and earth separated. The Emperor is Heaven – descended, divine and sacred."

Hirobumi Ito, *Commentaries on the Constitution of the Empire of Japan* (1889)

READINGS

G.B. Sansom's **A Short Cultural History of Japan** (1931) is an outstanding single-volume study.

R. Benedict's **The Chrysanthemum and the Sword** (1946) is the classic Western account of Japanese values.

H. Cortazzi's **Isles of Gold** (1983) is a superb introduction to Japanese cartography.

The Cambridge History of Japan (1993–) now nearing completion, is a splendid multi-volume history of Japan.

by one ruler. The Universe is great and wide, and the various countries are created each to have a share in ruling it." By the 1590s, the Japanese war-dictator, Hideyoshi, could dream of "crushing China like an egg" and "teaching the Chinese Japanese customs". This was a remarkable (though not a sustained) reversal of previous norms.

The traditions were summarized and taken to a further stage by the Confucian astronomer, Nishikawa Joken (1648–1724), under the impact of contacts with the West and the revelation of the vastness of the world disclosed by Western cartography. He pointed out that no country was literally central in a round world, but that Japan was genuinely divine and inherently superior on allegedly scientific grounds: the climate was best there, which was proof of heaven's favour. From the time of the Meiji restoration in 1868, a myth of modern concoction, recycling traditional elements, assumed the role of a state-building ideology: all Japanese descend from the sun goddess. The emperor is her senior descendant by the direct line. His authority is that of a head of family. The 1889 constitution called him "sacred and inviolable", the product of a continuity of succession "unbroken for eternal ages".

195

Technological supremacy
In the second half of the 20th century, Japanese electronic goods came to dominate world markets.

Noble Education

THE MERITOCRATIC IDEA

CONNECTIONS

For related, see **The Family Silver** (p.36), **Eat, Drink** (p.54), **The Curse of Work** (p.70), **Watching the Flock** (p.80), **Human Bondage** (p.150), **Class Struggle** (p.292), **Hero Inside** (p.304), and **The Intelligence Test** (p.382).

Education for all
In developing countries like Botswana, education is highly valued. Schools and teachers are often provided by local communities.

A society of opportunity could never develop freely where ancient riches or blood determined rank and the elites were impenetrable except by individuals of exceptional prowess, virtue, or genius.

China, in this as so many respects, was way ahead of the West in the Middle Ages. Because the imperial elite was selected by examination in an arduous, humanistic curriculum, clans could club together to pay for the training of intelligent poor relations. In the West, where no such system existed, government was revolutionized in the 14th and 15th centuries by the use first of paper, then of printing. Princes' commands could be cheaply and speedily transmitted to the furthest corners of every state. The consequent bureaucratization added another avenue of social advancement to the traditional routes via the Church, war, commerce, and adventure. The magnate ranks of Western countries were everywhere supplemented – and in some areas almost entirely replaced – with new men. To suit their self-perceptions, Western moralists embarked on the redefinition of nobility.

"Only virtue is true nobility," proclaimed a Venetian ambassador's coat of arms. In 1306, a Parisian academic declared that "intellectual vigour" best equipped a man for power over others. A few years later a German mystic dismissed noble blood, among qualifications for office, as inferior to the "nobility of the soul". "Letters", according to a Spanish humanist of the 15th century, ennobled a man more thoroughly than "arms". Gian Galeazzo Visconti, the strongman who seized Milan in 1395, could be flattered by an inapposite comparison with the exemplary self-made hero of humanists, the Roman orator, Cicero. Antonio de Ferraris, a humanist of Otranto whose very obscurity is a guarantee that he was typical, declared that neither the wealth of Croesus nor the antiquity of Priam's blood could replace reason as the prime ingredient of nobility.

This doctrine, however, was resisted in eastern Europe. In Bohemia, nobility was simply ancient blood. In the Kingdom of Hungary, only nobles constituted the nation; their privileges were justified by their presumed descent from Huns and Scythians whose right to rule was founded on the right of conquest; other classes were tainted with disgraceful ancestry from natural slaves who had surrendered their rights. Even here, however, the doctrine was tempered by the influence of humanism. Istvan Werboczy, the early 16th-century chancellor of the kingdom, who was the great apologist of aristocratic rule, admitted that nobility was acquired, not only by "the exercise of martial discipline", but also by "other gifts of mind and body" including learning. But he saw this as a means of recruitment to what was essentially a caste – not, as in the thought of Western humanists, a method of opening up an entire estate of society.

This bifurcation of Europe had important consequences. The term "eastern Europe" came to have a pejorative sense in the West, denoting a laggard land of arrested social development, held back during a protracted "feudal age", with a servile peasantry and a tightly closed elite.

Spread the word
The development of the printing press in Europe in the mid 15th century allowed the production of numerous copies of religious and "humanist" books, helping to nourish new generations of self-educated men (and women).

Christopher Marlowe (1564–93), English playwright, poet, and spy.

"Virtue solely is the sum of glory,
And fashions men with true nobility."

Christopher Marlowe, *Tamburlaine the Great* (1590)

READINGS

P.O. Kristeller's **Renaissance Thought** (1961) is an unsurpassed brief introduction.

R. Black's **Humanism and Education in Medieval and Renaissance Italy** (2001) is an exhaustive and powerful revisionist study.

M. de Montaigne's **Essays** (1580) provide well-informed opinions on nearly everything.

Noblesse Oblige

THE IDEA OF CHIVALRY

In the heaven-bound space-race of the European Middle Ages, laymen were at a disadvantage. The religious life opened heaven's gates; the warrior's life, stained with bloodshed, closed them. However, the religious model suggested the idea that the lay life could be sanctified – like those of monks and nuns – by obedience to rules.

The first formulators of such rules or "codes of chivalry" in the 12th century were the pious nobleman Hugh de Paynes and St Bernard of Clairvaux. They realized that warriors tended to savagery in the heat of battle and the euphoria of victory. Knights needed civilizing. Discipline could save them. The earliest rules reflected religious vows of chastity, poverty, and obedience, but lay virtues soon gathered prominence. The prowess that fortified the knight against fear could be adapted to confront temptations: largesse against greed, equanimity against anger, loyalty against lies and lust. Chivalry became the common aristocratic ethos of the age.

In the pulp fiction of the late Middle Ages, heroes of the kingship of a pre-chivalric age, including Alexander the Great, King Arthur, and Brutus of Troy, were transformed into exemplars of chivalric values. Even the Bible was ransacked for recruits and King David and Maccabeus joined the canon. Ritual jousts and accolades became focuses of political display in every princely court. Chivalry was a powerful force. It could not, perhaps, make men good, as it was intended to do, but it could win wars and mould political relationships. Thanks to knightly tales of seaborne derring-do, it was probably the main ingredient in Europe's culture of overseas expansion, inspiring adventurers such as Columbus, and making Christendom reach out further in exploration than better-equipped neighbours to the East, such as China and the Islamic world.

Ethos is more powerful than ideology in shaping behaviour because it supplies individuals with standards by which to appraise their actions. Chivalry did that job for medieval Europe and has continued as a spur to Western actions and self-perceptions ever since, compensating the "knights of the air" of the Battle of Britain for their generally modest social origins and shaping the heroics of the golden age of Hollywood. Today, it has dwindled to almost nothing.

198

Be prepared
The idea of chivalry hardly exists anymore, although it can still be found in the founding principles of the scouting movement. Set up by Sir Robert Baden-Powell in 1908 to establish an honour-code for boys in the chivalric tradition, it has become an influential worldwide movement for both boys and girls.

Charles Kingsley
(1819–75) was an
exponent of romantic
nostalgia.

"The Age of Chivalry is never past, so long as there is a wrong left unredressed on earth."

Charles Kingsley, *Westward Ho!* (1855)

Knight in shining armour
In the late Middle Ages, chivalry became a powerful force for shaping courtly behaviour. In Britain, the ancient Arthurian legend of Camelot was reworked to create a bygone era of chivalric heroics. This Pre-Raphaelite painting of Sir Galahad by George Frederic Watts reflected a Victorian sensibility towards knights in shining armour.

NOBLESSE OBLIGE

READINGS

M. Keen's **Chivalry** (1984) is the standard work, while M. Girouard's **The Return to Camelot** (1981) is a fascinating and stimulating account of the revival from the 18th to the 20th century.

See J. Goodman's **Chivalry and Exploration** (1998) on the explorers' inspiration.

The universally recognized "greatest" book about chivalry, M. Cervantes's **Don Quixote** (1615) satirizes it, while P.G. Wodehouse's **The Code of the Woosters** (1938) is perhaps the most amusing of the many re-workings of the idea that have followed.

Love Conquers All

THE IDEA OF MARRYING FOR LOVE

CONNECTIONS

For related ideas, see
Sex Laws (p.40),
Getting Together (p.86),
The Second Sex (p.268),
and **The Doll's
House** (p.288).

Matrimony – in most opinions – is too important
to be left to the young. The idea that love, an
unstable emotion, is a good basis for marriage is
scorned in most cultures, but is considered inviolable
in the modern West.

Over the centuries, in fiction and biography,
romantic love has traditionally been extra-marital and
therefore doomed: that is what makes it romantic.
Married lovers – like the Roman Christian poet
Ausonius and his wife – fall in love after the
wedding or marry in defiance of society with
generally tragic consequences. The first great
vindication of free choice of marriage partner was
perhaps Héloïse's in her 12th-century letters to
Abelard (though their authenticity has been called
into question). He was her former tutor, with whom
she eloped. Her father punished the groom with
castration. Separated and forced into religious lives, the
couple continued a chaste correspondence, full of guilt on
Abelard's part, but characterized on that of Héloïse, even
after she became abbess of her convent, by the frank
assertion of the sanctity of a union hallowed by love.

Strictly speaking, her view was orthodox: like all the
sacraments, marriage was effective in conferring grace only if
freely undertaken. Marriages were "made in heaven", not by
worldly matchmaking. The Church never admitted parental
dissent or communal disapproval as lawful impediments
and Romeo and Juliet had many real-life counterparts
in the medieval and early modern periods. In practice,
however, even at quite modest social levels, such
marriages invited ostracism, disinheritance, and

Frank Sinatra
(1915–98), US singer
and film actor.

*"Love and marriage go together like a
horse and carriage... You can't have one
without the other."*

Sammy Cahn, "Love and Marriage", sung by Frank Sinatra (1955)

Love match
*Love as a basis for
matrimony is a recent
phenomenon. In the West
wedding cake figurines
portray an ideal couple.*

revenge. Moreover, as the Church bayed for the right to licence marriage, "clandestine" weddings, contracted out of public gaze, were outlawed. In consequence, opportunities for people to marry in defiance of society diminished in the 16th and 17th centuries.

Simultaneously, however, evidence accumulated of families anxious to arrange marriages in which their children's affections would, at least, be engaged: this is intelligible in the context of changing family life, as parents and children spent more time in private with each other and became emotionally closer. Inter-generational tensions in the crises of adolescence – of which the choice of marriage-partner usually precipitated the worst – became a dominant theme of Western literature in the 18th and early 19th centuries. Though romantic writers wished otherwise, wealth still determined who married whom, and the greatest freedom occurred in circumstances of greatest poverty.

From one point of view, the modern history of marriage is a tale of conflict between a religiously enshrined principle – that of freedom for the couple concerned – and a discipline considered vital for society: regulation by the families of the intending partners. Love triumphed in the West gradually, in the 19th and 20th centuries: romanticism made young people's feelings seem important; individualism privileged private preferences; social mobility loosened the bonds of collective decision-making in families. In practice, however, people continued to choose in traditional ways, according to calculations of social or economic advantage rather than unalloyed love. Most societies maintained, in addition, traditional family disciplines. Immigrant communities in the modern West often face conflicts as their children grow up with distinctive expectations about how their partners will be selected. "It's an old-fashioned idea, marrying for love," according to Irving Berlin. Actually, it is rather new-fangled and still relatively little-tried.

Burton and Taylor
In a business largely based on the propagation of the idea of romance, film actors Elizabeth Taylor and Richard Burton were one of the most famous show-business couples of the mid 20th century. They married twice, once (shown here) in 1964 and, following a divorce, again in 1975.

READINGS

P. Aries and G. Duby's five-volume **A History of Private Life** (1987–91) is fundamental, while R. Outhwaite's (ed.) **Marriage and Society** (1981) is a valuable collection of essays.

W. Shakespeare's **Romeo and Juliet** (1597) is the classic tale of star-crossed lovers from warring families.

Mu

THE IDEA OF ZEN

The Indian philosopher Nagarjuna was the most innovative Buddhist thinker after Buddha. In the early 2nd century AD he systematized traditional thinking about the illusory nature of perceived reality. This led followers over the next couple of hundred years to question even the reality – or at least, the individuality – of the doubting mind.

Buddha-nature, the perfection of being at which Buddhist meditation aimed, was the recognition of non-being, immersion in a self-descriptive "void". Enlightenment is therefore literally inexplicable. This was the doctrine of Bodhidarma, who arrived in China in the early 6th century AD and founded the tradition now generally known by its Japanese name, Zen. A 12th-century Japanese definition called it "a special transmission outside the scriptures, not founded on words or letters, which allows one to penetrate the nature of things by pointing directly to the mind".

Today, Zen is the favourite "orientalism" of Western travellers in uncertainty because it seems to represent perfectly an ancient tendency of Buddhist thought: the claim that every insight is evanescent and that none is objectively correct. You have "no wandering desires at all," according to Robert Pirsig, author of *Zen and the Art of Motorcycle Maintenance*, "but simply perform the acts of… life without desire."

But Zen is really a corpus of stories of masters who baffled their pupils into enlightenment. They answered questions with meaningless noises – usually the utterance, "Mu" – or enigmatic gestures, or gave answers unrelated to the questions. Or they gave the same answer to different questions, or mutually contradictory answers to the same question, or no answer at all.

The enlightenment imparted by Zen is similar to the indifference enjoyed by Ancient Greek and Roman sceptics – "forgetfulness of the sky, retirement from the wind". Yet there is a difference. Ancient Western sceptics professed contentment with things as they seemed, on the grounds that appearances could do duty for truths that are impossible to know. The indifference of Zen is the conviction of self-extinction, the inertia of non-being, beyond thought and language. It sounds negative, but it has a plausibility hard to resist: without consciousness, we would not be trapped in subjectivism; without language, we would not be separated from the ineffable. Zen is a bid by mere humans for the reality

The art of archery
The Japanese art of kyudo (archery) evolved into a Zen-like discipline of self-development, in which negative thoughts and physical challenges are viewed as an opportunity for personal growth.

READINGS

H. Dumoulin's **Buddhism** (1990) and T. Hoover's **Zen Culture** (1977) are good introductions.

R. Pirsig's **Zen and the Art of Motorcycle Maintenance** (1974) is the classic story of the author's trans-American pilgrimage in search of a doctrine of "quality".

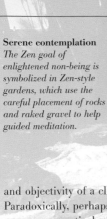

Serene contemplation
The Zen goal of enlightened non-being is symbolized in Zen-style gardens, which use the careful placement of rocks and raked gravel to help guided meditation.

and objectivity of a clod or a rock. Paradoxically, perhaps, it had enormous practical consequences: it contributed to the warrior-ethic of medieval Japan, because discipline, self-abnegation, and willingness to embrace extinction are martial virtues; it generated great art, from gardens of meditation to mystical poetry; and it was part of the vanguard of the reconquest of Western intellectuals by oriental influences in the late 20th century.

Moments of enlightenment can strike us like a bolt of lightning.

"As a dream or as the lightning flash, so should one look at all things, which are only relative."

Nagarjuna (2nd century AD)

Sacred Art

THE IDEA OF ICONS

Hostility to religious imagery goes back at least as far as two ancient Jewish ideas which are amply documented in law-codes attributed to the time of Moses. First, the idea that God is too holy even to be named, let alone represented; secondly, the idea that idols are enemies of believers in one God.

In Jewish contexts – perhaps in partial consequence – the visual arts have always been relatively weak. The same prejudice was inherited in Islam. Muhammad regarded statues as "an abomination" on a par with games of chance, and vowed punishment for image-makers at the Day of Judgement. This does not necessarily mean he was against all representational art. In the 10th century, Abu Ali al-Farisi pointed out what is surely a commonsensical reading of these texts: they ban images of deities in order to forestall idolatry. They are not meant to ban all naturalistic illustration and some Islamic schools allowed the natural world and the creatures in it to be depicted in a purely artistic spirit. Still, as a result, it is in non-representational work that Muslim artists have generally excelled.

Christian thought might have taken the same line. In AD 726 the Byzantine emperor, who still claimed nominal authority throughout Christendom, abolished religious images and ordered existing examples to be destroyed. Some Protestants at the time of the Reformation proclaimed similar rules and practised similar destruction: others simply abolished practices that suggested "that most detestable offence of idolatry", such as kissing images and burning candles before them.

In the 12th century in the West, rival monastic orders bickered over whether artworks were a good use of the Church's money. Mainstream Christian tradition took the line that representational art was useful, as long as images were not worshipped. Indeed, in the Middle Ages, art in churches made a vital contribution to instructing

Sacred Sphinx
In many religious traditions art becomes sacred by virtue of the sanctity of the beings it represents. Perhaps the Sphinx is a representation of the Egyptian sun-god Re?

READINGS

R. Cormack's **Painting the Soul** (1997) is a lively introductory survey, while T. Ware's **The Orthodox Church** (1991) is the best general book on the history of orthodoxy.

R. Grierson's **Gates of Mystery** (1993) is a superb illustrated account of the legacy of Russian medieval painting.

17th-century Russian icon of the **Virgin of Vladimir** covered in gold leaf.

"Those who look on art… are deeply stirred by recognizing the presentation of what lies in the idea, and so are called to recognition of the truth – the very experience out of which Love rises."

Plotinus, *The Six Enneads* (AD 250)

congregations: they were "the books of the unlettered". And art was valuable in inspiring worship: images of holy realities could properly be adored and revered – short of worship – "for the honour paid to the image passes to the original". The Orthodox Church went even further. The most precious relic of the cathedral of Constantinople was a portrait of the Virgin "not made with human hands", but painted by an angel for St Luke while he rested.

In consequence, the Church has been overwhelmingly the biggest source of art patronage in Christendom for centuries – indeed, almost the only source. Medieval artists shared the functions of priests and sometimes achieved the rank of saints, for they brought people in touch with the inhabitants of heaven. When artists began to paint nature in the 13th century, it was not for the intrinsic interest of the subject but as a means of glorifying God by depicting creation: a thought almost inconceivable to a Muslim or Jew. The concern of later Western artists to create "realistic" images derives from the late medieval demand for vivid, convincing depictions of sacred subjects as aids to prayer.

Kitsch Christ
Christian tradition believes religious art is useful, providing the images are not worshipped. The huge demand for mass-produced images of Christ, like this porcelain figure, reflects a need for objects of devotion.

Holy Terror

THE IDEA OF SACRED WAR

Christian crusaders
The Crusades to the Holy Land started in the 11th century as acts of penance, but perhaps through Islamic influence or perhaps because they were waged over lands sanctified by divine and saintly associations, they became "holy wars". This 14th-century painting shows the crusaders being urged on by mounted bishops.

War as a religious obligation was a theme of the sacred history of the ancient Jews. The 3rd-century BC Indian emperor Asoka even managed to justify his wars as fought for the sake of Buddhism. But it was one thing to use religion to justify war, another to sanctify it.

"Jihad" literally means "striving". Muhammad used the word in two contexts: first, to mean the inner struggle against evil, which Muslims must wage for themselves; secondly, to denote real war, fought against genuine enemies posing a real threat to Islam. But since in Muhammad's day the community he led was frequently at war, these terms of reference have always been quite generously interpreted. Chapter nine of the Quran seems to legitimize war against all "polytheists" and "idolaters". After the prophet's death, the doctrine was turned against the "apostates" who left the camp, believing their obligations to their acknowledged leader had lapsed at his demise. It was then used to proclaim a series of highly successful wars of aggression against Arabian states and the Roman and Persian empires. The rhetoric of jihad has often been abused by Muslims to justify their wars against each other. It is used to this day to dignify shabby squabbles, like those between tribal strongmen in Afghanistan, and terrorist campaigns against innocent people in areas singled out for enmity by self-appointed Islamist leaders.

Nevertheless, the term "holy war" seems an appropriate translation for jihad: the enterprise is sanctified by obedience to what are thought to be the prophet's commands and rewarded by the promise of martyrdom. According to a saying traditionally ascribed to Muhammad, the martyr in battle goes straight to the highest rank of paradise, nearest to the throne of God, and has the right to intercede for the souls of his own loved ones. It is worth observing that Muhammad laid down strict laws of war, which ought surely to define a jihad: "in avenging injuries inflicted on us, do not harm non-belligerents in their houses, spare the weakness of women, do not injure infants at the breast, nor those who are sick. Do not destroy

Formal, geometric, **Islamic gardens** aimed to reflect a vision of paradise.

"Those who believe with the Prophet strive with their wealth and lives. Allah hath made ready for them gardens where rivers flow... That is the supreme triumph."

Quran, 9: 88–9 (7th century AD).

Twin Towers terror
The rhetoric of holy war is still employed today. It was used to justify the al-Qaeda attacks on the World Trade Center and Pentagon in the USA on 11 September 2001, in which over 3,000 people died.

READINGS

C. Hillenbrand's **The Crusades: Islamic Perspectives** (1999) and K. Armstrong's **Holy War** (2001) are both highly readable and highly reliable.

G. Keppel's **Jihad** (2001) is an interesting journalistic investigation of the holy-war idea in contemporary Islam

the houses of those who offer no resistance, and do not destroy their means of life, neither their orchards nor their date-palms." These limitations effectively outlaw all terrorism and most state violence.

Abuses apart, the idea of jihad has been influential in two main ways. First, and more importantly, it fortified Muslim warriors, especially in the early generations of the expansion of Islam. In the 100 years or so after the death of Muhammad, it is hard to imagine how Islam could have achieved its successes of scale – which turned the Mediterranean into a "Muslim lake" – without it. Secondly, the jihad idea came to be copied in Christendom. Christians started the crusades with the notions of just war, waged to recover lands "usurped" by their Muslim occupants, and of armed pilgrimage, undertaken as a religious obligation to do penance for sin. Until crusaders began to see themselves in terms analogous to those applied to Islamic warriors – as potential martyrs for whom "the blood of the Saracens washes away sins" – there was no idea of holy war, though the objective was hallowed in the sense that the disputed territory had borne the blood and footprints of Christ and the saints.

CONNECTIONS

Other ideas about war are considered in **No Mercy** (p.76), **Noblesse Oblige** (p.198), **By Other Means** (p.310), and **War Is Good** (p.314). For a connection with modern anti-Americanism, which jihad rhetoric has tainted, see **The Great Satan** (p.388).

Christian Soldiers

THE IDEA OF SPIRITUAL CONQUEST

READINGS

S. Neill's **A History of Christian Missions** (1965) is the best short account of the spread of Christianity, while R. Ricard's **The Spiritual Conquest of Mexico** (1981) clearly sets the terms of debate on spiritual conquest.

B. Moore's **Black Robe** (1991) makes good use of detailed Jesuit histories of mission activity in its gripping tale of a Jesuit priest's test of faith in 18th-century Canada.

CONNECTIONS

Ideas fundamental to the rise of proselytizing religions are raised in **Universal Rule** (p.84) and **No God but God** (p.158). On the weakening of the missionary idea in modern times, see **Many Ways** (p.362) and **Global Village** (p.390).

To judge from the appeal of the Hebrew God, Judaism could have been a great world religion. In terms of the numbers of adherents, however, it remained small because Jews generally shunned proselytization. Islam grew slowly to its present massive dimensions. Richard W. Bulliet calculates for Persia that 2.5 per cent of the population were converted to Islam by 695; 13.5 per cent by 762; 34 per cent by 820; another 34 per cent by 875; and the remainder by 1009. As well as being slow-growing, Islam has remained culturally specific: extremely popular across a broad area of the world, but virtually unable to penetrate elsewhere except by migration.

Buddhism seems infinitely elastic, to judge from the worldwide appeal it demonstrates today, but it was checked for a long time. After huge successes in India, China, Japan, and south-east Asia, it retreated from India and achieved only brief but promising bouts of expansion thereafter: first in Tibet in the 11th and 12th centuries, then in a Tibet-based mission to central Asia from the 16th to the 18th centuries.

Early Christendom was fired with missionary zeal, but this flagged after the 11th century AD: the Crusades produced few converts. But a new sense of mission grew in the Church in the late Middle Ages: a conviction that the godly elite had an obligation to spread a more dogmatically informed Christian awareness to parts of society and places in the world

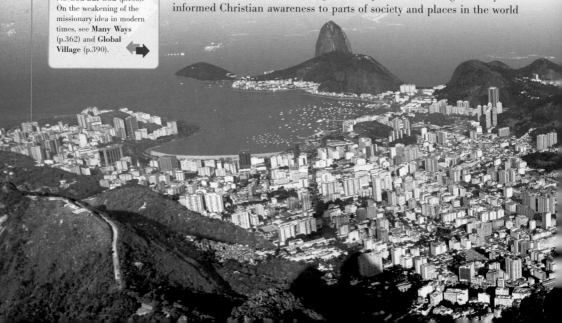

> *"Go into the highways and byways and compel them to come in."*

Christianity was always promoted as a **religion for everyone.**

The Master's injunction to his servants in Christ's parable of the Wedding Feast, *Luke 14: 23* (c. AD 80)

where, so far, evangelization had hardly reached or only superficially penetrated. This involved a new conversion strategy addressed to people low down the social scale: the deracinated masses of the growing cities and the peoples of forest, bog, and mountain, along with the vast, unevangelized world revealed by exploration. The rise of the mendicant orders, with their special vocations for missions to the poor and unbelieving, helped the trend along.

The outward drive revived thanks to a new idea of what conversion meant, formulated at the end of the 13th century by the Majorcan Ramon Llull. He realized that proselytization had to be culturally adjusted. You need to compromise with the culture you are converting people from. Above all, you have to address people in their own terms. So he instituted language schooling for missionaries, and suggested that "indifferent" elements of native culture could be left undisturbed. In consequence, the Christianity of "converted" societies normally exhibits original features that are perhaps examples of two-way cultural exchange.

Christianity – unlike Islam and, so far, Buddhism – has effected "spiritual conquests" in every type of cultural environment. The comparison raises the presumption that a the more culturally adaptable a religion is, the further it spreads.

"Hare rama, hare rama!" *The International Society for Krishna Consciousness actively seeks converts among educated young people, disillusioned with the Western lifestyle, in the USA and Europe.*

Christ the Redeemer *This vast statue of Christ on Mount Corvocado towers over Rio de Janeiro, celebrating the conversion to Christianity of much of the southern hemisphere.*

BACK TO THE FUTURE

1400–1800

5

Renewal and Enlightenment

Renaissance, Reformation, Enlightenment: the conventional catchwords of the history of the 16th, 17th, and 18th centuries make it sound as if the period was dominated by ideas, crafted by minds. In fact, the biggest transformations happened by accident and owed little to conscious human agency.

First there was the "ecological revolution". Living organisms from the different continents crossed the oceans with the circumnavigations of colonizers and explorers. Many were carried deliberately by settlers, but some vital seeds, germs, insects, predators, and stowaway pets made "incredible journeys" in seams and pockets, or in ships' stores or bilges, to new environments where their effects were transforming. The unforeseen result was the biggest evolutionary event since the invention of farming. A divergent pattern, many millions of years old, in which the plants and animals of the various continents had gradually grown unlike each other, yielded to a new, convergent trend, the result of which has been to spread similar life forms across the planet.

Priests in Peking
The handover of the Peking (Beijing) observatory to Jesuit priests in 1674 symbolized a turning-point in the shift of power from East to West.

Meanwhile, for reasons we still do not understand, the world of microbial evolution changed to the advantage of humankind. An "Age of Plague" had begun in the 14th century, when the Black Death wiped out great swathes of people – a third of the population in the worst-affected regions – in Eurasia and North Africa. For the next 300 years, baffling plagues recurred frequently in all these areas. In the 16th century, Old-World diseases spread to the Americas, killing off up to 90 per cent of the indigenous population in areas where the effects were most concentrated. In the 18th century, however, things began to get better and the plagues retreated. Populations boomed almost everywhere, especially in some of the former plague trouble spots, such as Europe and China.

Traditionally, historians have ascribed this change to human cleverness: better food and hygiene, and medical science depriving the deadly microbes of ecological niches in which to breed. Now, however, awareness is spreading that this explanation will not do. Areas of poor food, medicine, and hygiene benefited almost as much as their advanced counterparts. Where the industrial revolution threw up slums, which were ideal environments for germs to breed in, the death-rate declined nonetheless and the population continued relentlessly upwards. The main explanation lies with the microbes

Naval armament
Advances in seafaring technology and warfare, such as this ship's cannon, formed part of Europe's "great leap forward".

Chinese capitalism
Chinese technology led the world until the 18th century. Paper money, first printed in 1107, formed the basis of capitalism.

themselves, which seem to have diminished in virulence or deserted human hosts. So this was an age when environment exceeded intellect in its impact on the world. Nevertheless, there were still plenty of world-changing ideas around. Indeed, perhaps because ever-increasing populations caused new problems and demanded new solutions, output was faster than ever – certainly faster than in any earlier period that is comparably well-documented.

The new ideas were concentrated, disproportionately, in a region where demographic buoyancy was greatest and most unfamiliar: Europe. Partly because of this intellectual fertility, and partly because of the export of European ideas by trade and imperialism, these centuries were also a long period of gradual but unmistakeable shift in the worldwide balance of inventiveness, innovation, and influential thinking. For thousands of years, historical "initiative" – the power of some human groups to influence others – had been concentrated in the civilizations of Asia, such as India, the world of Islam, and, above all, that of China.

In technology, China had generated most of the world's most impressive inventions. Paper and printing were the foundation of modern communications; paper money was the basis of capitalism; gunpowder ignited modern warfare; in the blast furnace, modern industrial society was forged; and the compass, rudder, and separable bulkhead laid the foundations for modern shipping. Meantime, glass-making was

A pox on you
Infectious diseases wreaked havoc on an unprepared New World in the 16th century.

the only key technology in which the West was superior (except perhaps for mechanical clock-making, which became a Western speciality).

By the late 17th century, however, the signs were accumulating that Chinese supremacy was under strain from European competition. The symbolic turning-point occurred in 1674, when the Chinese emperor took control of the imperial astronomical observatory out of the hands of native scholars and handed it over to the Jesuits. Throughout the 18th century, Europeans continued to look to China for lessons in aesthetics and philosophy; and Chinese economic superiority, measured by the balance of trade across Eurasia in China's favour, was not reversed until well into the 19th century. It was increasingly evident, however, that the big, new ideas of the period – those that challenged habits and changed societies, now came overwhelmingly from the West.

Europe's "great leap forward" was indeed, after the ecological revolution and the end of the Age of Plague, the third great transformation of the time. This was a period of paradox: world-changing ideas were at their most prolific, but least impactful, compared with the vast ecological changes with which the multiplication of ideas only kept pace.

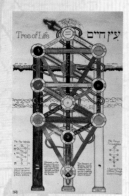

Tree of Life עץ חיים

Hidden meanings
Attempts at producing magical formulae, such as this cabbalistic chart (1604), went hand in hand with more scientific efforts to understand the world.

READINGS

F. Yates's **Giordano Bruno and the Hermetic Tradition** (1964) and **The Art of Memory** (1966) are both fundamental.

J. Spence's **The Memory Theatre of Matteo Ricci** (1984) is a fascinating study.

R.J.W. Evans's **Rudolf II** (1973) is a brilliant study of esoteric philosophy in a European court of the late 16th century.

Fool's Gold

THE IDEA OF MAGIC AS SCIENCE

One of the long-abandoned or dormant notions the Renaissance recovered was that ancient peoples had possessed magic formulae: in pharaonic Egypt, priests had supposedly brought statues to life with arcane talismans; at the dawn of Greece, Orpheus had written incantations that could cure the sick; the ancient Jews had a method of manipulating signs – the cabbala – to invoke powers normally reserved to God. Renaissance research in ancient texts inspired these claims by unearthing "magical" texts of late antiquity, which the piety of the Middle Ages had condemned as nonsensical or demonic. Starting, however, with Marsiglio Ficino, a Florentine priest who worked for the Medici family, Renaissance writers argued that magic was good if it was used for healing or for gaining knowledge of nature, and that some ancient magical texts were lawful reading for Christians.

The most influential text was the work attributed to a legendary Ancient Egyptian magus, Hermes Trismegistus, but which was actually the work of an unidentified Byzantine forger in the 2nd or 3rd century AD. It arrived in Florence among a consignment of books brought from Macedonia for the Medici Library in 1460, and caused a sensation. Renaissance magi felt inspired to pursue "Egyptian" wisdom in search of an alternative to the austere rationalism of classical learning – a fount of older and supposedly purer knowledge than could be had from the Greeks. The distinction between magic and science as a means of attempting to control nature almost vanished in the 16th century.

Dr Faustus, who sold his soul to the devil in exchange for magical access to knowledge, was a fictional character, but he was emblematic of a real yearning. In the Faustian world, wisdom was occult knowledge. The Holy Roman Emperor Rudolf II (1552–1612), who patronized esoteric arts, was hailed as the new Hermes. In his castle of Hradschin, magi

19th-century scientist **Jean Foucault** used a pendulum to show the rotation of the Earth.

"If two things don't fit, but you believe both of them, thinking that somewhere, hidden, there must be a third thing that connects them, that's credulity."

Umberto Eco, *Foucault's Pendulum* **(1988)**

Quest for knowledge
Magic exercised a powerful hold on the Renaissance imagination, and alchemists, who sought to turn base metal into gold, became a popular subject in the art of the period. David Teniers the Younger's The Alchemist *dates from 1645.*

gathered to elicit "secrets" from nature and to practise astrology, alchemy, cabbalism, and pansophy (universal knowledge) – in an attempt to classify knowledge and so gain access to mastery of the Universe.

None of this magic worked, but the effort to manipulate it was not wasted. Alchemy fed into chemistry, astrology into astronomy, cabbalism into mathematics, and pansophy into the classification of nature. The magi constructed what they called "theatres of the world", in which all knowledge could be compartmentalized and displayed, and "wonder-chambers" where specimens of everything in nature could be gathered: the outcome included the methods of classification for life-forms and languages that we still use today, as well as the idea of museums.

Many of the great figures of the Scientific Revolution in the Western world of the 16th and 17th centuries either started with magic or maintained an interest in it. Johannes Kepler was one of Rudolf's protégés. Isaac Newton was a part-time alchemist. Gottfried Leibniz was a student of hieroglyphs and cabbalistic notation. Historians used to think that Western science grew out of the rationalism and empiricism of the Western tradition. That may be, but it certainly also owed a lot to Renaissance magic.

Secret society
Interest in ancient magic led to the growth of societies, such as the Freemasons, whose badge motifs refer to their mythic origins as the builders of Solomon's temple.

Small World

THE MISTAKEN IDEA OF A SMALLER EARTH

CONNECTIONS

Columbus's thinking can be compared with other revisions of the world-picture in **Here Comes the Sun** (p.220). Consequences of his discovery are pursued in **Brotherhood of Man** (p.234).

Animal transportation
Columbus's "mistake" not only transformed the human demography of the Americas, but also altered the eco-systems through the introduction of livestock and Old World microbes.

Knowledge of how big the world is deterred exploration. Then, by imagining a small world, Columbus inspired efforts to "put a girdle round the Earth", surely producing the best example in history of how a wrong idea can change the world.

The size of the globe was worked out with remarkable accuracy by Eratosthenes, a librarian in Alexandria, around 200 BC, using a mixture of trigonometry, which was infallible, and measurement, which left room for doubt. Controversy over his findings remained academic until Christopher Columbus challenged them, nearly 1,700 years later. He proposed an alternative calculation, according to which the world seemed about 25 per cent smaller than it really is. His figures were all hopelessly wrong but they convinced him that the ocean that lapped western Europe must be narrower than was generally believed. This was the basis of his belief that he could cross it. He was saved from disaster only because an unexpected continent lay in his way: if America had not been there, he would have faced an unnavigably long journey. His miscalculation led to the

"The world is small... Experience has now proved it. And I have written the proof down... with citations from Holy Scripture... I say the world is not as big as commonly supposed and that one degree measured along the Earth's surface at the Equator equals fifty-six and two thirds miles, as sure as I stand here."

Christopher Columbus, *Letter to Ferdinand and Isabella* (1503)

exploration of a previously untravelled route linking the New World to Europe. Previously, Europeans had been unable to reach the western hemisphere, except by the unprofitable Viking route, current-assisted, around the edge of the Arctic, from Norway to Newfoundland. Columbus's route was wind-assisted, therefore fast; and it linked economically exploitable regions with large populations, ample resources, and big markets. The impact was such that Columbus's achievement has often been acclaimed as one of the greatest turning points in history.

The consequences included the reversals of three great historical trends. The world balance of economic power, which had long favoured the Chinese, began gradually to shift in favour of western Europeans, once they got their hands on the resources and opportunities of the Americas. Missionaries and migrants revolutionized the world balance of religious allegiance by making the New World largely Christian. Before, Christendom was a beleaguered corner; henceforth, Christianity became the biggest religion.

Meanwhile, evolution went – in one respect – into reverse: previously, for millions of years, life-forms in different parts of the world had tended to diverge, as the eco-systems of the various continents grew ever more unlike each other; now they began to converge as European ships shifted species back and forth. Not only were the same plants and animals now found on both sides of the Atlantic: the same human cultures and political systems accompanied them, as did the microbes that wiped out millions of Native Americans and changed the demographic profile of the planet. Vast migrations took place – some forced, like those of black slaves from Africa, some voluntary, like those of the settlers whose descendants founded and fought for the states of the modern Americas. A false idea about the size of the globe was the starting-point for all these processes. The effects of Columbus's mistake are still resonating as the influence of the New World on the old becomes ever more thorough and profound.

Promised land
This romanticized 19th-century depiction of Columbus's landing in the New World captures later generations' sense of the importance of the event.

READINGS

W.D. and C.R. Phillips's **The Worlds of Christopher Columbus** (1992) and F. Fernández-Armesto's **Columbus** (1996) are both up-to-date biographies of Columbus.

E. O'Gorman's **The Invention of America** (1972) is a controversial and stimulating study.

A.W. Crosby's **The Columbian Exchange** (1972) is the essential starting-place for understanding the idea's significance.

Here Comes the Sun

THE IDEA OF A SUN-CENTRED UNIVERSE

Islamic universe
*This heliocentric
representation of the
Solar System comes from
a 16th-century Ottoman
manuscript. Muslim
astronomers enjoyed the
world's highest reputation
from the 10th century to
the 17th century.*

God is easy to fit around the cosmos. The problem for
religion is where to fit humans inside it. The geocentric
theory of the Universe put our planet, and therefore
our species, at its heart. Ancient Greeks had
debated it but most upheld it. The most
influential synthesis of ancient astronomy,
made by Ptolemy in Alexandria in the
2nd century AD, ensured that geocentrism
would be the orthodoxy of the next
thousand years. Towards the end of
the 10th century, Al-Biruni, the great
Persian geographer, questioned it,
and in the 14th century in Paris
Nicolas of Oresme thought the
arguments finely balanced.

By the 16th century, so
many contrary observations had
accumulated that a new theory
seemed essential. The Polish
astronomer Nicolaus Copernicus
proposed re-classifying the Earth
as one of several planets revolving
around the Sun. This theory of
heliocentrism was formulated
tentatively, propagated
discreetly, and spread slowly.
He received the first printing
of his great book on the heavens
(*De revolutionibus orbium coelestium*), on
his deathbed in 1543. It took nearly 100 years
to remould thoroughly people's vision of the
Universe. In combination with the work early in

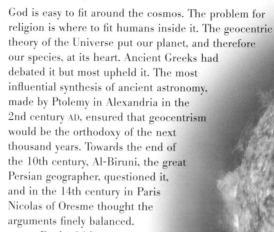

Fiery centre
*By casting the Earth (and
therefore humans) from
the centre of the Universe,
Copernicus began a process
that some people believed
could threaten Christianity.*

Galileo Galilei
(1564–1642) was an
Italian astronomer and
physicist.

"Yet it does move."

**Galileo Galilei, after being forced by the Inquisition to recant
his theory of a heliocentric Universe (1632)**

the 17th century on the mapping of orbits around the Sun by Johannes Kepler, and the observations of Galileo, the Copernican revolution expanded the limits of the observable heavens, substituted a dynamic for a static system, and wrenched the perceived Universe into a new shape around the elliptical paths of the planets.

This shift of focus from the Earth to the Sun was a strain on eyes adjusted to a self-centred galactic outlook. The process displaced the planet we live on from its central position, and every subsequent revelation of astronomy has reduced the relative dimensions of our dwelling-place and ground its apparent significance into tinier fragments. Religion often seems to go with a human-centred outlook: the notion that everything was made for us and that human beings have a privileged rank in the divine order. Science has made such a cosmos incredible. Therefore – it is tempting to conclude – religion is now purposeless and incapable of surviving the findings of science. So how did the Christian understanding of human beings' place in the Universe survive heliocentrism?

Religion, I suspect, is not necessarily an inference from the order of the Universe: it can be a reaction against chaos. Although medieval Christians had a geocentric mental map, it would be wrong to suppose that the "medieval mind" was focused on humans. The centre of the composition was God. The world was tiny compared to heaven. Time was dwarfed by eternity. The part of creation inhabited by man was a tiny blob in a corner of an image of God at work on creation; Earth and firmament together were a small disc trapped between God's dividers, like a bit of fluff trapped in a pair of tweezers.

Clockwork universe
By the 18th century, clockwork orreries like the one above, showing the Sun at the centre of the Solar System, were an accepted method of teaching astronomy.

READINGS

J.M. Dietz's **Novelties in the Heavens** (1993) is an engaging introduction.

A. Koestler's **The Sleepwalkers** (1959) is a spellbinding account of the early Copernican tradition.

T. Kuhn's **The Copernican Revolution** (1957) is a particularly interesting account.

CONNECTIONS

Earlier ideas on the heavens appear in **No Dice** (p.28), **Reading the Stars** (p.44), and **Universal Rule** (p.84). For the interaction between science and religion, see **Scientific Method** (p.132) and **Against Supernature** (p.128).

Prove Me Wrong

THE IDEA OF THE INDUCTIVE METHOD

Separation of light
Isaac Newton, part-time alchemist and amateur biblical scholar, developed scientific laws about the nature of light and gravity by applying experimental method and mathematical principles to the study of physical phenomena.

The English polymath Francis Bacon is often said to have expressed the scientific temperament of the early 17th century. He was an unlikely revolutionary. His life was mired in bureaucracy, from which his philosophical enquiries were a brilliant diversion, until at the age of 60 he was arraigned for corruption. His defence – that he was uninfluenced by the bribes he took – was typical of his robust, uncluttered mind. He is credited with the phrase "knowledge is power", and his contributions to science reflect a magician's ambition to seize nature's keys as well as a Lord Chancellor's natural desire to know her laws. He prized observation above tradition and was said to have died a martyr to science when he caught a chill while testing the effects of low-temperature "induration" on a chicken. This was an appropriate end for a scientist who recommended that "instances of cold should be collected with all diligence".

He devised the method by which scientists turn observations into general laws: the so-called "inductive method". A general inference is made from a series of uniform observations, then tested. The result, if it works, is a scientific "law", which can then be used to make predictions. Experience was a better guide than reason. Bacon took from the Dutch scientist, J.B. van Helmont, the trenchant motto, "Logic is useless for making scientific discoveries".

For over 300 years after Bacon's time, scientists claimed, on the whole, to work inductively. The reality is very different from the claim: no one ever really begins to make observations without already having a hypothesis to test. The best criterion for whether a proposition is scientific was identified by the 20th-century philosopher Karl Popper, who argued that scientists start with a theory, then try to prove it false. The theory is scientific if a test exists capable of proving it false; it becomes a scientific law if the test fails to do so.

CONNECTIONS

Scientific laws can be compared with man-made – laws: see **Written in Stone** (p.88). On the earlier history of scientific thinking, see **The New Illusion** (p.108), **Against Supernature** (p.128), and **The Scientific Method** (p.132). ➤

READINGS

F. Bacon's **The New Organon** (1620) is the fundamental text – especially Book One.

L. Jardine and A. Stewart's **Hostage to Fortune** (1998) is the best life of Bacon.

S. Gaukroger's **Francis Bacon and the Transformation of Early Modern Philosophy** (2001) takes a philosophical approach.

Thomas H. Huxley (1825–95) was a British biologist and a staunch Darwinist.

"The great tragedy of science: the slaying of a beautiful hypothesis by an ugly fact."

T.H. Huxley, *Biogenesis and Abiogenesis* (1870)

Scientific proof
*Using conclusions drawn
from particular evidence,
the inductive method can
generate hypotheses that
may form the basis
of new scientific
laws.*

The Thinker
Thought, most famously represented by Auguste Rodin's The Thinker (1880), was the only thing of which 17th-century philosopher Réné Descartes believed he could be certain – but for him this was enough to confirm his existence.

READINGS

R. Descartes' **Discourse on Method** (1637) is the key work, setting out the Cartesian division of a soul/body dualism.

R. Foley's **Working without a Net** (1993) is a provocative study of Descartes' context and influence. while S. Gaukroger's **Descartes' System of Natural Philosophy** (2002) is a challenging investigation of the philosopher's thought.

Cogito Ergo Sum

THE IDEA THAT INDIVIDUAL EXISTENCE IS VERIFIABLE

Réné Descartes made doubt the key to the only possible certainty. Striving to escape from the suspicion that all appearances are delusive, he reasoned that the reality of his mind was proved by its own self-doubts.

His starting-point was the age-old problem of epistemology: how do we know that we know? How do we distinguish truth from falsehood? "Suppose," he said, "some evil genius has deployed all his energies in deceiving me." It might then be that "there is nothing in the world that is certain" except that "without doubt I exist also if he deceives me, and let him deceive me as much as he will, he will never cause me to be nothing so long as I think that I am something." This perception was distilled into Descartes' famous aphorism "I think, therefore I am". A further problem remained: "What then am I? A thing that thinks. What is a thing that thinks? It is a thing that doubts, understands, conceives, affirms, denies, wills, refuses, that also imagines and feels."

Thought proceeding from such a conviction was bound to be subjective. Political and social prescriptions developed from such a starting-point tended to be individualistic. It remains true that by comparison with other cultures, Western civilization has been the home of individualism, and never more so than in the 18th century, which produced laissez-faire economics and the doctrine of human rights. Determinism had been attractive to constructors of cosmic systems: in the previous century, Spinoza implicitly denied free will and Leibniz eliminated it from his secret thoughts. However, it became a marginalized heresy in an age that made freedom its highest value among a strictly limited range of "self-evident truths".

CONNECTIONS

Descartes' doubts can be usefully compared with ancient and medieval forms of scepticism, subjectivism, and introspection, found in **Man is the Measure** (p.118), **Happiness First** (p.142), and **Mu** (p.204); and with their modern counterparts in **Road to Freedom** (p.374).

Sense deception
How do we know what we know when our senses are so easily deceived? Fairground mirrors use concave and convex curvatures to distort our perception of self. Only our memory of what we look like convinces us that the reflected image is wrong.

"Who is this I or he or it which thinks it is?"

Immanuel Kant
(1724–1804) doubted Descartes' doubts and preferred intuition.

Immanuel Kant, *Critique of Pure Reason* (1781)

Fallen Apple

THE IDEA OF AN ENGINEERED UNIVERSE

In a bout of furious thinking and experimenting, beginning in the 1660s, Isaac Newton seemed to discover the underlying, permeating "secret of the Universe" that had eluded the Renaissance magi. He imagined the cosmos as a mechanical contrivance – like the wind-up orreries, in brass and gleaming wood, which became popular toys for gentlemen's libraries. It was tuned by a celestial engineer and turned and stabilized by a ubiquitous force, observable in the swing of a pendulum or the fall of an apple, as well as in the motions of moons and planets.

Newton was a traditional figure: an old-fashioned humanist and an encyclopedist, a biblical scholar obsessed by sacred chronology, even, in his wilder fantasies, a magus hunting down the secret of a systematic Universe, an alchemist seeking the Philosophers' Stone. He was also a representative figure of a trend in the thought of his time: empiricism, the doctrine beloved in England and Scotland in his day, that reality is

READINGS

R. Westfall's two-volume **The Life of Isaac Newton** (1994) is the best biography.

M. White's **The Last Sorcerer** (1998) is a popular work intriguingly slanted towards Newton's alchemical interests.

H. Gilbert and D. Gilbert Smith's **Gravity: the Glue of the Universe** (1997) is an engaging popular history of the concept of gravity.

Sir Isaac Newton
(1642–1727), British
scientist, made key
discoveries in the
laws of mechanics.

"To myself I seem to have been only like a boy playing on the seashore... whilst the great ocean of truth lay all undiscovered before me."

Isaac Newton, quoted in *Memoirs of Newton* edited by D. Brewster (1855)

observable and verifiable by sense-perception. The Universe was seen as consisting of events "cemented" by cause and effect, for which Newton found a scientific description and exposed the laws. "Nature's Laws," according to the epitaph Alexander Pope wrote for Newton, "lay hid in Night" until "God said, 'Let Newton be!' and there was Light." It turned out to be an act of divine self-effacement. Newton thought gravity was God's way of holding the Universe together, but many of his followers did not agree on that point. Deism (belief in God not dependent on organized religion) thrived in the 18th century in Europe, partly because the mechanical Universe could dispense with the divine "Watchmaker" after He had given it its initial winding. By the end of the 18th century, Pierre-Simon de Laplace, who interpreted almost every known physical phenomenon in terms of the attraction and repulsion of particles, could boast that he had reduced God to "an unnecessary hypothesis".

CONNECTIONS

On the relationship between science and materialism, see **The New Illusion** (p.108), **Matter Matters** (p.124), and **Invisible Powers** (p.228). For the overlap between science and magic, see **The Golden Key** (p.24) and **Fool's Gold** (p.216).

Microscopic power
The discoveries of the scientific revolution provided the theoretical foundations for the technological developments of the industrial revolution.

Full steam ahead
Watt's discovery of invisible atmospheric pressure allowed the power of steam to be fully exploited. Railway-led transportation across vast distances was one consequence.

Invisible Powers

THE IDEA OF HARNESSING NATURAL ENERGY

Industrialization was one of the great technological revolutions of history. The suspicion is strong that some scientific idea must have underlain it, or even sparked it off. But if there was such an idea, what was it?

At first sight, the industrial revolution looks like one of those great transformations of history that "just happen" because of impersonal forces beyond human control – economic, demographic, and environmental – necessities that mother invention. No "idea of industrialization" seems detectable until the process had begun to unfold. Yet industrialization was preceded and accompanied by a conspicuously active and fruitful period in the history of Western science; historians have therefore looked for some connection.

The scientific revolution extended the reach of the senses to what had formerly been too remote or too occluded. During the 16th century, Galileo Galilei could see the moons of Jupiter through his telescope, Anton van Leeuwenhoek saw microbes through his microscope, and Marin Mersenne could hear harmonics that no one had noticed before and measured the speed of sound. In the 17th century, Isaac Newton could wrest the rainbow from a shaft of light or feel the force that bound the cosmos in the weight of an apple, and Robert Hooke could sniff "nitre-air" in the acridity of vapour from a lighted wick. A century later, Antoine

"We may justly look upon the steam engine as the noblest machine ever invented by man – the pride of the machinist, the admiration of the philosophers."

James Watt, *Notebooks and Papers* **(1761–1819)**

James Watt (1736–1819), Scots engineer, radically improved the steam engine.

READINGS

R. Spangenburg and D. Moser's **The History of Science in the Eighteenth Century** (1993) is a short popular introduction.

A. Donovan's **Antoine Lavoisier** (1993) is a fine biography, which sets the subject against a clear account of the science of the time.

R.E. Schofield's **The Enlightenment of Joseph Priestley** (1998) is the first volume of an equally impressive biography of Lavoisier's rival.

Lavoisier proved the existence of oxygen by isolating it and setting it on fire, and Luigi Galvani could feel the thrill of electricity in his fingertips. Also in the 18th century, Friedrich Mesmer thought hypnotism was a form of detectable "animal magnetism", and Benjamin Franklin demonstrated that lightning is a kind of electricity through life-threatening experiments with a kite and keys. Their triumphs made credible the cry of empiricist philosophers: "Nothing unsensed can be present to the mind!" This is surely part of the essential background of the industrial revolution.

Although industrialization was not an idea, mechanization, in some sense, was. In part, its origins lie in the idea that barely detectable forces can have enormous power, just as the strength of the body reposes in thread-like sinews. Steam, the first such power-source in nature to be "harnessed" to replace muscles, was a fairly obvious case: you can see it and feel its heat, even though it takes some imagination to believe that it can work machinery and impel locomotion. But James Watt's purely scientific discovery of atmospheric pressure, which is invisible and undetectable except by experiment, made steam power exploitable.

CONNECTIONS

It is worth tracing this idea back to remote antiquity. See **All Things Invisible** (p.18), **May the Force…** (p.26), and **No Dice** (p.28). On the relationship between the histories of science and materialism see **Matter Matters** (p.124).

Little Pests

THE IDEA OF MICROSCOPIC LIFE-FORMS

Adam had 'em
This engraving by the 17th-century Dutch microscopist Anton van Leeuwenhoek was one of many that recorded the first visual evidence of micro-organisms.

Germ-free environment
The realization that germs could be carried from place to place has helped medical science develop sterile or protective environments – like this incubator – to protect the vulnerable.

Louis Pasteur
(1822–95) identified the link between germs and disease.

Here was an idea that was to prove equally serviceable to theology and science, by illuminating the causes of decay and disease, while preserving the mystery of the origins of life. If God did not get life going, it must have arisen from spontaneous generation. At least, that was what everybody – as far as we know – who thought about it at all thought for thousands of years. For Ancient Egyptians, life came out of the slime of the Nile's first flood. The standard Mesopotamian narrative resembles the account favoured by many modern scientists: life took shape spontaneously in a swirling primeval soup of cloud and condensation mixed with a mineral element, salt. To envisage the "gods begotten by the waters", Sumerian poets turned to the image of the teeming alluvial mud which flooded up from the Tigris and Euphrates. The language is sacral, the concept scientific. Challenged by theology, common sense continued to suggest that the mould and worms that are visibly associated with putrescence generate spontaneously.

When microbes became visible under the microscope of Anton van Leeuwenhoek, therefore, it hardly seemed worth asking where they come from. "Freethinking" atheism got a boost from the microbial world, with its apparent evidence of spontaneous generation. The very existence of God – or, at least, the validity of claims about His unique power to create life – was at stake until, in 1799, with the aid of a powerful microscope, Lorenzo Spallanzani observed fission – cells reproducing by splitting. He demonstrated that if bacteria – or "animalculi", to use the term favoured at the time, or "germs", as he called them – were killed by

> *"I was hoping to mark a decisive step by solving... the celebrated question of spontaneous generation... what is there in air that provokes organization? Are they germs? Is it a solid? Is it a gas? Is it a fluid? Is it a principle such as ozone? All was unknown and invited experiment."*
>
> **Louis Pasteur, *Reflections on my Life* (1908)**

READINGS

R.W. Reid's **Microbes and Men** (1975) is a readable history of germ theory.

A. Karlen's **Man and Microbes** (1995) is a controversial, doom-fraught survey of the history of microbially inflicted plagues.

L. Garrett's **The Coming Plague** (1995) is a brilliantly written admonition to the world about the current state of microbial evolution.

Unspontaneous life
Observations of cell division at the end of the 18th century showed that micro-organisms – such as these listeria bacteria – did not appear spontaneously but could only grow in an environment where they were already present.

heating, they could not re-appear in a sealed environment. He concluded that living organisms did not appear from nowhere: they could only germinate in an environment where they were already present. Gradually, as his discovery came to be recognized, belief in the spontaneous generation of life waned.

Science is still grappling with the consequences. As far as we know, bacteria-like single-celled life-forms were the first on our planet. The earliest evidence of them dates from at least 500 million years after the planet was formed. They were not always around. So where did they come from? A "chemical accident" of the sort Ancient Egyptian and Sumerian science postulated seems indicated, but is still not proven.

The "germ theory" also had enormous practical consequences: almost at once, it transformed the food industry by suggesting a new way of preserving foods in sealed containers. In the longer term, it opened the way for the conquest of many diseases, as the suspicion that germs caused disease in the body as well as corruption in food turned out to be largely true.

CONNECTIONS

On early medicine, see **Good Humours** (p.134). For other thinking on the origins of life, see **All Things Invisible** (p.18), **Nothing Matters** (p.130), **The Power of Thought** (p.156), **Tooth and Claw** (p.320), and **Intelligence Test** (p.382).

State First

THE IDEA OF THE OVERRIDING INTEREST OF THE STATE

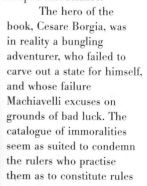

Original "Prince"
Cesare Borgia (1475–1507), the illegitimate son of Pope Alexander VI, was renowned for his ruthlessness, and provided a model of misbehaviour for Machiavelli's great work.

The Watergate hearings
According to Machiavelli, a ruler's only responsibility was to keep power. Republican US President Richard Nixon was caught doing just this, after he ordered a burglary of the Democratic Party's headquarters during the 1972 election campaign. He was forced to resign in disgrace.

The purpose of the state – ancient moralists decreed – is to make its citizens good. But whose job is it to make states good? Political theorists of antiquity and the middle ages recommended various kinds of state but they all agreed that the state must have a moral purpose: to increase virtue or happiness, or both. Even the "Legalist" school in Ancient China advocated oppression in the wider interest of the oppressed.

When Niccolò Macchiavelli wrote *The Prince*, his rules for rulers, in 1513, the book seemed shocking to readers not just because the author recommended lying, cheating, ruthlessness, and injustice, but because he did so with no apparent concession to morality. Machiavelli cut all references to God out of his descriptions of politics and made only mocking references to religion. The only basis of decision-making was the ruler's own interest and his only responsibility was to keep hold of his power. He should keep faith only when it suits him. He should feign virtue. He should affect to be religious.

Later thinking borrowed two influences from this: first, the doctrine of "realpolitik": the state is not subject to moral laws and serves only itself; secondly, the claim that the end justifies the means and that any excesses are permissible for the survival of the state.

But did Machiavelli really mean what he said? He was a master of irony, who wrote plays about behaviour so revoltingly immoral that they could make men good. His book for rulers is full of contemporary examples of rulers of ill-repute, whom many readers would have despised: yet they are portrayed as models to imitate with deadpan insouciance.

The hero of the book, Cesare Borgia, was in reality a bungling adventurer, who failed to carve out a state for himself, and whose failure Machiavelli excuses on grounds of bad luck. The catalogue of immoralities seem as suited to condemn the rulers who practise them as to constitute rules of conduct for their imitators. The real message of the book is perhaps concealed in the final chapter, in which Machiavelli appeals to "Fame" as an end worth striving for and calls for the unification of Italy and the expulsion of the French and Spanish "barbarians" who had conquered parts of the country. It is significant that he explicitly deals only with monarchies. In the rest of his works he clearly preferred republics and thought monarchies were suited only to degenerate periods in the history of civilization. Republics were best because the sovereign people were wiser and more faithful than monarchs. Yet, if *The Prince* was meant to be ironic, a greater irony followed: it was taken seriously by almost everyone who read it, and started two traditions that have remained influential to this day: a Machiavellian tradition, which exalts the interests of the state, and an anti-Machiavellian quest to put morals back into politics.

CONNECTIONS

Comparable ideas can be pursued in **Nasty, Brutish, Short** (p.238), **Brother Knows Best** (p.306), **Master Morality** (p.312), and **Axe in the Sticks** (p.364). Ideas for making the state virtuous are explored in **Philosopher-kings** (p.152) and **Neverland** (p.250).

READINGS

D. Wootton's translation of Machiavelli's **The Prince** (1995) is the best, while Q. Skinner's **Machiavelli** (1984) is a basic but useful short introduction to the man and his thought.

H.C. Mansfield's **Machiavelli's Virtue** (1998) is a profound and challenging re-assessment of the sources of his thought.

Machiavellian mogul
The epithet "machiavellian" is now applied to any overt displays of scheming behaviour. The character of Texas oil tycoon J.R. Ewing, from the hit 1980s US TV soap Dallas, *embodied this perfectly. He once said, "A conscience is like a boat or a car. If you feel you need one, rent it."*

Niccolò Machiavelli (1469–1527) was a Florentine diplomat and political theorist.

"A ruler… must be a fox to recognize traps and a lion to frighten off wolves."

Niccolò Machiavelli, *The Prince* (1513)

Brotherhood of Man

THE IDEA OF HUMAN UNITY

Separate lives
Racist laws remained in force in South Africa and parts of the USA, until the late 20th century. These were only repealed with the success of the Anti-Apartheid and Civil Rights movements respectively.

READINGS

B. de Las Casas's **Apológetica historia sumaria** (1551) is the fundamental text, but has never been translated into English.

L. Hanke's **The Spanish Struggle for Justice in the New World** (1966) is a classic work on the context.

T.L. Peacock's **Melincourt** (1817) offers a satirical sidelight on Lord Monboddo's theories and is a masterful comic novel.

"All the peoples of humankind are human," said the Spanish moral reformer, Bartolomé de Las Casas, in the mid 16th century. It sounds like a truism, but it was an attempt to express one of the most novel and influential ideas of modern times.

Legendary monsters are evidence of people's inability to conceive of strangers in the same terms as themselves. It is probably true that in most languages no term for human exists that encompasses those outside the group. There is, as it were, no middle term between brother and other. The inclusive doctrine of humanity – our sense of the human species as a unified whole – is a relatively recent innovation in the way we think of each other.

Although sages of the Axial Age had expatiated on the unity of humankind, and Christianity had made belief in our common descent a religious orthodoxy, the trouble was that no one knew where to draw the line between humans and supposed sub-species. Medieval biology imagined a "chain of being" in which humans were separated from animals by an intermediate, monstrous category of "similtudines hominis" – creatures resembling men but not fully human. It took a papal Bull to convince some people that Native Americans were truly human (even then, some Protestants denied it, suggesting that there must have been a second creation of a different species or a demonic engendering of deceptively human-like creatures in America). Similar doubts were raised concerning "negroes", "Hottentots", and "pygmies". There was a protracted debate concerning apes in the 18th century, and the Scots jurisprudentialist Lord Monboddo championed the orang-utan's claim to be considered human.

These were questions of vital importance to those who, if unfairly classified, would be excluded from human rights. Darwin's theory of evolution complicated the problem in two ways: first, it suggested that there was no clear dividing line between our species and the rest of creation. Campaigners for animal rights have concluded from this that even our present broad category of humankind is too inelastic. Secondly, awareness of human evolution has raised the problem of how far back

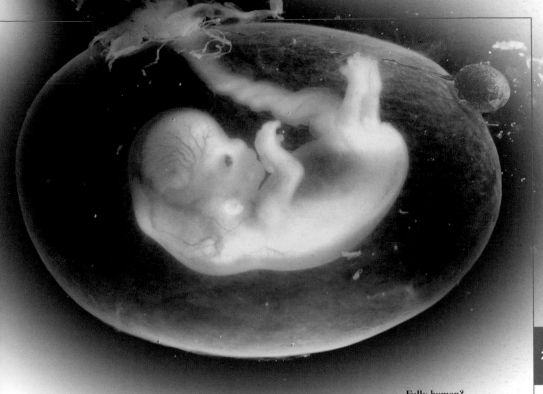

Fully human?
All humans look and behave alike in the early stages of their embryonic development. Differences come later. But we still seek ways of excluding some human beings from human rights.

should we project our human category. What about the Neanderthals? What about early hominids? Even today, when we set the limits of humanity more generously, perhaps, than at any time in the past, we have really only shifted the terms of the debate: the questions of how far the unborn and the moribund share human "personhood" and have human rights remain unresolved.

Bartolomé de Las Casas (1474–1566) was a priest who championed the rights of Native Americans.

"For all the peoples of the world are men, and the definition of all men, collectively and severally, is one: that they are rational beings... Thus all mankind is one, and all men are alike in what concerns their creation... "

Bartolomé de Las Casas, *Apologética historia sumaria* (1551)

CONNECTIONS

On the Christian background and its context in other faiths, see **Love Above** (p.160). On evolution, see **Tooth and Claw** (p.320). An important episode in the development of the tradition is described in **The Noble Savage** (p.258).

Law of Nations

THE IDEA OF INTERNATIONAL ORDER

The spoils of exploration
In an agreement brokered by the Pope, Spain and Portugal allotted each other zones of exclusive navigation in the Treaty of Tordesillas (1494). This gave access to the entire New World (minus Brazil) to Spain, and Africa and India to Portugal.

Most political theory has been concerned with peace and equity within the state. But what about between states? The world needs a way of escape from chaotic, anarchic international relations.

When Thomas Aquinas summarized the state of thinking in the Western world in the 13th century, he distinguished the laws of individual states from what he called the *ius gentium* (the law of nations), which all states must obey and which governs the relationships between them. Yet he never said what this *ius gentium* was or where or how it could be codified. Many jurists assumed it was just "natural law" or the basic, universal principles of justice – but this is also hard to identify in complex cases. In the late 16th century, the Spanish Jesuit theologian Francisco Suárez solved the problem in a radical way. The law of nations "differs in an absolute sense from natural law," he said, "[and] is simply a kind of positive human law". In other words, it says whatever people agree it should say.

This made it possible to construct an international order along lines first proposed earlier in the 16th century by one of Suárez's predecessors at the University of Salamanca, the Dominican Francisco de Vitoria, who advocated laws "created by the authority of the whole world" – not just pacts or agreements between states. In 1625, the Dutch jurist Hugo Grotius worked out the system that prevailed until the late 20th century: by natural law, states were obliged to respect each other's sovereignty; their relations were regulated by the mercantile and maritime laws that they had previously ratified or traditionally embraced, and by treaties they made between themselves, which had the force of contracts and which could be enforced by war.

US President **John F. Kennedy** (1917–63) found peace is easier to call for than to keep.

"Mankind must put an end to war or war will put an end to mankind."

John F. Kennedy, speech to UN General Assembly (25 Sept, 1961)

READINGS

H. Bull et al (eds) **Hugo Grotius and International Relations** (1990) is valuable.

J. Laurence and A. Pagden's (eds) **Vitoria: Political Writings** (1991) is useful on de Vitoria's contribution to international law.

This system did not need ideological concurrence. It would remain valid, Grotius said, even if God did not exist. It was fairly successful in limiting warfare in the 18th century and maintaining peace – at least in Europe – for much of the 19th. It did not, however, prevent horrific wars in the 20th century. From the 1950s to the 1990s, the "Cold War" kept an uneasy peace. When it ended, a new approach became urgent.

Most people assumed a "new international order" would be a collaborative system in which international relations would be brokered and enforced by the United Nations. In practice, however, it meant the hegemony of a single superpower, acting as a "global policeman". This role, exercised by the USA to an even greater degree after the events of September 11, 2001, is unsustainable because, although American policy is generally benign, it cannot be immune to the distortions of self-interest or escape the outrage of those who feel unfairly treated. The US monopoly of superpower status may come to an end and, in any case, the power of the USA – measured as a proportion of the wealth of the world – is already in decline. The search is on for an international system that will succeed American guardianship, but no solution is in sight.

Terms of victory
Relations between states have often been defined by postwar treaties. This historic photograph shows the signing of the Versailles treaty (1919), famous for its punitive terms.

Keeping the peace
Founded in 1945, the UN exists to promote peace and co-operation in the world. It deploys peacekeeping forces made up of soldiers from member countries.

Nasty, Brutish, Short

THE IDEA OF A SAVAGE "STATE OF NATURE"

What you think about politics derives from what you think about people: are they naturally good, and so best left free? Or do they need a strong state to redeem them from natural wickedness?

In the 16th and 17th centuries in Europe, the tradition that the state originated in a contract raised the presumption that the condition of humankind in the remote past must have been extremely grim: misery induced people to get together and sacrifice freedom for the common good. Meanwhile, the unfolding evidence accumulated by explorers and ethnographers suggested that "natural man" was no noble savage.

These influences came together in the mind of Thomas Hobbes, who was an extreme royalist in politics and an extreme materialist in philosophy. His natural inclinations were authoritarian: after living through the bloodshed and anarchy of the English Civil War (1642–49), he was left with a strong preference for order over freedom. He imagined the "state of nature" that preceded the political state as "a war of every

Civilized veneer
According to Hobbes, humans living in a "state of nature" would be engaged in a state of constant war with each other. This scene from the 1963 film of the book Lord of the Flies *depicts the rapid descent into savagery of boys stranded on a desert island.*

The frontispiece of **Leviathan** gives a visual representation of Hobbes's theory.

"The condition of man… is a condition of war of everyone against everyone."

Thomas Hobbes, *Leviathan* (1651)

READINGS

J.C.A. Gaskin's (ed.) **The Elements of Law, Natural and Politic** (1994) is an excellent introduction to Hobbes's thought.

A. Rapaczynski's **Nature and Politics** (1987) sets Hobbes in the context of Locke and Rousseau.

W. Golding's **Lord of the Flies** (1954) is a disturbing story of a Hobbesian-style state of nature.

man against every man", where "force and fraud are the two cardinal virtues" and "the life of man is poor, nasty, brutish, and short". This was quite different from the state of nature of traditional political theory, which was simply a state – presumed to have prevailed in the past – when the laws of nature or the rule of reason meant that man-made laws were unnecessary. It was also a refreshing contrast to the myth of a "golden age" of primitive innocence when people lived harmoniously, uncorrupted by civilization.

Unlike ants and bees, Hobbes continued, which form society instinctively, people had to grope their way by the use of reason, which inspired them to find the only workable way out of the state of nature. They agreed with one another to forfeit their freedom to an enforcer, who would compel observance of the contract, but who would not be a party to it. Instead of a compact between rulers and ruled, the founding covenant of the state became a promise of obedience. By virtue of belonging to the state, subjects renounced their liberty. As for their rights, the right of self-preservation is the only one subjects retain: they never had any others to renounce in the first place, for in the state of nature there was no property and no justice. People had only what they could grab by force.

Free for all
Hobbes argued that a state wielding absolute power was the only alternative to mob rule. Looting during the Los Angeles riots of 1992 exemplified one outcome of anarchy: selfish, anti-social behaviour.

This idea changed the language of politics for ever. Contract theory lost its hold over the power of the state: the sovereign is not bound by the contract and so is not bound to keep it. It was now possible to believe in the equality of all men – indeed, Hobbes assumed that all were naturally equal – and yet leave them at the mercy of the state. Finally, the doctrine had chilling implications for international politics: states were in a state of nature with respect to each other. There were no constraints on their capacity to inflict mutual harm, except the limitations of their own power. From one point of view, this justified wars of aggression; from another, it necessitated some contractual arrangement to ensure peace.

Heaven's Order

THE CHINESE IDEA OF POPULAR SOVEREIGNTY

In the mid 17th century, the Manchus conquered China and took over the empire. They were herdsmen from the steppelands of central Asia, whom the Chinese despised as barbarians. The shock made Chinese intellectuals rethink the whole basis of political legitimacy. The most startling and innovative result was the development of a doctrine of the sovereignty of the people, similar to that of western Europe. Huang Tsung-hsi postulated a state of nature where "each man looked to himself" until benevolent individuals created the empire. Corruption set in and "the ruler's self-interest took the place of the common good… The ruler takes the very marrow from people's bones and takes daughters and sons to serve his

Jade pendant in the shape of a dragon from the Manchu period of political upheaval.

"Heaven's order and Heaven's justice are not things rulers and ministers can take and make their own."

Lü Liu-liang, *Commentaries on the Four Books* (1670s)

Barbarian rule
Chinese ideas of popular sovereignty were devised to legitimize the "upstart", warlike Manchu dynasty. This 18th-century painting depicts the mobilization of imperial troops at Sichuan.

READINGS

W.T. de Barry and R. Lufrano's (eds) **Sources of Chinese Tradition** (1960) includes a useful selection of sources.

Liang Chi-chao's **History of Chinese Political Thought** (2000) is a good short introduction.

F. Wakeman's **The Great Enterprise** (1985) is the best introduction to Chinese history of the period.

debauchery." Lü Liu-liang went further: "The common man and the emperor are rooted in the same nature… It might seem as though social order was projected downwards to the common man [but, from the perspective of heaven] the principle originates with the people and reaches up to the ruler."

Yet, whereas in the West this sort of thinking helped to justify republics and generate revolutions, nothing comparable happened in China until the 20th century, when a great deal of Western influence had done its work. There were plenty of peasant rebellions but, as throughout the Chinese past, they aimed to renew the empire and replace the dynasty, not end the system and transfer the "mandate of heaven" from a monarch to the people. Unlike the West, China had no examples of republicanism or democracy to look to in history or idealize in myth. Still, the work of Huang, Lü, and the theorists who accompanied and followed them was not without practical consequences: it passed into Confucian tradition, helped to keep radical criticism of the imperial system alive, and helped to prepare Chinese minds for the later reception of Western revolutionary ideas.

People power
When Chinese communist revolutionaries took power in 1949, they followed in a tradition of ideas about popular sovereignty.

Price for Everything

THE IDEA OF MONETARY THEORY

The idea that price is a function of the supply of money was first proposed in the middle of the 16th century by a group of theologians known as the School of Salamanca. The chief exponents of the idea, Domingo de Soto and Martín de Azpilcueta Navarro, were particularly interested in what we might now call problems of the morality of capitalism.

While studying business methods they noticed a connection between the flow of gold and silver from the New World and the inflation of prices in Spain. "In Spain," observed Navarro, "in times when money was scarcer, saleable goods and labour were given for very much less than after the discovery of the Indies, which flooded the country with gold and silver. The reason for this is that money is worth more where and when it is scarce than where and when it is abundant." The usual explanations were that value was a purely mental construct, reflecting the irrationally different esteem the market applied to intrinsically equivalent products in different times and places; or to link price to the supply and demand of goods rather than of money; or to assume that

Golden gate
In the 16th century, Spanish economists noticed a direct link between the inflation of local prices and the import of bullion wrested from Spain's empire in the New World and channelled through Seville, depicted above.

Worthless money
The hyperinflation of post-WWI Germany led to a massive over-supply of paper money as it lost more and more of its value. Here, a shopkeeper stashes his Deutschmarks in a tea chest.

242

"*Wealth rides upon the wind. It takes the form of papers and contracts... silver and gold, instead of products that... add value and attract riches from abroad, sustaining our people at home.*"

Martín González de Cellórigo, *Politica necessaria y util retauración* (**1600**)

Anything can become **currency** by consent: base metals, even bits of paper.

Confidence trick
A market economy is influenced by supply and demand, but stock market values may fluctuate according to perceived "confidence", rather than any underlying economic strength or weakness.

"just" value was fixed by nature and that price fluctuation was the result of greed. In 1568 a similar observation to Navarro's was made in France by Jean Bodin: he thought he was the first to make this connection but the Salamanca theorists anticipated him by some years.

A by-product of the theory was to show that money is like other commodities and can be traded for, as Navarro put it, a moderate profit – without dishonour. "All merchandise," wrote Navarro, "becomes dearer when it is in great demand and short supply, and... money... is merchandise, and therefore also becomes dearer when it is in great demand and short supply." At the same time, the theory reinforced ancient moral prejudices about money: you can have too much of it; it is "the root of evil"; the wealth of a nation consists in the goods produced there, not the cash collected there. This opinion resonates in modern disquiet over the displacement of manufacturing by financial services. It also fuelled criticism of imperialism, which seemed to have impoverished Spain by flooding the country with money. Martín González de Cellórigo, one of the subtlest economists of the period, coined a famous paradox: "The reason why there is no money, gold or silver in Spain is that there is too much, and Spain is poor because she is rich."

Ironically, economic historians now mistrust the observations of the School of Salamanca and suspect that 16th-century inflation was the result of increasing demand rather than of the growth of the money supply. The theory, however, irrespective of the soundness of its foundations, has been immensely influential. Indeed, it would hardly be possible to imagine the development of modern capitalism without it.

READINGS

M. Grice-Hutchinson's **The School of Salamanca** (1952) is fundamental.

Some early sources are collected in A.E. Murphy's **Monetary Theory: 1601–1758** (1997).

D.H. Fischer's **The Great Wave** (1996) is a controversial but highly stimulating history of inflation.

243

PRICE FOR EVERYTHING

CONNECTIONS

Other ideas about economics are reviewed in **Fair Exchange** (p.56), **A Capital Idea** (p.144), **Tight Money** (p.244), **Laissez-faire** (p.246), **Workers Unite** (p.248), **Spending for Wealth** (p.366), **A Better World** (p.368), and **Solid Foundations** (p.370).

Tight Money

THE IDEA OF MERCANTILISM

For centuries, the European economy laboured under the burden of an adverse balance of trade with China, India, and the Near East. It was a matter of concern in Ancient Rome. It drove late-medieval explorers to

search the oceans for new sources of gold and silver. By the 16th century, when European travellers were able, in large numbers, to cast envious eyes on the riches of the East, it induced two obsessions in Western minds: bullion is the basis of wealth; and to grow rich an economy must be businesslike and sell more than it buys.

The Spanish moralist Tomás de Mercado perfectly expressed this doctrine – now known to economists as mercantilism – in 1569: "One of the principal requisites for the prosperity and happiness of a kingdom is always to hold within itself a great quantity of money and an abundance of gold and silver… And the thing which destroys this abundance and causes poverty is the export of money." All European governments believed it. In consequence, they tried to evade impoverishment by hoarding bullion, limiting imports and exports, regulating prices, defying the laws of supply and demand, and founding empires to create controllable markets. The consequences were woeful. There could be no overseas investment, except in imperial ventures. The protection of trade nourished inefficiency and squandered resources on policing. Competition for protected markets caused wars and, consequently, waste. Money drained out of circulation. These conditions, which clearly inhibited economic growth, were much criticized from the late 17th century onwards by advocates of free trade and "laissez-faire", but they remained the prevailing orthodoxy until the late 18th century.

Solid gold
The gold reserves governments use to support the value of their currency are a relic from the time when banknotes had to be backed by "solid" value.

John Locke
(1632–1704) was a political philosopher and founder of empiricism.

"Gold and silver, though they serve for few, yet command all the conveniences of life, and therefore in a plenty of them, consist riches."

John Locke, *Second Treatise on Government* (1690)

Wealth of nations
The first proponents of mercantilism argued that a well-stocked national "treasure chest" was the main foundation for economic health.

Modern economics has inherited two concerns from the mercantilist era. The first of these is the idea of "sound money", though this is no longer pegged to the gold and silver content of the coinage or the redeemability of promissory notes in precious metals, but rather to the total performance of the economy. The second is the "balance of payments" between what an economy earns from other economies and what is paid out to external suppliers of goods and services. It is still considered important to monitor this balance, but it is no longer treated as a "sacred cow" or as an infallible index of economic propriety.

We still overvalue gold – which is really rather a useless material, undeserving of its privileged position as the commodity in terms of which all other commodities – including money – are still commonly valued. But it is hard to say whether this is a relic of mercantilism or of gold's ancient, magical reputation as a uniquely untarnishable substance.

READINGS

L. Magnusson's **Mercantilism** (1994) is a good introduction.

I. Wallerstein's **The Modern World-system (Vol. 2)** (1980) is fundamental for the historical background, as is F. Braudel's three-volume **Civilization and Capitalism** (1983).

CONNECTIONS

On the origins of ideas about commerce, see **Fair Exchange** (p.56) and **A Capital Idea** (p.144). Other important economic ideas are explored in **Outside Eden** (p.66), **Laissez-faire** (p.246), **Workers Unite** (p.248), and **Solid Foundations** (p.370).

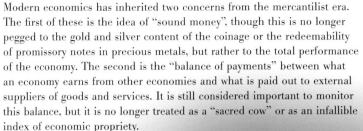

Laissez-faire

THE IDEA OF THE FREE MARKET

Trickle-down effect
Like a champagne pyramid, Smith's theory of an "invisible hand" suggested that wealth created by the rich would eventually trickle down to the poor.

The name of the Scots professor of moral philosophy, Adam Smith, has been linked with the cause of economic freedom ever since he published his *Inquiry into the Nature and Causes of the Wealth of Nations* in 1776. He had a lofty view of the importance of the law of supply and demand, believing that it affected far more than the market. "The natural effort of every individual to better his own condition" was the foundation of all political, economic, and moral systems.

In Smith's view, taxation was essentially an evil: first, it is an infringement of liberty; secondly, it distorts the natural operation of the market. He confidently believed that self-interest could be safely left to serve the common good. "It is not from the benevolence of the butcher, the brewer or the baker that we expect our dinner, but from their regard to their own interest." "In spite of their natural selfishness and rapacity," Smith declared, "[the rich] are led by an invisible hand to make nearly the same distribution of the necessaries of life which would have been made, had the earth been divided into equal portions among all its inhabitants."

In the long run, this optimistic view of the natural flow of wealth from rich to the poor has been proved false: the industrial revolution of the 19th century and the "knowledge economy" of the 20th opened glaring wealth gaps between classes and countries. But for a long time, Smith's formula seemed only slightly exaggerated: the rich of the industrializing era, for

"There is no art which one government sooner learns of another than that of draining money from the pockets of the people."

Adam Smith, *Inquiry into the Nature and Causes of the Wealth of Nations* (1776)

Adam Smith
(1723–90) was a key
exponent of the free
market idea.

instance, increased their workers' wages to stimulate demand; for a while, economists seriously hoped to eliminate poverty, as medical researchers hoped to eliminate disease.

Smith's *Inquiry into… the Wealth of Nations* appeared in the year of the American Declaration of Independence and should be counted among that nation's founding documents. It encouraged the revolution, for Smith said that government regulations limiting the freedom of colonies to engage in manufacture or trade were "a manifest violation of the most sacred rights of mankind". The USA has remained the homeland of economic liberalism ever since and a shining example of how laissez-faire can work. Meanwhile, wherever "planning", government regulation, or the "command economy" have displaced Smith's doctrines, economic progress has failed.

The idea of enlightened self-interest effectively means that greed is good. Smith had no place for pure altruism. He thought that merchants and usurers served their fellow men by buying cheap and selling dear. This was one defect of his thought. Another error was to assume that people can be relied on to predict their own best interests in the marketplace. In reality, people act irrationally and impulsively far more often than rationally or consistently. The market is more like a betting ring than a magic circle. Its unpredictability breeds lurches and crashes, insecurities and fears.

Smith's principles, strictly interpreted, would leave even education, religion, medicine, and the environment at the mercy of the market. In some respects, this has indeed come to pass. Gurus have become entrepreneurs, universities now resemble businesses, conservation is costed, and you can buy health even in systems expressly designed to treat it as a right. The world is still seeking a "third way" between unregulated and over-regulated markets.

Boston Tea Party
In 1773 American protestors destroyed British tea imports, setting the stage for the American Revolution. Their grievances anticipated Smith's arguments against government regulation.

LAISSEZ-FAIRE

Anti-globalization protest
Anti-capitalist marchers today aim their protests at "free-market" institutions, such as the World Bank, which they claim act against the interests of smaller economies.

Workers Unite

THE IDEA OF THE LABOUR THEORY OF VALUE

Valuable work
The price of this antique Chinese ivory casket would originally have reflected the cost of the labour invested in the elaborate carving.

David Ricardo recognized a principle of economics – that labour adds value to a product. He turned this insight into a law: value is proportional to the labour invested in it, "labour… being the foundation of all value, and the relative quantity of labour… almost exclusively determining the relative value of commodities".

In its crude form, the theory is wrong. Goods are not always exchanged at values proportionate to the labour invested in them; capital plays a part (and is not always just stored-up labour, since extremely valuable natural assets can be almost instantly realized for cash). The way the goods are perceived is also a factor. Rarity-value – which Ricardo did recognize, citing objects of art and "wines of a peculiar quality", but only as a short-term distorter – is

Joining forces
In the 19th century, workers, as well as capitalists, began to perceive the value of labour in the industrial process. This gave them the confidence to unite in their claims for better pay. This seminal image of workers is Il Quarto Stato by Giuseppe Pelizza.

"Wages should be left to the fair and free competition of the market, and should never be controlled by the interference of the legislature."

David Ricardo, *On Wages* (1817)

David Ricardo
(1772–1823) was an English banker and important economist.

the most obvious example; value added by advertising and recommendation is another. Still, the principle is right. Ricardo drew from it a counter-intuitive conclusion: if labour makes the biggest contribution to profits, one would expect high wages to reflect this – as generally, in modern industrial societies, they do. Ricardo, however, thought that in order to maximize profits, capitalists would always keep wages low. "There can be no rise in the value of labour without a fall in profits." Marx believed him, but both were ultimately proved wrong, since capitalists also recognized that it could be in their interests to pay well, not only to secure industrial peace and avert revolution, but also to improve productivity and increase demand.

However, an idea does not have to be right to be influential. The essential features of Ricardo's thoughts on labour – the labour theory of value and the idea of a permanent conflict of interest between capital and labour – passed via Marx to animate revolutionary unrest in late 19th-century Europe and the 20th-century world.

Priceless
In contradiction to the labour theory of value, the sale of Sunflowers *for £24m in 1987 in no way reflected the cost of Van Gogh's time.*

READINGS

D. Ricardo's **Principles of Political Economy and Taxation** (1817) is the basic work on the subject.

G. A. Caravale's (ed.) **The Legacy of Ricardo** (1985) is a collection of essays on his influence.

S. Hollander's **The Economics of David Ricardo** (1979) is an exhaustive study.

K. Marx's **Capital** (1867) re-interpreted the value of labour as the basis of society, history, and morality, as well as economics.

Neverland

THE UTOPIAN IDEA

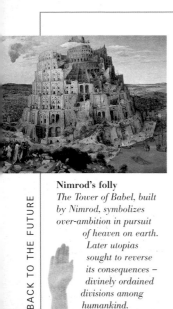

Nimrod's folly
The Tower of Babel, built by Nimrod, symbolizes over-ambition in pursuit of heaven on earth. Later utopias sought to reverse its consequences – divinely ordained divisions among humankind.

Utopias are ideal lands imagined in order to make implicit criticisms of real countries. In modern times, equality has been the main objective of utopians. In a Chinese fiction, the *Lieh Tzu*, complete by about 200 BC, Yu the Great discovered a land where "people were gentle, following nature without strife", practising free love, and devoted to music. But in individual Western imaginations, most utopias turn out to be dystopias in disguise: deeply repellent, albeit advocated with impressive sincerity. Plato imagined an ideal society, in which arts are outlawed and weak or unwanted infants are killed.

The tradition really got going with the work that gave the genre its name, Thomas More's *Utopia* (1516). Here there were golden chamber-pots and no pubs. Successor-utopias were even more unappealing. In Tommaso Campanella's *Citta del Sole* (1580), sexual couplings had to be licensed by astrologers. In the 1760s, Bougainville thought he had found a real-life sexual utopia in Tahiti: on departure, his ships' crews were raddled with sexually transmitted diseases.

Hitlerjugend
Utopias have a habit of degenerating into tyranny. Hitler's "New World Order" turned equality into uniformity.

William S. Gilbert
(1836–1911), librettist
in the operetta-writing
partnership of Gilbert
and Sullivan.

*"The Earl, the Marquis, and the Duke,
the Groom, the Butler and the Cook...
All shall equal be."*

W.S. Gilbert, *The Gondoliers* (1889)

From the 16th to the 19th centuries, many
projects were launched to create egalitarian
utopias in Europe and America, usually by
religious fanatics in a Christian tradition, or by
secular reformists, influenced by traditions that go back to Classical
antiquity: "The same law for all", for instance, was a principle the Stoics
advocated. Their justification for this was that men were "naturally" equal,
that inequalities were historical accidents, and that the state should try to
redress them. Some have gone further in demanding equality of
opportunity, or of power, or of actual material well-being for all. In
practice, this tends to lead to communism – since communal ownership
is the only guarantee against the unequal distribution of property – or to
dreariness. In America, as John Adolphus Etzler proposed to remodel it
in 1833, mountains are flattened and forests "ground to dust" to make
building-cement: something like this has actually happened in parts of
modern America. In Etienne Cabet's utopia, Icaria, clothes had to be
made of elastic to make the principle of equality "suit people of different
sizes". No one has seriously recommended equalization of age, brainpower,
beauty, stature, fatness, or luck; some inequalities genuinely are "natural".

The state always has an equalizing role to play in society. For those
who believe in the "natural" equality of all, the state is there to enforce
it; for those who do not, it has a moral role, levelling the "playing field",
redressing the imbalances between the strong and the weak, the rich and
the poor. However, the idea that this function of the state exceeds all
others in importance is dangerous, because equality enforced at the
expense of liberty can be tyrannous. Utopians usually display misplaced
faith in the power of society to improve citizens. They want us to defer
to guardian-dictators, intrusive computers, know-all theocrats, or
paternalistic sages, who do your thinking for you, over-regulate your life,
and crush or stretch you into comfortless conformity. The nearest
approximations to lasting realizations of utopian visions in the real world
were built in the 20th century by the Bolsheviks and Nazis. The search
for an ideal society is like the pursuit of happiness: it is better to travel
hopefully, because arrival breeds disillusionment or worse.

Sardine solutions
*Clusters of concrete dystopias
over the world's urban areas
are a legacy of 20th-century
modernism's attempts to
build "ideal" communities.*

READINGS

T. More's **Utopia** (1516) is the
starting-point of the modern
tradition of utopian writings.

J. Carey's (ed.) **The Faber
Book of Utopias** (1999) is
a superb anthology.

J.-J. Rousseau's **The Origins
of Inequality** (1754) is a
fundamental text.

R.W. Fogel's **The Fourth
Great Awakening** (2000)
is a provocative work, linking
radical American
egalitarianism to the
Christian tradition and
arguing for a future in which
equality will be attainable.

A. Sen's **Inequality
Reexamined** (1992) is an
arresting essay that brings
the story up to date and
poses challenges for future
thinking on the subject.

Getting Better

THE IDEA OF PROGRESS

CONNECTIONS

For the idea of linear time, see **Time's Arrow** (p.112). The idea of change is discussed in **All Change** (p.110). For a counter-perspective, see **Good and Evil** (p.48) and **A Golden Age** (p.90). See also **Class Struggle** (p.292) and **Tooth and Claw** (p.320).

The idea that in general, allowing for fluctuations, everything is always – and perhaps necessarily – getting better is so contrary to the experience of most of humankind that it is not surprising that it arose so late in history.

For most of the past, people stuck to the evidence and assumed they were living in times of decline or a world of decay – or of indifferent change, where history is just "one damn thing after another". To make progress credible, someone had to think up a way of comprehending evil that made all the woes of the world seem somehow for the best.

This was a long-unfulfilled task of theologians, who never satisfactorily answered the atheists' challenge: "If God is good, why is there evil?" In the 17th century, the growth of atheism made the task urgent. "To justify the ways of God to man" was the objective Milton set himself in his epic poem, *Paradise Lost* (1667). But it is one thing to be poetically convincing, quite another to produce a reasoned argument. In 1710, Gottfried Wilhelm Leibniz did so. He started from everyday experience. Good and evil are inseparable, because each is meaningless without the other. Freedom is good, but includes freedom to do evil; altruism is good only if selfishness is an option. Of all logically

Herbert Spencer (1820–1903), English evolutionary philosopher.

"Progress is not an accident but a necessity. It is part of nature."

Herbert Spencer, *Social Statics* (1850)

conceivable worlds, ours has, he submitted, the greatest possible surplus of good over evil. So – in the phrase Voltaire used to lampoon this theory – "all is for the best in the best of all possible worlds". In Voltaire's novel, *Candide* (1759), Leibniz is satirized as "Dr Pangloss", the hero's tutor, whose infuriating optimism is equal to every disaster.

Leibniz wanted to show that God's love was compatible with human suffering. It was not his purpose to endorse progress, and his "best world" could have been interpreted as one of static equilibrium, in which the ideal amount of evil was inbuilt. But, in alliance with the conviction of human goodness, which most thinkers of the Enlightenment shared, it made a secular millennium possible, towards which people could work by using their freedom (from divine predestination) to adjust the balance, bit by bit, in favour of goodness. The Marquis de Condorcet, for instance, thought he could see "the human race... advancing with a sure step along the path of truth, virtue and happiness", because political and intellectual revolutions had broken the hold of religion and tyranny on a human spirit "emancipated from its shackles [and] released from the empire of fate". Ironically, he wrote this endorsement of progress while under sentence of death from the French revolutionary authorities. The Revolution and the wars it provoked dissolved the optimism of the Enlightenment in blood.

Yet the idea of progress survived. In the 19th century it strengthened and fed on the "march of improvement" – the history of industrialization, the multiplication of wealth and muscle power, and the insecure but encouraging victories of constitutionalism against tyranny. It became possible to believe that progress was irreversible by human failings: programmed into nature by evolution. It took the horrors of the late 19th and 20th centuries – a catalogue of famines, failures, inhumanities, and genocidal conflicts – to unpick the idea from most people's minds.

READINGS

J.B. Bury's **The Idea of Progress** (1920) is an unsurpassed classic, stimulatingly challenged by R. Nisbet's **History of the Idea of Progress** (1980), which attempts to trace the idea back to Christian traditions of providence.

G.W. Leibniz's **Theodicy** (1710) is the classic statement, while J.M. de Condorcet's **The Future Progress of the Human Mind** (1794) is an eloquent and, in the circumstances, poignant history of progress.

W .Groom's **Forrest Gump** (1986), adapted for film in 1994, is an amusing modern interpretation of Voltaire's **Candide** (1759).

A type of progress
Just as handwritten scripts were adapted for type, which later evolved to meet changing fashions and the demands of technology, so over the centuries, human life and thought evolved. In both cases there have been those who maintain the changes represent a constant improvement, while others see no such progression.

Cleansing the Temple

THE IDEA OF ANTICLERICALISM

Scourge of intolerance
*Voltaire (1694–1778)
gained much admiration
for his involvement in
several anticlerical causes,
including the affair of the
Calas family (depicted
here), who were accused
of killing one of their sons
to prevent him from
becoming a Catholic.*

254

READINGS

P. Dykema and H. Oberman's
(eds) **Anticlericalism in
Late Medieval and Early
Modern Europe** (1993)
is an important collection
of essays.

S.J. Barnett's **Idol Temples
and Crafty Priests** (1999)
tackles the origins of
Enlightenment anticlericalism
in a fresh way.

P. Gay's two-volume
The Enlightenment (1996)
is a brilliant work with a
strong focus on the secular
thinking of the *philosophes*.

Voltaire was the best-connected man of the 18th century. He corresponded with Catherine the Great, corrected the King of Prussia's poetry, and influenced monarchs and statesmen all over Europe. His works were read in Sicily and Transylvania, plagiarized in Vienna, and translated into Swedish. The *Encyclopédie*, the great systematization of the thought of the Enlightenment, projected to every part of Europe. Because Voltaire and his collaborators regarded the Church as the great obstacle to reform on enlightened principles, the progress of the Enlightenment can be measured in anticlerical acts.

Voltaire erected his own temple to "the architect of the universe, the great geometrician", but regarded Christianity as an "infamous superstition to be eradicated – I do not say among the radical, who are not worthy of being enlightened and who are apt for every yoke, but among the civilized and those who wish to think". In 1759, the Jesuits were expelled from Portugal. In 1761, the Tsar secularized a great portfolio of Church property. Between 1764 and 1773, the Jesuit Order was abolished in most of the rest of the West. In the 1780s, 38,000 members of religious orders were forced into lay life. A Spanish minister proposed the forfeiture of most of the Church's land. In 1790, the King of Prussia proclaimed absolute authority over clergy in his realm. Meanwhile, at the most rarefied levels of the European elite, the cult of reason was taking on the characteristics of an alternative religion. In the rites of freemasonry a profane hierarchy celebrated the purity of its own wisdom, brilliantly portrayed in Mozart's *The Magic Flute* (1791).

The Enlightenment turned to darkness in the French Revolution and the wars that followed. The churches survived and in many ways recovered. But elite anticlericalism remained a feature of European politics and, in particular, the claim that in order to be liberal and progressive a state must be

Denis Diderot
(1713–84), French
writer and
encyclopedist.

"We must show that we are better than Christians and that science makes more good men than grace."

Denis Diderot, letter to Voltaire (1762)

secular has maintained an ineradicable hold. Modern attempts to rehabilitate Christianity in politics – such as the Social Catholic, "Social Gospel", and Christian Democrat movements – have had some electoral success and have influenced political rhetoric without reversing the effects of the Enlightenment. Indeed, the country where Christian rhetoric is loudest in politics is the one with the most rigorously secular constitution and public institutions, and has a political tradition most closely representative of the Enlightenment: the United States of America.

Religious satyrs
During the French Revolution of the 1790s, satirical pornographic prints featuring the clergy in compromising positions were distributed in an attempt to discredit and denigrate a corrupt Church.

A secular language
Mustapha Kemal Atatürk (1881–1938) made Turkey a secular republic in 1923, launching a programme of social and political reform, which included the Westernization of the Turkish (Arabic) language.

Forced to be Free

THE IDEA OF THE GENERAL WILL

Vive la République!
The doctrine of the general will promised an end to tyrant-kings, leading to the execution of Louis XVI (above), but it also opened the way to the tyranny of factions (like the Jacobins) and mobs.

Jean-Jacques Rousseau regarded the state as a corporation, or even a sort of organism, in which the individual identities of the citizens are subsumed. At a previous stage of history, the act occurred "by which people become a people… the real foundation of society… The people become one single being… Each of us puts his person and all his power in common under the supreme direction of the general will."

Citizenship is fraternity: an organic bond, equivalent to the blood-bond between brothers. The commands of the general will are perfect freedom – "social" or "civil" freedom, Rousseau calls it – and anyone constrained to obey them is simply being "forced to be free". Apart from an obviously fallacious argument ("to be governed by appetite alone is slavery, while obedience to a law one prescribes for oneself is freedom"),

Jean-Jacques Rousseau (1712–78) outlined the terms for membership of society.

> "Whoever refuses to obey the general will shall be constrained to do so by the whole body, which means nothing other than that he shall be forced to be free."

Jean-Jacques Rousseau, *The Social Contract* (1763)

CONNECTIONS

Other aspects of Rousseau's thought are covered in **The Noble Savage** (p.258), **We, the People** (p.260), and **Inalienable Rights** (p.264). For related ideas, see **My Country** (p.286), **Extreme Optimism** (p.290), and **Brother Knows Best** (p.306).

Rousseau was vague about the moral justification for this obviously dangerous doctrine. Immanuel Kant, however, provided one. By setting aside one's individual will or interests and exercising reason instead, one can identify objective goals of a kind whose merit is discernible by everybody. Submission to the general will limits one's own freedom in deference to the freedom of others. In theory, the general will is different from unanimity, sectional interests, or individual preferences. In practice, however, it just means the tyranny of the majority: Rousseau admitted that "the votes of the greatest number always bind the rest".

In Rousseau's version of the way his system works, political parties are outlawed because "there should be no partial society within the state". The same logic would proscribe trade unions, religious communions, and reformist movements. This is a licence for totalitarianism, and indeed all the movements shaped in whole or part by Rousseau's influence – the French Jacobins and communards, the Bolsheviks, the modern fascists, and the Nazis – have suppressed individual liberty. Yet the passion with which Rousseau invoked freedom has made it hard for his readers to see how illiberal his thought really was. The opening words of his essay of 1762 – "Man is born free and everywhere he is in chains!" – have been adopted as a slogan by countless revolutionaries.

READINGS

J.-J. Rousseau's **The Social Contract** (1762) is the defining work on the subject.

A. Levine's **The General Will** (1993) traces the concept from Rousseau to modern communism.

P. Riley's **The General Will before Rousseau** (1986) is a superb study of its origins.

Marching orders
In the 1980s, the Solidarity movement sought reform of the Communist regime in Poland, reflecting the "general will". However, Rousseau would not have approved of this "partial society" within the state.

Sticking together
A natural parallel for the idea of the general will can be found in the behaviour of fish that form large schools, within which individuals react and move together as one organism.

257

FORCED TO BE FREE

The Noble Savage

THE IDEA OF PRIMITIVE VIRTUE

Civilization has always had its malcontents. Moralists have frequently berated each other with examples of virtuous outsiders, who possess natural virtues that make up for lack of education, or of the goodness of a simple life uncorrupted by commerce and comfort.

In the 15th and early 16th centuries, European overseas exploration began to accumulate examples of ways of life supposedly close to those of "natural man" – naked, untutored, dedicated to foraging, and dependent on God. At first, these discoveries seemed disappointing. The Golden Age of primitive innocence was nowhere to be found. But clever scrutineers could find redeeming features in "savages". In the mid 16th century, the sceptic French essayist Michel de Montaigne argued that even so repugnant a practice as cannibalism had moral lessons for Europeans, whose mutual barbarities were much worse.

In the 17th century, however, missionaries believed they really had found the good savage of legend among the Hurons of North America. This tribe practised appalling barbarities, yet their egalitarian values and technical proficiency, compared with their neighbours, combined to make them seem full of natural wisdom. In the early 18th century, Louis-Armand de Lahontan made an imaginary Huron a spokesman for his own anticlerical radicalism. Voltaire made a hero of an

Natural nobility
The perceived virtues of American Indians impressed 18th-century Europeans. This idealized view was at odds with rival portrayals of them as subhuman barbarians.

CONNECTIONS

On the issue of the natural goodness of mankind, see **Good and Evil** (p.48) and **Ethical Beings** (p.136). For ideas that reflect the expanding panorama of mankind in European minds, see **Brotherhood of Man** (p.234) and **Nasty, Brutish, Short** (p.238).

Paradise lost?
The discovery of the South Seas gave Westerners an "Eden" on to which they could project visions of a tropical paradise. French artist Paul Gauguin portrayed the island of Tahiti as a place of innocence and abundance.

"Ingenuous Huron" who criticized kings and priests. The Jesuit Joseph-François Lafitau praised the Huron for practising free love, and in a play performed in Paris in 1768, a Huron-hero led an assault on the Bastille.

The socially inebriant potential of the Huron myth grew as more "noble savages" appeared during the exploration of the South Seas, a voluptuary's paradise of liberty and licence. In the mind of Jean-Jacques Rousseau, the idea of the noble savage blended into that of the common man, and the idea of "natural wisdom" licensed that of popular sovereignty. Without the Huron and the South Sea Islanders, perhaps, the French Revolution would have been unthinkable.

Yet the savage Eden proved full of serpents. The Huron died out, ravaged by European diseases. The "savage" became a subject for anthropology rather than ideology. The South Seas were corrupted by European venal habits and venereal diseases. Romantics continued to be drawn back there, however, and the noble savage reappeared in Margaret Mead's influential *Coming of Age in Samoa* (1928). She got the facts wrong, but that did not seem to matter. She depicted a sexually unrepressive paradise, uncompetitive, creatively fertilized by freedom, protected from the restraints and inhibitions that psychologists were uncovering in the West. Western adolescence was re-shaped in consequence by uncompetitive schooling, rod-sparing discipline, and cheap contraception.

Jean-Jacques Rousseau (1712–1778), French writer and political theorist.

"I dared to strip man's nature naked… and showed that his supposed improvement was the fount of all his miseries."

Jean-Jacques Rousseau, *Confessions* (1781)

READINGS

T. Ellingson's **The Myth of the Noble Savage** (2001) is a radical revision, while H. Fairchild's **The Noble Savage** (1925) is an elegant history of the concept.

A. Pagden's **The Fall of Natural Man** (1982) is an invaluable study of the ideas generated by early ethnography.

M. de Montaigne's **Essays** (1580) have barely dated in their perceptive commentaries on cannibalism and other relevant matters.

We, the People

THE IDEA OF REPRESENTATIVE DEMOCRACY

Democracy as we know it today – a system of representative government elected by universal or near-universal suffrage – was really an American invention. Attempts to trace it from the Ancient Greek system of the same name or from the French Revolution are misleadingly romantic.

While democracy was growing up in America in the late 18th and early 19th centuries, almost everyone in Europe was against it. Even advocates of popular sovereignty hesitated to recommend a system Plato and Aristotle had condemned. Rousseau detested it. As soon as representatives are elected, he thought, "the people are enslaved". Edmund Burke – the voice of political morality in late 18th-century England – called the system "the most shameless in the world". Even Immanuel Kant, who was once an advocate, reneged on democracy in 1795, branding it as the despotism of the majority. The political history of Europe in the 19th century is of "mouldering edifices" and democracy deferred, where the ruling elite were mindful of the terror of the scaffold and the menace of the mob.

In America, democracy "just growed": it took a European visitor to observe it and refine the idea. By the

Set in stone
At Mount Rushmore, giant busts of presidents George Washington, Thomas Jefferson, Theodore Roosevelt, and Abraham Lincoln commemorate the founders of the USA's democratic institutions.

> "*Americans of all ages, all stations of life, and all types of disposition are forever forming associations... In democratic countries knowledge of how to combine is the mother of all other forms of knowledge; on its progress depends that of all the others.*"

Alexis de Tocqueville (1805–59) was a perceptive writer on American politics.

Alexis de Tocqueville, *Democracy in America* (1835)

time the aristocratic French historian Alexis de Tocqueville went to America to research democracy in the 1830s, the USA had an exemplary democratic franchise in the sense that almost all adult white males had the vote. The exception was Rhode Island, where property qualifications for voters were still fairly stringent. De Tocqueville was wise enough, however, to realize that democracy really meant something deeper and subtler than that: "a society which all, regarding the law as their work, would love and submit to without trouble", where "a manly confidence and a sort of reciprocal condescension between the classes would be established, as far from haughtiness as from baseness". Meanwhile, "the free association of citizens" would "shelter the state from both tyranny and licence". Democracy, he concluded, was inevitable. "The same democracy reigning in American societies" was "advancing rapidly toward power in Europe", and the obligation of the old ruling class was to adapt accordingly: "to instruct democracy, reanimate its beliefs, purify its mores, regulate its movements" – in short, to tame it without destroying it.

America never perfectly exemplified the theory. De Tocqueville was frank about the shortcomings, some of which are still evident today: the costliness and inefficiency of government; the venality and ignorance of many public officials; the high levels of political bombast; the tendency for conformism to counterbalance individualism; the peril of the "tyranny of the majority"; the tension between crass materialism and religious enthusiasm; the threat from a rising plutocracy that could gain control of the state. Nevertheless, the advantages of democracy outweighed the defects. They could be computed in dollars and cents, and measured in splendid monuments erected in newly transformed wildernesses. Achievements included the strength of civic spirit, the spread of respect of law, the prospect of material progress, and, above all, the liberation of effort and energy that results from equality of opportunity.

Helping hand
The ideal of free elections has often suffered at the hands of corrupt ruling elites. This voter is taking part in Zimbabwe's general election in 2000 under the watchful eye of a government official.

261

WE, THE PEOPLE

READINGS

C. Williamson's **American Suffrage from Property to Democracy** (1960) traces the history of the American franchise.

H.C. Mansfield and D. Winthrop's (eds.) **Democracy in America** (2000) provides an interesting introduction to de Tocqueville's seminal text.

J. Bryce's **The American Commonwealth** (1888) sheds fascinating light on the reception of American democratic ideas in Europe.

Nation in Arms

THE IDEA OF THE CITIZEN-WARRIOR

Comrades at arms
Armed citizens often provided "cannon fodder" for revolution and its aftermath. These Red Army conscripts are rallying to the defence of the fledgling Bolshevik state against the Tsarist White Army during the Russian Civil War (1918–20).

More than Machiavellianism, Machiavelli's great contribution to history was his work on *The Art of War* (1520), in which he proposed that citizen-armies were best. There was only one thing wrong with this idea: it was impracticable. Gonzalo de Córdoba invited Machiavelli to instruct his troops and the result was a hopeless parade-ground tangle.

The reason why states relied on mercenaries and professional soldiers was that soldiering was a highly technical business; weapons were hard to handle and experience was essential seasoning for battle. The result was a "Machiavellian Moment" in the history of the Western world, where yeomanries and militias of dubious efficacy were maintained for essentially ideological reasons, alongside regular, professional forces. This

Training targets like this are regularly used by civilians as well as police marksmen.

> "A well-regulated militia being necessary to the security of a free state, the right of the people to keep and bear arms shall not be infringed."

US Constitution, 2nd Amendment (1791)

Citizen's army
France's late-18th-century revolutionary army was composed of conscripts from every walk of life.

probably contributed to political instability in the early modern West: armed citizenries could and sometimes did provide "cannon fodder" for revolution. By the late 18th century, however, the game had changed. Technically simple firearms could be effective even in ill-instructed hands. The impact of large masses of troops and intense fire-power counted for more than expertise. The American Revolutionary War was a transitional conflict: militias defended the revolution with help from professional French forces. By the time of the French Revolution, newly liberated "citizens" had to do all their fighting for themselves. "The Nation in Arms" won most of its battles and the era of mass conscription began. It lasted until the late 20th century, when rapid technical developments made large conscript forces redundant, though some countries retained compulsory military service in order to maintain a reservoir of manpower for defence or in the belief that military discipline is good for young people. Another, apparently ineradicable relic of the Machiavellian Moment is that "peculiar institution" of the USA, its loose gun laws, which are usually justified on the grounds that tight regulation of the gun trade would infringe the citizen's constitutional right to bear arms.

READINGS

J.G.A. Pocock's **The Machiavellian Moment** (1975) is the essential work.

G.Q. Flynn's **Conscription and Democracy** (2002) is an interesting study of the history of conscription in Britain, France, and the USA.

V. Davis Hanson's **Why the West Has Won** (2001) is a provocative argument in favour of the view that Western military culture is fundamentally democratic and freedom-loving – and therefore successful.

263

NATION IN ARMS

Bearing arms
For many US citizens, the right to bear arms is a fundamental freedom, and teaching the younger generation how to use them safely is seen by some as responsible citizenship.

Inalienable Rights

THE IDEA OF HUMAN RIGHTS

Fraternal thinker
Rousseau was one of the 18th-century thinkers who helped to formulate the idea of inalienable rights.

READINGS

J.-J. Rousseau's **Emile** (1762) outlines his ideas on people's rights in this novel about education, while T. Paine's **The Rights of Man** (1791) remains a classic polemic.

H. Lee's **To Kill a Mockingbird** (1960) depicts racial injustice in the American South through the eyes of a young girl.

N. Mailer's **An American Dream** (1965) is a black comedy that exposes the sacrifice of personal integrity in the pursuit of material success.

Most states throughout history demanded ultimate power over subjects who surrendered rights. In 18th-century Europe and America, the assertion of liberties beyond the state's reach began to turn subjects into citizens. French philosopher Jean-Jacques Rousseau and English political writer Tom Paine formulated the idea that there are human rights too important for the state to overrule. It was the climax of a long search by radical thinkers for ways of limiting rulers' absolute power over their subjects.

Revolutionaries in France and America seized on the idea, but the rights in question were easier to assert than to identify. The US Declaration of Independence in 1776 identified the key rights as "life, liberty and the pursuit of happiness". The first was ignored by all states, which continued to put people to death when it suited them. The second and third seemed, at first, too vague to change the course of history; they could be ignored on the specious grounds that different people had conflicting claims to liberty and happiness. In France, they were repeatedly sidelined by illiberal governments until well into the 20th century. Even in America, the founding Declaration's supposedly "human" rights were long denied to slaves and their descendants.

But the idea acted on the world in an unexpected way. In the late 19th and 20th centuries, it became the basis of the "American dream", according to which everyone in America could pursue a kind of happiness – material prosperity – with encouragement from the state, instead of the usual interference. In partial consequence, the USA became the richest and, therefore, the most powerful country. By the turn of the millennium, the American example was a magnet for the world. Most countries copied

The **US flag** is recognized worldwide as a symbol of wealth and freedom.

"We hold these truths to be self-evident, that all men are created equal, that they are endowed by their Creator with certain unalienable rights, that among these are life, liberty and the pursuit of happiness."

US Declaration of Independence (4 July, 1776)

An American Dream
For many Americans, life, liberty, and happiness is manifested in the achievement of material prosperity.

the institutions – a free market, a democratic constitution, and the rule of law – that made the American dream deliverable.

In the same period, most states signed up, with varying degrees of commitment, to the "Helsinki Process" (1975–83), which defined further human rights: of immunity from arbitrary arrest and imprisonment; of peaceful association; of self-expression within the limits of public order; of immunity from persecution on grounds of race, sex, creed, or disability; of education; and of a basic level of shelter, health, and subsistence. Life and liberty, however, remained problematic: life, because of abiding disputes over whether the right applies to criminals, the unborn, and victims of euthanasia; liberty, because of disparities of power. These continued to leave many people effectively defenceless against predatory states, criminal organizations, and rich corporations. In the early 21st century, the rhetoric of human rights has triumphed almost everywhere, but the full reality has yet to reach most of the world.

CONNECTIONS

On the authoritarian background against which the rights-theorists rebelled, see **Watching the Flock** (p.80) and **Nasty, Brutish, Short** (p.238). For Rousseau's other ideas, see **Forced to be Free** (p.256) and **The Noble Savage** (p.258).

Promontory of Asia

THE IDEA OF EUROPE

European union?
Around the 18th century, the appearance of maps showing Europe as a distinct entity coincided with a widely held conviction of European superiority.

"I must begin with Europe," wrote the Greek geographer Strabo about half a century before the birth of Christ, "because it is both varied in form and admirably adapted by nature for the development of excellence in men and governments." After a long period of near-oblivion, the name and idea of Europe revived between the 15th and 18th centuries, as European self-confidence recovered. The divisions of Europe did not heal (rather, they got worse). Agreement about where the frontiers of the region lay was never achieved. Yet the sense of belonging to a European community and sharing a Europe-wide culture became typical of elites. The uniformity of enlightened taste in the 18th century made it possible to glide between widely separated frontiers with little more cultural dislocation than a modern traveller feels in a succession of airport lounges. The historian Edward Gibbon – Strabo's devoted reader, who made his stepmother send him his copy to study while he was at a militia training camp – was mid-way through his *History of the Decline and Fall of the Roman Empire* (1788) when he formulated a European idea: "It is the duty of a patriot to prefer and promote the

---

CONNECTIONS

No other continent can be so identified with an idea – perhaps because other continents have more obviously definable geographical characters. Compare: **Out of Africa** (p.378), **American Dream** (p.336), and **Centre of the World** (p.182).

The **European Union** parliament building is situated in Brussels, Belgium.

"We must build a kind of United States of Europe."

Winston Churchill, speech in Zurich (19 September 1946)

exclusive interest of his native country: but a philosopher may be permitted to enlarge his views, and to consider Europe as one great republic, whose various inhabitants have attained almost to the same level of politeness and cultivation."

Like Strabo's, his belief in this common European culture was inseparable from a conviction of European superiority, "distinguished above the rest of mankind". The re-emergence of the idea of Europe was fraught with menace for the rest of the world. Yet the overseas empires founded from Europe in the 18th and 19th centuries proved fragile; their moral records were not good enough to sustain the notion of European superiority. In the first half of the 20th century, the idea of a single Europe dissolved in wars and subsided in the fissures of ideological quakes. It became commonplace to acknowledge the fact that "Europe" is an elastic term, a "mental construction" that corresponds to no objective geographical reality and has no natural frontiers. Europe, said the poet Paul Valéry, was merely "a promontory of Asia". The form in which the idea was revived in the European Union movement of the late 20th century would have been unrecognizable to Gibbon: its unifying principles were democracy and a free internal market; but its member-states' choice of how to define Europe, and whom to exclude from its benefits, has so far remained as self-interested as ever.

READINGS

D. Hay's **Europe: the Emergence of an Idea** (1957) is an excellent history of the concept.

Long and short histories respectively can be found in N. Davies's **Europe: a History** (1995) and F. Fernández-Armesto's **The Times Illustrated History of Europe** (1995).

Common culture
Young aristocratic imaginations, moulded by the experience of the "Grand Tour", identified the 18th-century idea of Europe with a common cultural heritage derived from classical antiquity.

The euro
In 2001, the adoption of a single European currency (the euro) by many European countries marked the first stage of European Monetary Union, and a further stage towards an ever-closer and growing European Union.

The Second Sex

THE IDEA OF FEMINISM

CONNECTIONS

Ideas particularly related to women and their role in society can be followed in **A Family Affair** (p.40), **God Is a Woman** (p.72), **Just Like a Woman** (p.74), **Love Conquers All** (p.200), and **Many Mouths** (p.270).

The doctrine that women collectively constituted a class of society, historically oppressed and deserving of emancipation, was a product of late 18th-century preoccupations with the rights "of man and the citizen".

Olympe de Gouges and Mary Wollstonecraft launched a tradition, recognizable in feminism today, in two works, both published in 1792: de Gouges' *Declaration des Droits de la Femme et de la Citoyenne* and Wollstonecraft's *Vindication of the Rights of Women*. Both authors had to struggle to earn their living; both led unconventional sex lives; both lives ended tragically. De Gouges was guillotined in 1793 for defending the King of France; Wollstonecraft died in childbirth in 1797. Both rejected the entire previous tradition of female championship, which eulogized women for their virtues. Instead, they admitted their vices and blamed male oppression.

This view was uninfluential at first. Gradually, however, in the 19th and 20th centuries, men found a use for feminism as a justification for re-incorporating women into the labour market and so exploiting their productivity more effectively. When feminism became fashionable in the 1960s, it was after two World Wars had demonstrated the need and efficacy of contributions by women in realms formerly reserved or privileged for men. The French writer Simone de Beauvoir launched the new feminism one day in 1946, when, she said, "I began to reflect about myself and it struck me with a sort of surprise that the first thing I had to say was, 'I am a woman'."

Feminists claimed to be able to force men to change the rules in women's favour. At least they succeeded in persuading women to try to make the most of social changes and opportunities that would have occurred anyway. Some critics bemoaned the unintended effects: by competing with men women gave up some traditional advantages – male deference and much informal power; by joining the workforce they added another level of exploitation to their roles as home-makers and mothers, with consequent stress and overwork. Some women, who wanted to remain at home and dedicate themselves to their husbands and children, found themselves doubly disadvantaged: exploited by men and pilloried by "sisters". Society still needs to strike the right balance: liberating all women to lead the lives they want, without having to conform to roles devised for them by intellectuals of either sex.

Having it all
In the early 21st century, a wish for financial independence has led increasing numbers of women to combine the traditional role of mother with a demanding career.

"*Women may mount the scaffold: they should also be able to ascend the bench.*"

Olympe de Gouges (1792)

Olympe de Gouges
(1745–93) was a
prolific writer of
political pamphlets.

Votes for women!
In the West, calls for votes for women were resisted until the social changes brought about by WWI made reform inevitable. Emmeline Pankhurst (pictured here in 1914) was Britain's leading campaigner for women's suffrage.

READINGS

M. Wollstonecraft's **Vindication of the Rights of Woman** (1792) and her novel **Maria, or the Wrongs of Woman** (1798) – and O. de Gouges's **Rights of Woman** are the fundamental texts.

C. L. Johnson's (ed.) **The Cambridge Companion to Mary Wollstonecraft** (2002) is wide-ranging and helpful.

Many Mouths

THE IDEA OF OVERPOPULATION

One-child family
Some states have taken drastic measures to try to avoid overpopulation. Since 1979, China has actively encouraged one-child families with a range of campaigns and incentives.

In the second half of the 18th century, world population boomed. The reasons for this, still poorly understood, may be connected with a reduction in disease, resulting from evolutionary changes in microbes that had previously targeted humans. Between about 1750 and 1850, the population of China doubled, that of Europe nearly doubled, and that of the Americas doubled and doubled again. The doom-fraught theories of Thomas Malthus were therefore of their time – a voice crying for the want of a wilderness, an earnest, rational clergyman peering with anxious charity into a grave new world of overpopulation tempered by disaster.

Previously, no one had believed there could be any such thing as overpopulation. More people meant more economic activity, more wealth, more manpower, more strength. In his *Essay on Population* of 1798, Malthus drew the statistical basis of his new idea from the work of the arch-optimist, the Marquis de Condorcet, who cited rising population as evidence of progress. Malthus re-filtered the statistics through his own pessimistic vision. He concluded that population was rising so much faster than food production that humankind was bound for disaster. "The power of population is indefinitely greater than the power in the earth to produce subsistence for man." Only "natural checks" – an apocalyptic array of famine, plague, war, and catastrophe – could keep numbers down to a level at which people could be fed.

Malthus wrote so convincingly that the elites of the world panicked into believing him. His view, according to William Hazlitt, was "a ground on which to fix the levers that may move the world". Among the disastrous consequences were the wars and imperial ventures provoked by people's fear of running out of space, such as the German drive in the 19th century for *Lebensraum* (living space). A new wave of Malthusian apprehension hit the world in the mid 20th century as world population again surged forward; the results were again disastrous.

READINGS

A. Pyle's (ed.) **Population: Contemporary Responses to Thomas Malthus** (1994) is a fascinating compilation of early criticism.

S. Hollander's **The Economics of Thomas Robert Malthus** (1997) provides an exhaustive and authoritative overview.

M.L. Bacci's **A Concise History of World Population** (2001) offers a useful introduction to demographic history.

Family planning
It is only since the second half of the 20th century that reliable forms of contraception, such as the contraceptive pill, have had far-reaching effects on the size of human populations.

The so-called "green revolution" smothered
the world in pesticides and chemical fertilizers in
an effort to boost food production; some countries
introduced compulsory family-limitation policies, including
sterilization programmes; enormous investments were made in
contraceptive research, which produced dubious moral and medical side-effects.
But Malthusian anxieties have always proved false: demographic statistics are subject to
fluctuations, and trends are never sustained for long. Overpopulation is a rare phenomenon
in history; as an ever higher proportion of the world's population attains prosperity, the
paradox is that people breed less.

Thomas Malthus
(1766–1834) warned
of the dangers of
overpopulation.

*"Population, when unchecked, increases in a
geometrical ratio. Subsistence only increases
in an arithmetical ratio."*

Thomas Malthus, *Essay on Population* (1798)

A tide of humanity
*Malthus's apocalyptic view
of rapid population growth
has not been borne out.
However, in developing
countries, such as
Bangladesh (above), rates
of population increase are
still high.*

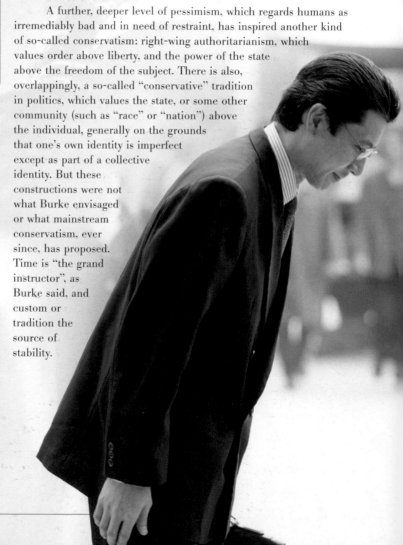

If It Ain't Broke

THE CONSERVATIVE IDEA

CONNECTIONS

On the problem of humans' mortal nature, see **Ethical Beings** (p.136). For other manifestations of political pessimism, see **Legalism** (p.146), and **Nasty, Brutish, Short** (p.238). On recent conservative ideas, see **Solid Foundations** (p.370).

Conservatism is part of a pessimistic disposition: unwillingness to tamper radically with things as they are, in case they get worse. In 1790 Edmund Burke re-formulated this tendency as an idea, in recoil from the excesses of the French Revolution.

A further, deeper level of pessimism, which regards humans as irremediably bad and in need of restraint, has inspired another kind of so-called conservatism: right-wing authoritarianism, which values order above liberty, and the power of the state above the freedom of the subject. There is also, overlappingly, a so-called "conservative" tradition in politics, which values the state, or some other community (such as "race" or "nation") above the individual, generally on the grounds that one's own identity is imperfect except as part of a collective identity. But these constructions were not what Burke envisaged or what mainstream conservatism, ever since, has proposed. Time is "the grand instructor", as Burke said, and custom or tradition the source of stability.

French writer and
satirist **Alphonse Karr**
(1808–90).

"Plus ça change, plus c'est la même chose"
(The more things change, the more they
remain the same)

Alphonse Karr, *Les Guêpes* (1849)

READINGS

E. Burke's **Reflections on the Revolution in France** (1790) is the founding text of the conservative tradition.

T.L. Peacock's **Melincourt** (1830) is a novel that brilliantly satirizes, though perhaps rather caricatures, Burke's idea of conservatism.

M.Oakeshott's **Rationalism in Politics** (1962) and R. Scruton's **The Meaning of Conservatism** (1980) are outstanding modern statements.

Order is essential, but not for its own sake – only to equalize the opportunities of all of a state's subjects to exercise liberty. Although there must be a bias towards the status quo, a state must be willing to reform itself when necessary; otherwise revolution, with all its evils, will ensue. When Robert Peel founded the British Conservative Party in 1834, he enshrined this balance in his party's programme: to reform what needed reforming and to "conserve" what did not – a formula with the flexibility to endure change. In partial consequence, most successful governments in modern times have adopted broadly conservative strategies, although they have not always admitted as much. Distrust of ideology is another feature modern conservatism inherited from Burke, who declared peace better than truth, and "metaphysical distinctions" to be "a Serbonian bog". Theorizing, he said, is "one sure symptom of an ill-conducted state".

Bowing to the past
Conservatism aims to preserve
traditional values and customs
where they serve present needs.
Modern Japanese businessmen
still greet each other with a
respectful bow.

The Big Idea

THE IDEA OF IDEALISM

In everyday language, "idealism" means an approach to life targeted on lofty aspirations. Philosophical idealism is different: the idea that only ideas exist. It would be easier to understand, perhaps, if it were re-named "idea-ism". From an idealist point of view, everything that exists would be a proper subject for this book.

There are stray indications in texts of the first millennium BC that a notion along these lines had occurred to thinkers in Ancient India, China, and Greece. At first glance, this idea so closely resembles Plato's theory that only ideal

Brain waves
According to idealism, mental perceptions are the only realities we know. Technological devices, such as this early EEG machine – a device to trace currents in the brain – prove the reality of mental activity but are incapable of telling us that this is all there is.

> *"The idea is the notion of the Idea... whose object is the Idea as such... the absolute and all truth, the Idea which thinks itself."*
>
> **Georg F.W. Hegel, *The Science of Logic* (1812–16)**

According to idealism, **ideas** are the only reality, however fleeting or fragile,

READINGS

Bishop George Berkeley's theory appeared in **The Dialogues between Hydas and Philonous** (1713).

F.H. Bradley's **Appearance and Reality** (1893) is a classic statement of an extreme form of idealism.

G. Vesey's (ed.) **Idealism: Past and Present** (1982) treats the subject historically.

"forms" are real that some people have confusingly called this "idealism", too. In the strict sense of the term, however, idealism was not systematically formulated until the Anglo-Irish philosopher Bishop George Berkeley did so in the early 18th century. Our assumption that material objects are real, he reasoned, derives from our mental registration of them; but those mental perceptions are the only realities of which we have evidence. Therefore, we cannot know that there are real things outside our minds, "nor is it possible that they should have any existence, out of the minds or thinking things which perceive them". In other words, there may be no such thing as a rock – just the idea of it. Dr Johnson claimed to be able to refute this theory by kicking the rock.

This thinking was taken much further by German theorists of the 19th century and led to a sometimes furious and still unresolved debate among philosophers about whether it is possible to distinguish "things in themselves" from the ideas of them that we have in our minds. As with many of the theoretical debates of the past – over theological arcana in antiquity, for instance, or the proper dress for clergymen in the 17th century – it seems hard to see, at first glance, what the fuss was and is about, since, as a working hypothesis, the assumption that perceptions reflect realities beyond themselves seems unavoidable. But the debate matters because of its serious implications for the organization and conduct of society.

Taken to one possible logical conclusion, idealism would lead us into the desperate cul-de-sac of denying the existence of anything outside our own minds. This has played a part, as a trend or tendency, in inspiring modern anarchism, subjectivism, and other kinds of extreme individualism. To escape this consequence, some philosophers proposed, in effect, the annihilation of the concept of self: to be real, ideas had to be collective. This claim fed corporate and totalitarian doctrines of society and the state. Ultimately, idealism led some of its proponents into a kind of modern monism according to which the only reality is "the absolute" – a consciousness that we all share. Self is part of everything else. This doctrine sounds benevolent, but is vulnerable to appropriation by self-appointed leaders of religious cults and others who claim to be able to embody, represent, or interpret the absolute.

CONNECTIONS

For further examination of Plato's ideas, see **Not a Horse** (p.116) and **The New Illusion** (p.108). For related ideas, see **Reality Unveiled** (p246) and **My Country** (p.286). On "heroes", see **Hero Inside** (p.304).

275

THE BIG IDEA

A mysterious web
A micrograph of brain cells provides an intriguing physiological picture of thought processes in action.

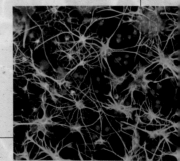

Reality Unveiled

THE IDEA OF ABSTRACTION

Abstraction – inferring universal realities from the common qualities of particular objects – has reformed the way we view the world. First, in the 18th century, through scientific systems of classification, and then in the 20th, through artists' re-depictions of reality.

Whether abstractions exist, or, if they do, whether it is useful to speak of them, is the subject of an old philosophical debate. For example, we are aware of various blue objects, but are they instances of a universal "blueness", with which we have no direct contact? Can we infer the reality of mathematical concepts like "three" or "triangles" from our apparent ability to identify sets of three or to group them in a triangular fashion? Do what mammals or flowers have in common make them in some sense the same thing as each other or, if we think so, are we mistaking categories of convenience for realities?

Thanks in part, perhaps, to the powerful arguments formulated in 1689 by John Locke, who revered abstraction as a uniquely human power of thought, most 18th-century scientists believed that by classifying one could expose the true nature of the objects of enquiry. The society portraitist, Sir Joshua Reynolds, applied the idea to art, arguing that the role of the artist was to abstract from his subject the universal qualities undiscernible to the common eye: heroism, greatness, or something else equally flattering to the sitter. In the 19th century, Schiller and Schopenhauer, among other thinkers, went further, reviving, with the help of a great deal of technical philosophical language, one of the great principles of the artistic theory of the Renaissance: the reality the artist depicts is not in the appearance of the object depicted, but its underlying

"Art is not the expression of the appearance of reality as we see it, nor of the life which we live, but of true reality and true life."

Piet Mondrian, *Circle* (1937)

Perfect Harmony

THE IDEA OF CLASSICAL PRINCIPLES IN ART

European artists had always admired and imitated the art of Ancient Greece and Rome. The great innovation of the Renaissance was that theorists of aesthetics worked out the principles that, by the 17th century, were being called "classical", and these were adopted by artistic academies as rules to be enforced.

These rules included: mathematical proportion as the secret of beautifully arranged shapes (and harmonious music); the privileging of certain shapes – such as the circle, the triangle, the square, the spiral, the "serpentine line", the "golden" rectangle (whose short sides were two-thirds the length of the long ones) – which varied at different times with different schools; the observation of mathematically calculated perspective (first explained by Alberti in 1418); and the embodiment of ancient philosophical ideas – such as Plato's "ideal form" or Aristotle's inner "substance" – which a work of art should seem to wrest from whatever part of nature it represented.

The demand that an artist should, as Shakespeare said, "surpass life" in depicting perfection meant, above all, that realism should mean more than the mere imitation of nature – but attempt to reach a transcendent reality. "To those who know and study the works of the Greeks," said the German art critic Johann Winckelmann, who codified classicism in his *Thoughts on the Imitation of the Works of the Greeks* (1755), "… their masterpieces reveal not only Nature in its greatest beauty, but something more than that… certain ideal beauties of Nature which… exist only in the intellect."

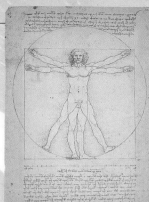

Perfect proportions
One of the greatest theorists of "classical" aesthetics was the Renaissance artist and engineer, Leonardo da Vinci. Da Vinci's Vitruvian man focused on the ideal proportions of the human figure.

Church within a temple
Renaissance architecture, such as the Church of San Lorenzo in Rome, used classical proportions to lend elegance and style.

READINGS

L. Alberti's **On Painting** (1435) and A. Palladio's **The Four Books of Architecture** (1570) are a good starting-place for the new ideas of "harmonious" construction.

F. Haskell's **Patrons and Painters** (1980) distils the work of the foremost scholar in the field.

J. Mordant Crook's **The Greek Revival** (1995) focuses with panache on Greek models in architecture.

Organic proportions
"Classical" rules, based on mathematical calculations, helped to determine the proportional lengths of an organ's windpipes, needed for perfect pitch.

Johann Winckelmann
(1717–68) articulated the neoclassical revival.

"To take the ancient models is our only way to become great."

J.J. Winckelmann, *Thoughts on the Imitation of the Works of the Greeks* (1755)

Back to Nature

THE IDEA OF ROMANTICISM

"Natural" landscape
In his quest for a more "natural" landscape, in reaction against the prevailing Classical style, William Kent (1684–1748) scattered temples and rustic grottoes in his landscapes, as here at Stowe in the UK.

In 1800, the introspective German poet Novalis created one of Romanticism's most potent symbols, the *blaue Blume*, the elusive "blue flower" that has symbolized Romantic yearning ever since.

The 18th century in Europe was supposedly the "Age of Reason". But its failures – its wars, its oppressive regimes, its disappointment with itself – suggested the idea that reason alone was not enough. Intuition was at least its equal. Feelings were as good as thought and nature still had lessons to teach civilization. One factor underlying this new perception was closer contact between Europe and previously unknown worlds and cultures. In the New World, explorers found an inspiring wilderness. The scientific drawings made on an expedition to Quito, Ecuador, by Spanish engineers in the mid 1700s seem calculated to arouse the senses with awe and reverence for nature. Meanwhile the "noble savage" (see p.258) seemed to disclose wisdom that reason and learning could not unlock without the help of simple passions. The prevailing mood of the 19th century in the West was romantic, sentimental, enthusiastic, nostalgic, chaotic, and self-critical, whereas that of the 18th century, at its most characteristic, had been rational, ordered, detached, passionless, complacent, and assertive. The change that overtook Beethoven's music or Goya's painting during the Napoleonic Wars was symptomatic of the transformation of a whole culture.

The Romantic movement was not just a reaction against informally deified reason and classicism: it was also a re-blending of popular sensibilities into the values and tastes of educated people. Its poetry was "the language of ordinary men"; its grandeur rustic; its religion was "enthusiasm", which was a dirty word in the salons of the Ancien Régime but which drew crowds of thousands to popular preachers. The music of

Baron d'Holbach (1723–89) was a leading French anti-clerical philosopher.

"Return to Nature! She will… drive from your heart… the anxieties which rend you… the hatreds that separate you from Man whom you must love!"

Baron d'Holbach, *System of Nature* (1770)

Romanticism ransacked traditional airs for melodies. Its theatre and opera borrowed from the cacophonous serenades of street mummers. Its prophet was the German philosopher Johann von Herder, who praised the moral power of the "true poetry" of "those whom we call savages". Its philosopher was Rousseau, who taught the superiority of untutored passions over contrived refinement. Its slogan was devised by the collector of folk-tales Jakob Grimm: "*Das Volk dichtet*" ("The people make poetry"). Its portraiture showed society ladies in peasant dress in gardens "landscaped" to look natural, re-invaded by romance. "The people" had arrived in European history as a creative force and as a re-moulder of its masters in its own image.

The 19th century, the century of Romanticism, would also awaken democracy, socialism, industrialization, "total" war, and "the masses" – backed by far-seeing members of the elite – "against the classes".

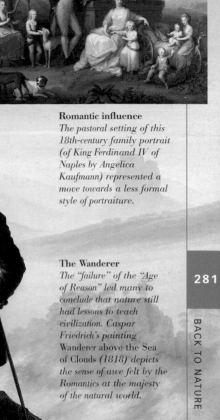

Romantic influence
The pastoral setting of this 18th-century family portrait (of King Ferdinand IV of Naples by Angelica Kaufmann) represented a move towards a less formal style of portraiture.

READINGS

I. Berlin's **The Roots of Romanticism** (1965) is a challenging collection of lectures, while W. Vaughan's **Romanticism and Art** (1994) is a spirited survey, and D. Wu's **Companion to Romanticism** (1999) is a useful background guide.

J. Goethe's **The Sorrows of Young Werther** (1774) is the archetypal tale of a tragic romantic hero.

The Wanderer
The "failure" of the "Age of Reason" led many to conclude that nature still had lessons to teach civilization. Caspar Friedrich's painting Wanderer above the Sea of Clouds *(1818) depicts the sense of awe felt by the Romantics at the majesty of the natural world.*

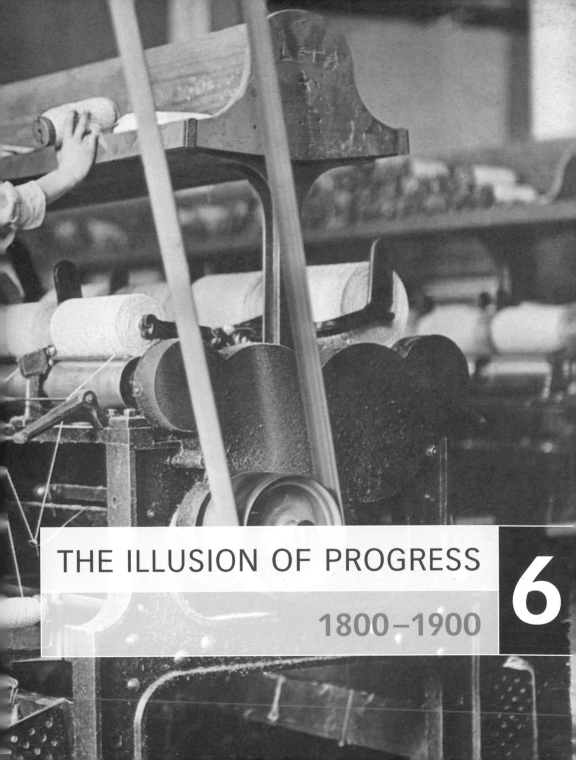

THE ILLUSION OF PROGRESS

1800–1900

6

19th-Century Frustrations

The French Revolution streaked the Enlightenment with shadows, scarring it with the slashes of the guillotine. In 1798, Etienne Gaspard Robertson displayed a freak light-show in Paris, making monstrous shapes loom at the audience from a screen or flicker eerily, projected on to clouds of smoke. Meanwhile, in electrifying demonstrations of the newly discovered wonders of galvanization, real-life precursors of Frankenstein made corpses twitch to thrill audiences.

It was not the "sleep of reason" that produced monstrosities like these. They were creatures of its most watchful hours: the hideous issue of scientific experimentation, tortured by "crimes committed in the name of liberty". They were pre-figurations and predictors of how monstrous modernity could be.

Meanwhile, the failures of humankind provoked Romanticism – a reaction in favour of nature. Sentiment, enthusiasm, and angst replaced 18th-century reason, dispassion, and complacency. Was humankind lord of creation or subject to nature? Yet one feature of the thought of the pre-revolutionary world survived, bloodied but unbowed: the belief in progress.

Driven by ambition
Napoleon Bonaparte emerged from the shadows of the French Revolution to impose his will on the changing map of Europe.

Instead of a golden age of the past – the normal locus of utopias in earlier periods – the "perfectibilians" of the 19th century thought the golden age was still to come.

Progress, however, could no longer be seen as a function of human reasoning: the collapse of the Enlightenment had brought down the house of reason, exposing human violence and irrationality. All that remained were "crooked timbers" with which "nothing straight" could be made. Improvement came to be seen as driven by vast impersonal forces – "laws" of nature, of history, of economics, of biology, of "blood and iron" – instead of by reason. The result was a mechanized and brutalized world picture.

But the illusion of progress was sustained by staggering conquests in in the realms of science and technology. An industrial revolution driven by steam immeasurably multiplied the power of muscle. Science discovered formerly invisible worlds – exposing the fossil record of the Earth, perceiving links between species, magnifying microbes, manipulating gases, measuring previously ill-known forces, such as magnetism, electricity, and atmospheric pressure.

Every advance was adapted for evil as well as good. People's intellects and morality registered none of the expected improvements. Like the Enlightenment that preceded it, the 19th-century "age of progress" dissolved in blood – in the cataclysm of World War I and the horrors of the 20th century. Those excesses flowed from 19th-century ideas of

Beethoven's Fifth
Nineteenth-century Romanticism can be heard in the impassioned compositions of Ludwig van Beethoven.

nationalism, militarism, the value of violence, the rootedness of race, the sufficiency of science, the irresistibility of history, and the cult of the state. A chilling fact about the ideas in this chapter is that most of them generated appalling effects. The 19th-century mind shaped the future of the world. Its ideas had, however, relatively little influence on the age in which they took shape. That is not surprising for there is bound to be a time-lag between the birth of an idea and the engendering of its own progeny. The philosophies that seem best to characterize the industrial phase of Western history – utilitarianism, pragmatism, Marxism – were among its results, not its causes.

The factories went up in what was still a Renaissance world, as far as the elite were concerned – "always talking about the Greeks and Romans", as William Hazlitt observed. Even scientific thought contributed surprisingly little to industrialization. The late 18th-century inventors of the processes that made the industrial revolution possible – coke smelting, mechanized spinning, steam pumping, and the steam-driven loom – were all heroes of "self-help": self-taught artisans and engineers with little or no scientific formation. It would be truer to say that European science was hijacked for the aims of industry – bought by money for "useful research", diverted by dogmas of social responsibility – than that it had an inbuilt practical vocation. At the start of the 19th century, William Blake

Imperial traces
The British Empire reached its apogee in India, leaving its legacy in the country's infrastructure, such as Victoria Memorial Hall, Calcutta.

could still draw Europe as a "Grace" among equals, supported, arm-in-arm, by Africa and America. Over the century as a whole, however, unprecedented demographic, industrial, and technical strides opened new gaps.

Industrialized parts of the world – mainly the "white man's" world in Europe and North America – drew apart and ahead. The result was a relatively brief period of European hegemony when European influence and "business imperialism" extended over much of the world. It was a brief hegemony. By the end of the century, the USA and, to a lesser extent, Japan, had overtaken most European countries in industrial prowess and capacity for war – which, to most people, was the criterion that really counted. Later, European empires would collapse as spectacularly as they had arisen.

Still, the 19th century remains a century of "European miracle": the culmination of Europe's long commercial "out-thrust", imperial initiatives, and scientific achievements. Most of the world-shaping ideas that arose in Asia were responses or adjustments to the unaccustomed power, receptions, or rejections of European exhortations or examples.

My Country

THE IDEA OF NATIONALISM

Limits of geography
The imposition of national boundaries is no guarantee that the peoples living within them will share a common identity. In 1994 in ethnically divided Rwanda, hundreds of thousands of Tutsi people were massacred by their Hutu neighbours.

READINGS

E. Gellner's **Nationalism** (1998) is a superb introduction, while B. Anderson's **Imagined Communities** (1991) is a pioneering study of nationalism and identity.

E. Hobsbawm and T. Ranger's (eds) **The Invention of Tradition** (1983) and D. Simpson's **Romanticism, Nationalism and the Revolt against Theory** (1993) are both useful reference works.

H. Cogniard's play **La Cocarde Tricolore** (1831) personifies nationalism in the character of Nicolas Chauvin.

Even the most impassioned nationalists disagree about what a nation is and no two analysts' lists of national characteristics ever quite match.

Johann Gottfried von Herder, who is usually credited with starting the modern tradition of nationalist thought, preferred to speak of "peoples". More recent nationalists have used the term as a synonym for various entities: states, historic communities, races. Herder's concept, in essence, was that a people who shared the same language, historic experience, and sense of identity constituted an indissoluble unit, linked (to quote the Finnish nationalist, A.I. Ardwisson) by "ties of mind and soul mightier and firmer than every external bond". Nationalism in the 19th century was the doctrine that everyone must belong to a nation of this kind, and that every nation collectively had to assert its identity, pursue its destiny, and defend its rights.

Though validated – some advocates claim – by history and science, nationalism was usually couched in mystical or romantic language apparently ill adapted to practical ends. Infected by romantic yearning for the unattainable, it was doomed to self-frustration. Indeed, like the passion of the lover on Keats's Grecian urn, it would have been killed by consummation. German nationalism thrived on unfulfilled ambitions to unite all German-speakers in a single Reich. That of Serbs was nourished by inexhaustible grievances. Even in France – the land of "chauvinism", which proclaimed, more or less, "My country, right or wrong" – nationalism would have been weakened if the French had ever attained frontiers that satisfied their rulers.

Powerful symbols
National emblems need not be glamorous to be effective. The Citroën 2CV was simply designed to transport French farmers to and from market, and its distinctive shape has become associated with rural France.

Because nationalism was a state of romantic yearning rather than a coherent political programme, music expressed it best. *Ma Vlast* by the Czech composer Anton Dvořák or *Finlandia* by Jean Sibelius have outlasted their era as no nationalist literature has done. Nationalism belonged to the values of "sensation, not thought" proclaimed by Romantic poets. "The voice of God" told Giuseppe Mazzini, the republican fighter for Italian unification, that the "Nation" supplied individuals with the framework of potential moral perfection.

Nationalism was obviously false. There is no innate spiritual bond between people who happen to share elements of common background or language, their community is simply what they choose to make of it. Yet for an idea so incoherent, nationalism had amazing effects. It played a part in justifying most of the wars of the 19th and 20th centuries and inspiring people to fight in them. Together with the doctrine of "national self-determination", it shaped Europe after World War I and the world after the retreat of European empires. It seems increasingly irrelevant today, in a world of globalization and internationalization, but some politicians, threatened with the need to pool their power, have re-discovered a certain nostalgia for the nation-state. A reaction against immigration, internationalization, and multi-culturalism has made nationalist parties popular again in Europe, threatening both cultural pluralism and the project of European unification.

"A nation is a society united by delusions about its ancestry and by common hatred of its neighbours."

Dean W.R. Inge

Dean W.R. Inge
(1860–1954), English cleric and writer.

The Doll's House

THE NEW IDEAS OF CHILDHOOD AND WOMANHOOD

The re-evaluation of the role of children and women in 19th-century Europe was an effect of industrialization. The exploitation of children's and women's labour was one of the scandals of the early phases, but the gradual effect of mechanization was to take these groups out of the labour market. Womanhood was placed on a pedestal and children were treated as a distinct rank of society – almost a sub-species of humankind – whereas formerly they had just been little adults. Both women and children were deified by artists and advertisers and confined to their special shrines in the home.

These were uniquely Western cults, barely intelligible in cultures where women and children were still men's partners in production. The status looked enviable in artists' images of delicately nurtured femininity or cherubic childhood. But there were disadvantages. Societies that freed children from the workplace tried to pen them inside schools. Chimney sweeps did not naturally change into water-babies and the romantic ideal of childhood was more often coerced than coaxed into being. In his play *A Doll's House*, of 1879, Henrik Ibsen captured the new role in which women had been cast; in some respects they had similar rights to those of children. For them the fall from the pedestal could be bruising. Like adulteresses depicted in terrible stages of decline and destitution in paintings and melodramas, or like the sexually louche operatic heroines of *Manon* and *La Traviata*, the fallen woman became the favourite villainess of the age. The "doll's house" and the "secret garden" proved, in practice, to be oppressive pens from which the women and children of 20th-century Europe would have to struggle to escape.

Child labour
Women and children alike were exploited by industrialists until the increasing mechanization of factories reduced the need for their cheap labour. Children were still working cotton looms in Britain as recently as 1908.

288

READINGS

E.O. Hellerstein's **Victorian Women** (1981) is a valuable collection of evidence.

L. de Mause's (ed.) **The History of Childhood** (1974) is a pioneering collection of essays.

F.H. Burnett's **The Secret Garden** (1911) is a novel that explores the mysteries of childhood by treating growing up as a magical experience.

Women and children's special status meant they were saved first from a sinking ship.

"Women and children first – that phrase which exempts the adult male from sanity."

E.M. Forster, *Abinger Harvest* (1936)

Forever blowing bubbles
During the late 1800s, the changing status of children was mirrored by the use of romanticized images of youth in advertising. This poster for Pears' soap was based on a J.E. Millais painting, Bubbles (1886).

Ideas into action
Socialist revolution has often been associated with the violent overthrow of the status quo. Here, Cuban revolutionaries pose with weapons captured from the forces of General Batista in 1958.

CONNECTIONS

Related ideas can be investigated in **Big Brotherhood** (p.166), **Workers Unite** (p.248), **Neverland** (p.250), **Class Struggle** (p.292), **The Third Way** (p.296), and **Peasant Socialism** (p.372).

Extreme Optimism

THE IDEA OF SOCIALISM

The clash of political visions in 19th-century Europe was the echo of a mightier clash of rival philosophies of man. Was he ape or angel? Was he the image of God or the heir of Adam? Would the goodness inside him emerge in freedom or was it corroded with evil, which had to be controlled? Politics of fear and hope collided.

Socialism was an extreme form of optimism. In Milan in 1899, Giuseppe Pelizza, a convert from a guilt-ridden bourgeois background, began his vast symbolic painting on the subject. The scene depicted in *Il Quarto Stato* (shown on page 248) was a vast crowd of workers, advancing, the artist said, "like a torrent, overthrowing every obstacle in its path, thirsty for justice". Their march is relentless, their solidarity intimidating. But, except for a madonna-like woman in the foreground – who seems bent on a personal project, appealing to one of the rugged

George Orwell
(1903–50), British
socialist, essayist,
and novelist.

*"As with the Christian religion, the worst
advertisement for socialism is its
adherents."*

George Orwell, *The Road to Wigan Pier* (1937)

leaders at the head of the march – they are
individually characterless, moving like parts of a giant
automaton, with a mechanical rhythm, slow and pounding.

No work of art could better express the grandeur and
grind at the heart of socialism: noble humanity, mobilized by
dreary determinism. In the history of socialism, the nobility
and humanity came first. They were expressed in the ideals
of equality and fraternity, proclaimed by utopians of the
Enlightenment and applied in the practices of sharing and
co-operating of early socialist communities, like the "Icaria" of the
19th-century French philosopher Etienne Cabet, where he proposed that
envy, crime, anger, and lust would be abolished by the proscription of
rivalry and the abolition of property.

A very different kind of socialism – "accountants' socialism" – was
expounded by the English writer Thomas Hodgskin. He pointed out that
workers' labour added the greater part of the value of most commodities,
so they should get the lions' share of the profits. This was a capitalist's
kind of socialism, in which ideals carried a price-tag. Once socialist
economics had become conventional, the French historian Louis Blanc
made its politics conventional, too. He convinced most socialists that
their ideals could be entrusted to the state, to be imposed on society.
John Ruskin echoed these arguments in England. For him "the first duty
of a state is to see that every child born therein shall be well housed,
clothed, fed and educated" and he relished the prospect of increased state
power to that end. Meanwhile, Karl Marx predicted the inevitability of
socialism's triumph through a cycle of class conflicts; as economic power
passed from capital to labour, so workers – degraded and inflamed by
exploitative employers – would seize power in the state.

Early socialist experiments had been peaceful, with no land to
conquer except in the open spaces of the wilderness, and no human
adversaries except selfishness and greed. In the industrial era,
transformed by the language of conflict and coercion, socialism became
an ideology of violence, to be resisted vigorously by those who valued
property above fraternity and liberty above equality.

Workers united
*The hammer and sickle,
familiar as the emblem
of the communist regime
in the former Soviet Union,
symbolically unites
industrial workers with
farm labourers in the
struggle against capitalist
oppression.*

EXTREME OPTIMISM

READINGS

L. Kolakowski and
S. Hampshire's (eds) **The
Socialist Idea** (1974) is
a critical introduction.

C.J. Guarnieri's **The Utopian
Alternative** (1991) is a good
study of backwoods
socialism in America.

C. Northcote Parkinson's **Left
Luggage** (1967) is perhaps
the funniest critique
of socialism.

Class Struggle

THE IDEA OF HISTORICAL DIALECTIC

Marching for jobs
Marx argued that workers would eventually wield power. But industrialization also created unemployment, which in 1936 drove these men to march from Jarrow to London in protest.

READINGS

K.R. Popper's **The Open Society and its Enemies** (1945) is a brilliant study and a devastating critique.

D. McLellan's **Marx: Selected Writings** (1999) is a good introduction to Marx.

F. Wheen's **Karl Marx** (2000) is a lively, insightful biography.

Karl Marx (1818–83),
German philosopher,
emphasized economic
factors above all else.

According to Marx's theory of historical change, every instance of progress is the "synthesis" of two preceding, conflicting events or tendencies. He based it on a method of thinking, devised by the German philosopher Friedrich Hegel, called "dialectic": everything is part of something else. So if x is part of y, you have to understand y in order to think coherently about x. You cannot know either without knowing $x + y$: the "synthesis" that alone makes perfect sense. This seems unimpressive: a recipe for never being able to think coherently about anything in isolation.

As well as "dialectical", Marx's scheme was "materialist": change was economically driven (not, as Hegel thought, by "spirit" or "ideas"). Political power, for instance, ended up with whoever held the sources of wealth. Under feudalism, land was the "means of production", so landowners ruled; under capitalism, money counted for most, so financiers ran states; under industrialism, as the British economist David Ricardo had shown, it was labour that added value, so the society of the future would be ruled by workers in a "dictatorship of the proletariat". A further, final synthesis remained vaguely delineated in Marx's work: a classless society in which the state would "wither away", everybody would share wealth equally, and all property would be common.

Apart from this last, perfect consummation, each transition from one type of society to the next, Marx thought, was inevitably violent: the ruling class strove to hold on to power, while the rising class struggled to wrest it. So he tended to agree with the thinkers of his day who saw violence as conducive to progress. The effect of his idea was therefore generally baneful, helping to inspire revolutionary violence, which sometimes succeeded in changing society, but never seemed to bring the communist utopia into being. All his predictions proved false. If he had

"What the bourgeoisie produces, above all, are its own gravediggers. Its fall and the victory of the proletariat are equally inevitable."

Karl Marx and Friedrich Engels, *The Communist Manifesto* **(1848)**

More equal than others
*Lenin, who led the Bolsheviks during
the Russian Revolution of 1917,
attempted to put Marx's ideas into practice.
The society that resulted was beset by as
many injustices as the one it had replaced.*

been right, the first great proletarian
revolution ought to have happened in
America, the vanguard-society of
capitalism. In fact, America remained the
country where Marxism failed to take root on
any great scale, whereas the great revolutions of
the early 20th century were essentially traditional
peasant rebellions in the largely unindustrialized
societies of China and Mexico. Russia, which
Marxists saw for a while as an exemplary case
of Marxism in action, was only very patchily
industrialized in 1917, when the state was seized
by Marxist revolutionaries. But even there
the master's principles were honoured in the
breach: it became a dictatorship, but not of
the proletariat. The ruling class was replaced,
but only by a ruling party. Instead of
discarding nationalism, Russia's new rulers
soon reverted to traditional policy-making
based on the interests of the state, and the
exploitation of workers by the bourgeoisie
was succeeded by the oppression of
almost everybody by the state.

Mexican revolution
*The first successful revolution of the 20th century
was the peasant uprising in Mexico (1910–20),
which resulted in a major land redistribution.*

Bull versus Man
*In Bentham's utilitarian
terms, the bull's pain
is outweighed by the
crowd's pleasure. This
"low" pleasure might
not have been so highly
rated by John Stuart Mill.*

Preserved for posterity
*Jeremy Bentham
(1748–1832), the founder
of utilitarianism, believed
that the state should
provide the greatest
happiness for the
greatest number.*

The Greatest Good

THE IDEA OF UTILITARIANISM

Jeremy Bentham is treated as a kind of secular saint – his body is preserved at University College, London (see left), exhibited as encouragement to students – and his philosophy, usually called "utilitarianism", is a creed for the irreligious.

He thought good could be defined as a surplus of happiness over unhappiness. The aim of the state was "the greatest happiness of the greatest number". This was not liberalism – social "utility" came above individual liberty – but it was radical, because it proposed a new way of evaluating social institutions without deference to their antiquity or authority or past success. The doctrine was also thoroughly secular: Bentham's standard of happiness was pleasure and his index of evil was pain. He was the most eloquent member of a British elite engaged in a retreat from romanticism; instead, he and his friends attempted rational and scientific thinking about how to run society.

Bentham's most effective and devoted disciple, John Stuart Mill, could not quite escape romantic yearnings. At the age of 20, he experienced a vision of a perfect world in which all his prescriptions had been adopted, and recoiled in horror from the prospect. The greatest happiness of the greatest number means sacrifices for some. It is strictly incompatible with human rights, because the interest of the "greatest number" will always tend to leave some individuals bereft of benefits. Instead, Mill adopted a scale of values with freedom at the top. Liberty, he thought, is absolute, except where it impinges on others. "The only purpose," he wrote, "for which power can be rightfully exercised over any member of a civilized community, against his will, is to prevent harm to others [not] to make him happier [or] because, in the opinions of others, to do so would be wise or even right." For Bentham's greatest number, Mill substituted a universal category: the individual. "Over himself, over his own body and mind, the individual is sovereign."

Mill's individualism was never so rampant as to exclude social priorities. "For the protection of society [the citizen] owes a return for the benefit." He can be made to respect others' rights and to contribute a reasonable share of taxes and services to the state. Nor was Mill's liberalism consistent. At times he veered wildly between extremes of rejection and praise for socialism. In consequence of his influence, the British political elite adopted what might be called a modified liberal tradition, which responded undogmatically to change and helped to make the country uniquely impervious to violent revolutions, by European standards, in the 19th and 20th centuries.

Meanwhile, utilitarianism was amazingly influential. The British state was re-organized along lines Bentham recommended: the penal code was reformed to minimize unhelpful "pain"; new poor laws aimed to abolish misfortune by making it unbearable; the administration was re-staffed with good examinees. Capitalist and libertarian prejudices could never quite exclude "public interest" from legislators' priorities, even under nominally right-wing governments. The radical tradition in Britain was preponderantly Benthamite, even when it called itself "socialist", until well into the 20th century.

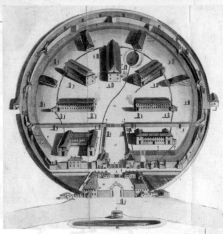

Perfect prison
Bentham measured "good" with a "hedonistic calculus" and applied this to his ideas on punishment. He planned a prison, the Panopticon (above), where the severity of punishment would be decided according to the amount of pain caused by the offence.

John Stuart Mill
(1806–73), English philospher, modified the utilitarian idea.

"The liberty of the individual must thus far be limited: he must not make himself a nuisance to other people."

J.S. Mill, *On Liberty* (1859)

READINGS

J. Bentham's **Principles of Morals and Legislation** (1789) is his key text, while G.J. Postema's (ed.) **Bentham** (2002) is a useful collection of essays.

J.S. Mill's **On Liberty** (1859) is indispensible, while A. Ryan's **The Philosophy of John Stuart Mill** (1987) is an outstanding work, and M. Cowling's **Mill and Liberalism** (1990) is a superb and cogent study.

E. Halévy's **The Growth of Philosophic Radicalism 1901–04** (1952) is the great classic study of utilitarianism in context.

The Third Way

THE IDEA OF CHRISTIAN SOCIALISM

"I have a dream"
The radical conscience of black American Civil Rights leader Martin Luther King was firmly rooted in his Christian faith as pastor.

CONNECTIONS

On Church and state, see **Render unto Caesar** (p.186). For Christian communitarianism, see **Love Above** (p.160) and **Big Brotherhood** (p.166). For the socialist context, see **Extreme Optimism** (p.290) and **Class Struggle** (p.292).

William Blake (1757–1827), English mystical visionary, artist, and poet.

Early Christianity abjured the state. Medieval Christianity erected an alternative church-state. The challenge for modern Christianity in a secularizing age has been to find a way of influencing politics without getting engaged and perhaps corrupted.

Potentially, Christianity has something to contribute to all the major political tendencies represented in modern industrial democracies. It is conservative, because it preaches absolute morality. It is liberal, because it stresses the supreme value of the individual and affirms the sovereignty of conscience. It is socialist, because it demands service to the community and "bias to the poor", and recommends the shared life of the apostles and Early Church. It is therefore a possible source of the "third way" eagerly sought in a world that has rejected communism but finds capitalism uncongenial.

The most convincing route to a third way lies through the idea – known as "Christian socialism" in the Anglican tradition and as "Catholic syndicalism" or "social Catholicism" in the Catholic Church – of combining the communitarian values of socialism with insistence on individual moral responsibility. The term "Christian socialism" was coined in the 1840s by the Anglican priest, F.D. Maurice; at the same time, the Sisters of Charity exercised a practical mission among the poor of Paris, and Archbishop Affré died at the barricades in the revolution of 1848. After Pope Leo XIII's pragmatic accommodation with the modern world after 1878, it was possible for Catholic priests to take part in workers' political movements. The hierarchy encouraged this simply in order to "save" workers from communism, but the inevitable result was that Catholic political groupings and trade unions multiplied under lay leadership. Some of them became powerful mass movements and electorally

"Both read the Bible day and night,
But thou read'st black where I read white."

William Blake, *The Everlasting Gospel* (1810)

successful parties. Social Catholicism really became orthodoxy in the 1960s, under the reformist leadership of Pope John XXIII. In his encyclical of 1961, *Mater et Magistra*, he outlined a vision of the state enhancing freedom by assuming social responsibilities and "enabling the individual to exercise personal rights". He approved state intervention in health care, education, housing, work, and the provision of leisure activities. Some of the vocabulary of current political discourse in Europe – including "subsidiarity" and "common good" – is drawn from Catholic social theory. The secular socialist parties are in danger of conversion to, or replacement by, politics in this tradition.

Catholic conscience
Christian values of self-sacrifice and service to the poor have brought about the involvement of members of Roman Catholic orders in social and political reform. Sister Irma Dulce is pictured here with one of the Brazilian orphans in her care.

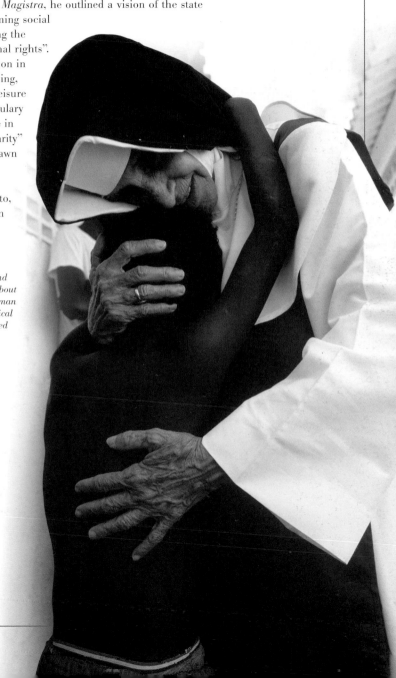

READINGS

A.R. Vidler's **A Century of Social Catholicism** (1964) is the single most important work, followed by P. Misner's **Social Catholicism in Europe** (1991).

L.P. Wallace's **Leo XIII and the Rise of Socialism** (1966) supplies important context, while W.D. Miller's **Dorothy Day** (1982) is a good biography of a leading Catholic social activist of modern times.

A. Wilkinson's **Christian Socialism** (2002) traces the Christian influence on labour politics in Britain.

Less Is More

THE IDEA OF ANARCHISM

CONNECTIONS

"Mainstream" socialism is
introduced in **Extreme
Optimism** (p.290). For
more on the violent side
of anarchism, see **Will to
Power** (p.302). Peaceful
resistance to state tyranny
is discussed in **Just Say
No** (p.308).

Running battles
*Anarchists' rejection of the
state in favour of a more
informal type of society has
frequently led to violent
clashes with the authorities.
Self-styled anarchists
brought their brand of
confrontation to recent
anti-globalization protests.*

If humans are naturally moral and reasonable, they should be able to get
along together without the state. Belief in progress and improvement in
18th-century Europe made this ancient ideal seem realizable.

In 1793, William Godwin (who later married Mary Wollstonecraft)
proposed to abolish all laws on the grounds that they were derived from
ancient compromises, botched in a state of savagery, that progress
rendered obsolete. Small, autonomous communities could resolve all
conflicts by face-to-face discussion. The term "anarchism" was invented
by Pierre Joseph Proudhon, in 1840, to mean a society run on principles
of reciprocity, like a mutual society. Many experimental communities
of this sort followed, but none on a scale to rival the conventional state.
Meanwhile, the socialist mainstream was seized by followers of the French
historian Louis Blanc, who put their faith in a strong, regulatory state to
realize revolutionary ambitions, and social democrats, who proposed to
capture the state by mobilizing the masses. Anarchists became marginalized
as leftist heretics. Under the influence of Mikhail Bakunin's writings, in
particular, they became associated with what seemed the only practical
alternative revolutionary programme: violence by terrorist cells.

Peter Kropotkin was the last great theorist of anarchism. His
Mutual Aid (1902) was an effective riposte to social Darwinism, arguing
that collaboration, not competition, is natural to humankind, and that the
evolutionary advantage of our species consists in our collaborative nature.
So social coercion is unnecessary and counter-productive.

Anarchism has seceded from the political forefront since failure
in its last great battles, fought during the Spanish Civil War (1936–39),
against authoritarianism of left and right alike; in the student revolutionary
movements of 1968, it contributed rhetoric, but little effectiveness. Its
appeal has always been problematical because the whole Western tradition,
since Aristotle first exalted the state as an agent of virtue, has tended
to denigrate anarchy. However, it contributed reckless idealism to the
ideological struggles of the earlier 20th century. It is possible that the
growing strength of concern for freedom on the political left in Europe
in the late 20th century was due less to the influence of the libertarian
right (as is commonly supposed) than to a lingering anarchist tradition.
Certainly a preference for human-scale solutions to social problems,
rather than the grand planning advocated by communists and socialists
of the past, has become a major theme of the modern left.

LESS IS MORE

Power to the people
The idea of anarchy reached its most organized manifestation during the Spanish Civil War, in which numerous left-wing militias fought on the Republican side. This poster promoted the cause of three anarchist organizations: the CNT, AIT, and FAI. Its slogan reads: "The invincible power of the proletariat against the military ideology of killing."

READINGS

D. Morland's **Demanding the Impossible** (1997) examines 19th-century anarchism with a psychological perspective.

C. Cahm's **Kropotkin and the Rise of Revolutionary Anarchism** (1989) is a useful historical survey.

P. Kropotkin's **Memoirs of a Revolutionist** (1899) is now also available in a translated version.

A. Kelly's **Mikhail Bakunin** (1987) is the best book on this revolutionary anarchist.

Mikhail Bakunin (1814–76) was one of the founding fathers of anarchism.

"No theory, no ready-made system, no book that has ever been written, will save the world. I cleave to no system. I am a true seeker."

Mikhail Bakunin, *God and the State* (1916)

Climate of Fear

THE IDEA OF TERRORISM

Explosive measures
*Government buildings
(such as this French
cultural centre in Berlin,
bombed in 1982 by "Carlos
the Jackal") have often
been targeted for their
symbolic significance.*

"Cold terrorism of the brain not the heart", in defence of the victims
of oppression, was first proposed as a guerrilla tactic by Carlo Bianco,
the early 19th-century Italian revolutionary advocate of partisan warfare.
But most revolutionaries of his day were idealists repelled by terror-
tactics. Insurrection had to be moral. It had to tackle the armed forces
of the enemy and spare the civilian population and the innocent.

The German anarchist Johannes Most disagreed. The entire elite –
including their families, servants, and all who did business with them –
were, for him, legitimate targets of armed struggle, to be killed at every
opportunity. Anyone else caught in the crossfire was a sacrifice in a good
cause. He devised the phrase "propaganda of the deed" and, in 1884,
published a handbook on how to make bombs explode in churches,

READINGS

W. Laqueur's **The Age of Terrorism** (1987) is a fine introduction.

W. Laqueur's (ed.) **The Guerrilla Reader** (1978) and **The Terrorism Reader** (1979) are useful anthologies.

P. Wilkinson's **Political Terrorism** (1974) is a practical-minded survey.

Joseph Conrad's **The Secret Agent** (1907) and Graham Greene's **The Honorary Consul** (1973) are among the most perceptive novelistic treatments of terrorism.

> *"We kill the kings of the infidels, kings of the crusaders, and civilian infidels in exchange for those of our children they kill. This is permissible in Islamic law and logically."*
>
> **Osama bin Laden, interview with al-Jazeera TV (21 October 2001)**

Osama bin Laden (1957–) uses terrorism in his war against the "enemies of Islam".

ballrooms, and public places, where the "reptile brood" of aristocrats, priests, and capitalists might gather. He also advocated exterminating policemen on the grounds that these "pigs" were not fully human.

The book was written from a socialist perspective, but it nourished a nationalist terror-movement. The first guerrilla movement systematically to adopt terror tactics as its main means of expression was founded in 1893 by Damian Gruev, which eventually came to be known as the Internal Macedonian Revolutionary Organization. Its slogan was "Better a horrible end than endless horror". Gruev's guerrillas resorted to what would become the classic terrorist method: using murder, looting, and rape to intimidate communities into bankrolling, sheltering, and supplying them.

The idea of terrorism has continued to reverberate in the world. "Liberation struggles" regularly become terrorist campaigns. Criminals sometimes affect political postures in order to justify ruthlessness and emulate terror tactics. It is hard to distinguish criminal from political motives in the drug wars of Colombia and Northern Ireland. The ideological posture of the al-Qaeda team that destroyed New York's World Trade Center in 2001 seems confused, at best: some of these supposed martyrs for Islam prepared for their feat by heavy drinking – these enemies of Westernization led consumerist lives.

For its practitioners, the appeal of terrorism seems in general to be psychological, not intellectual or practical. Usually, it fails; but it satisfies psychotic needs among alienated, frustrated constituencies for violence, secrecy, self-importance, and defiance.

CONNECTIONS

Revolutionary movements of the period are described in **Class Struggle** (p.292), **Less Is More** (p.298), and **Peasant Socialism** (p.372). It is also worth comparing terrorism with a peaceful doctrine of resistance; see **Just Say No** (p.308).

301

CLIMATE OF FEAR

Catalyst for war
Terrorist acts can have momentous consequences. Here, a suspect is arrested after the assassination of Archduke Franz Ferdinand in 1914 – the event that lit the fuse for WWI.

Freedom fighters
ETA's campaign of bombing and assassination in Spain's Basque Country shows how struggles for independence may develop into terrorist campaigns.

Will to Power

NIETZSCHE'S IDEA OF THE PRIMACY OF THE WILL

Leni Riefenstahl's great propaganda film for Hitler was called *Triumph of the Will*, in tribute to the 19th-century genealogy of the Fuhrer's self-image. The begetter of this savagery was a rather self-indulgent, mystical, and reclusive philosopher of the mid 19th century, Arthur Schopenhauer.

Philosophers had tried without success to isolate something – anything – that could be agreed to be "real": matter, spirit, the self, the soul, thought, God. Schopenhauer hit on "the will". It was never clear quite what he meant by this, but it was obviously meant to be something different from reason or morals. It led by "subterranean passage and secret complicity akin to treachery" to self-knowledge so distinct as to be convincing. The ultimate purpose of the will was the extinction of everything – which, he claimed, was what Buddha meant by nirvana.

This sort of nihilism is usually advocated only by the embittered and the failed, but it had an obvious appeal for the "great dictators" of the 20th century. Schopenhauer did not mean it literally: he was aiming at a mystical ascent, through the abnegation of the external world, towards a state of ecstatic self-realization, but his philosophy could be mistaken for a celebration of destructiveness. G.K. Chesterton chillingly satirized it in his story, *The Swami's Secret*, in which the protagonist – an amoral, murderous nihilist – declares, "I want nothing. I *want* nothing. I want *nothing*." The shifts of emphasis indicate the slide from egotism, to will, to nihilism.

Friedrich Nietzsche mediated Schopenhauer's rather vague and spineless doctrine to the would-be supermen who rose to power in the 20th century. He suggested that the primacy of the will committed people to mutual struggle; these power-relationships could not be resolved except through the victory and domination of some over others. To minds like Hitler's and Mussolini's, this was a justification for imperialism and war.

No pain, no gain
Nietzsche was concerned with human psychology as much as grand theories, and he articulated, through his notion of the "will to power", the belief that people would only feel real achievement if they had to struggle to attain a goal.

READINGS

A. Schopenhauer's **The World as Will and Idea** (1818) and F. Nietzsche's edited notebooks **The Will to Power** (1911) are the fundamental texts.

B. Magee's **The Philosophy of Schopenhauer** (1983) is the best introduction, while J.E. Atwell's **Schopenhauer on the Character of the World** (1995) focuses on the doctrine of the will.

D.B. Hinton's **The Films of Leni Riefenstahl** (1991) is a straightforward introduction to her work.

Force of will
Although Nietzsche was never a champion of violence, his celebration of the domination of the weak by the (will of) the strong was seized on by fascist dictators of the 20th century as justification for their own aggressive behaviour. Here, the Italian dictator Benito Mussolini is shown imposing himself through his demagoguery.

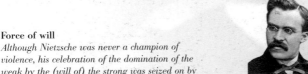

Friedrich Nietzsche
(1844–1900) argued that people should live for themselves.

"The world is the will to power – and nothing beside! And you are also this will to power – and nothing beside!"

F. Nietzsche, *Will to Power* (1911)

Hero Inside

THE IDEA OF THE SUPERMAN

Heroic ideal
Napoleon Bonaparte inspired hero-worship both during and after his lifetime as a "world-historical individual". As Nietzsche might have said, he gave "style" to his character, as a shaper of events rather than a pawn of history.

The 19th century was obsessed with heroes, and personality cults re-shaped whole cultures. English schoolchildren modeled themselves on the Duke of Wellington. Bismarck became a role-model for Germans. The name of Louis-Napoleon Bonaparte, unknown at the time of his election as French president, inspired reverence. Abraham Lincoln was a hero for Americans.

Georg Hegel was the Superman's begetter. He thought most people were incapable of worthwhile achievement. He also thought we are the playthings of history and that vast, impersonal, inescapable forces control our lives. Occasionally, however, "world-historical individuals" of extraordinary wisdom or prowess could embody the spirit of the times and force the pace – though not alter the course – of history. His heroes were all blood-soaked despots. As heroes displaced saints in popular estimation, the world got worse.

The dangers of Superman-worship should have been apparent in the work of Friedrich Nietzsche, who thought "the anarchical collapse of our civilization" was a small price to pay for such a genius as Napoleon. "The misfortunes of… small folk do not count for anything except in the feelings of men of might." He thought that the "artist-tyrant" was the noblest type of man, and "spiritualized and intensified cruelty" the highest form of culture.

The Superman may have been created and moulded by German thinkers, but he was worshipped elsewhere. The toweringly influential British writer, Thomas Carlyle, who did much of his thinking under a German spell, thought history was little more than the record of the achievements of great men. He advocated hero-worship as a kind of secular religion of self-improvement. "The history of what Man has accomplished in this world," he wrote, "is at bottom the History of the Great Men who have worked here." "Worship of a Hero is transcendent admiration of a Great Man… there is, at bottom, nothing else admirable… Society is founded on hero-worship" and "submissive admiration for the truly great." He believed that time does not make greatness; the great make it for themselves. History does not make heroes; heroes make history. This was hard to reconcile with the burgeoning democracy of the late 19th century. The consequence was that in the belief that great men could save society, democracies entrusted ever more power to their leaders, surrendering, in many cases in the 20th century, to demagoguery and dictators.

READINGS

T. Carlyle's **Of Heroes and Hero-Worship** (1841) is a representative text.

F. Nietzsche's **Thus Spake Zarathustra** (1883) contains his thinking on the subject.

O. Chadwick's **The Secularization of the European Mind in the Nineteenth Century** (1975) is a brilliant study.

"I teach you the Superman. Man is something to be surpassed."

Friedrich Nietzsche
(1844–1900) famously
articulated the ideal of
the "Superman".

F. Nietzsche, *Thus Spake Zarathustra* (1883)

Superheroes to the rescue
*The 19th-century idea that
society could be moulded
by the actions of a few
exceptional individuals was
echoed in 20th-century
comics and films featuring
superheroes, such as
Wonderwoman (pictured
here). Their extraordinary
powers allowed them to
defeat the enemies of
humanity.*

CONNECTIONS

For more on Hegel and
Nietzsche, see **The Big
Idea** (p.274), **My Country**
(p.286), **Brother Knows
Best** (p.306), **Master
Morality** (p.312), and
War Is Good (p.314). For
a discussion of fascism, see
Axe in the Sticks
(p.364).

Lone protest
Hegel argued that the state's "will" always took precedence over its citizens. But individuals may feel compelled to defy the state's power when pushed too far, such as this student during the Chinese pro-democracy protests of 1989.

Brother Knows Best

THE IDEA OF THE UNCHALLENGEABLE STATE

CONNECTIONS

The idea of the "general will" is covered in **Forced To Be Free** (p.256). For other related ideas, see **Legalism** (p.146), **I Am the State** (p.190), **State First** (p.232), **My Country** (p.286), **Master Morality** (p.312), and **Axe in the Sticks** (p.364).

"The state is the divine idea as it exists on Earth," said Hegel. This sounds like empty rhetoric, but he really meant it. He thought that it made no sense to speak of individuals: you are only complete in the context of the political community to which you belong. The state, however, is perfect (this was illogical, because states are part of an even wider community – that of the entire world, but Hegel chose to ignore this point). "The state is the reality of the moral idea – the moral spirit, the manifest will, self-evident, which thinks and knows itself."

What the state wills – in practice, what the elite or ruler wills – is the "general will" and takes precedence over what individual citizens want, or even what they all want.

This mystical idea proved strangely attractive and influential; but it only confirmed a trend to absolute state power that was already happening. The state had been constrained by notions of natural law and divine law, administered by an institution independent of the state, such as the Church in medieval Europe. But by Hegel's time, "positive law" – the law the state made for itself – was effectively all that mattered. Moreover, the sheer power of the state to enforce obedience grew with taxes and technologies. States had ever more manpower, more intelligence-gathering machinery, more means of punishment at their command.

Fortified by changes in technology and by the power that increasing tax yields bought in a productive century, the state became stronger vis-à-vis citizens, traditional institutions, associations, and regional power structures. Conflicts ensued: in Germany, Japan, Italy, and the USA, civil wars were won by centralizers. "Culture-struggles" between Church and state or between state and trade-syndicates were common. Every change that hoisted the state above the law multiplied the prospects of injustice. This outcome often occurred in democracies; it was the normal state of affairs in dictatorships. Not until the late 20th century did pooled sovereignty in an ever closer-knit world and the resistance of citizens and communities to the intrusiveness of government begin to result in the imposition of limitations to the power of the state.

The all-seeing eye
New technology, such as this CCTV surveillance camera, has dramatically increased the power of the state over its citizens in a way that Hegel could not possibly have foreseen.

Name and number
Attempts by states to exert ever greater control have often met with stiff resistance. Some people argue that being forced to carry identity cards is an erosion of civil liberties.

READINGS

S. Avineri's **Hegel's Theory of the Modern State** (1974) is a clear introduction to the key concepts, while E. Weil's **Hegel and the State** (1998) discusses some of the lineages of political thought that Hegel fathered.

G. Orwell's **1984** (1949) offers a nightmare vision of a totalitarian dystopia, while A. Solzhenitsyn's **One Day in the Life of Ivan Denisovich** (1962) starkly depicts life in a Soviet penal colony.

G.W.F. Hegel
(1770–1831), German philosopher, idealized the role of the state.

"The State is the reality of the moral idea... the moral spirit, the manifest will."

G.W.F Hegel, The Philosophy of Law (1821)

Just Say No

THE IDEA OF CIVIL DISOBEDIENCE

CONNECTIONS

Contrast **Brother Knows Best** (p.306), **Master Morality** (p.312), and **War Is Good** (p.314). For other challenges to the state contemporary with Thoreau's, see **Less Is More** (p.298) and **Climate of Fear** (p.300).

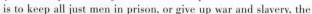

Henry David Thoreau was an utterly impractical man, yet his thought re-shaped the world. He was an incurable romantic who advocated – and for a long time practised – economic self-sufficiency "in the woods". However, his disciples included some of the dynamic figures of the 20th century: Mahatma Gandhi, Emma Goldman, and Martin Luther King.

His most important essay on politics was written in revulsion from the two great injustices of the antebellum USA: slavery, at the expense of blacks; and imperialist warmongering, mainly at the expense of Mexico. He decided that he could not support such immoral politics. He would "quietly declare war with the state", renounce allegiance, and refuse to pay taxes if they were used to pay for the oppression or dispossession of innocent people. If all just men did likewise, the state would be compelled to change. "Under a true government which imprisons any unjustly, the true place for a just man is also a prison... If the alternative is to keep all just men in prison, or give up war and slavery, the

"Let your conscience be your guide."

Jiminy Cricket, *Pinocchio* (1940)

In *Pinocchio*, **Jiminy Cricket** (© Disney Enterprises, Inc.) urges Pinocchio to follow his conscience.

Red Emma
The anarchist Emma Goldman was one of early 20th-century America's most notable advocates of civil disobedience.

READINGS

H.D. Thoreau's **On the Duty of Civil Disobedience** (1849) is the classic text.

J.M. Washington's (ed.) **A Testament of Hope** (1990) is a good collection of King's speeches and writings.

J.M. Brown's **Gandhi and Civil Disobedience** (1977) is the leading study.

A. Camus's **The Rebel** (1951) advocates just saying "no".

State will not hesitate which to choose." He was actually imprisoned for withholding his taxes, but "someone interfered, and paid the tax", and he was let out after one night. He commended the American system – "... even this state and this American government are in many respects very admirable and rare things, to be thankful for" – and he recognized that it was the duty of the citizen to do "the good the state demands of me". But he had an important insight to contribute into the nature of representative democracy. The citizen alienates his power to the state, but not his conscience. Conscience is essentially an individual responsibility, which cannot be delegated to an elected representative. It was better to dissolve the state than to preserve it in injustice. Referring to the war with Mexico, Thoreau wrote, "This people must cease to hold slaves and to make war on Mexico, though it cost them their existence as a people."

Thoreau insisted on assent to two propositions: that civil disobedience was a duty for the correction of injustice; and that such disobedience had to be non-violent and prejudicial only to the resister and those who freely associated themselves with him. These conditions were the basis of Gandhi's campaign of "moral resistance" to British rule in India and Martin Luther King's of "non-violent non-cooperation" for civil rights in the USA. Both of those campaigns succeeded without recourse to violence. Thoreau's doctrine was endorsed by the late John Rawls – probably the most respected political philosopher in the world in the early 21st century. Civil disobedience of the kind Thoreau urged is justified, he said, if the majority in a democracy deny equal rights to a minority.

PACIFIC TEAL
BARROW

NUCLEAR FREE

Peaceful protest
As part of his non-violent campaign against British rule in India, in 1930 Gandhi and his followers marched peacefully in protest against the tax on salt.

David and Goliath
Obstruction is one of the most used strategies of civil disobedience. Here, Greenpeace environmental campaigners attempt to block the passage of a ship carrying nuclear materials.

Women at war
*In an age of total war,
there is no such thing as
a non-combatant. Here,
Iranian women abandon
their traditional passive
role and train as soldiers.*

By Other Means

THE IDEA OF TOTAL WAR

In the 1790s, the French Revolution introduced mass conscription.
Henceforth, war was waged by "the nation in arms", not just a professional
elite. Napoleon mobilized populations on a scale unseen in Europe since
antiquity, and engaged in battles of unrestrained violence, unlike the
modest encounters of the previous century when generals were more
concerned to conserve their forces than to destroy vast numbers of
enemies. The idea of total war – waged actively between entire societies,
in which there is no such thing as a non-combatant or an illegitimate
target – was bound to follow, mirroring the new reality.

Carl von Clausewitz, the Prussian general who formulated this
idea, assumed that states were permanently and inherently disposed to
fight each other, because their underlying interests consisted in gaining

"War is an act of violence pushed to its utmost bounds."

Carl von Clausewitz, *On War* (1832)

Dresden, destroyed by Allied bombing in 1945, was a victim of total war.

CONNECTIONS

For related ideas about war, see **No Mercy** (p.76), **All Change** (p.110), **Holy Terror** (p.208), **Law of Nations** (p.236), **Nation in Arms** (p.262), **War Is Good** (p.314), and **Axe in the Sticks** (p.364). On the link with German nationalism, see **Master Race** (p.328).

an advantage at each other's expense. Rational action was action adjusted to its ends. So the only rational way to wage war is "to the utmost". "He who uses force unsparingly, without reference to the bloodshed involved, must obtain a superiority." Clausewitz advocated a strategy of attrition and general destruction to wear down the enemy. The ultimate objective (though, to be fair to Clausewitz, he did point out that this was not always necessary) was to leave the enemy permanently disarmed. This encouraged belligerents to fight for unconditional surrender when they were winning, to resist defeat obstinately when they were losing, and to impose vindictive and burdensome terms when they achieved victory. He insisted that war should not be waged for its own sake, but only for political objectives that were unrealizable using other methods. "War is a mere continuation of politics by other means" was his most famous utterance.

In practice, however, Clausewitz was so convinced of the ubiquity and necessity of war that this qualification had little restraining effect on his readers, who included the entire military and political establishment of Europe and America for the century and a half after publication of his *On War* in 1832. The results of his influence were to make war worse – multiplying the victims, spreading the destruction – and more frequent, by encouraging pre-emptive attacks.

READINGS

C. von Clausewitz's **On War** (1832) is the classic text, B. Heuser's **Reading Clausewitz** (2002) explains his thought and influence.

M. Howard's **Clausewitz** (2002) is a pithy and satisfying introduction.

P. Bobbitt's **The Shield of Achilles** (2002) is a spectacular, hawkish history of war in international relations.

Total victory
For Clausewitz, the purpose of war was total defeat of the enemy, there being little point in partial victory. Here, Napoleon is depicted after his 1805 victory over Austria and Russia at Austerlitz, receiving captured officers.

Master Morality

THE IDEA THAT MIGHT IS RIGHT

The powerless are wrong
Nietzsche's view that conquerors are inherently superior to their victims, has sometimes been used by powerful groups to justify the displacement of unwanted minorities (like these Kosovan Albanians, forced by the Serbs to flee their village in 1999).

Friedrich Wilhelm Nietzsche solved the problem of truth by denying its existence. One interpretation should be preferred to another only if it is more self-fulfilling to the chooser. The same applied to morals. All moral systems, he thought, are "tyrannies" contrived to deprive us of freedom. "Consider any morality with this in mind: [it] teaches hatred of the *laisser-aller*, of any all-too-great freedom, and implants the need for limited horizons and the nearest tasks – teaching the narrowing of our perspective and thus in a certain sense stupidity." According to Nietzsche, love of neighbour was just a euphemism for fear of neighbour. In this, as in all his repulsive doctrines, he was alone in his day but ominously representative of the future.

In works mainly of the 1880s, he called for the reclassification of revenge, anger, and lust as virtues; he advocated slavery, the subjection of women to "the whip", the rule of "artist-tyrants", the refinement of the human race by gloriously bloody wars, the extermination of millions of inferior people, the eradication of Christianity with its contemptible bias to the weak, and an ethic of "might makes right". He claimed this was scientifically justified, on the grounds that conquerors are necessarily superior to their victims and so should enjoy power and precedence and priority of interest. "I... entertain," he wrote, "the hope that life may one day become more full of evil and suffering than ever."

All this made him Hitler's favourite philosopher. Yet Hitler misunderstood him. Nietzsche's hatreds were broad enough to encompass the state; individual strength was what he admired, and state-imposed morality the kind he most detested. Like that of so many great thinkers misread by Hitler, his work was twisted to serve Nazism.

> *"All these moralities... what are they but... recipes against the passions?"*
>
> **Friedrich Nietzsche, *Beyond Good and Evil* (1886)**

Friedrich Nietzsche (1844–1900) believed that innovators should make their own values.

CONNECTIONS

For more ideas on the state, see **Less Is More** (p.300). For Hitler's ideology, see **Axe in the Sticks** (p.364). For more on Nietzsche's philosophy, see **Will to Power** (p.302) and **Hero Inside** (p.304). For more on slavery, see **Human Bondage** (p.150).

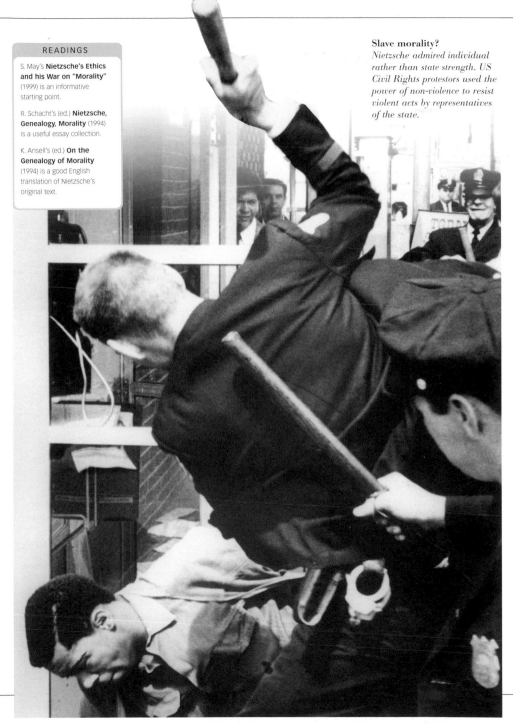

READINGS

S. May's **Nietzsche's Ethics and his War on "Morality"** (1999) is an informative starting point.

R. Schacht's (ed.) **Nietzsche, Genealogy, Morality** (1994) is a useful essay collection.

K. Ansell's (ed.) **On the Genealogy of Morality** (1994) is a good English translation of Nietzsche's original text.

Slave morality?
Nietzsche admired individual rather than state strength. US Civil Rights protestors used the power of non-violence to resist violent acts by representatives of the state.

Chosen Victims

THE IDEA OF ANTI-SEMITISM

CONNECTIONS

On racism, see **Inferior by Nature** (p.318) and **Good Breeding** (322). For other forms of subjugation, see **Just Like a Woman** (p.74) and **Human Bondage** (p.150). On ideas of genocide, see **No Mercy** (p.76) and **Axe in the Sticks** (p.364).

In the ghetto
The Nazis brought technological efficiency to their persecution of the Jews. They were deported in vast numbers (like these Jews in Warsaw) to the concentration camps, then systematically maltreated and massacred

The origins of modern anti-Semitism are fiercely disputed among historians. A well-supported view is that it originated in Christian hostility to the Jews, who were held to have been responsible for the death of Jesus, and that it developed in the Middle Ages, when Jews – together with some other "outsider" groups and ghetto-dwellers in Europe – experienced increasing persecution. There are two good reasons for modifying (without entirely rejecting) this theory. First, though never completely emancipated, Jews benefited from the 18th-century Enlightenment, getting a share of the "rights of man" and, in many cases, emerging from the ghettos into the social mainstream.

After this break with the past, anti-Semitism, when it re-emerged in the 19th century, seemed different. The tolerance of host societies cracked as Jewish numbers grew. This coincided with

Badge of shame
During WWII, Jews were forced to wear the yellow star of David as part of their "Special Treatment", which also included revoking their citizenship and isolating them from the rest of society.

a period in Europe when pseudo-scientific racism became noisily popular. Anti-Semitic violence, sporadic in the early part of the century, became commonplace in Russia from the 1870s and Poland from the 1880s. Partly under pressure of the numbers of refugees, it spread to Germany and even, in the 1890s, to France, where Jews had previously seemed well integrated and established at every level of society.

As adverse economic conditions became generalized in Europe in the 1920s and 1930s, anti-Semitism became uncontainable, exploited by politicians, some of whom seem to have believed their own rhetoric and genuinely to have regarded a Jewish presence as incompatible with welfare or security. Demagogues of the right denounced Jews as indelibly communist; for those of the left they were incurably capitalist. Anti-Semitic regimes had always tried to "solve the Jewish problem" by eliminating it – usually through hermetic sealing in ghettos, forced conversion, or mass expulsion.

The Nazi project for eliminating the Jews by extermination – the "Final Solution" – was an extreme development of a long tradition. About 6,000,000 Jews perished at Nazi hands in one of the most purposeful campaigns of genocide in history. Throughout Europe west of the Soviet border, fewer than 2,000,000 survived. It was an act of European self-amputation of a community that had always contributed disproportionately to the intellectual and artistic life of the continent as well as to wealth-creating economic activity.

Le Rire

World domination?
From the 19th century, anti-Semitism often focused on fear of a supposed Jewish conspiracy for global economic domination. This French magazine cover from 1898 shows the Jewish banker Alphonse de Rothschild grasping the world in his "claws".

317

CHOSEN VICTIMS

READINGS

D. Cohn-Sherbock's **Anti-Semitism** (2002) is a balanced and rigorous history, while N. Cohn's **Europe's Inner Demons** (1975) is a classic and controversial investigation of the lineage of anti-Semitism.

P. Pulzer's **The Rise of Political Anti-Semitism in Germany and Austria** (1988) is well-informed and convincing.

H. Walser Smith's **The Butcher's Tale** (2002) is a fascinating case-study.

A. Frank's **The Diary of a Young Girl** (1947) has become the classsic account of a Jewish family's unsuccessful attempt to survive the Holocaust.

Adolf Hitler (1889–1945), Nazi leader, wished to "purify" Europe of the Jews.

"They are just pure parasites... They had to be treated like tuberculosis bacilli... That was not cruel... Why should the beasts who wanted to bring us Bolshevism be spared more? Nations which did not rid themselves of Jews perished."

Adolf Hitler, in minutes of meeting with Admiral Horthy of Hungary (17 April 1943)

Inferior by Nature

THE IDEA OF SCIENTIFIC RACISM

No-go area
Scientific racism has been used to justify imperialism, state-sponsored repression, and even genocide. In South Africa, the policy of apartheid, or separate development, denied many rights to non-whites.

An apologist of slavery, Edward Long, had justified it in 1774 on the grounds that blacks were differentiated from other peoples by – among other offensive ideas – a "narrow intellect", so as almost to constitute a different species. Henry Home in the same year went further: humans constituted a genus in which there were numerous different species. This view was generally rejected, since it was obvious that humans of all kinds are capable of breeding with one another. However, the search was on for a way of characterizing the diversity of humankind in a manner that was consistent with the science and the prejudices of the times.

In 19th-century Europe, the classification of humankind into races was thought to be scientific by analogy with botanical taxonomy. Various methods were proposed, according to pigmentation, hair type, nose shape, blood type (once the development of serology made this possible), and, above all, cranial measurements. This last method was devised by the late 18th-century Leiden anatomist, Pieter Camper, who carefully arranged his large collection of skulls "in regular succession", with "apes, orangs, and negroes" at one end and central Asians and Europeans at the other. There was obviously an underlying agenda: a desire not only to classify races, but also to rank them in terms of superiority and inferiority. Hence the emphasis on the shape and dimensions of the skull, which were alleged to affect brain-power.

The Comte de Gobineau, who died in 1882 – the same year as Darwin – relied more on what was then beginning to be called anthropology rather than on biology to work out a ranking of

"All is race. There is no other truth."

Benjamin Disraeli (1868)

Benjamin Disraeli
(1804–81), a Jewish
British Prime Minister.

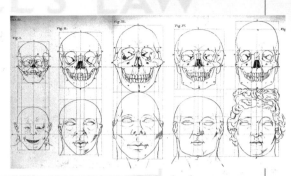

Head-to-head
*Early anatomists believed
that their efforts to classify
different human races were
perfectly scientific. This
comparative study of
human skulls was made by
Pieter Camper in 1791.*

races in which "Aryans" came out on top and
blacks at the bottom. Gregor Mendel, the kind
and gentle Austrian monk, whose experiments
with pea plants established the foundation of
the science of genetics, died two years later. Mendel's work was not
followed up until the end of the century and then the implications of
his findings were distorted. Along with the contributions of Darwin and
de Gobineau, Mendel's research was used to help complete a supposedly
scientific justification of racism. Genetics provided an explanation of
how one man could, inherently and necessarily, be inferior to another
by virtue of race alone.

In partial consequence, the first half of the 20th century was
an age of empires at ease with themselves, where critics of imperialism
could be made to seem sentimental and unscientific, in a world sliced by
the sword and stacked in order of race. Just when white power was at its
most penetrative and most pervasive, scientific theory helped to ram it
home. Inferior races were doomed to extinction by natural selection, or
could be actively exterminated in the interests of progress.

It might be argued that racism is timeless and universal. It is said
that in most human languages the word for "human being" denoted only
members of the tribe or group; outsiders are classed as beasts. Contempt
is a common mechanism for excluding the stranger. What the 19th
century called "race" had been covered earlier by terms like "lineage"
and "purity of blood". No earlier idea of this kind, however, had the
persuasive might of scientific racism, nor the power to cause so much
oppression and so many deaths.

319

READINGS

A. de Gobineau's **The
Inequality of Human Races**
(1855) is the starting point.

C. Bolt's **Victorian
Attitudes to Race** (1971)
and L.K. Uper's (ed.) **Race,
Science and Society** (1975)
are excellent modern studies.

INFERIOR BY NATURE

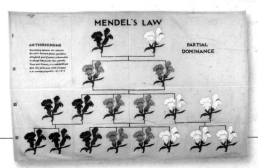

MENDEL'S LAW

ANTIRRHINUMS

PARTIAL
DOMINANCE

Family tree
*Through his experiments
with plants, Gregor Mendel
showed that characteristics
are passed from "parent" to
"offspring" in a predictable
fashion – insights later
misused by proponents
of scientific racism.*

CONNECTIONS

To compare the idea of
scientific racism with anti-
Semitism, see **Chosen
Victims** (p.316); to compare
with eugenics: see **Good
Breeding** (p.322). For a
discussion of the political
manifestation of racism,
see **Axe in the
Sticks** (p.364).

Tooth and Claw

THE IDEA OF NATURAL SELECTION

The air of Charles Darwin's day was thick with comprehensive schemes for classifying the world. George Eliot satirized them in the obsessions of the characters in her novel *Middlemarch* (1852): Mr Casaubon's "key to all mythologies" and Dr Lydgate's search for "the common basis of all living tissues". Most scientists already believed that life had evolved from, at most, a few primitive forms. What they did not know was "the mystery of mysteries": how new species arose.

In 1839 on Tierra del Fuego, at the southern tip of South America, Darwin encountered "man in his savage state". The indigenous inhabitants taught him two things: that a human is an animal like other animals – "a foul, naked, snuffling thing with no inkling of the divine" – and that the environment moulds us. The Fuegians adapted to their icy climate so perfectly that they could endure it naked. Later, in the Galapagos Islands, he observed how small environmental differences cause marked biological mutations. A theory of evolution embracing all species occurred to him back home in England, among game birds, racing pigeons, and farm stock. Nature selects strains, as breeders do. The specimens best adapted to their environments survive to breed and pass on their characteristics. Darwin held the struggle of nature in awe, partly because his own sickly offspring were the victims of it. He wrote, in effect, an epitaph for his dying children: the survivors would be more healthy and most able to enjoy life. "From the war of nature," according to *On the Origin of Species* (1859), "from famine and from death, the production of higher animals directly follows."

As his theories became accepted, other thinkers proposed refinements that came to be known as "social Darwinism". Such extrapolations included the idea that conflict is natural, therefore good; that society is well served by the elimination of anti-social or

Well bred
Humans have long used selective breeding to enhance characteristics they wished to promote, like the folds of baggy skin of this Shar Pei puppy.

READINGS

C. Darwin's **On the Origin of Species** (1859) and **The Descent of Man** (1871) set out the theory and placed humankind in its context.

N. Eldredge's **Time Frames** (1986) is the best modern critique.

A. Desmond and J. Moore's **Darwin** (1992) is an exciting biography, while J. Brown's **Charles Darwin** (2003) is more exhaustive but staid.

In this 19th-century satirical sketch, the ape-like **Darwin** is portrayed holding up a mirror to another ape.

"We must, however, acknowledge, as it seems to me, that man with all his noble qualities… still bears in his bodily frame the indelible stamp of his lowly origin."

Charles Darwin, *The Descent of Man* (1871)

weak specimens; and that "inferior" races are justly exterminated. Hitler made the last turn in this twisted tradition: "War is... the prerequisite for the natural selection of the strong and the elimination of the weak."

It would be unfair to blame Darwin for this. By advocating the unity of creation, he implicitly defended the unity of mankind. He detested slavery. Nevertheless, he thought Africans would have evolved into a separate species if imperialism had not ended their isolation. In any case he thought they were doomed to extinction. There was no clear dividing line between social Darwinism and the original "scientific Darwinism". Darwin was the father of both.

The fact that the theory of evolution has been abused should not obscure the even more important fact that, broadly speaking, it is true. Natural selection probably does not account for every aspect of evolution: there seem to be random mutations; mating habits can be capricious and unsubmissive to natural selection's supposed laws. It is reasonable, however, to conclude that species originate naturally and divine intervention does not have to be invoked to explain the differences between them.

CONNECTIONS

On the early search for order in creation, see **No Dice** (p.28). For related ideas, see **Deo Volente** (p.96), **Top Ape** (p.138), **Good Breeding** (p.322), and **The Great Chain** (p.380).

Fish out of water
In the 19th century it was considered shocking that humans could have evolved from apes, yet less than 150 years later it is largely taken for granted. These images by Daniel Lee give an artist's view of evolution.

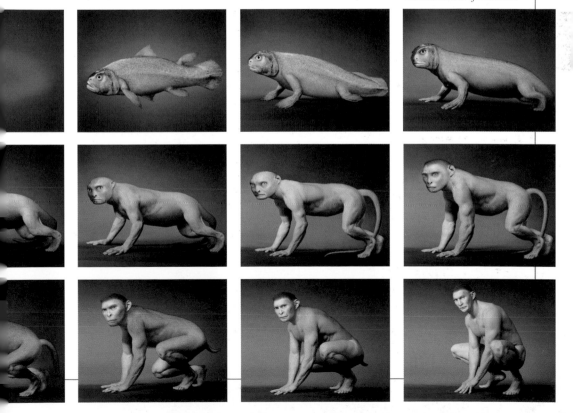

Good Breeding

THE IDEA OF EUGENICS

CONNECTIONS

For more on the background to "new eugenics", see **The Great Chain** (p.380) and **Intelligence Test** (p.382). For the context in which scientific racism developed, see **Inferior by Nature** (p.318) and **Tooth and Claw** (p.320).

READINGS

F. Galton's **Essays in Eugenics** (1909) is now available in a recent edition, while M.S. Quine's **Population Politics in 20th Century Europe** (1996) brilliantly defines the context.

M. Kohn's **The Race Gallery** (1995) studies the rise of racial science, while C. Clay and M. Leapman's **Master Race** (1995) is a chilling account of one of Nazism's eugenics projects.

A. Huxley's **Brave New World** (1932) imagines a dystopic future where children are bred in bottles for specific roles.

We are all the way we are because of a mixture of inherited characteristics and environmental factors. The importance of heredity was obvious to common observation for thousands of years before genetic theory produced a convincing explanation of why, for example, some looks, skills, quiddities, diseases, and deficiencies run in families.

Plato's proposals in *The Republic* (380 BC) for a perfect society were based, in part, on the assumption that it should be composed of perfect individuals: the best citizens should be encouraged to reproduce. The children of the dim and deformed should be exterminated to stop them from breeding. This was a glaringly bad idea: quite apart from its moral repugnance, it would be unlikely to work. Mental or physical qualities, even if they could be satisfactorily identified, constitute only a small part of character and make only a partial contribution to an individual's worth. Plato's idea was shelved for many centuries and not revived until the 19th century. At that time in Europe and North America, racism blamed heritable deficiencies of character for the supposed inferiority of non-whites, while a form of Darwinism suggested that the supposed advantages of natural selection might be helped along by

Eggs for sale
Today, eugenics has taken a new form. It is possible to create babies to order by purchasing eggs and sperm on internet sites such as the example pictured here.

"If a twentieth part of the cost and pains were spent on measures for the improvement of the human race that is spent on the improvement of the breed of horses and cattle, what a galaxy of genius might we not create!"

Francis Galton, *Hereditary Talent and Character* (1865)

Sir Francis Galton (1822–1911) advocated selective breeding to enhance humankind.

human agency. In 1885, Darwin's cousin, Sir Francis Galton, proposed what he called eugenics: the human species could be perfected by the elimination of undesirable mental and moral qualities, and this could be achieved by selective control of fertility and marriage.

Within a couple of decades, this became one of the orthodoxies of the age. In early Soviet Russia and parts of the USA in the same period, the right of marriage was denied to people officially classified as feeble-minded, criminal, and even (in some cases) alcoholic. By 1926, compulsory sterilization of people in some of these categories had been adopted in nearly half the states of the USA.

The eugenic idea was most enthusiastically adopted in Nazi Germany, where its internal logic was fulfilled – the best way to prevent people from breeding was to kill them. Anyone in a category that the state deemed genetically inferior, including Jews, gypsies, and homosexuals, was liable to extermination. Meanwhile, Hitler tried to perfect what he thought would be a "master race" by selective breeding between people supposedly of the "purest" German physical type. Children born of the experimental copulation encouraged between big, strong, blue-eyed, blonde-haired human guinea-pigs did not, on average, seem any better or any worse qualified for citizenship, leadership, or strenuous walks of life than other people.

Nazi excesses made eugenics unpopular for generations. But the concept is now back in a new guise: the reproduction of "genetically engineered" individuals. Indeed, sperm banks of semen donated by people allegedly of special prowess or talent have long been available to potential mothers willing to shop for a genetically superior source of insemination. The isolation of particular genes associable with various inherited characteristics has, moreover, made it theoretically possible for undesirable characteristics to be "filtered out" of the genetic material that goes into a baby at conception. Today, the consequences are incalculable.

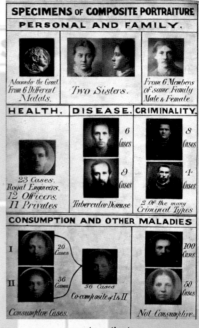

An evil science
One of the main aims of eugenics was to identify and eliminate undesirable qualities. This chart appeared as the frontispiece to one of Sir Francis Galton's treatises.

Atheist Faith

THE IDEA OF GODLESS HUMANISM

"Enemy of religion"
The philosopher Bertrand Russell (1872–1970) asserted that organized Christianity was "the principal enemy of moral progress in the world".

READINGS

M. Knight's (ed.) **Humanist Anthology** (1961) is a useful collection of texts.

O. Chadwick's **The Secularization of the European Mind in the Nineteenth Century** (1990) is an excellent account of the 19th-century "crisis of faith", echoed in A.N. Wilson's **God's Funeral** (2000).

F. Dostoevsky's **The Brothers Karamazov** (1880) brilliantly articulates the search for faith.

A. Maslow's **Towards a Psychology of Being** (1968) offers a humanist psychology of self-actualization.

Appeals to reason and science justified atheism in every age. Even for believers, confidence or resignation that humans can or must manage without divine help has always been a practical recourse from our inability to harness God for our purposes.

Only in the 19th century did the idea arise of combining these strands and inaugurating a quasi-religion of atheists to rival real religions. Four circumstances help to explain the phenomenon and its emergence, initially and especially in France, the USA, and Britain. First, the "Cult of the Supreme Being", begun by the Jacobin leader Maximilien Robespierre, in revolutionary France, suggested – despite its short life and risible failure – that it was possible to start an anti-Christian religious-style movement from scratch. Early in the 1850s, Auguste Comte proposed "a religion of humanity" with its own calendar of secular saints (including Adam Smith and Frederick the Great). Secondly, the dazzling success of Christian evangelism in industrializing environments in the 19th century awakened proselytizing atheists to the need and opportunity to fight back. Thirdly, within Christian Unitarianism – a form of radical Protestantism that denied the divinity of Christ – dissenting congregations multiplied, carrying scepticism to new extremes and finding in dedication to social welfare an ethos that did not need any religious basis. Finally, Darwin's theory of evolution suggested a new scientific explanation for life without religion: the impersonal force of evolution might replace the majesty of divine providence. If science could explain a problem as "mysterious" – to use a term Darwin used himself – as the diversity of species, it might yet be able to explain everything else.

Numerous other quasi-religious movements followed Comte's. The most influential was that of the Ethical Societies, launched in New York in

Felix Adler (1851–1933), US reformer and founder of the Ethical Societies.

"Morality is the law which is the basis of true religion."

Felix Adler

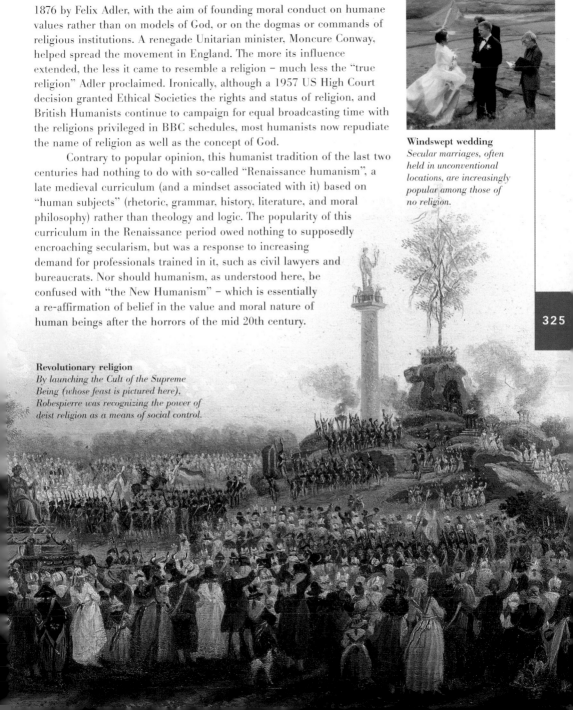

1876 by Felix Adler, with the aim of founding moral conduct on humane values rather than on models of God, or on the dogmas or commands of religious institutions. A renegade Unitarian minister, Moncure Conway, helped spread the movement in England. The more its influence extended, the less it came to resemble a religion – much less the "true religion" Adler proclaimed. Ironically, although a 1957 US High Court decision granted Ethical Societies the rights and status of religion, and British Humanists continue to campaign for equal broadcasting time with the religions privileged in BBC schedules, most humanists now repudiate the name of religion as well as the concept of God.

Contrary to popular opinion, this humanist tradition of the last two centuries had nothing to do with so-called "Renaissance humanism", a late medieval curriculum (and a mindset associated with it) based on "human subjects" (rhetoric, grammar, history, literature, and moral philosophy) rather than theology and logic. The popularity of this curriculum in the Renaissance period owed nothing to supposedly encroaching secularism, but was a response to increasing demand for professionals trained in it, such as civil lawyers and bureaucrats. Nor should humanism, as understood here, be confused with "the New Humanism" – which is essentially a re-affirmation of belief in the value and moral nature of human beings after the horrors of the mid 20th century.

Windswept wedding
Secular marriages, often held in unconventional locations, are increasingly popular among those of no religion.

Revolutionary religion
By launching the Cult of the Supreme Being (whose feast is pictured here), Robespierre was recognizing the power of deist religion as a means of social control.

Calculating Machine

THE IDEA OF ARTIFICIAL INTELLIGENCE

CONNECTIONS

Materialist thinking is explored in: **Matter Matters** (p.124), **The Great Chain** (p.380), and **Intelligence Test** (p.382). For more ideas about numbers and logic, see **Seeing Double** (p.46), **Count on This** (p.120), and **If *x* then *y*** (p.122).

Number cruncher
Since the earliest times, humankind has developed time-saving aids for calculation. In the 1830s, Charles Babbage constructed a mechanical "analytical engine" that could solve complex mathematical problems reliably and rapidly.

George Boole was a prodigy in mathematics but, because his formal education was patchy and poor, and because he lived in relative isolation in Ireland, he was always making, on his own initiative, discoveries that were already familiar to the rest of the mathematical world. Yet in the 1820s, he managed some suggestive work on binary notation – the number system based on units of two instead of 10, which results, for example, in the number 27 being expressed as 11011 (the righthand digit representing 1 x 1, the next 1 x 2, the next 0 x 4, and so on). This system put a new idea into the head of the mathematician Charles Babbage.

Babbage, was engaged at the time on a scheme for improving astronomical tables by calculating them mechanically and so eliminating human error. The idea of calculating machines was long familiar, and commercially viable machines capable of simple arithmetical functions were already in production. But Babbage's thinking was subtler than any predecessor's: he turned complex trigonometrical operations into simple addition and subtraction, which could be performed by cogs and wheels.

The British government invested heavily in his efforts because of the importance of such tables for navigation and imperial mapping. But in 1833, the insight Babbage got from Boole made him abandon work on the relatively simple "difference engine" he had in mind, and turn to the construction of what he called an "analytical engine". This, though operated mechanically, anticipated the modern computer, using the

binary system to generate computations of amazing range and speed. In a method echoed by early electronic computers, the operations were controlled by holes punched in cards. The British government declined to help, and Babbage had to rely on his own fortune and the support of Byron's daughter Ada Lovelace, a gifted amateur mathematician.

The machine was never finished, but the idea was obviously workable and awaited only two conditions – the appropriation of the power of electricity and the revival of government interest – to be carried forward. These conditions were not met until well into the next century, but thereafter the development of computers unfolded rapidly. Computers revolutionized the world, in combination with microtechnology, which made small computers viable (the early specimens made in Manchester and Harvard were the size of small ballrooms), and telecommunications technology, which made it possible to link computers along telephone lines and by radio signals, so that they could exchange data. By the early 21st century, it really had become possible to re-imagine the world as a "global village", where every part of the globe could be in virtually instant contact with every other part. This has been both a disaster and an opportunity: "information overkill" has glutted minds and, perhaps, dulled a generation, but the Internet has multiplied useful work, diffused knowledge, and served freedom.

The speed and universality of the computer revolution raised the question of how much further it could go, and prompted speculation that machines could emulate human intelligence, as well as controversy over whether this was a threat or a promise. In fact, human intelligence is probably fundamentally unmechanical: in other words, there is – contrary to the assertion of the British philosopher Gilbert Ryle – a "ghost in the machine". But computers can certainly extend minds and change them in ways we have only begun to explore. A new psychology is being forged in cyberspace.

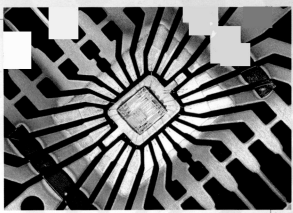

Chips with everything
The miniaturization of the humble silicon chip was at the heart of the computer revolution. Today, we are increasingly dependent on machines, tools, and gadgets that depend on silicon chips for their operation.

Alan Turing (1912–54) was a pioneer of both computer science and artificial intelligence.

"I believe that at the end of the century we will be able to speak of machines thinking without being contradicted"

Alan Turing, *Mind* (1950)

READINGS

D.R. Hofstadter's **Gödel, Escher, Bach** (1979) is the most brilliant – though ultimately unconvincing – apologia for "artificial intelligence" ever penned.

K. Hafner and M. Lyon's **Where Wizards Stay Up Late** (1996) is a lively history of the origins of the Internet.

J.M. Dubbey's **The Mathematical Work of Charles Babbage** (1991) is probably the best book on Charles Babbage.

Master Race

THE IDEA OF GERMAN SUPERIORITY

In the opening years of the 19th century, Germany was a stomping ground for French and Russian armies. This humiliating experience provoked an intensely nationalist reaction: an attempt to show that, like all history's best victims, Germans were really superior to their conquerors.

Germany, in many Germans' opinion, needed to unite and organize for resistance and counter-attack. Meanwhile, inspired by Plato's theory of forms, German philosophers saw the *Volk* (people) as an ideal – a transcendent, immutable reality. The first rector of the University of Berlin, Johannes Göttlieb Fichte, thought German identity was eternal

Ein Volk! Ein Reich!
During the 1930s, the idea that the German people were morally superior to those of other states was expressed in the militarism of the Third Reich. Triumphalist Nazi Party rallies (like this one at Nuremberg in 1936) served to reinforce this perception.

*"Germany will be a world
power or she will be nothing."*

Adolf Hitler, *Mein Kampf* (1925)

**Adolf Hitler's (1889–
1945) powerful oratory
fuelled support for
German expansionism.**

and unchanging. "To have character and be German"
were "undoubtedly one and the same thing". The
Volksgeist – the "Spirit of the Nation" – was essentially good and
insuperably civilizing. Hegel thought that the Germans had replaced the
Greeks and Romans as the final phase in "the historical development of
Spirit". "The German spirit is the spirit of the new world. Its aim is the
realization of absolute Truth as the unlimited self-determination of
freedom." This sounds very grand and a bit scary. There was no good
reason behind it except for intellectual fashion.

The problem arose of who belonged to this "German nation".
The most widely accepted definition was linguistic, formulated by the
poet Ernst Moritz Arndt: "Germany is there wherever the German
language resounds and sings to God in heaven." This did not, however,
displace the racial definitions that became increasingly popular in the
course of the century. In practice, it meant that many – at times, perhaps,
most – Germans came to think that Jews and Slavs could not be fully
their fellow-countrymen even if they spoke the language; but the German

state had a right to rule wherever
German was spoken, even if only by
a minority. The implications were
explosive: centuries of migration had
strung German-speaking minorities
across eastern Europe – along the
Danube and into the southern Volga
valley – as well as into parts of what
were usually considered to be France
and Belgium, setting the scene for
the traumatic armed confrontations
of the 20th century.

The Iron Chancellor
*Prince Otto von Bismarck (1815–98)
revenged past humiliations inflicted on
the German people by defeating their
enemies to create a unified state in 1871.*

Ancient authority
*The imposing, temple-like
façade of Berlin's Reichstag
(the main legislature of the
German state) emphasized
Germany's claims to be a
natural successor to the
traditions of Ancient Greece
and Rome.*

CONNECTIONS

Compare the German *Volk*
to ideas of superiority in
China (**Centre of the World**,
p.182), Japan (**Scattered
Grains**, p.194), and Britain
(**Rule, Britannia**, p.330).
For essential context, see
My Country (p.286) and
The Big Idea
(p.274).

READINGS

G. Fichte's **Reden an die
Deutsche Nation** (1808)
is the basic text.

A.J.P. Taylor's **The Course
of German History** (1945)
is a brilliant polemic.

A.J. La Vopa's **Fichte, the
Self and the Calling of
Philosophy** (2001) is the
first volume of what looks
like being a magisterial life
of Gottlieb Fichte.

Rule, Britannia

THE IDEA OF BRITISH SUPERIORITY

The British Empire
This 1886 world map shows the full extent of the British Empire in pink. By the early part of the 20th century, over a third of the globe was "pink".

330

CONNECTIONS

For other nations' ideas of superiority, see **Centre of the World** (p.182), **Scattered Grains** (p.194), and **Master Race** (p.328). See **Promontory of Asia** (p.266), **American Dream** (p.336), and **Black Is Beautiful** (p.376) for related ideas.

In November 1848 Thomas Babington Macaulay, English historian, sat in his study congratulating himself on living in a country that had escaped the revolutionary convulsions of continental neighbours "impatient to demolish and unable to construct".

Since he belonged, in his own estimation, to "the greatest and most highly civilized people that ever the world saw", he might have accepted British superiority as needing no explanation. Instead, he stopped to enquire rationally why he had been spared the sight of "the pavement of London piled up in barricades, the houses dented with bullets, the gutters foaming with blood". His answer, crudely summarized, was that Britain had pre-enacted the struggles of her neighbours between constitutionalism and absolutism, and settled them, a century and a half before, in favour of "the popular element in the English polity".

The English Revolution had established that "kings reigned by a right in no respect differing from the right by which freeholders chose knights of the shire or from the right by which judges granted writs of *habeas corpus*". Macaulay thought, that the European revolutionaries of his day were trying to implement what had become an English shibboleth: that the rights of governments were limited by law and conferred by merely human grace. He was no democrat. He was haunted by nightmares of a Europe engulfed in a new barbarism, inflicted by under-civilized masses. At the same time he was confident of the progress of history and of the long-term perfectibility of man.

It was England's destiny to pioneer progress and approach perfectibility: the whole of English history had been leading up to such

"Rule, **Britannia,** Britannia rule the waves" starts a famous British patriotic song.

"The British race is sound to the core and... dry rot and dust are strangers to it."

Cecil Rhodes, quoted in T. Ranger's *Rhodes, Oxford and the Study of Race Relations* (1987)

a consummation, ever since the Anglo-Saxons had brought a tradition of liberty, born in the Germanic woods, to Britannia, where liberty blended with the civilizing influences of the Roman Empire and Christian religion. Britain was simply the arena of England. These were, at best, crudely oversimplified versions of the British past, but they had the power of myth to explain the present for 19th-century Britons: the extraordinary facts that Britain had become a superpower, the "workshop of the world", and the "mother-country" of the world's most extensive empire.

Playing the game
One of British culture's most enduring legacies around the world has been the game of cricket and the sense of fair play with which it is associated.

READINGS

T.B. Macaulay's **History of England** (1849) is the starting-point of the 19th-century British myth.

D. Gilmour's **Rudyard Kipling** (2002) is the best biography of the greatest celebrant of Britishness.

N. Davies' **The Isles** (2000) is the best, as well as the most controversial, single-volume British history.

Imperial nostalgia
In one of the few regular displays of overt patriotism in modern Britain, the crowd at the Last Night of the Proms indulge in a, perhaps ironic, flag-waving celebration.

Bollywood dreams
No aspect of Indian life demonstrates the appropriation of Western culture so clearly as the Mumbai (Bombay) film industry, which has created its own imagery and values from a distant Hollywood model.

CONNECTIONS

For the British imperial background, see **Rule, Britannia** (p.330). On comparable ideas in China and Japan, see **Asian Renaissance** (p.334). On black responses to white hegemony, see **Black Is Beautiful** (p.376).

East Meets West

THE INDIAN IDEA OF WESTERNIZATION

Raja Rammohun Roy was the herald and representative thinker of Westernization in India. His West was Enlightenment Europe. He made an almost divine cult of human nature, prescribed Voltaire for his pupils, and replied, when the Bishop of Calcutta mistakenly congratulated him on converting to Christianity, that he had not "laid down one superstition to take up another". Yet the roots of his rationalism and liberalism pre-dated his introduction to Western literature: they came from Islamic and Persian traditions and he knew about Aristotle from Arabic works before he encountered the original works. The movement he founded in 1829, which became known as Brahmo Samaj, was a model of "modernization" for societies that had been "left behind" by the headlong progress of the industrializing West, but which wanted to catch up without forfeiting their own traditions and identity.

This was characteristic of cultural cross-fertilization in 19th-century India. In the next great figure in Roy's tradition, Isvarcandra Vidyasagar, indigenous roots are even more conspicuous. He did not learn English until he was on the verge of middle-age. When he argued for widow re-marriage or against polygamy, or when he advocated relaxing caste discrimination in the allocation of school places, he did not hold up the West as a model to be imitated, but marshalled ancient Indian texts in support of his suggestions. On the other hand, he dismissed the claims of some pious Brahmins who insisted that every Western idea had an Indian origin. He was an atheist in effect, "challenging God for the sake of improving man's condition". He resigned the secretaryship of the Sanskrit College of Calcutta in 1846 because of opposition from the Hindu establishment to his programme of including "the science and civilization of the West" in the curriculum. But this commitment to reform must be seen in the context of Vidyasagar's major project – the revitalization of native Bengali tradition. "If the students be made familiar with English literature," he claimed, "they will prove the best and ablest contributors to an enlightened Bengali renaissance." He was right. In the next generation, the Bengali renaissance was going the way of earlier European counterparts in generating a vernacular revival.

The British in India were like many foreign "barbarian" conquerors before them, adding a layer of culture to the long-accumulated sediments of the sub-continent's past. More than in China and Japan, Western traditions could be appropriated by Indians without a sense of submission, because of the myth of the "Aryan race". These supposed original speakers of Indo-European languages, who spread across Eurasia thousands of years ago from the Bay of Bengal to the Atlantic, created the possibility of thinking of Indian and European cultures as kindred and sprung from the same origin. The great advocate of the equal value of Indian and European thought, Swami Vivekananda, called Plato and Aristotle "Yavana gurus". In consequence, India could accept selective Westernization without sacrifice of identity or dignity.

Father of modern India
Raja Rammohun Roy (1772–1833) founded the Brahmo Samaj in 1829, a movement that promoted a vague theism. He viewed Western Enlightenment values as part of a continuum of ancient Eastern traditions.

Space-age currency
At the start of the 21st century, India's techno-logical revolution is symbolized by its nuclear-weapon capability and multi-million-dollar satellite programme – celebrated here on a two-rupee note (the price of two cups of tea).

READINGS

D. Kopf's **The Brahmo Samaj and the Shaping of the Modern Indian Mind** (1979) is a profoundly insightful work.

G. Haldar's **Vidyasagar: a Reassessment** (1972) is an outstanding portrait.

M.K. Haldar's **Renaissance and Reaction in Nineteenth-Century Bengal** (1977) is brisk, perceptive, and provocative.

Asian Renaissance

THE CHINESE IDEA OF SELF-STRENGTHENING

East meets West
In a departure from Japan's isolationist past, Crown Prince (future Emperor) Hirohito (far left) toured Western countries in 1921.

Show of force
China's resurgence over the last century has sought to combine technological prowess, on show in this huge military parade, with traditional Chinese values.

In November 1861, Wei Mu-ting, an Imperial censor with a taste for history, wrote a memorandum that laid out the principles of what came to be called "self-strengthening" in China. He stressed the need to learn from and catch up with the latest "barbarian" military technology, but represented this programme as the retrieval of what had originally been Chinese. In his view, which became a commonplace of Chinese literature on the subject for the rest of the century, Westerners had borrowed their first knowledge of ordnance from the Mongols, who had picked it up in China. Most of the military and maritime technology of which China was the victim had been developed from prototypes that had originally been developed by the Chinese.

This is curiously reminiscent of the terms in which Western apologists nowadays denounce Japanese "imitations" of Western technology. It is also probably true: Western historians of the diffusion of Chinese technology are now saying something similar themselves. Once China had recovered her lost sciences, Wei Mu-ting believed, it would again resume its customary supremacy.

The essence of self-strengthening as it was understood in China was that superficial technical lessons could be learned from the West, without prejudice to the essential verities on which Chinese tradition was based. Tseng Kuo-fan, the model administrator responsible for modernizing China, uttered the language of Western conservatism. "The mistakes inherited from the past we can correct. What the past ignored, we can inaugurate." But he insisted on the perfection of imperial rule and rites, and saw political decline as a product of moral degeneracy. "Propriety and righteousness" came above "expediency and ingenuity". New arsenals, shipyards, and technical schools teetered precariously on the edges of traditional society.

Meanwhile, the Japanese version of "self-strengthening" took a somewhat different course. The revolutionaries of 1868 proclaimed the restoration of a supposedly ancient order of imperial government, and promised to "expel the barbarians" as well as "enrich the country and strengthen the army". In practice, however, Okubu Toshimichi, the main author of the new policies, realized the samurai – the hereditary warrior class – would be transformed unrecognizably by mass mobilization of conscript soldiers. The new ruling classes confirmed foreign treaties, unknotted their hair, rode in carriages, flourished umbrellas, and invested in railways and heavy industries. Japan became the "Britain" or "Prussia" of Asia and launched a new career as a major modern power.

Today's "Asian Renaissance" – the prominence of Japan; the rise of "tiger economies" in South Korea, Singapore, and Hong Kong; the hectic development of Pacific-side China; and the progress of economic development in many parts of Southeast Asia – is the latest phase of self-strengthening. It has the same watchwords: selective Westernization, defence of "Asian values", and a determination to rival or eclipse Westerners at their own games of economic power.

Bright lights, big city
Since the revolutionary upheavals of 1868, Japan has taken less than 150 years to transform itself from a backward, agrarian state into a highly urbanized economic powerhouse.

READINGS

F. Yukichi's **Autobiography** (1966) is a fascinating memoir of one of Japan's "discoverers of the West".

I. Hsu's **The Rise of Modern China** (1970) is the best general history of China throughout the relevant periods.

S.A. Leibo's **Transferring Technology to China** (1985) is an excellent study of one strand in the self-strengthening movement.

CONNECTIONS

Contrast traditional Chinese and Japanese notions of superiority in **Centre of the World** (p.182) and **Scattered Grains** (p.194). For other ideas formulated in response to the white Western world, see **Black Is Beautiful** (p.376) and **Out of Africa** (p.378).

Rudyard Kipling (1865–1936) doubted Asia's ability to match British military might.

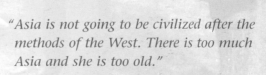

"Asia is not going to be civilized after the methods of the West. There is too much Asia and she is too old."

Rudyard Kipling, *The Man Who Was* (1907)

American Dream

THE IDEA OF AMERICAN EXCEPTIONALISM

On the right track
America's self-confidence and pioneering spirit found expression in the heroic construction of railroads across the country's wild interior from the mid 1800s to the early 1900s.

336

READINGS

J. Farina's (ed.) **Hecker Studies: Essays on the Thought of Isaac Hecker** (1983) is a good introduction, while P. Gleason's **Keeping Faith** (1987) is a good history of Catholicism in the USA.

F. Scott Fitzgerald's **The Great Gatsby** (1925) describes American re-invention, while T. Wolfe's **The Right Stuff** (1979) eulogizes the courage of a new breed of American hero – test pilots and astronauts.

The idea that America is a unique country, beyond comparison with others, is older than the USA. It was part of the "pioneer spirit" – the shining-face enthusiasm that saw America as a promised land for chosen people. In the 19th century, some "different" expectations seemed fulfilled. The USA became successively a model republic, an exemplary democracy, a burgeoning empire, a magnet for migrants, a precocious industrializer, and a great power. America, according to Americanism, could learn nothing from the rest of the world.

Unfairly, perhaps, an extreme form of this idea was ascribed to the Catholic reformer, Father Isaac Hecker, who argued that progressive enrichment of divine grace accompanied modern progress, so that, by implication, Christian perfection was more easily attainable in the USA. Pope Leo XIII thought this was American arrogance, an attempt to devise a special form of Catholicism for America, painting the Church red, white, and blue. It undermined Americans' awareness of dependence on God and made the Church redundant as a guide for the soul. These suspicions may have been partly justified.

Two related heresies have helped to define American culture: the Lone Ranger heresy and the Donald Duck heresy. According to the Lone Ranger heresy, every hero has to be an outsider, whom society needs but who does not need society; he does what a man's gotta do, even if it means shoot-outs or show-downs along the way. Almost every American hero, from the pioneer pathfinder to Rambo, exemplifies this trait.

The Donald Duck heresy, meanwhile, sanctifies impulses by representing them as outpourings of natural goodness, feeding the conviction of self-righteousness that so often got Donald into trouble. Belief that our impulses are naturally good is part of the

American icon
Donald Duck (© Disney Enterprises, Inc.) reflects the US values of cussed-ness, individualism, and warmheartedness.

Israel Zangwill's play *The Melting Pot* upheld the benefits of American immigration.

"America is God's Crucible."

Israel Zangwill, *The Melting Pot* (1908)

American dream, for individual
liberation is only justifiable if
one believes in the essential
goodness of man – or, in Donald's
case, of duck. And it is remarkable
that Donald, despite all his
vices of individualist excess –
his irrational self-reliance, his
opinionated noisiness, his trigger-
happy gun-toting, his fits of
temper, and his indulgent self-
image – is at bottom warm-
hearted and well-disposed.

The same sort of self-
righteousness, and obedience to
impulse, makes American policy-
makers, for instance, bomb people
from time to time – but always
with good intentions. The
"feelgood society", from which
personal guilt is excised and
self-satisfaction made a virtue,
is among the other consequences.
In America, confession is replaced
by therapy and self-reproach by
self-discovery.

Still, if America was ever exceptional,
it is so no longer, as the rest of the world
strives to imitate its success. Genuine
historic communities always differ from
their neighbours in some ways. But when
exceptional cases are examined in detail, the
similarities usually outweigh the differences.
Believers in American exceptionalism now
tend to see that "specialness" as a double-
edged sword that is both a source of weakness
and of strength. It distinguishes the USA in evincing
extreme forms of commonplace vices, such as myopic
patriotism, morbid religiosity, and confrontational
insistence on one's rights, but is also characterized
by the widely celebrated human qualities of
civic-mindedness, neighbourly values, love of
freedom, and devotion to democracy.

One small step...
*America, more than any other
country, has often claimed to act
on behalf of humankind rather than
from narrow self-interest, as when the
astronauts from Apollo 11 landed on
the Moon in July 1969.*

Symbolic greeting
*The Statue of Liberty
provides a symbolic
welcome to new migrants
arriving in New York. This
model also shows the twin
towers of the World Trade
Center destroyed in 2001
in a terrorist attack.*

Little house on the prairie
*Midwestern homesteaders
seeking a better life laid
the foundations for the
USA's self-image as a
"can-do" culture.*

Manifest Destiny

THE IDEA OF AMERICAN EXPANSIONISM

Ideas sometimes take a long time to fulfil in practice. Even while the USA
was experiencing its founding revolution, some Americans imagined their
"nation" filling the hemisphere, but it seemed a vision impossible to
realize. Once Alexander Mackenzie had crossed North America in 1793,
in latitudes still under British sovereignty, it became an urgent matter for
the fledgling republic to reach "from sea to shining sea". The Louisiana
Purchase in 1802 made it a theoretical possibility, and a transcontinental
expedition in 1803 sketched out a route. But in the first half of the 19th
century, there were Mexicans and Native Americans to be swept aside.
During the feverish hostility and war against Mexico in the 1830s and
1840s, the journalist John L. O'Sullivan propagated the idea that America's
"manifest destiny" was "to overspread the continent allotted by Providence
for the free development of our yearly multiplying millions".

There was still, however, an unconquerable environment to be
traversed, then known as the "Great American Desert", which occupied
most of the region between the exploitable lands of the Mississippi
basin and the territories of the Pacific coast. In the Midwest, virtually
nothing grew naturally that human stomachs could digest; except in
a few relatively small patches, the unyieldingly tough soils could not
be broken without industrial technology. To the writer James
Fenimore Cooper, it seemed a place without a future, "a vast
country, incapable of sustaining a dense population".

Then steel ploughs began to bite into sods too tough to
yield to earlier farming technologies. Rifles drove off the Native
Americans and killed off the undomesticable
fauna: the great herds of buffalo, which were
slaughtered almost to extinction. Cheap nails
and machined planks made it possible to build
balloon-framed, "Chicago-built" cities in
treeless places. Railroads could carry the grain
to where it was saleable. Grain elevators,
introduced in 1850, made it possible to grow
and store the grain without vast amounts of
labour. Giant flour mills processed them into
marketable wares. Wheat was the edible grass,
new to the region, which made the land yield
efficient plant food for humans.

"We, the American people, are the most independent, intelligent, moral, and happy people on the face of the Earth."

The United States Journal (1845)

READINGS

R. Horsman's **Race and Manifest Destiny** (1990) is a lively and controversial inquiry into the subject.

W. Cronon's (ed.) **Under an Open Sky** (1994) is a superb study of westward colonization in the USA, and its ecological effects.

L. L'Amour's **How the West was won** (1963) inspired Hollywood's romantic vision of the making of America.

The domestication of the prairie turned the region into the granary of the world and an arena of cities. The USA and Canada became continent-wide countries and real world powers, with power over the price of food. Among the consequences was that the hitherto most underexploited of North America's resources – space – was put to productive use, soaking up migrants to make the USA a demographic giant, generating wealth to help put it and keep it economically ahead of all rivals.

Into the unknown
When explorers Lewis and Clark, pictured here, began their famous expedition to map out the uncharted American West in 1805, the USA's destiny to "overspread" the entire continent was by no means certain.

339

Dr Strangelove

THE IDEA OF A WEAPON TO END WAR

Never again
Fear of the apocalyptic power of nuclear weapons, used on Hiroshima (above) and Nagasaki, Japan, in August 1945, has so far prevented any further world-scale conflict.

Keeping the peace
Alfred Nobel (1833–96) proposed that states should possess massive bombs as a deterrent to war. His prize-giving foundation (Nobel Prize medal, above) was established to further research into such weaponry.

The notion of a weapon so terrible that it would frighten people into peace seems counter-intuitive, but it is the logical consequence of the Roman saying: "Let him who desires peace, prepare for war."

Towards the end of the 19th century, the Swedish philanthropist Alfred Nobel was one of the richest men in the world, but he was lonely, morbidly cynical, and, for two reasons, wracked by guilt. First, he had blown up his own brother in an accident during an experiment with high explosives. Secondly, he had made his fortune in death-dealing trades: the manufacture of dynamite and the traffic in arms. He took refuge in extravagant and sometimes alarming projects for world peace. Most of the (largely self-elected) delegates who frequented the "Peace Congresses" of late 19th-century Europe believed the way to secure lasting peace was to improve the system of international law and to devise institutions to arbitrate in peace-threatening disputes. Others, more crankily, hoped to improve human nature by education or eugenics – filleting out or repressing people's instinct for violence.

Nobel disagreed. War would "stop short, instantly", he promised during a Congress in Paris in 1890, if it were made "as death-dealing to the civilian population at home as to the troops at the front". Consistent with his vocation as an explosives expert – and perhaps in an effort to assuage his own conscience – he dreamed of a super-weapon so destructive that no one would dare to start a war for fear of unleashing its power. In the absence of such a bomb, the best hope he could see for peace was spreading the fear of germ warfare. The prizes he endowed for contributions to peace and science were in fact intended to promote research towards the development of super-weapons.

His idea was flawed. In practice, there are always lunatics or fanatics for whom no destruction is a deterrent and no weapon too terrible. The Nobel Prizes have encouraged work in the theory of science, the conquest of disease, and the peaceful resolution of conflicts – all more useful to the world than the war-killing weapon Nobel dreamed of. Still, his vision did help to influence scientists who worked on nuclear weapons; and, against the balance of probabilities, the atom and hydrogen bombs did contribute to limiting war in the second half of the 20th century, when the equipoise of "mutually assured destruction" (MAD) deterred the hostile great powers of the day from engaging one another directly. However, "nuclear proliferation" magnifies the risk, and in the early 21st century the danger is growing that a "rogue state" or terrorist network will start a nuclear war.

Nuclear deterrent
In 1985, President Reagan of the USA and Mikhail Gorbachev of the USSR signed an important treaty limiting the size of their nuclear arsenals.

READINGS

K. Fant's **Alfred Nobel** (1993) is the most useful biography.

R. Rhodes's **The Making of the Atomic Bomb** (1986) and L.S. Wittner's **The Struggle Against the Bomb** (1997) are both informative.

P. George's **Red Alert** (1958) is a powerful satire on the Cold War, on which S. Kubrick based **Dr Strangelove** (1964).

Dr Strangelove
(as played by Peter Sellers) is the archetypal mad scientist.

"Heck, I reckon you wouldn't even be human beings if you didn't have some pretty strong personal feelings about nuclear combat."

T.J. "King" Kong, in the film *Dr Strangelove or How I Learned to Stop Worrying and Love the Bomb* **(1964)**

Doomsday scenario
Some defence analysts fear that a ruthless government or terrorist group may one day be tempted to deploy a nuclear weapon, with unimaginable consequences.

THE AGE OF UNCERTAINTY

1900–2000

7

Chaos Restored

Historians have a habit of tampering with commonsense chronology: treating the 20th century as starting in 1914, for instance, as if the trenches of the Great War were a crucible for the world. The years preceding the war become a period of inertia when nothing much happened – a golden afterglow of the Romantic Age, turned blood-red by the real agent of change: the war itself. Yet in the history of ideas, the period between 1900 and the outbreak of the war was startlingly innovative.

During that decade-or-so, a scientific counter-revolution exploded certainties inherited from the 17th and 18th centuries. Relativity made absurdities credible. Primitivism subverted racial hierarchies. Cubism disordered perceptions. Science subsided to the level of convention. Common sense crumbled. Notions that had prevailed since the time of Newton turned out to be misleading. By 1914, "the spirit of unrest", – it could be said – had "invaded science".

Potentially devastating philosophical malaise eroded confidence in traditional notions about language, reality, and the links between them. The spread of Freudian psychology – which claimed to expose the world of the subconscious – undermined conventional ideas of experience, and, in particular, of sex and childhood. Meanwhile, a revolution in anthropology, which made cultural relativism the only credible basis on which a serious study of human societies could be pursued, spread gradually from America.

20th-century design
The invention of Bakelite (an early form of plastic) allowed the creation of affordable radios to "receive" the first wireless broadcasts.

The period was both a graveyard and a cradle: a graveyard of certainties, the cradle of a civilization of crumbling confidence, in which it would be hard to be sure of anything. The unsettling effect can be literally seen in the work of painters of the time. Never more than in the 20th century, painters tended to paint not the world as they saw it directly, but as science and philosophy displayed it for their inspection. The revolutions of 20th-century art exactly match the jolts and shocks administered by science and philosophy.

In 1907, Cubism held up to the world images of itself reflected as if in a distorting mirror, shivered into fragments. Mondrian, who had painted the trees along the river Geyn with romantic fidelity, splayed and atomized them into new versions. Meanwhile, in 1911, Kandinsky read Rutherford's description of the atom, "with frightful force, as if the end of the world had come. All things become transparent, without strength or certainty". The effects fed into the new style, in which he suppressed every reminiscence of real objects in his work. The effects of anthropology on art are even more explicit than those of science: Picasso, Braque, Brancusi, and the Blue Rider school copied the arts of "primitive" cultures, demonstrating the validity of alien aesthetics, and drawing lessons from the formerly despised. The syncopations of jazz and the new noises of atonal music – released by Schoenberg in Vienna in 1908 – subverted the harmonies of the past as surely as quantum mechanics began to challenge its ideas of order.

Reaching for the sky
In the 20th century, skyscrapers came to dominate urban skylines. The 443-metre (1,454-ft) high Empire State Building in New York, which was erected in 1930–31, was the world's tallest building for over 50 years.

Technology – the characteristic science of the century – hurtled into a new phase. The 20th century would be an electric age, much as the 19th had been an age of steam. In 1901, Marconi broadcast by wireless. In 1903, the Wright brothers took flight. Plastic was invented in 1907. The curiosities of late 19th-century inventiveness, such as the telephone, the car, and the typewriter, all became commonplace. The other essentials of technologically fulfilled 20th-century lifestyles – the atom-smasher, the ferro-concrete skyscraper-frame, even the hamburger and Coca-Cola – were all in place before the outbreak of World War I.

In politics, too, the new century opened with new departures. The world's first fully fledged democracies – fully fledged in the sense that women had equal political rights with men – were founded in Norway and New Zealand in 1901. In 1904, Japanese victories over Russia foreshadowed the fate of white imperialism. Ultimately, the challenge of Japanese power would begin the unravelling of European empires by making British, French, and Dutch imperialism unsustainable in the Far East. Encouraged by Japan's example, independence movements leapt into action. Apologists for the equality of races took new heart. In 1911, the first great "rebellions of the masses" began: the Mexican and Chinese revolutions. These were seismic convulsions, compared with which, in the long run, World War I would seem like only a short, sharp shock to the existing world-system, and the later communist revolutions would resemble a brief blip.

By 1914, the world seemed stripped for action: atomized, chaotic, seething with rebellion, raw-emotioned, and equipped with terrible technologies. Most of the great themes of the 20th century were anticipated by the developments of its first few years. The worldwide ideological struggle, between fascism, communism, and democracy, which overshadowed the 20th century, was fought between 19th-century ideas, or, at least, between ideas of 19th-century origin.

Advanced robotics
In 100 years, the world has advanced from primitive transistor-valve radios to highly complex silicon-chip-controlled robots, such as Honda's humanoid ASIMO.

Warped Universe

THE IDEA OF RELATIVITY

The theory of relativity is an outstanding example of an idea that changes the world by changing the way we perceive and picture it. In 1901 Albert Einstein was a second-class Technical Officer in the Swiss Patent Office – penned in a corral for the containment of genius. He had been expelled from school as disruptive and suspected of arrogance at university. Donnish jealousy had excluded him from an academic career and buried him in obscurity. In 1905 he emerged, like a sapper from a mine, to detonate a terrible charge.

He produced a theoretical solution to an experimental paradox: measured against moving objects, the speed of light never seemed to vary, no matter how fast or slow the motion of the source from which it was beamed. If the speed of light is constant, Einstein inferred, time and distance must be relative to it. At speeds approaching that of light, time must slow down and distance shorten. We assume that space and time are absolute only because, compared with light, we never go very fast. Einstein liked to explain his theory of relativity by way of fantastic analogies with trains. His most graphic example, however, was the paradox of the twins: the twin who left on an ultra-fast journey would return home younger than the one who stayed behind. In Einstein's universe, every appearance deceived. Mass and energy were mutually convertible. Parallel lines met. Commonsense perceptions vanished as if down a rabbit-hole to Wonderland.

The theory of relativity shook confidence in traditional certainties. It transformed the way people perceived reality and measured the Universe. It unlocked the new paradoxes of quantum mechanics for the next generations of scientists to explore. It made possible, for good and ill, a new phase of practical research in the conversion of mass into energy: atomic power.

Relatively near
Einstein revolutionized our understanding of time and distance and, by extension, our relationship with the vastness of the Universe. At over two million light years away, the Andromeda Galaxy is our nearest neighbouring galaxy.

READINGS

L.C. Epstein's **Relativity Visualized** (1985) is one of the clearest explanations around, while J.R. Lucas and P.E. Hodgson's **Spacetime and Electromagnetism** (1990) is more advanced.

E.A. Abbott's **Flatland** (1884) is a thought-provoking visualization of two- and three-dimensional space.

346

German-born **Albert Einstein** (1879–1955) won the Nobel Prize for physics in 1921.

"When a man sits with a pretty girl for an hour, it seems like a minute. But let him sit on a hot stove for a minute and it's longer than any hour. That's relativity."

Albert Einstein, *On the Effects of External Sensory Input on Time Dilation* (1938)

Warp speed
Einstein stated that it is not possible to travel faster than the speed of light. The creators of television's Star Trek invented "warp speed", in which distances are compressed to allow spacecraft to reach their destinations faster than the speed of light.

Uncertainty

THE IDEA OF THE IMPLICATED OBSERVER

Can science solve all the problems of the world? In the 18th and 19th centuries it was easy to hope so, but ideas that were developed in the 20th century made it ever harder for science to do so.

Between 1911 and 1913, work on atomic structures revealed that electrons appear to slide erratically between orbits around a nucleus. Findings that followed from the attempt to track the elusive particles of sub-atomic matter were expressed in the new discourse of "quantum mechanics". Its forms were paradoxical – like those employed by the Danish Nobel Prize-winner Niels Bohr, who described light as both waves and particles. By the middle of the 1930s, more contradictions piled up. When the motion of sub-atomic particles was plotted, their positions seemed irreconcilable with their momentum. They seemed to move at rates different from their measurable speed and to end up where it was impossible for them to be. Working in collaborative tension, Bohr and German colleague Werner Heisenberg enshrined these incompatible

Quantum mechanic
Danish physicist Niels Bohr (1885–1962) conducted pioneering research into the behaviour of sub-atomic particles and was a key contributor to the development of quantum mechanics.

Unwanted interference
In many cases, the observer determines the outcome of an experiment due to the limitations inherent in the scientific process. Here, ripples in water are used to study the behaviour of waves, but because they are artificial, the observer has influenced the results.

"The nature of our epoch is multiplicity and indeterminacy... Foundations that other generations believed to be firm are really only sliding."

Hugo von Hofmannsthal, *Ein Brief* (1905)

values in a principle they called "Uncertainty" or "Indeterminacy". Their debate provoked a revolution in thought. Scientists who thought about it realized that the world of big objects is continuous with the sub-atomic world. Experiments in both spheres are vitiated by the same limitation: the observer is part of every experiment and there is no level of observation at which his findings are objective. This insight threatened to put scientists back on a par with their predecessors – the alchemists – who, because they worked with complex distillations under the mercurial influence of the stars, could never repeat the conditions of an experiment and, therefore, never predict its results.

This was of enormous importance because practitioners of other disciplines tended to treat science as a benchmark of objectivity. Historians, anthropologists, sociologists, linguists, and even some students of literature called themselves scientists in proclamation of their intention to escape their status as subjects. It turned out that what they had in common with scientists was the opposite of what they had hoped: they were all implicated in their own findings. Contributions later in the century only seemed to put more space between subject and object. In 1960, in one of the most influential works ever written by a philosopher about science, the American Thomas Kuhn argued that scientific revolutions were identifiable with what he called "paradigm shifts" that changed our ways of looking at the world through the construction of new imagery or language in which to describe it.

Kuhn always repudiated the inference that most people drew: that the findings of science depended not on the objective facts but on the perspective of the enquirer. Yet increasingly in the 20th century, ordinary people and non-scientific intellectuals lost confidence in science. Faith that it could solve the world's problems and de-code the secrets of the cosmos evaporated. In part, this was the result of science's practical failures: every technological advance unleashed its own problems and side-effects. In the century that saw two world wars, science seemed best at devising horrors and engines of destruction. In part, however, the process was one of intellectual disintegration, as uncertainty corroded the unassailability of "hard facts" with which scientific investigation was formerly associated.

READINGS

T. Kuhn's **The Structure of Scientific Revolutions** (1962) is fundamental.

A. Pais's **Niels Bohr's Times** (1991) is a superb biography.

G. Zukav's **The Dancing Wu-Li Masters** (1979) attempts to express modern physics in terms of oriental philosophy.

P. Auster's **New York Trilogy** (1987) examines identity from an observer's point of view.

349

UNCERTAINTY

CONNECTIONS

Other ideas of the 20th century contributed to the undermining of certainty. See, for example: **Warped Universe** (p.346), **Chaos Theory** (p.350), **Common Sense** (p.352), **Their Own Terms** (p.354), and **Road to Freedom** (p.374).

Chaos Theory

THE IDEA OF UNPREDICTABILITY

Traditionally, science has aimed to expose "nature's laws" in order to make the way the world works predictable and therefore, perhaps, manageable. In the 1980s, chaos theory proposed a science of unpredictability and inspired new kinds of awe and despair.

The search for predictability broke down first in meteorology. No matter how many statistics meteorologists compiled, the weather continued to surprise them. The disproportion between small causes and vast consequences was so great that some relationships of cause and effect were untraceable. In an image that captured the imagination of the world, "the flap of a butterfly's wings" could set off a series of events leading ultimately to a typhoon or tidal wave.

The model seemed universally applicable. Market fluctuations, ecosystems, political stability, and the survival of civilizations all seem vulnerable to sudden, effectively inexplicable fluctuations. Even the oscillations of a pendulum and the forces of gravity (since Newton, the sanctuaries of traditional science, whose vocation is to find order in the Universe) were shown by experiment to undergo chaotic distortions.

Chaos seemed to be a function of complexity. The more multifarious and interconnected the parts of a system, the greater the likelihood of some small, deeply, invisibly embedded alterations bringing down the whole structure. Paradoxically, the search for nature's laws became refocused on a quest for some deeper level of coherence that might make chaos itself seem systematic and its catastrophic interventions predictable in their turn.

Benjamin Franklin (1706–90) was an American philosopher, scientist, and statesman.

"... for the want of a nail the shoe was lost; for the want of a shoe the horse was lost; and for the want of a horse the rider was lost..."

Benjamin Franklin, *Poor Richard's Almanac* **(1757)**

More convincingly, however, the exposure of chaos looks like another nail in the coffin of "scientism" – yet more evidence that nature really is ultimately inexplicable by definitive forms of analysis, and therefore uncontrollable by human minds. Other discoveries and speculations of recent science reinforce this modest conclusion. The idea, for instance, that not all events have causes but can happen randomly, seems essential to understand the pace of evolution.

Strictly speaking, this understanding precludes explanation. Ultimately, random mutations just happen – that is what makes them random. Quantum physics can only be described – in the present state of our knowledge – with formulations that are strictly self-contradictory. Sub-atomic particles defy what were formerly thought to be laws of motion. What mathematicians now call "fractals" distort what were once thought to be patterns, such as the structures of snowflakes or spiders' webs or, indeed, of butterflies' wings. The engravings of M.C. Escher seemed to predict this impressive fact.

As the Nobel Prize-winning physicist Philip Anderson has pointed out, there appears to be no universally applicable order of nature: "When you have a good general principle at one level," you must not expect "that it's going to work at all levels." Science seems to be self-undermined, and the faster its progress, the more questions emerge about its own competence. And the less faith most people have in it.

CONNECTIONS

Other ideas related to chaos theory include **Warped Universe** (p.346) and **Uncertainty** (p.348). For early ideas of order, see **No Dice** (p.28). For an earlier debate about the sufficiency of science, see **Impossibilism** (p.202).

Random order
Chaos theory concerns the science of patterned disorder. Fractal patterns like that from the Julia Set (left) are of huge interest to mathematicians, since these geometric shapes have infinitely repeating patterns that do not follow linear formulas.

Common Sense

THE IDEA OF PRAGMATISM

CONNECTIONS

Relativism is explored in **Man Is the Measure** (p.118) and cultural relativism is covered in **Their Own Terms** (p.354). For a useful point of comparison with pragmatism's emphasis on utility, see **The Greatest Good** (p.294).

New from old
Recycling is a good example of pragmatism at work: one person's rubbish becomes another's raw material. These toy cars for sale in Madagascar started life as soft-drink cans.

William James was a child of privilege. In the mid 1840s, his rich father would take his family on cultural tours to Europe, and proudly take a nap at the Athenaeum club in London in an armchair next to the philosopher Herbert Spencer. Young James's dilemma was that he felt guilty when he was not earning his own living. Inside the contemplative, there was always a capitalist striving to get out. James wanted a distinctively American philosophy, reflecting the values of business and hustle. He resisted the attempts of his famous brother (the novelist Henry James) to Europeanize him, and always scampered back thankfully to "my own country".

But no one should expect James to be consistent. He was a physician wracked by disease, a psychologist struggling against insanity, a workaholic who knew he could be saved only by rest. He went through life abandoning vocations. He was a frustrated painter, forced to relinquish work through bad eyesight. He recoiled from practising as a doctor in a profession he regarded as humbug. He dabbled in Christian Science and psychical research, and had flashes of mysticism, even while cultivating a "tough-minded" approach to philosophy. On the recoil from the sublime and ineffable, he tried to make a home for himself in the grimy world of Charles Dickens' famous character, Mr Gradgrind. "Go back into reason," he advised, "and you come at last to fact, nothing more."

In his seminal work of 1907–07, James developed "old ways of thinking" formulated in America in the 1870s by the philosopher Charles Saunders Pierce. Philosophy should be practical. Usefulness is what makes truth true and right right. This was hailed as "the philosophy of the future". James sought reasons for making other people share his belief in God. He argued that: "If the hypothesis of God works satisfactorily in the widest sense of the word, it is true." But what works for one individual or group may be useless to another. James's claim that truth is a matter not of the reality of what is claimed, but of its conformity to a particular purpose, was one of the most subversive claims ever made by a philosopher. James, who had originally set out as an apologist for Christianity, ended up undermining it by relativizing truth.

READINGS

C.S. Pierce's **Collected Papers** (1933) and W. James's **Pragmatism** (1907) are the fundamental texts, while J.P. Murphy's **Pragmatism from Pierce to Davidson** (1990) is the best survey.

G.W. Allen's **William James** (1967) is a useful biography.

C. Dickens' **Hard Times** (1854) satirizes the "principles of Fact".

Whatever it takes
Pragmatism often involves expediency: choosing the best means of achieving an end, even if counter-cultural. If it works, do it.

353

William James (1842–1910), US philosopher, popularized the idea of pragmatism.

"A pragmatist turns... towards concreteness and adequacy, towards facts, towards action, and towards power."

William James, *What Pragmatism Means* (1906–07)

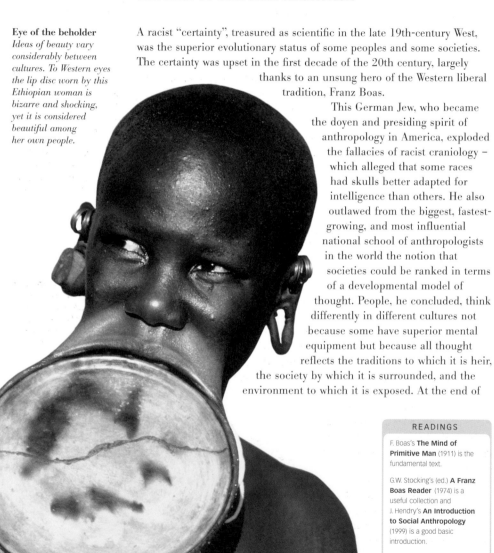

Their Own Terms

THE IDEA OF CULTURAL RELATIVISM

Eye of the beholder
Ideas of beauty vary considerably between cultures. To Western eyes the lip disc worn by this Ethiopian woman is bizarre and shocking, yet it is considered beautiful among her own people.

A racist "certainty", treasured as scientific in the late 19th-century West, was the superior evolutionary status of some peoples and some societies. The certainty was upset in the first decade of the 20th century, largely thanks to an unsung hero of the Western liberal tradition, Franz Boas.

This German Jew, who became the doyen and presiding spirit of anthropology in America, exploded the fallacies of racist craniology – which alleged that some races had skulls better adapted for intelligence than others. He also outlawed from the biggest, fastest-growing, and most influential national school of anthropologists in the world the notion that societies could be ranked in terms of a developmental model of thought. People, he concluded, think differently in different cultures not because some have superior mental equipment but because all thought reflects the traditions to which it is heir, the society by which it is surrounded, and the environment to which it is exposed. At the end of

READINGS

F. Boas's **The Mind of Primitive Man** (1911) is the fundamental text.

G.W. Stocking's (ed.) **A Franz Boas Reader** (1974) is a useful collection and J. Hendry's **An Introduction to Social Anthropology** (1999) is a good basic introduction.

"The general theory of valuation of human activities, as developed by anthropological research, teaches us a higher tolerance than the one we now profess."

Franz Boas, *The Mind of Primitive Man* (1911)

the first decade of the century, he summarized the findings or principles of the work in progress under his guidance: "The mental attitude of individuals who… develop the beliefs of a tribe is exactly that of the civilized philosopher."

The value that we attribute to our own civilization is due to the fact that we participate in this civilization, and that it has been controlling all our actions since the time of our birth. But it is certainly conceivable that there may be other civilizations, based perhaps on different traditions that are of no less value than ours, although it may be impossible for us to appreciate their values without having grown up under their influence.

Boas was a fieldworker in his youth and a museum-keeper in maturity – always in touch with the people and artefacts he sought to understand. His pupils had Native American peoples to study within little more than a railway's reach. The habit of fieldwork clinched the conclusion that cultural relativism was inescapable. It reinforced the relativistic tendency by piling up enormous quantities of diverse data intractable to the crudely hierarchical schemes of the 19th century. It took a long time to spread beyond the circles directly influenced by Boas, but it was already influencing British methods by the first decade of the 20th century. Cultural relativism soon reached France, too, where anthropologists commanded the greatest worldwide prestige, and from there it became a 20th-century orthodoxy.

It helped to undermine empires and build multicultural societies, but it also created unresolved problems. If no culture is objectively better than another, what about morality? Are cannibalism, infanticide, widow-burning, "gender" discrimination, head-hunting, incest, abortion, female circumcision, and arranged marriage all admissable under the rubric of cultural relativism? If not, how and where does one draw the line?

Traditional medicine
The sale of tiger parts for use in traditional Chinese medicine is condemned from a Western conservationist point of view. However, cultural relativism might argue that such traditional practices should be respected.

Freedom to die
From a Western perspective, the Hindu practice of suttee, in which a widow threw herself on the same funeral pyre as her dead husband, was thought barbaric. The British banned suttee in 1829, but this created resentment among some Hindus.

Sleeper

THE IDEA OF THE UNCONSCIOUS

Sigmund Freud was the model and mentor of the
20th century. His claim that the root of much human
motivation is buried in the unconscious successfully
challenged traditional notions about responsibility,
identity, personality, conscience, and mentality.

In an experiment he conducted on himself in 1896,
Freud exposed his own Oedipus complex (the attachment of
a son to his mother, with unconscious rivalry to his father).
The therapeutic effect of such an exercise seemed confirmed in
a series of patients who rose from his couch – or from that of his
mentor, Josef Breuer. Women who only a few years previously would
have been dismissed as hysterical malingerers became case studies
from whose example almost everyone could learn.

But Freud's "science" failed to pass the most rigorous tests.
When Karl Popper asked how to identify someone who did not have
an Oedipus complex, the psychoanalytic fraternity refused to take the
question seriously. They behaved like a religious sect or fringe political
movement – denouncing each other's heresies and issuing
expulsions from their self-elected bodies. Nevertheless, for
some patients, their efficacy was a convincing substitute
for scientific rigour and rational conduct.

Freud, with his genius for communicating ideas,
seemed able, from the evidence of a few burgesses of
pre-war Vienna, to illuminate the human condition. Every
child – he claimed to show – experienced before puberty

READINGS

S. Freud's **The
Interpretation of Dreams**
(1900) is his major work.

P. Gay's **Freud: a Life for
Our Time** (1988) should be
contrasted with J.M. Masson's
The Assault on Truth
(1983) and F. Forrester's
**Despatches from the
Freud Wars** (1997).

Sigmund Freud
(1856–1939), Austrian
doctor and founder of
psychoanalysis.

*"At bottom God is
nothing more than
an exalted father."*

S. Freud, *Totem and Taboo* (1913)

the same phases of sexual development; every adult repressed similar fantasies or experiences. Hypnosis or, as Freud preferred, the mnemonic effects of free association, could retrieve repressed feelings and thus ease their nervous symptoms. Introspection became a rite in the modern West, defining our culture, as dance or codes of gesture might define another. Repression became the modern demon and the analyst an exorcist.

The "feel-good society", which proscribes guilt, shame, self-doubt, self-reproach, and incomplete fulfilment, is among the consequences. So is the 20th- and 21st-century habit of sexual candour. So is the fashion – prevalent for much of the 20th century and still quite widespread among psychiatrists – to treat metabolic or chemical imbalances in the brain as if they were deep-rooted mental disorders. The balance of good and evil that has flowed from Freud's theory is nicely balanced and objectively incalculable. Psychoanalysis and other sub-Freudian schools of therapy have helped millions and tortured millions – releasing some from repressions and condemning others to illusions or unhelpful treatments.

CONNECTIONS

The question of the relationship of mind and brain is raised in **Cogito Ergo Sum** (p.224). For ideas about childhood, see **Little Man** (p.358) and **The Doll's House** (p.288). For ideas about medicine, see **Good Humours** (p.134).

357

SLEEPER

Just relax...
The claim that human behaviour is motivated by the unconscious challenged traditional ideas of human mentality. Freud formulated a system for tapping into repressed feelings. The patient lay on a couch and was invited, through free association, to "open up" to the psychoanalyst.

Little Man

THE IDEA OF CHILD DEVELOPMENT

Child prodigy
Piaget's theories do not allow for the existence of genius in young children. Wolfgang Amadeus Mozart (1756–91), shown here aged seven, was playing and composing for the harpsichord from the age of five and performing publicly the year after that.

CONNECTIONS

For the legacy of 19th-century thinking on childhood, see **The Doll's House** (p.288). For more on education, see **Noble Education** (p.196). On inheritance and nurture, see **The Family Silver** (p.36) and **Intelligence Test** (p.382).

In 1909, the Swedish feminist Ellen Key proclaimed the rediscovery of childhood: children were different from adults. This was, in effect, a summary of the 19th-century Western idea of childhood. Now that childhood disease spared more of them for longer lives, children were suitable objects for the investment of time and emotion and, of course, study.

The most influential student was the Swiss polymath, Jean Piaget. Generations of schoolchildren, deprived of challenging tasks because Piaget said they were incapable of them, bear the evidence of his impact. He was a child prodigy himself, but like most of his successors in educational psychology, he had a low opinion of the intellectual abilities of children. In 1920 he was helping to process the results of early experiments in intelligence-testing. The children's errors seemed to him to betray thought that was peculiar and structurally different from an adult's. From this insight he began to build up a picture of "mental

Even **toddlers** have an innate ability to interact with, and learn from, their environment.

"Children... have no use for psychology."

Isaac Bashevis Singer, speech (1978)

development" in predictable, universal stages, as people grow up. He suggested that learning operates mainly through a process of trial and error, rather than as a result of conditioning.

In fact, most of what Piaget took to be universal is indeed culturally conditioned; much of the rest is probably innate. The latest experimental data confirms what is suggested by common sense and parents' routine observations – that our capacity for thinking is innate, including its essential structures and even the universal grammar that underlies language. It is part of the equipment evolution has given us. What we acquire as we grow up are habits refined by experience, imposed by culture, and shaped, perhaps, by particular languages.

Nevertheless, Piaget was so persuasive that, even today, school curricula bear the marks of his influence. Though there is increasing recognition that children do not come in standard packages, it remains the case that school systems classify them according to age and prescribe the same sorts of lessons, at the same levels of supposed difficulty, in much the same subjects, for everybody at each stage. This has a retarding or alienating effect on some individuals and perhaps even an arresting effect on society generally. It is unfair to children and provides a dubious theoretical basis for treating them as inherently inferior to grown-ups.

Step by step
Swiss psychologist and child prodigy Jean Piaget (1896–1980) was particularly interested in the structured stages of childhood development.

Man-children
Piaget believed that children's thought differed fundamentally from that of adults. The duo of Laurel and Hardy owed much of their comic success to the contrast between their adult appearance but childlike behaviour.

READINGS

J. Piaget's **The Child's Conception of Physical Causality** (1930) is fundamental, while M. Boden's **Piaget** (1994) is an excellent short introduction.

P. Bryant's **Perception and Understanding in Young Children** (1984) and L.S. Siegel and C.J. Brainerd's **Alternatives to Piaget** (1978) are outstanding revisionist works.

P. Aries and G. Duby's **A History of Private Life** (1975–81) is a challenging, wide-ranging exploration of the history of family relationships.

L. de Mause's (ed.) **The History of Childhood** (1974) is a pioneering collection of essays.

Back to Basics

THE IDEA OF RELIGIOUS FUNDAMENTALISM

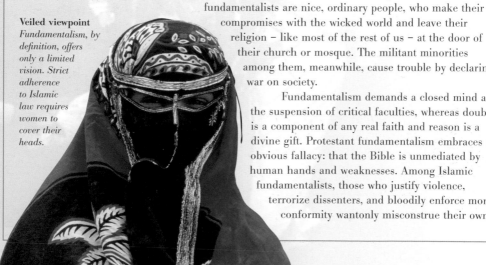

No room for doubt
An effigy of British author Salman Rushdie is burned by Muslims, protesting against "blasphemy" in his novel, The Satanic Verses.

CONNECTIONS

For ideas on written codes, see **Take a Letter** (p.78), **Written in Stone** (p.88), and **Books of Truth** (p.106). For ideas related to Islam and Christianity, see **Islam** (p.188) and **Love Above** (p.160). For the rejection of science, see **Impossibilism** (p.202).

Veiled viewpoint
Fundamentalism, by definition, offers only a limited vision. Strict adherence to Islamic law requires women to cover their heads.

Fundamentalism started at Princeton University, USA, in the early 20th century in intelligent minds, corrupted by literal-minded dogmatism in reaction against critical reading of the Bible. The idea was that there are fundamental truths in the text which cannot be questioned. What the text says is fact; the faith is founded on it. No critical exegesis can deconstruct it. No scientific evidence can gainsay it. This idea was termed "fundamentalism", and has been applied retrospectively to a similar doctrine, traditional in Islam, about the Quran. It can – and sometimes does – arise in the context of any religion that has a founding text or "holy scripture".

Karen Armstrong, one of the foremost authorities on the subject, sees fundamentalism as "modern": a scientific or pseudo-scientific attitude which treats religion as reducible to matters of incontrovertible fact. It is charmless and humdrum – religion minus the enchantment. Apart from the bleakness of modernity, fundamentalism's other begetter is fear. Fear of millennia, fear of Great Satans, fear of chaos, and, above all, fear of the unfamiliar. To fundamentalists, all difference is subversive. These facts help to explain why fundamentalism arose and throve in the modern world and has never lost its appeal.

All the movements we call fundamentalist are different but can be identified by the excesses they share: militancy, hostility to pluralism, and a determination to confuse politics with religion. Fundamentalists are self-cast as warriors against secularism. Yet, in practice, most fundamentalists are nice, ordinary people, who make their compromises with the wicked world and leave their religion – like most of the rest of us – at the door of their church or mosque. The militant minorities among them, meanwhile, cause trouble by declaring war on society.

Fundamentalism demands a closed mind and the suspension of critical faculties, whereas doubt is a component of any real faith and reason is a divine gift. Protestant fundamentalism embraces an obvious fallacy: that the Bible is unmediated by human hands and weaknesses. Among Islamic fundamentalists, those who justify violence, terrorize dissenters, and bloodily enforce moral conformity wantonly misconstrue their own

sacred texts. Some sects, with their crushing effects on individual identity, their ethic of obedience, their paranoid habits, and their campaigns of hatred or violence against the rest of the world, behave in frightening ways like the early fascist cells. If and when they get power, they tend to persecute everybody else. In the interim, their witch-huntings, book-burnings, and acts of terrorism continue.

In the early 21st century, Islamic and Christian fundamentalism are gaining support more rapidly than any other religious or political movements, with potentially dangerous consequences for the world.

Fanatical force
The fundamentalist general, Efraín Ríos Montt, was messianic in his pursuit of Guatemala's "civil war" (1982–83). His followers (above) were responsible for the deaths of thousands of native Mayans.

READINGS

K. Armstrong's **The Battle for God** (2000) is a fine survey, as are M.E. Marty and R.S. Appleby's (eds) **Fundamentalism Observed** (1991) and G.M. Marsden's **Fundamentalism and American Culture** (1980).

S. Rushdie's **The Satanic Verses** (1988) provoked a fundamentalist reaction.

W.J. Bryan (1860–1925), populist US politician and anti-evolutionist.

"The same science that manufactured poisonous gases to suffocate soldiers is preaching that man has a brutal ancestry and eliminating the miraculous and supernatural from the Bible."

William Jennings Bryan, speech (1920)

Many Ways

THE IDEA OF RELIGIOUS PLURALISM

Pluralist pioneer
*Swami Vivekananda,
founder of the
Ramakrishna Mission,
articulated ideas of
religious pluralism long
before they became
fashionable in the late
20th century.*

READINGS

R. Rolland's **The Life of
Vivekananda and the
Universal Gospel** (1953) is
a good introduction to the
Swami.

E. Hill's **The Wider
Ecumenism** (1968) broaches
the subject of inter-faith
ecumenism.

M. Braybrooke's **Inter-faith
Organizations** (1980) is a
useful history.

Fundamentalism means shutting the door on variety. An equal and opposite response to uncertainty is the call of the great spokesman of Hinduism and apostle of religious pluralism, Swami Vivekananda. We should, he said, acknowledge the wisdom of all religions and try a range of gateways to truth – "many ways to one truth" – simultaneously. This is an attractive option because it overtrumps relativism in its appeal to a multicultural, pluralistic world. Yet for the religious it is a fatal concession to secularism: it leaves you with no reason to prefer any religion over the rest, and raises the question of whether purely secular philosophies would not make equally good "gateways". On the ride towards the multi-faith rainbow's end, why not add more gradations of colour?

When religions dominate societies, they become triumphalist. In retreat, they become ecumenist, or more universal. Desire for "wide ecumenism", bringing together people of all faiths, was paralleled among rival Christian communions from the time of the Edinburgh Conference of 1910, which attempted to establish a basis of co-operation among Protestant missionary societies – though the Roman Catholic Church only began to take part in Christian ecumenism in the 1960s. In confronting irreligious values in the late 20th century, extraordinary "holy alliances" came into being, in which Catholics, Southern Baptists, and Muslims, for instance, joined to oppose relaxation of abortion laws in the USA, or collaborated in attempting to influence

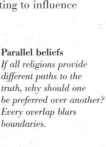

Pope Paul VI (1897–
1978) led many
initiatives for inter-
faith collaboration.

*"The Church is looking
for the world."*

Pope Paul VI

Parallel beliefs
*If all religions provide
different paths to the
truth, why should one
be preferred over another?
Every overlap blurs
boundaries.*

World Health Organization policy on birth control. Inter-faith organizations played a prominent part in promoting human rights and in organizing campaigns to restrain the possible excesses of genetic engineering. New political niches opened up for public figures with a role as spokesmen or -women for those of ill-differentiated faith. The Prince of Wales proposed himself in the role of "Defender of Faith" in multicultural Britain.

The idea has, therefore, an impressive recent past. But can it be sustained? The scandal of religious hatreds and mutual violence, which has so disfigured the past of religions, appears conquerable, but with every inch of common ground religions find between them, the ground of their claims to unique value shrinks.

Unbounded compassion
Charity does not recognize religious divisions. Here, a Catholic missionary brings comfort to a leper.

Axe in the Sticks

THE IDEA OF FASCISM

Might is right
"Fascist" comes from the fasces of Ancient Rome (shown here on a 1920s 2-lire coin). This was a bundle of sticks encircling an axe, which symbolized the power of magistrates to scourge people. The sticks represented individuals: weak on their own, but collectively strong.

Fascism was a political bias in favour of might, order, the state, and war. In as much as it was intellectual at all, it was a composite of ideas: ideological lego pieced together out of many corporate, authoritarian, and totalitarian traditions. Whether it was a splinter of socialism or not has been a matter of passionate debate. Fascists mobilized workers and petty bourgeois by advocating policies that could be crudely summarized as socialism without the surrender of property to the state. Fascism could as well be classified as an independently evolved doctrine, or just as a slick name for unprincipled opportunism.

Benito Mussolini adopted the Ancient Roman *fasces* (see left) as what would now be called the "logo" of his party; this image of bloodstained law-enforcement expresses the essence of fascism. Fascism was the weal of the rod and the gash of the axe – the smack of a system of values that put the group before the individual, authority before freedom, cohesion before

*"Fascism is not a new
order… It is the future
refusing to be born."*

Aneurin Bevan

Neo-Nazi salute
*Despite the destruction of
the fascist states at the end
of World War II, thousands
of organizations have since
sought to revive fascist
beliefs, often basing their
ideological programmes
around immigration issues.*

diversity, revenge before reconciliation, retribution before compassion,and the supremacy of the strong before the defence of the weak. It justified revocation of the rights of dissenters, misfits, and subversives. You could tell it by the effects you could feel – the sweat of the fear of it and the stamp of its heel.

Nazism shared all these characteristics, yet was something more than fascism because it actively imitated religion. It replaced God with history. It offered human sacrifices to this new god, speeding her purposes by immolating profane races. It adopted the framework of Christian millenarianism, promising the fulfilment of history in a "1000-year Reich". It had well-orchestrated liturgies, shrines and sanctuaries, icons and saints, processions and ecstasies, hymns and chants. It demanded irrational assent from its followers – submission to the infallibility of the Führer – and Nazis fantasized about restoring ancient folk-paganism.

Ideologies of order summed up the contradictions of modernity: technological prowess and moral regression. The "noisy little men" of fascism and Nazism failed in World War II, but the allure of "final solutions" has not entirely faded. As the chaos and complexities of society get more intractable, the pace of change more threatening, electorates may yet revert to totalitarian and authoritarian programmes.

Axis of evil
*The German and Italian
fascist leaders, Adolf Hitler
and Benito Mussolini
(shown together in Rome
in 1938) were opportunists
who seized power during
a time of economic unrest in
the aftermath of World
War I. They developed an
ideology based on strength
and authority.*

CONNECTIONS

Some of fascism's intellectual origins can be traced in **My Country** (p.288), **Extreme Optimism** (p.290), **Hero Inside** (p.304), **Brother Knows Best** (p.306), **War Is Good** (p.314), **Chosen Victims** (p.316), and **Good Breeding** (p.322).

AXE IN THE STICKS

READINGS

M. Blinkhorn's **Fascism and the Far Right in Europe** (2000) is a good introduction, while E. Nolte's **Three Faces of Fascism** (1965) and **Der Europaische Burgerkrieg** (2000) are brilliant histories of modern ideological conflict.

D. Mack Smith's **Mussolini** (1981) is both enjoyable and authoritative, while I. Kershaw's **Hitler** (2 vols) (2000) is a fine account.

C. Isherwood's **Goodbye to Berlin** (1939), a series of stories set in pre-Nazi Germany, inspired the musical *Cabaret* (1972).

Birth of suburbia
After the Great Depression of the early 1930s, Keynes advocated sustained public expenditure to stimulate the economy. In Britain, his ideas led to the state construction of suburban housing estates on an unprecedented scale.

J.M. Keynes
(1883– 1946) argued that states could "buy" economic recovery.

Spending for Wealth

THE IDEA OF WELFARE ECONOMICS

For most of the 20th century, economic policy in the developed world tacked back and forth between "planning" and "the market" as rival panaceas for economic problems. Keynesianism had the appeal of a modified form of capitalism, which, from the 1930s to the 1970s, seemed to work.

The 1920s were an era of capitalist complacency in industrialized economies. Automobiles became articles of mass consumption. Construction companies flung "towers up to the sun". Pyramids of many millions of shareholders were controlled by a few "pharaohs". A booming market

"There is no clear evidence… that the investment policy which is socially advantageous coincides with that which is most profitable."

John Maynard Keynes, *The General Theory of Employment* (1936)

Concrete achievement
President Roosevelt's "New Deal" anticipated Keynesianism with its ambition to revitalize the USA's economy through large capital projects, such as the Hoover Dam in Nevada.

held out prospects of literally universal riches. But, in 1929–33, the world's major markets crashed and banking systems failed or tottered. The world entered the most abject and protracted recession of modern times. In the USA, President Franklin D. Roosevelt put forward a "New Deal", in which government spending was used to kickstart the economy. His opponents denounced his modest scheme as socialistic, but it was more rhetorical than radical and left capitalism intact.

The comprehensive rethinking was done in England by John Maynard Keynes, who challenged the idea that the market naturally produces the levels of production and employment society needs. He identified two reasons for this. First, savings always render some economic potential immobile, creating a reservoir of under-utilized wealth. Secondly, the market is skewed by false expectations: people overspend in optimism and underspend when they get the jitters. Keynes believed unemployment is largely an unnecessary evil. By spending future revenues on public utilities and infrastructure, governments can get people back into work while also building economic potential. This, when realized, will produce tax yields that will pay the costs of the projects retrospectively.

This idea appeared in Keynes's *General Theory of Employment, Interest, and Money* in 1936. It seemed to work wherever it was applied, and therefore became a sort of orthodoxy, justifying ever higher levels of public expenditure all over the world in the course of the following half-century. But economics is a volatile science, and few of its laws last for long. Public expenditure is no more rational than the market and – although it was a saviour of those societies that tried it in the emergency conditions of the 1930s – it causes waste, inhibits production, and stifles enterprise in normal times.

In the 1980s, Keynesianism became a victim of a widespread desire to "claw back the state", "deregulate" economies, and re-liberate the market. We now seem to be in a new era of trash-capitalism, market volatility, and obscene wealth-gaps, when some of the salient lessons of Keynesianism need to be relearned.

READINGS

R. Skidelsky's **John Maynard Keynes** (2001) is an outstanding biography.

R. Lekachman's **The Age of Keynes** (1967) and J.K. Galbraith's **The Age of Uncertainty** (1977) are tributes to Keynes's influence.

J.A. Schumpeter's **Capitalism, Socialism, and Democracy** (1942) is an interesting and influential early answer to Keynesianism.

Slum-capitalism?
Economic deregulation often leads to obscene wealth gaps, clearly visible here in Mumbai (Bombay), India. A Keynesian approach might tackle the social problems of developing countries.

A Better World

THE IDEA OF UNIVERSAL WELFARE

Life on the margins
In Rio de Janeiro, Brazil, as in much of the developing world, the welfare state struggles to provide for the growing urban population.

READINGS

J. Harris's **William Beveridge** (1997) is a good biography.

D. Fraser's **The Evolution of the British Welfare State** (1973) traces the relevant traditions in modern social and political thought.

F.G. Castles and C. Pearson's **The Welfare State Reader** (2000) is a useful anthology.

J.C. Scott's **Seeing the State** (1999) is a brilliant, partisan indictment of state planning generally.

The first state insurance scheme was introduced by the German Chancellor, Otto von Bismarck, in the 1880s. But the welfare state, first proposed by the economist Arthur Pigou in Cambridge, UK, in the 1920s, was a much more radical idea – the state could tax the rich in order to provide benefits for the poor. In essence, this was not unlike the redistributive mechanisms that ancient despotisms used to guarantee the food supply.

The idea of the welfare state influenced John Maynard Keynes's arguments in favour of regenerating moribund economies by massive injections of public spending, but its main effect was on the UK economist William Beveridge. Commissioned during World War II to draft plans for an improved social insurance scheme, he projected "a better new world", in which universal health care, unemployment benefits, and retirement pensions were all to be funded from a mixture of national insurance contributions and taxation. Few government reports have been so widely welcomed or so resonant abroad. It encouraged President Roosevelt of the USA to proclaim a future "free from want". It was admired in Hitler's bunker. It was adopted by the postwar British government with near cross-party unanimity.

"The Beveridge Report" of 1942 was both a blessing and a curse. It has become impossible to call a society modern or just without a scheme broadly of the kind Beveridge devised. The benefits are incalculable – not only in delivering security and justice in individual lives but also in making society more stable and cohesive. The problem is that universal benefits are expensive. Two circumstances in the

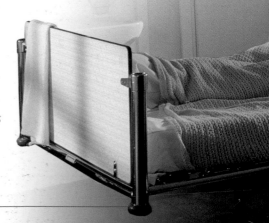

William Beveridge (1879–1963), social reformer and advocate of the welfare state.

"The purpose of victory is to live in a better world than the old world."

William Beveridge, speech (1945)

late 20th and early 21st centuries have threatened welfare states, even in the countries where they are best established. First, inflation made it hard for each generation either to save for its own future or to meet the costs of care for its elders. Then, no sooner had inflation been brought under something like control than the demographic balance of developed societies began to change drastically. The workforce got older, the proportion of retired people began to rise, and it became apparent that there would not be enough young, productive people to pay the escalating costs of social welfare in the future.

Governments have tried various ways of coping with the consequences, without dismantling the welfare state. There is, however, a general drift back to an insurance-based concept of welfare, in which individuals reassume responsibility for their own retirement and, to some extent, for their own health care costs and unemployment provision, while the state mops up marginal cases.

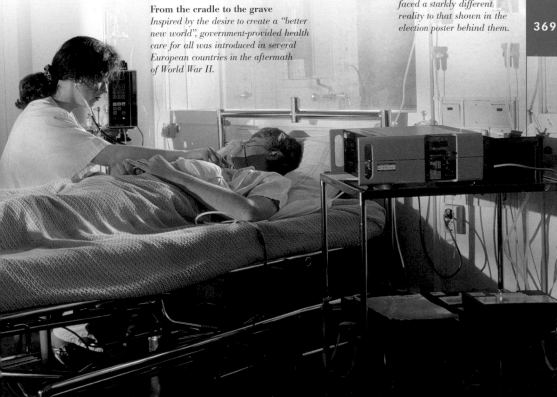

WORLD'S HIGHEST STANDARD OF LIVING

There's no way like the American Way

Double standards
Before the idea of "social security" became widespread, a state's citizens were at the mercy of events. In the USA in 1937, these displaced flood victims, queuing for food relief, faced a starkly different reality to that shown in the election poster behind them.

369

From the cradle to the grave
Inspired by the desire to create a "better new world", government-provided health care for all was introduced in several European countries in the aftermath of World War II.

Against intervention
*Friedrich von Hayek
(1899–1992) was opposed
to Keynesianism (state
intervention) and became
concerned about the
impact of increased
economic controls on
individual values.*

Icon of enterprise
*Bill Gates, billionaire
founder of Microsoft, the
leading software company
of the late 20th century,
was the embodiment of the
individualistic enterprise
culture espoused by Hayek.
He successfully fought off
state attempts to break up
his company's monopoly.*

Solid Foundations

THE IDEA OF SPONTANEOUS SOCIAL ORDER

Overplanned societies were the curse of much of the 20th century. They
worked badly. The "command" economies of eastern Europe, China, and
Cuba failed. In Scandinavia, mixed economies with a high degree of state
involvement produced "suicidal utopias" of frustrated and alienated
individuals. But the alternatives – anarchism, libertarianism, the
unrestricted market – were all condemned by history.

The economist Friedrich von Hayek led the developed world's
escape back into conservatism. During the overplanned years, Hayek was
a voice in the wilderness, long ignored but rediscovered in the 1970s to be
the theorist of a conservative revival. His key idea, which appeared in *The
Road to Serfdom* (1944), was that of "spontaneous social order", which is
not produced by conscious planning, but is the outcome of a long history –
a richness of experience unreproducible by any government intervention in
the short term. This comes close to defining the best argument for
conservatism: most government policies have good intentions and bad
effects. Therefore government is best "which governs least". Efforts to
improve society usually end up making it worse and the wisest course is
to tackle the imperfections modestly, bit by bit.

Hayek also tackled the problem of the tightrope act that usually
topples political conservatism: how to keep a balance between liberty and
order. His answer was a highly traditional one, which has been constantly
urged (though rarely observed) in the Western tradition since Aristotle:
the rule of law overrides the power of the state and sets proper limits
to individual freedom. "If individuals are to be free to use their own
knowledge and resources to best advantage, they must do so in a
context of known and predictable rules governed by law." Hayek
integrated this doctrine into his master-idea by suggesting that
law was the essence of the spontaneous social order, "part of
the natural history of mankind… coeval with society" and
therefore prior to the state. "It is not the creation of any
governmental authority and it is certainly not the
command of the sovereign."

In the past, doctrines of this kind always
foundered on the obvious problem: who but the
state is to say what these natural laws are? In the
late 20th century some hope of an escape from
the dilemma emerged from the development of

Edmund Burke
(1729–97), Irish
philosopher-statesman
and essayist.

*"To temper together these opposite elements of
liberty and restraint in one consistent work
requires much thought, deep reflection, a
sagacious, powerful, and combining mind."*

Edmund Burke, *Reflections on the Revolution in France* (1790)

READINGS

C. Kukathas's **Hayek and
Modern Liberalism** (1989)
and R. Kley's **Hayek's Social
and Political Thought**
(1994) are helpful studies.

J. Gray's **Hayek on Liberty**
(1998) is brilliant and
insightful.

G.R. Steele's **The
Economics of Friedrich
Hayek** (1996) is outstanding.

an international body of law connected with human rights. But I suspect
there was another, unacknowledged strand in Hayek's thinking – he
shared a traditional Christian prejudice in favour of individualism on the
grounds that sin and charity imply individual conduct, whereas "social
justice" diminishes individual responsibility.

His influence on the rightward drift of the political mainstream in
developed countries in the last two decades of the 20th century
was obvious. It was most marked on economic life, mediated
through Milton Friedman and other economists of the
Chicago School, who rehabilitated the idea of
the free market as an unsurpassable way
of delivering prosperity.

Good intentions and bad effects
*According to Hayek, state-planned economies
are doomed to failure. The demolition of these
state-built, high-rise blocks in London reflects
a recognition of their failure to balance
affordable housing with basic individual needs.*

CONNECTIONS

For previous conservative
thought, see **Laissez-faire**
(p.246) and **By Other
Means** (p.310). On non-
conservative liberalism, see
The Greatest Good (p.294).
For the ancient origins of
capitalism, see **A Capital
Idea** (p.144).

Peasant Socialism

THE MAOIST IDEA OF COMMUNISM

The Mexican and Chinese revolutions of 1911 seemed to show that Marx had been right about one thing: "proletarian" revolutions would not work with peasant manpower in unindustrialized societies. Mao Zedong was among those who thought otherwise.

Unlike communists better informed of Marxist orthodoxy, he was able to evolve a strategy of peasant revolution, independent of the Russian model and defiant of Russian advice, that best suited China's circumstances. "It was," Stalin said, "as if he doesn't understand the most elementary Marxist truths – or maybe he doesn't want to understand them."

During decades of limited success as a guerrilla leader, he survived by dogged perseverance

The Great Teacher
Chairman Mao's reputation was enhanced and preserved by the personality cult that grew up around him. In this archetypal image, he is portrayed as the benign elder statesman of the revolution.

CONNECTIONS

On Marx, see **Class Struggle** (p.292). On Chinese populist political thought before Mao, see **Heaven's Order** (p.240). For remoter precedents in Chinese philosophy, see **Legalism** (p.146) and **Centre of the World** (p.182).

"To read too many books is harmful."

Mao Zedong

(which he later misrepresented as military genius). He summed up his strategy in a much-quoted slogan: "When the enemy advances, we retreat; when he halts, we harass; when he retreats, we pursue."

From 1949, when the country was conquered and Mao was in control, he provoked endless new crises, because they were the milieu in which he thrived. He had no further ideas but lots of what he called "thoughts". Capricious campaigns of mass destruction were launched from time to time against dogs and sparrows, "rightists" and "leftists", "bourgeois deviationists" and "class enemies" – even at one point against grass and flowers. Official crime rates were low, but people were brutalized more by habitual punishment than occasional crime. Some of Mao's revolutionary principles were dazzlingly reactionary: class enmity was held to be hereditary. Romantic love was outlawed. Agriculture was wrecked by an age-old notion of the state as a hoarder and distributor of food. The most destructive campaign was the Great Proletarian Cultural Revolution of the 1960s: children denounced parents, students beat teachers, the educated were demoted to menial work, the ignorant were encouraged in the slaughter of intellectuals, antiquities were smashed, books burned, study subverted, and work stopped. The economy was broken. An efficient propaganda machine, however, presented fake statistics of progress to the world. The truth seeped out gradually. Meanwhile, the Chinese model encouraged much of the developing world to experiment with economically ruinous and morally corrupting programmes of political authoritarianism and command-economics.

China's re-ascent to her "normal" status as one of the world's most prosperous, powerful countries, and as an exemplary civilization, was indefinitely postponed. The signs of recovery are only beginning to be apparent in the early years of the 21st century. But Mao did more. His influence held back the world, blighting many new, backward, economically "underdeveloped" states with a malignant example.

Marching with Mao
The mythology of the Long March (1934–35), in which Mao led his followers 10,000 kilometres (6,000 miles) across China, continued to be evoked in propaganda posters like this one from the 1960s.

PEASANT SOCIALISM

READINGS

Mao's **Little Red Book of Quotations** (1966) is a fascinating compilation.

J. Spence's **Mao** (2000) is a fine short introduction.

S. Schram's **The Thought of Mao Tse-tung** (1989) is a valuable attempt at analysis.

J. Chang's **Wild Swans** (1991) is a personal memoir by a participant in and survivor of the Cultural Revolution.

Road to Freedom

THE IDEA OF EXISTENTIALISM

Preceding existence
Through his seminal work
Being and Time *(1927),*
German philosopher Martin
Heidegger (1889–1976)
was a crucial influence
on Jean-Paul Sartre.

For the Frankfurt School of philosophers, struggling in the 1930s and 1940s to find alternatives to Marxism and capitalism, the great problem of society was "alienation". Economic rivalries and short-sighted materialism sundered society. Individuals felt dissatisfied and unrooted. Martin Heidegger proposed a strategy for coping: accepting our existence between birth and death as the only immutable thing about us and tackling life as a project of self-realization, of "becoming". Who we are changes as the project unfolds. This "existentialism" represented the retreat of intellectuals into the security of self-contemplation, in revulsion from an uglified world.

In 1945, Jean-Paul Sartre relaunched it as a new creed for the postwar era. "Man," he said, "is only a situation" or "nothing else but what he makes of himself... the being who hurls himself towards a future and who is conscious of imagining himself as being in the future". Heidegger was shocked by the implications and explicitly repudiated Sartre's view: essence is "proximate" (near) to being, he contended, and individuals are the "shepherds", not the creators or "engineers" of their

own identity. By then, however, Heidegger had become tainted by his support for Hitler and Nazism, and his sensible observations were largely ignored.

For Sartre, self-modelling was not just a matter of individual choice: every individual action is "an exemplary act", a statement about humankind, about the sort of species you want us to be. Yet there is no objective way of testing such a statement. In Sartre's view, God does not exist, everything is permissible, and "as a result man is forlorn, without anything to cling to... If existence really does precede essence, there is no explaining things away by reference to a fixed... human nature. In other words, there is no determinism, man is free, man is freedom." According to Sartre, no ethic is justifiable except acknowledgment of the rightness of this.

Sartre's version of existentialism fed the common assumptions about life of educated but alienated young Westerners in the 1950s and 1960s. In the event, critics who denounced it as a philosophy of decadence were not far wrong, as it was used to justify every form of self-indulgence as part of a project of "becoming oneself". Sexual promiscuity, "revolutionary" violence, indifference to manners, defiance of the law, and drug-abuse were all characteristic existentialist vices. Beat culture and sixties permissiveness – ways of life adopted or imitated by millions – as well, perhaps, as the late 20th-century's libertarian reaction against social planning, would have been unthinkable without it.

Essence of protest
According to Sartre, you are defined by your actions. Such a view might be used to justify deliberate self-destruction, such as the self-immolation of this Kurdish demonstrator in Athens in 1999.

READINGS

J.P. Chiari's **Twentieth-Century French Thought** (1975) is a concise history.

C. Howells' (ed.) **The Cambridge Companion to Sartre** (1992) is an indispensable guide.

J.P. Sartre's **Nausea** (1938), A. Camus's **The Outsider** (1942), and Norman Mailer's **An American Dream** (1965) all tell the stories of existential anti-heroes.

Existential outlaws
The glamour of alienation permeates the iconic road movie Easy Rider (1969), in which the "hippy" protagonists search for freedom in a corrupt and bigoted society.

Jean-Paul Sartre
(1905–80), French thinker and writer.

"If existence really does precede essence, man is responsible for what he is."

J.P. Sartre, *Existentialism and Humanism* (1946)

Black Is Beautiful

THE IDEA OF PRIDE IN BLACK CULTURE

African origins
In the early 20th century, collectors and artists in the West (such as Pablo Picasso) began to appreciate and derive inspiration from African tribal art, such as this mask from Congo.

Colonialism made possible the idea that all black people share a common identity because of the colour of their skin. It was an identity imposed, in the first place, on blacks by whites – by slavers and imperialists, to whom blacks did indeed seem to have features in common: inferiority, exploitability, and unfitness for self-rule.

The experience of slavery, which forced blacks of widely differing homelands and cultures into a shared suffering, demonstrated that they could transcend their differences of origin and background to form united communities (including in some cases independent "maroon" kingdoms and republics in the Americas, and states founded by liberated returnees in Africa – in Liberia and Sierra Leone). They could also develop new, distinctively black cultures: black religious confraternities, churches, and cults; black music and dance; and black languages and literature written in those languages. The earliest such literature, as far as I know, appeared in Neger-engels, a language of Surinam, in the 1840s.

In the early 20th century, scholarship by blacks in newly independent Cuba began to treat such culture on terms of equality with white culture. Coincidentally, white musicians discovered jazz, and white "primitivist" artists began to esteem and imitate African tribal art. In 1916 in the USA, the Jamaican Marcus Garvey launched the slogan, "Africa for the black peoples of the world". The idea that black culture

READINGS

G. Davis's **Aimé Césaire** (1997) is the best study of the poet's thought.

L.W. Levine's **Black Culture and Black Consciousness** (1978) is an interesting history of the movement in the USA.

A.Haley's **Roots** (1977) was an influential, "factional" work by a Black American, reconciling African identity with the American dream.

Jamaican musician **Bob Marley** combined reggae music with tough, political lyrics.

Still in bondage
Militant black nationalist leader Malcolm X (1925–65) famously said, "If you're born in America with black skin, you're born in prison." For most of his career he preached racial separatism, although he became more conciliatory just before his death.

"It's not politic', it's really talkin' 'bout roots."

Bob Marley, *In His Own Words*, I. McCann (ed.) (1997)

embodied values superior to those of white was the next phase. It emerged during the 1920s in the work of a Cuban "generation of '98" of whom the critic Juan Marinello and the poet Nicolás Guillén were perhaps the most influential. The idea spread to wherever black people lived – transforming, on its way, the self-consciousness of blacks who were still under colonial rule or suffering under social inequalities. In French West Africa in the 1930s, Aimé Césaire and Léon Damas became brilliant spokesmen for what they called "Négritude".

The conviction grew and spread that blacks were at least the equals of whites in all areas of achievement. It fed into independence movements for colonized regions and civil rights movements in countries such as South Africa and the USA (where blacks were still denied equality under the law). Ultimately, in the late 20th century, when those battles were more-or-less won, it grew into the long struggle against racial prejudice and residual forms of discrimination against black people in predominantly white countries.

Young, gifted, and black
In the 1960s, black people living in America and Europe began to develop and celebrate their own "Afro-style", as exemplified here by US singer, Marsha Hunt.

CONNECTIONS

Ideas about how to rank humankind in terms of communities are broached in **No Mercy** (p.76), **Centre of the World** (p.182), **Scattered Grains** (p.194), **Chosen Victims** (p.316), **Inferior by Nature** (p.318), and **Master Race** (p.328).

The Great Chain

THE IDEA OF MANIPULATING THE CODE OF LIFE

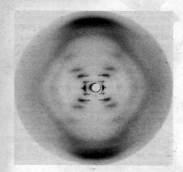

Crystal clear
Rosalind Franklin's X-ray crystallography images provided Crick and Watson with vital information on the structure of DNA.

Pandora's flock
Dolly the sheep was the result of a cloning technique that seemed to offer the possibility of replicating humans.

In lectures in Dublin in 1944, Austrian physicist Erwin Schrödinger speculated about what a gene might look like. He predicted that it would resemble a chain of basic units which connected like the elements of a code. The nature of DNA as a kind of acid was not yet known (Schrödinger expected a sort of protein), but the idea Schrödinger outlined galvanized the search for the basic "building blocks" of life.

A few years later, James Watson, a biology student in Chicago, read Schrödinger's paper. When he saw X-ray pictures of DNA, he realized that it would be possible to discover the structure Schrödinger had envisaged. He joined Francis Crick's project at Cambridge University to identify DNA's molecular form. They got a great deal of help from a partner laboratory in London, where work by Maurice Wilkins and Rosalind Franklin, who suspected that DNA had a helical structure, helped build up the picture of what it was really like. Subsequent challenges over whether the Cambridge team had played fairly could not obscure the importance of the outcome. Still, it took a long time for the significance of the results to emerge fully, with the growing realization that genes in individual genetic codes were responsible for some diseases and, perhaps, for many kinds of behaviour, which could be regulated by changing the code.

Similarly, the codes of other species can be modified to obtain results that suit humans. These include producing food crops that give higher yields, for instance, or animals designed to produce human food more cheaply or that is more palatable or more packagable. Progress in research in these fields has been so rapid that it has raised the spectre of a world re-crafted, as if by Frankenstein or Dr Moreau, with unforeseeable consequences. People now have the power to make their biggest intervention in evolution yet – selecting "unnaturally", not according to what is best adapted to the environment but according to what best matches agendas of human devising. "Designer" babies are already being produced in cases where genetically transmitted diseases can be prevented, and the prospect that some societies will want to engineer human beings along the lines prescribed in former times by eugenics is entirely likely. Morally dubious visionaries are already talking about a world from which disease and deviancy alike have been excised.

> *"Modern societies…
> have become as
> dependent on science
> as an addict on
> his drug."*

**J. Monod, *Chance
and Necessity*
(1970)**

The beast inside

*Frankenstein's monster, the fictional
creation of Mary Shelley, embodies
for many the inherent dangers of
meddling with nature. Perhaps we
risk creating a terrifying "creature"
beyond our control.*

CONNECTIONS

It is interesting to compare
gene-manipulation with
ideas on eugenics in
Good Breeding (p.322).
Tooth and Claw (p.320)
describes the essential
intellectual background
to Erwin Schrödinger's
thinking.

READINGS

J.D. Watson's **The Double
Helix** (1968) is the
unabashedly personal
account of one of the
discoverers of DNA and
should be read alongside
B. Maddox's **Rosalind
Franklin** (2002), which tells
the fascinating story of
Crick's and Watson's rival.

J. Enriquez Cabot's **As the
Future Captures You**
(2001) is brilliant on genome
technology.

Fire and rain
Forests are the "lungs of the planet". Their destruction, whether by accidental fires or through logging, is of prime concern to environmentalists.

Nowhere to go
Many plant and animal species are threatened by damage to their habitats. Eco-tourism enhances awareness of this, but also increases the threat.

Silent Springs

THE IDEA OF ENVIRONMENTALISM

All societies exploit their environments and all have to establish rational limits for the conservation of the resources they need. The search for the right balance has become one of the great projects for the global community in the 21st century. The idea that nature is worth conserving for its own sake, quite apart from its human uses, forms part of religious traditions in which nature is sanctified: Jainism, Buddhism, Hinduism, and Taoism, for example, and traditional Western paganism. In modern, secular traditions of thought, environmental concerns surfaced in the sensibilities of late 18th-century romanticism, which revered nature as a "book" of secular morality, and (so the historian Richard Grove has argued) may have developed among European imperialists awestruck at the custodianship of far-flung "Edens".

The era of global industrialization in the 19th century, however, was unpropitious for conservation. The 20th century experienced "something new under the sun" – environmental destruction so unremitting and extensive that the biosphere seemed unable to survive it. An early monitor or prophet of the menace was the Jesuit palaeo-anthropologist,

US biologist **Rachel Carson** inspired ecological angst.

"Spring now comes unheralded by the return of the birds and the early mornings are strangely silent."

Rachel Carson, *The Silent Spring* (1962)

READINGS

R. Carson's **The Silent Spring** (1962) revolutionized the agenda.

D. Worster's **Nature's Economy** (1994) is a brilliant history of environmentalist thinking.

J. McNeill's **Something New Under the Sun** (2000) is a wonderful, worrying history of 20th-century environmental mismanagement.

Pierre Teilhard de Chardin, who in the early 20th century was among the first to appreciate the complexity of the Earth's ecosystems. In the 1950s scientific publications began to reveal causes for concern, but environmentalism was viewed as a quirk of dewy-eyed romantics, or – what was worse – it had been a mania of some prominent Nazis, who nourished bizarre doctrines about the relationship of purity of "blood and soil". To become a major political movement, environmentalism needed a whistle-blower with gifts as a publicist. In 1962 Rachel Carson emerged.

Industrialization and intensive agriculture were spreading across the world. Two circumstances helped to provoke the new situation. First, decolonization created new governments in underexploited parts of the world, where elites were anxious to imitate the industrialized West, find new ways of exploiting their own environments, and "catch up" with the established economic giants. Secondly, world population was hurtling upwards and new farming methods, involving saturation with chemical fertilizers and pesticides, were needed to meet it. Rachel Carson's *Silent Spring* (1962) was one of those rare books that change minds. It sounded an alarm heard around the world, though it was directly addressed to America and chiefly focused on the effects of pesticide-profligacy. It was brilliantly written, conjuring an apocalyptic vision of a future America in which all the songbirds had died.

Environmentalism fed on pollution and thrived in the hothouse of climate debate. It rapidly became the orthodoxy of the scientific community and the rhetoric of politicians. Many doom-fraught predictions made in its name have been exaggerated; some of the mystics and cranks who have espoused it as a quasi-religion have restored part of its former disrepute. Some damaging environmental practices – dam-building, "greenhouse gas" emissions, unsustainable forestry, unregulated urbanization, inadequate testing of agrochemicals – have been slightly, or in some cases significantly, curtailed. The biosphere is showing powers of resilience surprising to some prophets. Despite efforts to interest the global public in "deep" – that is, disinterested – ecology, most environmentalism remains, however, of a traditional kind, more anxious to serve humans than nature. Conservation is popular, it seems, only when our own species needs it.

CONNECTIONS

For the Romantic idea, see **Back to Nature** (p.280). For human interventions on our environment, see **Outside Eden** (p.66) and **Lords of Creation** (p.68). On our relationships with other species, see **Top Ape** (p.138) and **Little Pests** (p.230).

385

SILENT SPRINGS

Poisoned land
In the aftermath of WWII, chemicals were seen as a "quick fix" for agricultural prosperity. This remains the case in parts of the developing world, but there is a heavy environmental price to pay.

Fast Talking

THE IDEA THAT LANGUAGE IS INNATE

The idea of innate language structures came from Noam Chomsky's observations on how quickly children learn to talk their language. He was impressed by the way children acquire speech, without having to be taught: "Children learn language from positive evidence only (corrections not being required or relevant), and they appear to know the facts without relevant experience in a wide array of complex cases." They can even combine words in ways they have never actually heard.

Chomsky also found it remarkable that the differences in languages appear superficial compared with the "deep structures" – the parts of speech and the relationships between terms, which we call "grammar" and "syntax" – that are common to all of them. This suggested a link between the structures of language and brain: we learn languages fast because their structure is already part of the way we think.

Chomsky's idea was revolutionary in 1957, when the prevailing orthodoxies – Freud's psychiatry, Sartre's philosophy, and Piaget's educational nostrums – suggested otherwise. Experience and heredity do not make us the whole of what we are. Part of our nature is hard-wired into our brains at birth. The way Chomsky saw it, at least at first, was that this "language instinct" or "language faculty" was untouchable – and therefore perhaps unproduced – by evolution. He has since proposed that other kinds of knowledge may turn out to resemble language in

READINGS

N. Chomsky's **Knowledge of Language** (1986) is a mature and judicious, though technically uncompromising, summary of his thought.

James Peck's (ed.) **The Chomsky Reader** (1987) is a useful resource.

S. Pinker's **The Language Instinct** (1994) is a brilliant and irresistible survey of the subject.

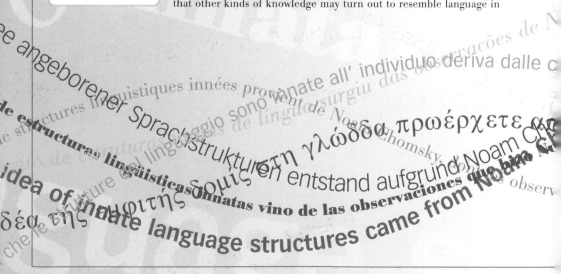

"Why does Homo sapiens…, this unified species, not use one common language?"

George Steiner, *After Babel* (1975)

CONNECTIONS

On Freud, see **Sleeper** (p.356). On Piaget, see **Little Man** (p.358). On Sartre, see **Road to Freedom** (p.374). Other material on language can be found in **Give Me a Sign** (p.14) and **Their Own Terms** (p.354).

these respects: that our "mental constitution" explains how we acquire all sorts of science. Experience, perhaps, is less important in learning than we thought, or, at least, does not have an exclusive role. It does not mediate knowledge directly to our minds, but triggers capacities latent in the structures of our mental faculties.

This may mean that our language prowess, on which we tend to congratulate ourselves as a species, and which some people even claim as a uniquely human achievement, is like the special skills of other species – that of cheetahs in speed, for instance, or cows in ruminating. Most people think that a basic distinction between humans and other animals is that the latter are creatures of instinct. This is why they are very good at tasks we think are instinctive (such as food-finding) and poor at, or ignorant of, others that we think are non-instinctive (such as art and science). On the other hand, humans, who are supposedly deficient in instinct, have "freedom" – we can think, imagine, discover, communicate. Chomsky doubts the validity of this distinction: our peculiar capacities, too, are innate.

In other words
Chomsky believed that whatever the language in which we express ourselves, all humans use the same inherent grammatical structures.

387

Chomsky sobre a ... on how quickly children learn to tal
Ky's observations ... wie schnell Kinder ihre eigene Sprache ... à parler leur langue
azio... Noam Chomsk... que ... fants apprenn...
...omsky sobre lo rápidamente que los niños aprenden a hablar su idi
...quelle les enfants ... ...tanças aprendem a falar a
montrent la ...idité avec la... su come i bambini imparano a parlare la lo... ...apidement a ...
ς παρατίρησις του Noam Chomsky για το πόσο γρήγ

The Great Satan

THE IDEA OF ANTI-AMERICANISM

Burger culture
Hamburgers have become a symbol of all that is best and worst about America: they are "fast", convenient, and generate huge profits, but at a high cost to the environment, health, and the local food cultures they displace.

READINGS

Z. Sardar and M. Wyn Davies's **Why Do People Hate America?** (2002) is a brilliant summation.

Granta 77: What We Think of America (2002) is a special issue of this review devoted to essays on the subject.

J.S. Nye's **The Paradox of American Power** (2002) is a searching and thoroughly compelling study.

As American power grew to eclipse that of other powers, resentment of the USA grew with it. After World War II, the USA enjoyed the hegemony of the world as far as the frontiers of communism. It interfered in other people's empires, treated much of the world as its "backyard", and legitimized illiberal regimes in American interests. The magnetism of the trashy culture of hamburgers and rock 'n' roll was as widely resented as it was irresistible. American GIs – whose presence in Europe was an irksome reminder of European impotence – were "over-paid, over-sexed, and over here". The relatively benign aspects of American policy, which supported war-weak economies with aid, were ungratefully received by some of their beneficiaries.

From 1958, the hero and spokesman of anti-Americanism was the French President Charles de Gaulle – a Samson in Dagon's temple, pushing at the pillars and striving to expel the Philistines. An unruly client of the USA, his critique was more effective than the propaganda of self-interested enemies who issued their denunciations from behind the Iron Curtain. More convincing still – and more disturbing from an American point of view – was the growing challenge from morally committed, politically neutral quarters. First, from within the liberal West, especially from within the USA itself, which became strident during the Vietnam War; and secondly, from the developing world. In the 1970s, as the USA began to get over the trauma of Vietnam, the initiative in the campaign of criticism passed to an exiled Iranian mullah, Ayatollah Khomeini. He hated other forms of modernization but was a master of mass communication, with an almost insane conviction of self-righteousness. His simple message was that the world was divided between oppressors and "dispossessed", and that the USA was the "Great Satan", corrupting humankind and suborning the species with crude force.

As the self-proclaimed champion of capitalism in successful global confrontations with rival ideologies, the USA invited this caricature. Moreover, American society had undeniable defects, as its critics from

British playwright
Harold Pinter (1930–) is a vociferous critic of US foreign policy.

"The 'rogue state' [the USA] has… effectively declared war on the world. It knows only one language – bombs and death."

Harold Pinter, article in *Granta 77: What We Think of America* (2002)

within well knew: the trash-capitalism, the excessive privileges of wealth, the selective illiberalism, the dumbed-down popular culture, the stagnancy of politics, the tetchiness and ignorance that veil the USA from the rest of the world, unquestioning patriotism, unhealthy religiosity, and aggressive insistence on one's rights. But these are vices other communities also have in abundance and the USA's virtues greatly outweigh them: the people's genuine commitment to freedom and democracy, and the relative restraint and disinterest with which the state discharges its superpower role.

It is hard to imagine any of the other contenders for unique superpower status in the 20th century behaving in victory with similar magnanimity. Yet hatred of America grows. Every American foreign-policy error and injudicious operation of "global policing" makes it worse. Anti-Americanism has become a breeding-ground of resentment and a source of recruitment for terrorists. In the early 21st century, it is a major problem for the world.

Whose freedom?
US military campaigns are often carried out in the name of "freedom", but others do not always see it that way. Here, Pakistanis opposed to the US military operation in Afghanistan in 2001 are burning the American flag.

Fundamentally opposed
In the 1980s, the Iranian leader Ayatollah Khomeini (1900–89) was Islam's loudest critic of the USA. He linked criticism of US power with accusations of cultural degeneracy.

It takes all kinds
*The 1970s pop group
Village People adopted
a plurality of American
archetypes to promote their
hit song "YMCA". It also
became a gay anthem,
marking a stage in the
acceptance of gay culture
into the mainstream.*

CONNECTIONS

For related cultural and
religious pluralisms, see
Their Own Terms (p.354)
and **Many Ways** (p.362).
For 20th-century ideas
hostile to pluralism,
see **Axe in the Sticks**
(p.364) and **Black Is
Beautiful**
(p.376).

Global Village

THE IDEA OF CULTURAL PLURALISM

For most of history, most states had to be "unitary", with one religion,
ethnicity, and identity. Large empires have always necessarily been multicultural, but they have usually had a dominant culture, alongside which
others are tolerated. In the 20th century, this would no longer do. The
aftermath of the era of global empires, the range and intensity of
migrations, the progress of ideas of racial equality, the multiplication of
religions, and the large-scale redrawings of state boundaries made multi-
culturalism essential to the peace of most states. Those that rejected the
need faced traumatic periods of "ethnic cleansing" – the standard late
20th-century euphemism for massacres and forced relocations of minority
communities. Meanwhile, the intense competition of rival ideologies could
only be contained in democracies by political pluralism – that is, the
admission to the lawful political arena, on equal terms, of parties
representing potentially irreconcilable views.

"I can enter into a value system which is not my own... for all human beings must have some common values... and also some different values."

Isaiah Berlin, *New York Review of Books* (1998)

Sir Isaiah Berlin
(1907–97), British
philosopher and
historian of ideas.

In philosophy, pluralism means the doctrine that reality cannot be contained by mònist or dualist thought. This claim, which is well documented in antiquity, helped to inspire the conviction that a plurality of cultures – religions, languages, ethnicities, communal identities, versions of history, value systems – could be accommodated on terms of equality in a single society, a single state. The idea grew up gradually, but the best formulation of it is usually attributed to Isaiah Berlin's *The Sense of Reality* (1996). In this work, he argues that there is a "plurality of values", which are numerous but not infinite. Human values, according to Berlin, are "values that I can pursue while maintaining my human semblance, my human character". Different people pursue different values, but all of us are capable of imagining what it would be like to pursue values other than our own, and why others make choices of values different from ours. Within limits set by our understanding of what it means to be human, we can accept, and even embrace, conflicts of values. "Hence the possibility of human understanding," Berlin concludes.

This differs from cultural relativism: it does not say, for instance, that all cultures can be accommodated. One might exclude Nazism, say, or cannibalism. It leaves open the possibility of peaceful argument about which culture, if any, is best. It claims, in Berlin's words, "that the multiple values are objective, part of the essence of humanity rather than arbitrary creations of men's subjective fancies." Together with cultural relativism, it contributes to making multi-cultural societies conceivable and viable.

Ironically, pluralism has to accommodate anti-pluralism, because not everybody likes it. In the early years of the 21st century, a detectable reaction called for policies of "cultural integration" of immigrants to replace those of multi-culturalism. In a world where globalization and other huge, integrative processes make most historic communities defensive about their own cultures, there is much evidence of the difficulty of persuading them to co-exist peacefully with the contrasting cultures of their neighbours. Still, the idea endures because pluralism is obviously the only practical future for a diverse world. Paradoxically, perhaps, it is the only truly uniform interest that all the world's peoples have in common.

READINGS

A. Lijphart's **Democracy in Plural Societies** (1977) is a thoughtful, cogent, hopeful study of the problems, while R.Takki's **A Different Mirror** (1993) is an engaging history of multicultural America.

I. Berlin's **Two Concepts of Liberty** (1959) is a key text, while J. Gray's **Isaiah Berlin** (1995) is a stimulating study of the great advocate of modern pluralism.

391

GLOBAL VILLAGE

Astride the divide
The fall of the Berlin Wall in 1989 has led to the assimilation of the communist culture of the former Eastern bloc into the dominant capitalist culture of the West. But there is still no cultural consensus, and deep differences remain between the German peoples.

Index

Acknowledgments

The publisher would like to thank the following for their kind permission to reproduce their photographs;
(Abbreviations key; t=top, b=below, r=right, l=left, c=centre, f=far, a=above, kb=knock back)

(Agency abbreviations key; BAL=Bridgeman Art Library, London/New York, MEPL=Mary Evans Picture Library, HIP=Heritage Image Partnership, RF=Rex Features, SPL=Science Photo Library)

2-3: Simon Stock; 8-9: Corbis/Archivo Iconografico, S.A.; 10: Corbis/Adam Woolfitt (br), British Museum (c); 11: Art Archive/Musée du Louvre Paris/Jacqueline Hyde (tr); 12: AKG London (bl, kb), Time Team/Channel 4 (tl); 13: Pitt Rivers Museum (tl), Kobal/Orion/Ken Regan; 14: Corbis/Gianni Dagli Orti (tl); 14-15: Getty Images/Hulton Archive/Picture Post (bc); 15: Corbis/Stapleton Collection (tl), Corbis/Ted Spiegel (br); 16: AKG London/Erich Lessing/Palazzo del Te, Mantua (kb, c); 17: Jerry Young (tr); 18-19: Masterfile UK/Mike Macri; 18: NASA (bl), Ann & Bury Peerless (tl); 20: AKG London/Herbert Kraft (bl, kb), Ashmolean Museum (l); 21: Corbis/Charles & Josette Lenars; 22: British Museum (tl, kb), Scala Group S.p.A. (bl); 23: Robert Harding Picture Library/Robert Frerck; 24: MEPL/Harry Price Collection (l); 25: CM Dixon (bl), Fortean Picture Library (tl, kb), Kobal/Lucas Film/20th Century Fox; 26: Corbis/Hulton-Deutsch Collection (bl), SPL/G. Hadjo/CNRI (tl, kb); 27: Kobal/Lucas Film/20th Century Fox, Masterfile UK/R. Ian Lloyd (c); 28: BAL (kb); 29: BAL (tr); 30-31: Das Fotoarchiv/SVT Bild (b); 31: Corbis/Roger Ressmeyer; 32: Corbis (bc), Natural History Museum (tl); 33: alamy.com/M-dash.com/Martin Wilson (tl), Robert Harding Picture Library/Sylvain Grandadam (bc); 34-35: Robert Harding Picture Library; 36: Getty Images/Hulton Archive (b), SPL/Novosti (tl); 37: Corbis/Eye Ubiquitous/Paul Seheult (tl), Corbis/Stefano Bianchetti (tl), Board of Trustees of the Armouries (br), SPL/Novosti (bl); 38: Corbis/Eye Ubiquitous/Paul Seheult (l); 39: Corbis/Michael S. Yamashita (bc); 40: Corbis/Johnathan Smith/Cordaiy Photo Library (tl, b), Art Archive/Museo Storico Italiano della Guerra Rovereto/Dagli Orti (kb, l); 41: Corbis/David Turnley (tr), Kobal/Phillip Caruso (br); 42-43: AKG London (b); 42: Ancient Art & Architecture Collection/R. Sheridan (tl); 43: Corbis/Hulton-Deutsch Collection (tl); 44: Art Archive/Bodleian Library Oxford (cl), HIP/British Library (tr, kb); 45: Corbis/Ira Nowinski (tl), SPL/Stanley B. Burns, MD & the Burns Archive, NY (c); 48: Corbis/Baldev (bl), Hulton-Deutsch Collection (tl, c); 49: Kobal/AKG London/Erich Lessing (r); 50: SPL (tr); 51: Getty Images (tl, kb); 52-53: Corbis/Kevin Fleming; 52: Das Fotoarchiv/SVT Bild (l); 53: Agence France Presse (tl), Associated Press AP (br); 54: BAL/Lambeth Palace Library, London (tl), Getty Images/Hulton Archive/Lambert (b); 55: BAL/Lambeth Palace Library, London (kb), Corbis/Lindsay Hebbard (tl); 56: Corbis/Michael S. Lewis, Danish National Museum (tl); 57: BAL/London/New York/Giraudon/Castello di Issogne, Val d'Aosta, Italy (bl), Corbis/Chris Rainier (br); 58-59: Getty Images/Ernst Haas (kb), Corbis/Galen Rowell (bl); 61: British Museum (tc); 62: INAH (bl), Magnum/Thomas Dworzak (tl, kb); 63: Corbis/Bettman (tr); 64: Corbis/Sandro Vannini (bl); 65: Art Archive/Musee de la Tapisserie Bayeux/Dagli Orti (tr); 66: Getty Images (tl); 68-69: Corbis/Joseph Sohm/ChromoSohm Inc. (bc); 68: Getty Images (l); 69: Ancient Art & Architecture Collection (r); 70: Getty Images/Hulton Archive (tl); 71: Corbis/Benjamin Lowy (tl), Lori Adamski Peek (tr); 72: Advertising Archives/Vanity Fair/Conde Nast/Contact Press Images/Annie Liebovitz (bl); 72-73: BAL/James Goodman Gallery, New York (b), CM Dixon (tl), Art Archive/Pinacoteca Virreinel Mexico City/Dagli Orti (kb); 73: Art Archive/Pinacoteca Virreinel Mexico City/Dagli Orti (l); 74: Corbis; 75: Corbis/Chris Hellier (tr), Getty Images/Hulton Archive/Lambert/Archive Photos (br, kb); 76: Corbis/Christel Gerstenberg (tl, kb), Bradbury Science Museum, Los Alamos (bl); 76-77: RF (b); 78: Corbis/Austrian Archives (l), Corbis/Gianni Dagli Orti (bl); 79: Corbis/Royal Ontario Museum (tr, kb), Digital Revolution (bc); 80: Corbis/Bettmann; 81: BAL/Lauros-Giraudon (tl), Corbis/Michael Freeman (tr), Getty Images (br, kb); 82-83: SOA Photo Agency/Rainer Jahns; 83: Art Archive/Museum/Dagli Orti (bc); 84: Art Archive/Bodleian Library Oxford; 85: Ancient Art & Architecture Collection (tl); 85: Corbis/Jose Fuste Raga (kb, r), British Museum (tr); 86: BAL/Lauros-Giraudon/Louvre, Paris (bl), Ronald Grant Archive (tl), RF/SIPA (kb); 87: Corbis/Bob Krist (t), RF/SIPA (tr); 88: BAL/Galleria Borghese, Rome, Italy (l); 89: alamy.com (br), BAL/Leeds Museum and Art Galleries (City Museum) (tl, kb), Art Archive/Museo Civico Pisa/Dagli Orti (A) (bl); 90-91: Popperfoto (b); 91: Katz/FSP/Jacques Prayer (tr); 92: Corbis/David Lees (tl); 92-93: Getty Images; 93: RF/Greg Williams (tl); 94: AKG London; 95: National Maritime Museum (bl), Kobal (tr, kb); 96: Corbis/Araldo de Luca (bl, kb); 97: Getty Images; 98: MEPL (l); 99: BAL/Los Angeles County Museum of Art, CA, USA/ADAGP,DACS 2003 (kb), BAL/Los Angeles County Museum of Art, CA, USA/ADAGP,DACS 2003 (r), Glasgow Museum (bl); 100-101: Getty Images/Hugh Sitton; 102: Art Archive/Archaeological Museum Chora Greece/Dagli Orti (tc), Art Archive/Dagli

Orti (bl); 103: BAL/Lauros/Giraudon (l), Art Archive/Topkapi Museum Istanbul/Dagli Orti (tr); 106: Corbis/Ted Spiegel (tl); 106-107: BAL/British Museum (cl); 107: Corbis/J.B.Russell; 108-109: Getty Images; 109: Fondation Le Corbusier/ADAGP, DACS 2003 (tr); 110-111: alamy.com (c); 110: Corbis (bl, kb); 111: Corbis/David Turnley; 112-113: Getty Images/Hulton Archive (b); 112: Hutchison Library/Osarah Errington (c); 113: BAL/Ognissanti, Florence, Italy (tl), Wellcome Institute Library, London (tr); 114: Corbis/Bettmann (bl), Corbis/Chris Hellier (tl); 114-115: Getty Images/Clint Eley (c); 115: SPL/Pascal Goetgheluck (bc); 116 alamy.com (bl); 117: SPL/Jerry Schad (bl, kb); 118: alamy.com (bl); 118-119: Das Fotoarchiv/SVT Bild (c); 119: BAL/Giraudon/Art Institute of Chicago, IL, USA (r); 123: Corbis/Najlah Feanny (tl), Ronald Grant Archive/Paramount Television (br); 124: Advertising Archives (bl), BAL/Bibliothèque Nationale, Paris, France/Archives Charmet (tl, kb), Institut für Plastination (bl); 125: BAL/Collection of the Earl of Pembroke, Wilton House, Wilts., UK (tr); 126-127: Getty Images; 127: Corbis/Bettmann (bl), SPL/Lawrence Berkeley Laboratory (tr); 128-129: BAL/National Gallery London, UK (bc); 128: Corbis/Michael Nicholson (bl), Getty Images (tl); 129: Science Museum (tr); 130-131: Getty Images; 131: Topham Picturepoint (tc); 132: Corbis/Historical Picture Archive (bl); 132-133: National Maritime Museum (tl); 134: HIP/British Library (tl), Kobal/Anglo Amalgamated (bl); 135: Art Archive/University Library Prague, Dagli Orti (b), HIP/Science Museum (tl), HIP/British Library (kb); 136: Art Archive (bl, kb), Summerhill School (cl); 137: Getty Images/Hulton Archive/Lambert/Archive Photos; 138: AKG London/Cameraphoto (cl, kb), Stephen Oliver (tl); 139: N.H.P.A./Andy Rouse; 140: Corbis/Hulton-Deutsch Collection (b), Corbis/Lindsay Hebberd (tl); 141: Masterfile UK/Miles Ertman; 142: Corbis/Archivo Iconografico, S.A. (bl); 142-143: Kobal/MGM (c); 144: Corbis/Francis G. Mayer (tl); 144-145: Corbis/John Van Hasselt; 145: Corbis/Adam Woolfitt (tl); 146: Getty Images/Hulton Archive/Fox Photos (kb); 146-147: 2000AD, Rebellion/Jock; 147: Getty Images/Hulton Archive/Fox Photos (tr); 148: BAL/Dept. of the Environment, London, UK (tl), Scala Group S.p.A./Palazzo Madama, Roma (bl); 149: Corbis/Archivo Iconografico, S.A.(tl); Corbis/Archivo Iconografrico (kb), Corbis/Peter Turnley (tr); 150: BAL (tl), Corbis (bl, kb); 150-151: Corbis/Bojan Brecelj (c); 151: BAL/Michael Graham Stewart (tr); 152-153: Getty Images/Hulton Archive (b); 153: Corbis/Miroslav Zajic (tl), Getty Images/Hulton Archive/Keystone (c); 154-155: Simon Stock; 155: Corbis/Bettmann (tl), Wellcome Institute/Science Museum (tr); 156: BAL/Private Collection (bl); 156: SPL/Wellcome Dept. of Cognitive Neurology (cl.); 156-157: SPL (c); 157: Corbis (br); 158-159: Agence France Presse (bc); 158: Art Archive/British Museum/Eileen Tweedy (b), Impact Photos (t); 159: Art Archive/British Museum/Eileen Tweedy (tl); 160: Corbis/Bettmann (bl, kb), Redfers/David Redfern (cl); 161: BAL/Museo del Prado, Madrid (c); 162-163: BAL/Giraudon; 164: Getty Images/ Nabeel Turner (c); 165: Corbis/Richard T. Nowitz (tr); 166: BAL/Skopje, Macedonia (bl), Corbis/Kimbell Art Museum (tl); 167: Corbis/West Semitic Research/Dead Sea Scrolls Foundation (c); 168: Corbis/National Gallery Collection; By kind permission of the Trustees of the National Gallery, London (bl, kb), Corbis/Owen Franken (tl); 169: BAL, London /New York/V&A Museum, London (br); 170: Art Archive/Museo Capitolino Rome/Dagli Orti (A) (tl), MEPL (kb); 171: Art Archive/Tempio di Canova Possagno/Dagli Orti (A) (br), MEPL (bl); 172: BAL/Prado, Madrid (bl), British Museum (tl); 172-173: Kobal/Paramount (bc); 174-175: BAL:/Santa Maria della Vittoria, Rome, Italy (c); 174: Getty Images/Hulton Archive (tl); 175: BAL/Tretyakov Gallery, Moscow, Russia (br); 176: Corbis/Dean Conger (tl, kb), Moviestore Collection (b); 177: Corbis/Bettmann; 178: Corbis (bl), Corbis/Jason Hawkes (tl); 179: Christie's Images Ltd (tr), Art Archive/Basilica San Giusto Trieste/Dagli Orti (tl); 180: Jane Burton (tl), Art Archive/Saint Stephen's Cathedral Vienna/Dagli Orti (A) (bl); 181: Corbis/Todd Haimann (br), ImageState/Pictor/AGE Fotostock (tr); 182: Antiquarian Images (tl); 182-183: Corbis/Liu Liqun (c); 183: BAL/Archives Charmet, Corbis (c); 184-185: BAL/Santa Maria delle Grazie, Milan, Italy (b); 184-185: Corbis/Kevin Fleming (tl); 185: Corbis/Craig Aurness (tl); 186: Corbis/Hulton-Deutsch Collection (tl); 187: Corbis (br), Art Archive/Galleria d'Arte Moderna Rome/Dagli Orti (A) (tl, kb); 188: BAL/Edinburgh University Library, Scotland (bl), Panos Pictures/Mark Henley (tl); 188-189: Panos Pictures/Dermot Tatlow (tl); 189: HIP/British Library (br); 190: BAL (kb), BAL /Fitzwilliam Museum, University of Cambridge (bl), Pa Photos/EPA European Press Agency (tl); 191: Art Archive/Musee du Chateau de Versailles/ Dagli Orti (r); 192: BAL/The Stapleton Collection (tl), Corbis/Archivo Iconografico, S.A. (bl), Corbis/Joseph Sohm/ChromoSohm Inc (kb); 193: Corbis/David Lees (tr), Corbis/Joseph Sohm/ChromoSohm Inc (br); 194: Getty Images/Hulton Archive (tl); 194-195: ImageState/Pictor/AGE Fotostock (c); 195: Corbis/Michael S. Yamashita (r), Art Archive/Private Collection Paris/Dagli Orti (tl); 196: Corbis/Hulton-Deutsch Collection; 197: Corpus Christi College (bl), Saint Bride Printing Library (tl); 198: MEPL (bl), Getty Images/Hulton Archive (tl); 199: Christie's Images Ltd (r); 200-201: Corbis/Araldo de Luca (tl), Corbis/Jon Feingersh (c); 200: Kobal/United Artists (bl); 201: Corbis/Araldo de Luca (tr), Getty Images/Hulton Archive/Express (cr); **202:** BAL/Private Collection (bl); **203:** Corbis/National Gallery Collection/By kind permission of the Trustees of the National Gallery (kb), Corbis/National Gallery Collection/By kind permission of the Trustees of the National Gallery, London (tl), Pa Photos/EPA (tr); **204:** Art Archive/Gunshots (tl), Zefa Picture Library/Nightlight (kb); **205:** Corbis/Charles & Josette Lenars (r), Zefa Picture Library/Nightlight (tl); **206–207:** alamy.com/plainpicture/R. Erwin, R; **206:** BAL/Private Collection (bl), Alistair Duncan (tl); **208:** HIP/ British Library (tl), Courtesy of the Trustees of the V&A (bl, kb); **209:** RF/SMM; **210–211:** Getty Images (bc); **211:** Corbis/Vince Streano (tl), Art Archive/San Angelo in Formis Capua Italy/Dagli Orti (A) (tl); **212–213:** BAL/Giraudon/Galleria degli Uffizi, Florence, Italy; **214:** Corbis/Bettmann (c), National Maritime Museum (bl); **215:** National Bank of China (tl), SPL/Eye of Science (tr); **216:** Corbis/Bettmann (bl, kb), Art Archive/Eileen Tweedy (tl); **217:** BAL/Library and Museum of Freemasonry, London, UK (tr), Scala Group S.p.A./Mauritshuis (b); **218:** Corbis/Historical Picture Archive (tl); **219:** BAL/Ayuntamiento de Coruna, Spain (r), Art Archive/Naval Museum Genoa/Dagli Orti (A) (tl, kb); **220:** BAL/Lauros-Giraudon/Bibliotheque Nationale, Paris (bl), Art Archive/Turkish and Islamic Art Museum Istanbul/Dagli Orti (A) (tl); **220–221:** SPL/NASA (c); **221:** National Maritime Museum (tr); **222:** BAL/Stapleton Collection (bl, kb), Corbis/Bettmann (tl); **223:** Getty Images/Hulton Archive/Lambert/Archive Photos; **225:** BAL/Private Collection (bl, kb), Corbis/Bettmann (br); **227:** Art Archive/Royal Society/Eileen Tweedy (tl); **228:** Judith Miller; **228–229:** Getty Images/Hulton Archive/Fox Photos (b); **229:** SPL/Sheila Terry (tl); **230:** Corbis/Lester Lefkowitz (cl), SPL/Custom Medical Stock Photo (bl), SPL/Custom Medical Stock Photo (kb); SPL/Dr Jeremy Burgess (tl); **231:** SPL/Dr.Gary Gaugler; **232:** Corbis (bl), Corbis/Archivo Iconografico, S.A.(tl,kb); **233:** Corbis/Archivo Iconografico, S.A.(br); **233:** Kobal (l); **234:** Corbis/Bettmann (tl); BAL;/Archivo de Indias, Seville, Spain (bl); **234:** SPL/Dr G. Moscoso (tl); BAL;/Archivo de Indias, Seville, Spain (bl); **236:** Corbis/Bettmann (bl), Art Archive/Marine Museum Lisbon/Dagli Orti (tl); **237:** Corbis/Underwood & Underwood (tl), Art Archive/Marine Museum Lisbon/Dagli Orti (cl), Getty Images (br); **238:** Kobal/Two Art/CD; **239:** BAL (tl, kb), Corbis/Peter Turnley (cr); **240–241:** Christie's Images Ltd/Christie's Images, Inc; **240:** HIP/British Museum (cl); **241:** Corbis/Baldwin H. Ward & Kathryn C. Ward (cr); **242:** BAL/Museo de America, Spain (tl), Getty Images/Hulton Archive (bl); **243:** alamy.com/Joseph Sohm (cr), BAL/Museo de America, Madrid, Spain (br); **244:** Corbis/Roger Garwood & Trish Ainslie (tl), BAL/Philip Mould, Historical Portraits Ltd, London, UK (bl); **245:** Corbis/Cooperphoto; **246:** Corbis/Hulton-Deutsch Collection (l); **247:** BAL/Private Collection (cr, kb); BAL/Scottish National Portrait Gallery, Corbis/Serra Antoine (br); **248–249:** Archivi Alinari/Galleria d'Arte Moderna, Milan, Italy; **248:** Corbis/Bettmann (bl); **249:** BAL/Royal Armoury, London (tr); **250:** BAL/Kunsthistorisches Museum, Vienna, Austria (tl), Getty Images/Hulton Archive (b); **251:** Corbis/Historical Picture Archive (tl, kb), View Pictures/Peter Cook (tr); **252:** BAL/London Library, St James's Square, London (bl, kb); **254:** BAL/Musee Antoine Lecuyer, Saint-Quentin, France (tl, kb), Corbis/Archivo Iconografico, S.A. (bc); **255:** MEPL (tl), Taschen (c); **256:** MEPL (tl); **256–257:** Malcolm Hey; **257:** BAL;/Musee Lambinet, Versailles, Corbis/Peter Turnley (br); **258:** Corbis; **259:** BAL/Musee Antoine Lucuyer, Saint-Quentin, France (bl); BAL/Museum of Fine Arts, Boston, Massachusetts, USA (t); **260–261:** Corbis/Joseph Sohm; ChromoSohm Inc.; **261:** BAL/Chateau de Versailles (tl), RF (r); **262:** Getty Images/Hulton Archive; **263:** BAL/Musee de la Ville de Paris, Musee Carnavalet, Paris, France (cr), Corbis/Mark Peterson (br), RF/Nils Jorgensen (tl); **264:** Corbis/Archivo Iconografico (bl), Corbis/George D. Lepp (bl, kb); **265:** Corbis/Bettmann; **266–267:** Corbis/Matthias Kulka (c); **266:** Art Archive/Bodleian Library Oxford (tl), RF/Lehtikuva Oy (bl, kb); **268:** Corbis/Jose Luis Pelaez, Inc (l); **269:** BAL/Musee de la Ville de Paris, Musee Carnavalet, Paris, France (tl), HIP/Museum of London (r); **270:** Corbis/Owen Franken (tl); **271:** BAL/Private Collection (bl); **272–273:** Getty Images/Nick Clements (c); **273:** Corbis/Hulton-Deutsch Collection (tl); **274:** Das Fotoarchiv/SVT Bild (tl); SPL/Nancy Kedersha (br), Getty Images/Gandee Vasan (tl); **279:** Artothek/Weimar, Kunstsammlungen (bl), BAL/Galleria dell' Accademia, Venice, Italy (tr); **280:** BAL/John Bethell (tl), MEPL (bl, kb); **281:** BAL/Hamburg Kunsthalle, Hamburg, Germany (c), BAL/Muso e Gallerie Nazionali di Capodimonte, Naples, Italy (tr); **282–283:** Corbis; **284:** Corbis/Austrian Archives (tc), Lebrecht Collection (b); **285:** Corbis/Jack Fields (br); **286:** Corbis/Vince Streano (br), RF/SIPA (tl, kb); **287:** Empics Ltd/Tom Marshall (r), National Portrait Gallery, London (tl); **288:** alamy.com/George Logan (bl, kb), Getty Images/Hulton Archive/George Eastman House/Lewis W. Hine/Archive Photos (tl); **289:** Advertising Archives (r); **290:** Getty Images/Hulton Archive/Archive Photos; **291:** Getty Images/Hulton Archive/Archive Photos (tl, kb); **292:** Corbis/Archivo Iconografico, S.A (bl), Corbis/Archivo Iconografico, S.A. (tl), Getty Images/Hulton Archive/Keystone (tl); **293:** David King Collection (r); **294:** Getty Images/Stuart Dee (t), University College London (bl); **295:** MEPL (tr, bl, kb); **296:** Art Archive/Jarrold Publishing (bl), Getty Images/Hulton Archive/Central Press (tl, kb); **297:** Corbis/Stephanie Maze; **298:** Corbis/Swim Ink (kb), RF/Ray

Tang (bl); **299:** BAL/Private Collection (bl), Corbis/Swim Ink (tl); **300:** Corbis/Rykoff Collection (b), RF/SIPA (tl); **301:** Corbis/Corbis Sygma (t), Corbis/Corbis Sygma/Christian Borderie (br); **302:** Getty Images/Hulton Archive; **303:** alamy.com (tr), Getty Images/Hulton Archive (bc, kb); **304:** BAL/Chateau de Versailles, France (tl); **305:** Corbis/Bettmann (tl), Kobal/Warner Bros TV/DC Comics (c); **306:** Corbis/Bettmann; **307:** Corbis/Bettmann (bl, kb), Corbis/Nogues Alain/Corbis Sygma (cr), Corbis/Philip Harvey (tr); **308:** Getty Images/Hulton Archive/Keystone; **309:** Corbis/Bettmann (br), Disney Enterprises, Inc (tl), Pa Photos/EPA (br); **310:** Corbis/Francoise de Mulder (br); **311:** Art Archive/Musée du Château de Versailles/Dagli Orti (bl), Getty Images/Hulton Archive/Evening Standard (tl); **312:** Corbis/Bettmann (bl, kb), Panos Pictures/Andrew Testa (cl); **313:** Corbis/Bettmann; **314:** alamy.com/Popperfoto (t), BAL/Ricahrd S. Zeisler Collection, New York, USA/ADAGP, DACS 2003 (kb); **315:** BAL/Richard S. Zeisler Collection, New York, USA/ ADAGP, DACS 2003; **316:** Corbis/Bettmann (bl); **316–317:** Imperial War Museum (c); **317:** alamy.com/Popperfoto (tr), Corbis/Bettmann (kb), MEPL (tr); **318:** Getty Images/Hulton Archive/ Keystone (bl); **319:** BAL/Philip Mould, Historical Portraits Ltd, Wellcome Institute Library, London (tr), Wellcome Institute Library, London/ The Galton Institute (bl); **320:** Tracy Morgan (tl), Wellcome Institute Library, London (bl, kb); **320–321:** Daniel Lee; **322:** Getty Images; (b); **323:** Corbis/Bettmann (tl), SPL/Stanley B. Burns, MD & The Burns Archive N.Y. (kb, r); **324:** British Humanist Society (tr); Corbis/Bettmann (tl), New York Historical Society (br); **325:** British Humanist Society (tr), Art Archive/Musée Carnavalet Paris/Dagli Orti (b); **326:** Science & Society Picture Library; **327:** SPL (bl), SPL/ Alfred Pasieka (tr, kb); **328:** Corbis/Bettmann; **329:** AKG London/Slg. E. Werner d. Johanniter-Ordens (bl), alamy.com/Popperfoto (tl, kb), Getty Images/Steven Weinberg (tr); **330:** Art Archive/Bodleian Library Oxford (N.12288b after p 88) (tl), MEPL (tr); **330–331:** RF; **331:** Corbis/Karan Kapoor (tr); **332:** Corbis/Abbie Enock/Travel Ink (t); **333:** Bank of India (bl), BAL/Bristol City Museum and Art Gallery, UK (tr); **334:** Corbis/China Features/Corbis Sygma (b), Getty Images/Hulton Archive/Central Press (tl); **335:** Corbis/Bettmann (bl), Getty Images/Hulton Archive/Central Press (kb), ImageState/Pictor/Brian Lovell (tr); **336:** Advertising Archives/Disney Enterprises, Inc. (br, kb), Corbis/E.O. Hoppé (bl), Michael Maslan Historic Photographs (tl); **337:** NASA; **338:** Corbis/Cathy Crawford (tl), Peter Newark's Pictures (bl); **339:** Peter Newark's Pictures (tl, b); **340–341:** Corbis (c); **340:** Getty Images/Hulton Archive/Keystone (tl); **341:** Kobal/Hawk Films Prod/Columbia (cl), RF/Greg Mathieson (tr); **342–343:** Corbis/Langevin Jacques; **344:** Science & Society Picture Library (c); **345:** Corbis/Bettmann (t); **346:** Corbis/Bettmann (bl, kb), SPL/Tony & Daphne Hallas (tl); **347:** Moviestore Collection; **348:** SPL (cl); **349:** MEPL (tl); **350:** Art Archive/Musee du Louvre Paris/Dagli Orti (bl); **350–351:** SPL/Alfred Pasieka; **352:** Corbis/Bettmann (bl), Corbis/Chris Hellier (tl); **353:** Corbis/Bettmann (b), Getty Images/Hulton Archive/Three Lions; **354:** ImageState/Pictor/AGE Fotostock; **355:** Corbis/Bettmann (b), Corbis/Historical Picture Archive (br, kb), Corbis/Tom Brakefield (tr); **356:** Corbis/Bettmann (bl); **356–357:** ImageState/Pictor; **358:** BAL/Mozart Museum, Salzburg, Austria (tl); **358–359:** Kobal/Hal Roach/UA (c); **359:** Corbis/Farrell Grehan (tr); **360:** Pa Photos/EPA (tl, kb), Corbis/Bettmann (bl), Getty Images (t); **362–363:** Corbis/Liz Barry/Eye Ubiquitous (b) **362:** Corbis/Bettmann (bl, kb), Vivekananda Centre London (tl); **363:** Corbis/Rykoff Collection (t); **364:** Getty Images/Hulton Archive/Keystone (b); **365:** Corbis/Condé Nast Archive (tl), British Museum (tl), RF/SIPA (tr, kb); **366:** Corbis/Bettmann (bl), Jason Hawkes Aerial Library (t); **367:** Getty Images (tr, br); **368:** alamy.com/Popperfoto (kb), Getty Images/David Frazier (t); **368–369:** Pix Gallery Agency AB (b); **369:** Peter Newark's Pictures (tr); **370:** Getty Images/Hulton Archive/Three Lions (tl), RF/Isopress (cl, kb); **371:** alamy.com/David Hoffman Photo Library (b), BAL/Royal Albert Memorial Museum, Exeter, UK (tl); **372:** Getty Images; **373:** Corbis/Swim Ink (tr, kb), Stephen Oliver (t); **374:** Corbis/Bettmann (bl); **374–375:** Kobal Columbia; **375:** Corbis/Apeiron/Sygma (tr); Gisèle Freund/Agency Nina Beskow Photos/Richard Saunders (br, kb), Redferns/Gelnn A. Baker (t); **377:** Camera Press/Justine de Villeneuve; **378:** Art Archive/Maritime Museum Prins Hendrik Rotterdam/Dagli Orti; **379:** Corbis/Bettmann (br), Art Archive/Maritime Museum Prins Hendrik Rotterdam/Dagli Orti (bl), MEPL (tl), SPL/John Reader (tr); **380:** Corbis/Corbis Sygma/McLeod Murdo (b), King's College London (tl); **381:** MEPL (tl), Kobal/Universal (c); **382:** Corbis/Hulton-Deutsch Collection (b); **382–383:** Science & Society Picture Library (c); **383:** alamy.com/Popperfoto (bc), Corbis/Bettmann (b); **384:** alamy.com/Bryan & Cherry Alexander Photography (bl), alamy.com/Photofusion Picture Library/Steve Morgan (t); **385:** alamy.com/Bryan & Cherry Alexander (kb), Corbis/Bettmann (br), Corbis/Nicole Duplaix (tr); **387:** Pa Photos/EPA (tl); **388:** RF/London Weekend Television (bl); **389:** Corbis/Brian A.Vikander (bl), RF/Sipa-e-Sahaba/Ilyas J Dean (bl); **390:** Corbis/Lynn Goldsmith; **391:** Corbis/Bassouls Sophie (t), Corbis/David Turnley (br, kb).

All other images © Dorling Kindersley.
For further information see: www.dkimages.com

The author would like to thank Jonathan Metcalf, who had the original idea for a book of ideas; Nigel Ritchie, who patiently, generously, and enthusiastically saw the project through to press; and all the team at Dorling Kindersley who helped to produce the book.

Dorling Kindersley would like to thank David Goldblatt for help with the original concept; Chuck Wills for ideas for additional readings; Ben Hoare and Christine Heilman for editorial help; and Christine Lacey and Vanessa Thompson for design assistance.